PRIVATE POLICING

Volume 23. **Sage** Criminal Justice System Annuals

#1939

PRIVATE POLICING

Clifford D. Shearing
Philip C. Stenning
Editors

SAGE PUBLICATIONS
The Publishers of Professional Social Science
Newbury Park   Beverly Hills   London   New Delhi

ACKNOWLEDGMENTS

We would like to thank Susan Addario for her assistance in the editing of this manuscript. We would also like to thank the Ministry of the Solicitor General of Canada who, through its Contributions Programme to the Centre of Criminology, assisted in the preparation of this book.

For information address:

SAGE Publications, Inc.
2111 West Hillcrest Drive
Newbury Park, California 91320

SAGE Publications Inc.
275 South Beverly Drive
Beverly Hills
California 90212

SAGE Publications Ltd.
28 Banner Street
London EC1Y 8QE
England

SAGE PUBLICATIONS India Pvt. Ltd.
M-32 Market
Greater Kailash I
New Delhi 110 048 India

Printed in the United States of America

Library of Congress Cataloging-in-Publication Data

Main entry under title:

Private policing.

    (Sage criminal justice systems annuals ; v. 23)
    Includes bibliographies and index.
    1. Police, Private. I. Shearing, Clifford
D., 1942-   . II. Stenning, Philip C. III. Series.
HV8290.P74 1986   363.2'89   86-15450
ISBN 0-8039-2688-X
ISBN 0-8039-2689-8 (pbk.)

CONTENTS

FOREWORD

DAVID H. BAYLEY

This book is much more important than its title suggests. It does not tell the story, now familiar through the pioneering scholarship of Shearing and Stenning, of the unexpected and dramatic development of private security. Instead, it demonstrates compellingly that to understand police institutions, entirely new analytic categories must be developed. Not that these unusually able essays ever say that explicitly. The authors were too intelligent, or subtle, to know how trite—indeed ritualistic—such assertions can be. But that is the cumulative message. And a great virtue of the book is that by juxtaposing current analytic categories with the empirical richness of "policing," readers will be prompted to take that next big step themselves.

The essays establish several important propositions about policing. They show that policing has been done under an enormous variety of auspices—national and local governments, revolutionary and nonrevolutionary parties, neighborhoods, churches, landowners, workers, peasants, businesses, and professional associations. Even more interesting, varieties of policing are complexly mixed. This complexity is not a modern phenomenon, but seems to have been common in other historical periods. Societies of very diverse sorts—as different as classical capitalism and socialism—are affected by similar policing imperatives, specifically the need to make it effective and legitimate. At the same time, differences in social structure affect the forms that policing takes. Although the proportions in the mixture vary, similar forms appear again and again. In particular, "public" and "private" policing never wholly supplant one another. Indeed, the distinction itself becomes problematic in many circumstances. Public and private police institutions cooperate, sometimes interpenetrate, and often share modes of operation. Today in North America, for example, public police are discovering the utility of ordering through compliance, whereas private police are recognizing obligations to deter. Finally, the creation of accountability over institutions should properly be seen as a form of policing. Policing is a reciprocating engine in that groups regulate individuals but individuals collectively regulate groups.

Paradoxically, then, these essays show that the notion of private policing crumbles when examined closely. So too does the more fundamental concept of "police." Significantly, Shearing and Stenning use the word "policing" in the book's title, indicating a concern with activity of a certain kind, not with particular persons. The other authors refer to "ordering," "regulating," and "controlling." So general becomes the concern that they might have included "governing," stripped of its connotative connection with states.

In exposing the intellectual constraints of the dichotomy between public and private forms of policing, the book forces the reader to confront general questions about social ordering. Taken together, the essays show that ordering may be a singular activity but one that is done by different people, to different people, in different ways, and on different occasions. Similar questions should be asked about it in all times and places, rather than assuming a priori that it comes in a few qualitatively different forms such as public or private. Harold Lasswell, the distinguished American political scientist, once said that the study of politics was about who gets what, when, and how. This book, then, suggests that the study of policing is about who, how, to whom, and when.

One might dismiss this broadening of intellectual focus as a commonplace instance of breaking out of inherited analytic categories. The gods of legend ate their children; intellectuals eat their parents. But there is more to it than that. The accumulating work on ordering by anthropologists, sociologists, historians, political scientists, criminologists, and legal scholars is forcing fundamental reconceptualization. The physical sciences, said Thomas Kuhn in *The Structure of Scientific Revolutions* (1962), advance in large jumps when existing theoretical formulations no longer accommodate diverse observations. The essays in *Private Policing* show that "contradictions" in the study of ordering are becoming clear to many people. What is especially promising is that reconceptualization is not taking place by fiat, each scholar creating a unique typology. Rather, the process is being informed by induction, through the astute insights of people working with different materials. At the risk of going out on a limb, these essays fortify my impression that we are in a period of unique intellectual creativity with respect to the study of authority and order, more narrowly policing and law, that may touch the foundation of disciplines. Whether this proves to be the case or not, *Private Policing* is remarkably successful in freezing for inspection the leading edge of the debate.

REFRAMING POLICING

CLIFFORD D. SHEARING
PHILIP C. STENNING

The decision by Sage to publish a collection of essays such as this on private policing is very timely for a number of reasons. In the first place, after a long period in which the phenomenon of private policing was almost totally ignored by criminologists and others, the last decade has seen a small but significant and growing number of scholars beginning to turn their attentions to this neglected topic. The result has been a steady flow of official (for instance, Kakalik and Wildhorn, 1971; U.S. National Advisory Committee on Criminal Justice Standards and Goals, 1976; Cunningham and Taylor, 1985), scholarly (Spitzer and Scull, 1977a, 1977b; Shearing and Stenning, 1981, 1983), and more popular (Draper, 1978) writing on the subject. Most of this work has been largely descriptive in character and it is only now, with our improved understanding of what private policing *is,* that we are in a position to ask the right questions about what it *means* for policing, for civil liberties and privacy, and for social control more generally. One objective of this collection is to pose, and suggest some tentative answers to, such questions.

Second, what the extant research on the subject plainly demonstrates is that in the years since World War II the phenomenon of private security has been growing exponentially, and continues to do so, not only in North America (as many non-North Americans would like to think) but in many other places in the world. Indeed, one of the most impressive (to some, even startling) features of modern private policing is its pervasive, international character. The analytical tools that scholars have applied to the understanding of public policing—confined, for the most part, to nationally based organizations—have for this reason become increasingly inadequate. Many of the implications of this pervasive, international character of private policing are specifically addressed in the essays collected in this volume.

More than this, however, our current understanding of private policing has alerted us to the fact that the development of this phenomenon in recent years has been changing the very nature and objects of policing itself, such that an appreciation of the character and meaning of policing in the latter half of the twentieth century can no longer afford to assume that it is most typically (or even most importantly) about crime, law enforcement, or punishment. Rather, as we have suggested in our own work and as reflected in many of the contributions in this volume, policing must nowadays be understood more broadly as quintessentially about *order,* and the myriad ways in which it can be established and maintained. At this point of our understanding, it is perhaps trite to say (although as recently as 15 years ago it would not have been) that "police" are no longer simply large men in somber uniforms who run around trying to catch criminals.

The study of private policing does not simply challenge our commonsense notions of what policing is, however. As many of the contributions in this volume testify, it also forces us to reconsider some of our most fundamental notions about what is "public" and what is "private," and into which of these categories the function of policing is most appropriately placed. The public-private distinction, in fact, has been central—albeit often implicitly rather than explicitly so—to most scholarly writing on the subject of policing.

In these introductory paragraphs, therefore, our primary focus will be on filling out this conceptual context by examining the way in which the public-private distinction has developed and been used in the study of policing.

Although it would be possible, and perhaps logically neater, to discuss the public-private distinction abstractly by showing how it is central to, and arises out of, a liberal-democratic philosophical framework, it is more useful in setting the context for the chapters in this volume to adopt a more pragmatic approach. This can be done by reviewing the way in which the private-public distinction has been used and developed in conventional, liberal histories of policing (Reiner, 1985). To do so we focus our attention on developments leading to the emergence of the public police as we now know them in the English-speaking world, for it is these histories that have established the conceptual frame within which modern policing is most commonly viewed. Although we restrict our attention here to English policing, the analysis these histories have generated can be used, as Bayley (1985a) makes clear, in articulating a much more generalizable conceptual framework.

The public-private distinction has been utilized in two interrelated ways by liberal historians to explicate the emergence of modern public policing: The first has to do with the definition of order, the second with the responsibility for maintaining it.

The origins of contemporary public policing have been sought in the development of the idea of a public peace. This notion arises through a process that began in antiquity when order was defined in terms of a multiplicity of private peaces (Keeton, 1975: chap. 1). Maitland (1913: 108) provided one of the most colorful (if historically questionable) descriptions of the process through which the notion of a single "public peace" was constructed when he wrote that the peace of the King "devours" competing private peaces to become *the* public peace. The political and territorial base for this process began with the development of kingdoms and was finalized with the emergence of the nation-state as a public authority that claimed to encapsulate all other authorities (Bayley, 1985b). The Mort d'Arthur legend describes the early period of this development in which rival kings struggled for political and territorial sovereignty in what is now Britain.

Inherent in the idea of a nation-state is the notion that the state is the public authority and all other authorities operating within its territory are subordinate to it. Private authorities can be authorized, at the discretion of the state, to define separate private peaces so long as they are not in conflict with the public peace. Bayley (1985b: 28) talks of the state "encapsulating" private authorities and of "groups capable of authorizing policing nesting inside one another like Chinese puzzle boxes" (1985a: 8). The space for private orders that the state permits determines the extent of private liberties. Hobbes (1968/1651: 264) provides one of the best-known statements of this principle within the liberal frame:

> The Liberty of the subject, lyeth therefore only in those things, which in regulating their actions, the sovereign hath praetermitted: such as is the liberty to buy, and sell, and otherwise contract with one another; to choose their own aboad, their own diet, their own trade of life and institute their children as they themselves think fit; & the like.

The oft-quoted adage that "a man's home is as his castle" is an expression of the understanding that in liberal societies individuals are accorded some space in which to act as private authorities. Their subordination to the state, and its definition of order, is clearly expressed in the remainder and less familiar portion of this quotation: "and *while he is quiet,* he is as well guarded as a prince in his castle" (Smith, 1978: 551, our emphasis).

In tracing the development of the nation-state and the movement from autonomous private peaces to a single dominant public peace, the implicit assumption has been that this is a linear, and irreversible, process. Within this context the public-private distinction becomes relevant primarily with respect to the distribution of responsibility for maintaining public order. Historical accounts written within this liberal frame have examined the emergence of modern public policing in terms of this dimension. The modern public police are viewed as the end point in a process whereby the state progressively accepted responsibility for maintaining public order, which had previously been delegated to (or simply left with) private entities. This process has been presented as one in which responsibility for the maintenance of order is made consistent with the source of its definition. These histories tend to adopt a normative implication: a "publicly" defined peace should properly be "publicly" maintained. Thus, the emergence of modern public police, as full-time salaried employees of the nation-state claiming a monopoly over order maintenance, is constituted as both proper and inevitable.

Within this context evidence that private organizations are doing a great deal of contemporary policing both in public and private places (for a review see Shearing and Stenning, 1981) comes as a bit of a shock. The conceptual consequences of this shock are minimized, however, if this evidence is absorbed into the above frame (see Kuhn's, 1970 discussion of how paradigm shifts are avoided). This can be done with the minimum of frame disruption by abandoning the assumption that the move from private to public responsibility for maintaining public order is linear and irreversible. When this is done private policing comes to be viewed as the reinvolvement of the private sector in assisting the state in maintaining public order. The presence of private policing is thus revealed as a sort of contemporary manifestation of frankpledge—an Anglo-Saxon system, formalized by the Normans, that required local communities to assist in the maintenance of the King's peace. When the ideology of policing is presented in this way, the vital liberal premise that the state is an encapsulating authority that monopolizes the definition of the peace remains intact.

This construction of private policing and its place in the contemporary context sets the parameters for debate about the evolution of policing, and more generally, control. Thus, the pivot around which debate has turned has been discussion about the extent to which private involvement in control signals a decline in, or an addition to, state control (see, for example, Cohen, 1985). Although this argument is not yet settled, the balance of evidence clearly favors those who take the latter position. This conclusion has directed attention to an examination of how public and private control mechanisms are, or should be, articulated.

The liberal construction and the debate and research it has generated have been of considerable heuristic value in drawing attention to questions about the scope and nature of contemporary control as well as the manner in which responsibility for it is shared between the public and private sectors. Research within this frame has dominated the exploration of private involvement within order maintenance and much has been learned from it. Several of the chapters within this volume—as well as much of our own work (see Shearing and Stenning, 1981)—operate within this frame and demonstrate its usefulness in raising critical questions. Gary Marx, for example, examines both the way in which public and private police agencies cooperate with each other in undercover work and the consequences of the strategies they use to do so for the nature of contemporary policing.

The advantages of operating within the previously mentioned frame have, however, not been without cost. What the retention of the liberal framework has done has been to direct our attention away from features of contemporary private policing that suggest that its consequences may be considerably more radical than the comparison with frankpledge allows. In other words, although the liberal frame has been maintained in a manner that has permitted scholars to question the assumption that the state has exclusive *responsibility* for maintaining public order, it has not permitted the more radical suggestion that contemporary private police are evidence of the reemergence of private authorities who sometimes effectively challenge the state's claimed monopoly over the *definition* of order. Yet, as we have argued elsewhere (1983, 1984), what is now known about private policing provides compelling evidence in support of precisely this conclusion, namely, that what we are witnessing through the growth of private policing is not merely a reshuffling of responsibility for policing public order but the emergence of privately defined orders, policed by privately employed agents, that are in some cases inconsistent with, or even in conflict with, the public order proclaimed by the state.

Once one begins to break out of the liberal frame in this way, it becomes apparent that other critical assumptions that have been taken for granted also require serious reexamination. Of particular importance in exploring the challenge that private policing represents is the manner in which the liberal frame structures the political-legal landscape. What it does is construct and juxtapose two ideal entities: the state and the individual. The category "individual" has taken on a residual character in that if a political legal entity is not part of the state it is then conceived of as an individual. This analytic strategy has made possible the political-legal sleight of hand through which corporations are treated, for certain important purposes, as "individuals" even though they are empirically very different from flesh and blood individuals and, indeed, very often are more similar to states. Although this piece of conjuring has maintained the liberal frame it has not been useful in facilitating an understanding of critical aspects of private policing. Most important, it has obscured the similarity between the state and large corporations as political-legal entities. The latters' stature as authorities with the resources and power to rival the influence of the state *and* with jurisdiction over substantial territories and communities has not been adequately explored. This has been particularly detrimental to our understanding of the role of corporations in defining and maintaining social order.

Thus, although the liberal frame has been heuristically useful in the ways we have noted, it is clear that if its assumptions continue to hold sway, it will not be possible to consider the more radical implications of private policing noted earlier. Shedding these assumptions is, however, as we know from our own experience, a slow and difficult process. Nonetheless, it is one that we need to begin. Several chapters in this volume begin to explore this uncharted terrain.

In suggesting the need to move beyond the liberal frame as an analytic base for the examination of private policing we, of course, do not wish to downplay in the slightest the importance of the liberal assumptions as the empirical context within which private policing has and continues to develop. Indeed, it is only by giving full recognition to the political-legal assumptions that the liberal frame makes possible that many of private policing's most enigmatic features can be understood. The lack of understanding (and concern) over the legal authority of private policing agents, for instance, is directly attributable to this ideological environment that they inhabit, as is much of the unquestioning legitimacy that the public, and governments, accord them (Shearing et al., 1985b).

Corporate orders are defended on the grounds that corporations, like any other "persons," have a right to a sphere of private authority over which they have undisturbed jurisdiction. Furthermore, this right is sacrosanct, for to encroach upon it would undermine the very freedoms that are definitive of liberal democracy. The irony is that it is the liberal frame itself (with its emphasis on the relative rights of "individuals," especially property-owning ones) that has legitimated the development of huge multinational corporations into powerful private authorities whose very existence, and activity, mock the liberal frame.

With contemporary corporations as the modern-day equivalents of feudal lords, reigning supreme over huge feudal estates, the search for a historical parallel leads us back beyond frankpledge to more ancient concepts of private peaces and conflicting private authorities. Indeed, the very distinction between private and public takes on a new significance that blurs, and contradicts, its liberal meanings. This is true not only because private "individuals" are engaged in the maintenance of public order but also because more and more public life is nowadays conducted on privately owned and controlled property. Because our definitions of public and private are so inextricably bound up with the ownership and control of property, however, the control of such essentially public life on privately owned property has continued to be treated as an essentially private matter.

However, to conclude from this disjuncture between ideology and the real world that the private-public dichotomy should be abandoned altogether as an analytical tool (Spitzer, 1982; Klare, 1981, 1982) would be premature. This distinction's roots are far deeper and more fundamental than the liberal frame that has simply shaped an ancient experientially based dichotomy for political and ideological purposes. A wiser course than scrapping the distinction altogether may be to explore the ways in which it has been successfully deployed to support political and economic orderings, and to see whether it cannot fruitfully be reframed as an analytically useful concept.

The essays in this volume serve this purpose well. The collection begins with a thoughtful chapter by Albert Reiss, in which he seeks to develop a conceptual framework for understanding the public and private realms within which policing (both public and private) is undertaken. Stuart Henry, in the chapter that follows, broadens the conceptual frame to encompass what he sees as a dialectical relationship between the public and private spheres in the production of order and justice.

These theoretical contributions are followed by a historical review by Nigel South in which he examines in some detail the circumstances surrounding the emergence of modern public police forces during the eighteenth and nineteenth centuries, and the underlying reasons for this apparent transfer of responsibility from the private to the public realm. Robert Weiss's chapter looks at this shift from the other side as it were, tracing how a large American corporation utilized its private policing resources during the mid-twentieth century, and the relationship between these in-house police and their public (state) counterparts in securing industrial discipline.

Both Austin Turk and Gordon West discuss the ambivalent character of collective or "community" policing. Turk critically considers the ideology behind such community policing in the context of a North American urban environment, whereas West examines the concept at work in the very different conditions of revolutionary Nicaragua.

Gary Marx's essay brings us right to the heart of the question of how (and how much) public and private police utilize each other's services in the investigation and prevention of various kinds of crime. The two pieces that follow (by Susan Shapiro, and John Braithwaite and Brent Fisse, respectively) take up this theme of public-private cooperation and competition as it applies to the policing of corporate crime and disorder. Each of these chapters considers how responsibility is divided (and shared) between public and private authorities and what explanations can be advanced for this allocation of responsibility.

Pursuing the theme of private corporate policing, Nancy Reichman illustrates the transformations that are occurring in the nature of policing methods to suit the needs and objectives of corporate "clients." This leads us to Michael Clarke's chapter which reflects on the question of why certain policing strategies (and certain allocations of responsibility between public and private authorities) make more sense than others in addressing particular policing problems. This is followed by Peter Manning's careful analysis of one such strategy (compliance policing), which he examines in the context of nuclear regulation. This raises the question as to whether policing strategies are related to the public-private character of those on whose behalf policing is undertaken.

The use of the term "regulation" in the preceding paragraph, and in several of the chapters in the volume, raises the question, "Is regulation different from policing?" Each term, as it is used in this volume, signifies activity that maintains order. What differentiates them is that they embody different evaluations of the nature of the order to be maintained and the relationship between those who maintain it and those whose activity is to be ordered. Policing signifies order maintenance that is coercive and has a top-down quality to it. It is something that is done *for* one group *to* another. In addition, for the reasons we have already noted, it is typically associated with government and the maintenance of public order.

In contrast, regulation signifies order maintenance that has a softer edge. There is a consensual connotation; it is not associated with state power (though this can be added as in the term "state-regulation") and it implies a sense of harmony. One regulates a clock, for example, so that it may work accurately.

These differences are significant and remind us of the necessity of paying attention to the terms actors choose in describing order maintenance. Nonetheless, it is important, analytically, to select a term identifying ordering as a generic activity whether it be hard or soft edged. To do this we have adopted the term "policing," partly for reasons of usage, and partly because it seems to us, at present, to embody the fewest disadvantages. Thus, in our terms, all the essays in this volume, whether they are about policing or regulation, are about policing.

We end the collection with a look into the future (which seems nevertheless to be already with us) as it is reflected in our own observations of private corporate policing at Disney World. Mickey Mouse and friends, it seems, are rather more than they appear to be. Like all good cartoon characters, they inform us about who we are, and where we are going, in the friendliest way.

REFERENCES

BAYLEY, D. (1985a) *Patterns of Policing.* New Brunswick, NJ: Rutgers University Press.
———(1985b) *Social Control and Political Change.* Center of International Studies, Research Monograph 19, Princeton University, Princeton, NJ.
COHEN, S. (1985) *Visions of Social Control.* Cambridge, England: Polity Press.
CUNNINGHAM, W. and T. TAYLOR (1985) *Private Security and Police in America.* Portland, OR: Chancellor Press.
DRAPER, H. (1978) *Private Police.* Harmondsworth, England: Penguin Books.

HOBBES, T. (1968) *Leviathan*. Harmondsworth, England: Penguin Books. (Originally published in 1651)

KAKALIK, J. and S. WILDHORN (1971) *Private Police in the United States,* vols. 1-5. Santa Monica, CA: Rand Corporation.

KEETON, G. (1975) *Keeping the Peace*. Chichester/London: Barry Rose Publishers.

KLARE, K. (1981) "Labor law as ideology: toward a new historiography of collective bargaining law." *Industrial Relations Law Journal* 4: 450-482.

———(1982) "The public private distinction in labor law." *University of Pennsylvania Law Review* 130: 1358-1422.

KUHN, T. (1970) *The Structure of Scientific Revolutions*. Chicago: University of Chicago Press.

MAITLAND, F. (1913) *Constitutional History.* Cambridge, England: Cambridge University Press.

REINER, R. (1985) *The Politics of the Police*. Brighton, England: Wheatsheaf Books.

SHEARING, C. and P. STENNING (1981) "Modern private security: its growth and implications," in M. Tonry and N. Morris (eds.) *Crime and Justice—An Annual Review of Research, vol. 3*. Chicago: University of Chicago Press.

———(1983) "Private security: implications for social control." *Social Problems* 30, 5: 493-506.

———and S. ADDARIO (1985a) "Police perceptions of private security." *Canadian Police College Journal* 9, 2: 127-153.

———(1985b) "Public perceptions of private security." *Canadian Police College Journal* 9, 3: 225-253.

SMITH, M. (1978) *The Writs of Assistance Case*. Berkeley: University of California Press.

SPITZER, S. (1982) "The dialectics of formal and informal control," pp. 167-205 in R. Abel (ed.) *The Politics of Informal Justice*, vol.1. New York: Academic Press.

———and A. SCULL (1977a) "Privatization and capitalist development: the case of the private police." *Social Problems* 25, 1: 18-29.

———(1977b) "Social control in historical perspective: from private to public responses to crime," in D. Greenberg (ed.) *Corrections and Punishment: Structure, Function and Process*. Beverly Hills, CA: Sage.

U.S. National Advisory Committee on Criminal Justice Standards and Goals (1976) Private Security: Report of the Task Force on Private Security. Washington, DC: Department of Justice.

Chapter 1

THE LEGITIMACY OF INTRUSION INTO PRIVATE SPACE

ALBERT J. REISS, Jr.

INTRUSION INTO PRIVATE SPACE

We each stake out for ourselves private space that covers our persons, our property, and their extensions, which we perceive as our territory and our rights. Phenomenologically, our sense of the private has an experiential base; our bodies are the residence for our unique identity as a self. I am my home and it is irreducibly a private place. Ordinarily we are not conscious of the many ways we bound our private space and guard it against intrusion. Our private personal space is with us when we go about, and we expect others to respect its boundaries.

Common etiquette, as well as the law, requires that each of us respect the other's private space. We expect that our private actions will be respected no matter where we are. For example, in Western societies, our toilet behavior is to be respected in public rest rooms as well as in our own bathroom. Closing the door to the booth in a public toilet, as well as to one's private bathroom, is more than a symbolic gesture; it announces that this is both a private matter and one's private place. Where that privacy cannot be so easily ensured, as in the congregation before urinals in public mens' rest rooms, common etiquette requires that each look straight ahead to avoid intruding upon the privacy of others. The covert glance may be tolerated without an overt display of disapproval; the stare ordinarily is not.

Etiquette usually protects our privacy. But when etiquette is not enough, we look for protection to more formal rule systems and

AUTHOR'S NOTE: I wish to express appreciation to the editors for their helpful suggestions.

their enforcement agents. We look to the law and its public enforcers to protect us against illegal intrusions into our private spaces, whether those intrusions are into our domicile or occur when going about in private or public places. We may also privately employ protection against intrusion or rely upon privately organized protective and security agents to do so.

Paradoxically, the very agents responsible for the protection of private spaces must invade some to do so. To protect against illegal intrusion or to ensure redress against it we empower our public police to search, seize, and arrest. To protect their interests against employees, we permit employers to develop files of personal information.

This chapter presents variations on a theme about the social construction of privacy and its manifestation in political, legal, and sociocultural arenas. It focuses on the nature of intrusions into private space, the ways intrusions are legitimated, and the means used to protect against unwarranted intrusion. Special attention is devoted to how the law and our public and private police legitimate and protect against intrusion.

PRIVACY AND THE LAW

Privacy encompasses those places, spaces, and matters upon or into which others may not normally intrude without the consent of the person or organization to whom they are designated as belonging. Our concern here is with the role that law plays in defining and protecting privacy and the conditions under which the law legitimates intrusion into or upon it.

The first way that the law plays a major role in privacy is by defining certain places, spaces, and matters as private, that is, by defining legally what privacy is.

The common law of trespass evolved to protect against intrusions that brought injury to person, property, and rights and for redress against such injuries. Its evolution is closely linked to the legal separation of private from public places, private from public property, and individual from collective or sovereign rights and matters.

The law distinguishes between the ownership of property and the right of access to it with and without the consent of owners. Whether the property is publicly or privately owned, access to it depends in large part upon whether it is at law a public or a private place. Much government property is regarded as a private place or matter and access is restricted. Military, intelligence, and police agencies are common examples of organizations that always restrict access to both places and matters. Every organization limits access by the public. Some, such as eating and drinking establishments, are regarded as public places when they are posted as open for business and as private places when they are closed. The kind of crime with which a person will be charged depends not only upon the harm done but often upon the legality of the access. The crimes of trespass and burglary, for example, presume access to private places. A robbery may be in a private or a public place, but the robber in a public place cannot be charged with unlawful entry. The way intrusions are defined depends then more upon the legal designation of place as private or public than upon who owns it. It goes, almost without saying, that one is permitted more privacy in a private than a public place.

Similarly, the law designates some matters as private and others as public. Often, part of one's behavior may be regarded as public whereas other aspects of it are not. One's voter registration and whether one signed the ballot registry are matters of public record; one's actual vote is not.

The second way that the law plays a major role in privacy is by defining what will be regarded as consent and as consent to intrude. The law may recognize both actual and implied consent. Thus, a contract may provide very explicitly for specific kinds of intrusion into private matters. We quite commonly abrogate some of our rights to privacy and its secrecy in making contracts. When applying for some privileged status—such as financial credit, employment, school admission, or a license—one not only provides private information but, if one furnishes a list of references who may be contacted, a grant is given to legitimately pry into one's private affairs by seeking information from others. Should one rent rather than own one's domicile, one contractually agrees to landlord provisions that intrude upon one's privacy—rights that one would retain were one the owner. A renter usually grants the landlord access to the rental quarters, with and without proper notice. No notice is required, for instance, to make emergency repairs, but notice may be required to make ordinary repairs or to show the dwelling to prospective tenants.

The law may also invoke a doctrine of implied consent. The issuance of a motor vehicle license, for example, may carry the implied consent to submit to a blood alcohol examination when a law officer has reason to conclude an operator is driving a motor vehicle while intoxicated.

Although privacy rests in consent to intrude, the granting of consent to intrude is often problematic. A simple illustration may make this plain. Ordinarily the right to keep domestic matters private is sacrosanct. One may even invoke spousal immunity in criminal matters. Yet, each spouse has the privilege to disclose domestic matters that are *jointly* private in a divorce action or a criminal proceeding. Private matters, jointly held, thus are vulnerable to public disclosure by each private party.

A third way that the law defines privacy is to permit certain activities or behavior only on the condition that one consents to some intrusion into privacy. This is often the case where governments promulgate rules to regulate conduct. For example, a condition for boarding many flights is that one submit to a search of one's property and, when deemed necessary, to a search of the person as well. Often one is required to identify oneself before being permitted to engage in some activity, such as entering or leaving a country or to be served an alcoholic beverage. In order to receive some government benefit one may be required to provide information on one's financial status or submit to a medical examination. The extent of such intrusions may be considerable, such as when one is investigated for a government security clearance in connection with one's employment.

Intrusions are not limited by law to government alone because private organizations often require consent for intrusion into privacy as a condition of receiving private access or benefit. One often has to allow such intrusions to secure private as well as public employment, and access to many private places often requires the limited intrusion of identifying oneself.

The law also defines privacy in a fourth way by requiring that certain people, under certain circumstances, disclose what are normally regarded as private matters, under penalty for refusing to do so. The law, under threat of penalty, may coerce disclosure when it would be voluntarily withheld. This is especially the case for legal proceedings. The subpoena that commands a witness to appear and give testimony or to produce evidence in his or her possession or control, discovery as part of a judicial course of action, and oaths, with their threats of perjury, are all examples of legitimate legal means compelling disclosure of private matters.

The law, finally, delegates authority to certain persons—sometimes public officials and sometimes private persons—to intrude, under certain circumstances, upon privacy *without* consent. The nature and scope of such authority will vary with the purpose advanced to justify intrusion. Among the major purposes advanced to justify such intrusion are the detection of crime and capture of criminals, the protection of state or organizational security, the efficient collection of taxes, and the mobilization of the population under emergency conditions, whether in war service or in disaster or accident in peacetime. Nowhere is the requirement of consent to intrude more vulnerable, perhaps, than in the sovereign power to intrude without consent when there is reason to believe a crime has been committed or is about to be so. Even one's domicile is not secured against search nor one's property against seizure. Search without a warrant is permissible in many democratic states when time is of the essence in criminal matters. Similarly, one's private conversations are not protected from a duly authorized wiretap.

Custom as well as law also plays a role in defining privacy, its protections against intrusion, and the conditions under which one may intrude upon the privacy of others with and without consent. Although our focus in this essay is upon the role of the law, it is important to bear in mind that these customary definitions may, and do, conflict with political and sociocultural constructions of privacy. They are open to challenge both within and without the law. A sit-in may be an unwarranted intrusion under the law; yet, it may be claimed as a moral right, as Martin Luther King and his followers demonstrated so eloquently in the civil rights movement in the United States.

LEGAL DOMAINS AND THE
LEGITIMACY OF INTRUSION

Each domain of law, as, for example, administrative, criminal, and private law, differs in how it limits intrusion into the same private matters. A few comparisons will illustrate how they commonly differ.

Searches of persons and their property, seizing or impounding property, and detaining persons may be handled quite differently under the authority of an administrative rather than a criminal law agency. The discretionary power of law enforcement agents to search, seize, and detain is less constrained by administrative than by criminal statutory and case law. A customs or airport security control agent can search all persons and their possessions with only the simple presumption that some persons might be violating the law and that implied consent is given; indeed, they assume that most searches are negative. The searches are not without implied coercion as well as implied consent. One must permit the search or one will be denied entry into one's country, a seat on a plane, or to take along personal possessions—even one's prescription medication. Where ordinarily one is entitled to keep knowledge of one's purchases and the price for the commodity a private matter, one is compelled to furnish that information and give evidence to a customs authority.

A public police officer has far less authority to make comparable searches and certainly not without a reasonable presumption that a crime has been or is about to be committed. To search everyone on the street or in a particular area because of a belief that someone within that aggregate might be preparing to commit a crime would not qualify as a reasonable presumption under the criminal law. Similarly, although a customs agent may detain one for a considerable period of time without formal charges, such lengthy detention is prohibited, at least in the United States, under police discretionary powers. It may be noteworthy that both the police and customs agents may deprive one of the use of one's property for considerable periods of time pending the outcome of some investigation or proceeding. Police agents, for example, may impound stolen property as evidence of the theft for a subsequent proceeding, thereby depriving the owner of its use.

BOUNDING PRIVATE SPACE
AND LEGITIMATING INTRUSION

Although definitions and rules bound private from public space, in practice boundaries are usually indeterminate. Yet, it is precisely at the margin that the legitimacy of intrusion is most likely to be challenged and tested. By law, police actions may fall at that margin. Was the force a police officer used necessary to sustain an arrest or an assault? Was the admission coerced or obtained by consent? Was there entrapment? Similarly, there are margins separating legitimate from illegitimate intrusions by citizens. Was the automobile stolen or its use simply unauthorized? Was the child assaulted or abused or simply punished? Did the child-care worker show care toward or, rather, molest the child? Was the disclosure permitted or prohibited? Did the employer sexually harass or simply show caring for the employee?

Questions such as these attest to the fact that the legitimacy of intrusion into private space often is problematic. What is also noteworthy about them is how the language in which they are framed implies a margin separating legitimate from illegitimate intrusion. Words such as harassment, molestation, and unauthorized necessitate evidence that one has crossed a particular margin. That is often no simple matter. What evidence is required to sustain a charge that a police officer used force unnecessarily or that someone was solicited or importuned for immoral purposes?

The law and its agents continually grapple with defining these margins so as to be able to interpret behavior; so do ordinary citizens in their everyday lives. There are a number of central concepts in the law that focus particularly on the legitimacy of intrusion. Some concepts, such as coercion, permission, and agreement, are used to determine whether there was *consent* to intrude upon private space. Others focus on the *legitimacy of the authority* of the intruder, such as whether one was authorized to take a particular action or whether the office has the authority to do so. Still others center on the *qualifications* to intrude, such as whether one is licensed or certified to take a particular action.

THE LEGITIMACY OF INTRUSION BY PUBLIC AND PRIVATE POLICE

Generally, administrative law enforcement agents and privately employed police have greater discretionary powers to intrude upon private space than do our public police, who are constrained by the criminal law. This greater discretion is partly due to the fact that compliance and deterrence forms of law enforcement have different objectives.

The principal objective of compliance law enforcement is to ensure conformity by a demonstration that the means are available to comply or that actions have been taken to prevent infractions of rules or violations of laws. Deterrence law enforcement's principal objective is to ensure conformity by detecting violations, determining who is responsible for them, and penalizing violators in order to deter the offender or others from committing violations in the future. Although both compliance and deterrence systems seek to prevent violations, compliance systems are premonitory and deterrence systems postmonitory. Hence, compliance systems manipulate means that induce conformity whereas deterrence systems react to events once they occur (Reiss, 1984a: 23-24).

Although both public and private police systems pursue both compliance and deterrence objectives, the public police are formally organized around the deterrence model of detection, arrest, and punishment, and, informally, around a peace-keeping model (Bittner, 1967a; 1967b; Reiss, 1984b). By contrast, private policing is formally organized around maintaining private orders and preventing their disruption. Their role in enforcing the criminal law is normally limited to mobilizing the public police (Shearing and Stenning, 1981: 210).

The organizational status of public and private police should not be confused with their policing role. We generally distinguish public from private police in terms of their ownership—whether that of a private capital organization or a public government. Yet, they are distinguished more by employer interest than ownership. The public police serve public rather than private interests. One must be careful, likewise, not to confuse a proprietary interest in police with the private or public character of their place of work. Governments in the United States, for example, often contract with private security firms to guard their property and to maintain order, and the public police often work for private places with most of their police powers intact.

It would be mistaken, however, to assume that these differences in organizational status are unimportant for the legitimation of intrusion. For example, when public police officers police for private interests, they may incur liabilities without the benefit of public protections. Correlatively, the private security firm that protects government property and personnel assumes at least some of the liability for those actions.

The legitimacy of actions is far more problematic for private than public police. As Ericson and Shearing note in "The Scientification of Police Work" (1986: 1), "the law allows the [public] police to legitimately claim that they are taking action within the rule of law, that is according to universal, general, uniform, and neutral criteria in the public interest." They go on to observe that the public police are able to act under the guise of legitimate authority because the rules of criminal procedure constrain rather than enable their actions (1986: 1). Noting that formal legal rationality helps the public police to legitimate their actions so that they meet formal standards of accountability (1986: 2), Ericson and Shearing astutely conclude that in everyday police work those formal rules are primarily an enabling resource to justify the particular actions a police officer wishes to take rather than determinative of those actions (1986: 3).

Legitimating their actions seems more problematic for private police because they lack the justification of the law (Ericson and Shearing, 1986: 1) and are publicly regarded as acting in private interests and maintaining private orders (Shearing and Stenning, 1981: 106). Because they cannot readily turn to a body of law or to legal rules and procedures to legitimate their actions, they normally justify their actions in terms of management practice rather than legal authority.

Given the necessity to legitimate their actions as lawful, deterrence-based systems formally provide more protections against intrusion into private space than do compliance-based systems. The reason for this lies in their contrasting conceptions of the problem of order. Order within criminal justice is fundamentally a moral problem, whereas within private control systems it is regarded as instrumental (Shearing and Stenning, 1984: 339). The authority to intervene, and consequently to intrude into private matters, must be legitimated primarily when matters are regarded as moral. When the focus is upon preventing and ordering relations so as to control behavior, legitimation usually is not required. Intrusion is regarded as necessary to prevent undesirable consequences; it is a means and not an action to be evaluated by itself. Consequently, private policing may be highly intrusive but with little public awareness that it is so. We shall return later to this question of the public visibility and awareness of intrusion by private and public police.

FEAR AND RESISTANCE TO INTRUSION
INTO PRIVATE SPACE
AND ITS PROTECTIONS

It is difficult to imagine any individual or organization that does not define a private space and matters and make efforts to protect it against intruders. A primary reason for this may be that no organization seems possible—whether that of the personality, a family or friendship, or more formal organizations, including the state— without its private matters or secrets. For the capacity to act is predicated in part on preserving a unique form of organization that sets it apart from others. Moreover, any competitive advantage one may have stems in part from being able to "keep others guessing." There appears to be an implied threat even in sharing that information with others; its disclosure makes one vulnerable. At the core, then, of one's private matters or space is a fear that one is vulnerable to others. Hence, one seeks to protect that space against intrusion.

Many, if not all, matters are commonly regarded as secrets. The word "secret" denotes something that is hidden from others, to be shared with no one or only a select few. Secrets are constructed so as to escape observation. But a secret connotes much more—the idea that one conceals and protects the matter and that it is a choice whether or not to disclose it to others.

I have used the term "private space" to denote not only these private and secret matters but perhaps an even more fundamental attribute of persons and organizations—a sense of territoriality. For people, there is a sense in which this is literally *my* territory, as it includes physical space—one's physical self, with and without clothes (for most Westerners, the private space is larger when one is unclothed) and some space that physical self inhabits. It is the property that one sees as being "territorially mine."

There are both fixed and mobile properties to that space. My domicile, for example, is a part of my private space. When I physically leave it, it nonetheless remains mine and can be intruded upon. I then may well feel *personally violated* even though I am not there when the intrusion occurs. We have found in studying victims that many persons who have experienced a burglary—and most especially women—experience the trespass as personal and report not only feeling violated in a deep personal sense, but feel that it is never quite the safe space one thought it was.

It appears, also, that I carry a sense of my territory with me when I leave my domicile and go about in public space. When strangers become physically very close, one becomes very conscious that one's personal territory is invaded. Most people will involuntarily withdraw when any physical contact ensues with strangers. One may even suspect the motives of the "intruder" when one perceives an invasion of *private* territory. Is it simply a breach of etiquette, and if so, why was there no excuse for it? Is it some form of sexual advance or impropriety? Are they about to harm me in some way?

But, the sense of private space may extend even farther. People expect the distance between themselves and others to vary according to circumstance. A woman walking on a dark street at night may want to maintain considerable distance between the strange man behind her and herself. She quickens her pace when it lessens. If he does likewise, she may be terror stricken. By contrast, one expects people to be much closer in crowd situations. Again, one's fear may be tied closely to circumstance. When exiting a stadium after a football game, one anticipates being in a "crush." Still, someone may panic if the crowd begins to move in an unpredictable way, such as it has at some soccer and football games. Similarly, if a police vehicle or officer appears to be following, one may either become anxious or feel safe, depending upon how one defines one's territory and whether or not the officer is protecting or intruding upon it.

This suggests that the definition of space, and others in relation to it, is a social construction of one's reality as one moves about in everyday life. Indeed, one of the explanations offered for the paradoxical finding that women who have lower actual rates of victimization by crime than men nonetheless report much higher levels of fear of victimization by crime is that they experience far more *threats* to their private space. They are more likely to infer such threats from the presence and behavior of men than women. Harassment, following, and suspicion of intruding are more commonly the experiences of women than of men. That is not to say, of course, that there is no basis in reality for their perceived threat. Whether men are more likely than women to intrude upon the private space of others in public is uncertain, but men are probably more likely to intrude upon the private space of women than vice versa. The perception of intrusion should vary with one's sense of protection against intrusion. In Western cultures, it appears that women have a lesser sense of self-protection in the face of threats by men than men do of women.

It seems central to human existence to protect one's private space against intruders, including one's natural predators. Animals as well as humans invade private space. Some people call the police because of the trespasses of a neighbor's dog. A barking dog can be as intrusive as a neighbor's radio or raucous party. If one calls the police, the disruption of one's private peace may be deemed a disturbance of the public peace.

The foregoing social constructions of private space are to some degree institutionalized in the law. Laws of sexual assault, disorderly conduct, and disturbing the peace are examples.

All of us develop forms of self-protection and rely upon others such as public and private police to protect us. Many people go to considerable effort to protect their private space. They install locks, bars, or alarms to protect their private domicile or other property; organizations do likewise. People may take their valuables to a safe-deposit box in a vault. Even when going about, they may take the somewhat irrational step of locking their suitcase or briefcase. Women may take care to purchase a handbag that is less vulnerable to a purse snatcher. Cars are locked when parked. Some people arm themselves with Mace, knives, or other dangerous weapons when they go out and a substantial proportion of people in high crime-rate areas keep a weapon at home, often in defiance of gun registration laws and at considerable risk to themselves. Moreover, when going about, they may exercise great caution, fearing their personal space will be violated, especially if the perceived harm is great. Avoidance behavior is common, such as crossing the street if one perceives someone is a suspicious or threatening person, walking through private arcades to avoid the public streets, or avoiding dark and unpeopled places.

CUES CONSTRUCT REALITY AS THREATENING TO PERSONAL SAFETY

We continually take cues from our environment to tell us how safe is our private space. And, reality itself is structured and organized in ways to provide us with those cues. Recent research on the fear of victimization by crime and of the flight from high crime-rate areas points to the importance of such cues in generating fear. It is the visible signs of a disorderly and dangerous physical environment that are perceived as threatening. Graffiti, littered lots, abandoned buildings, broken windows, destroyed public amenities in parks and playgrounds, and barred windows all characterize some areas as a citadel of iron gates—a place to be feared and avoided or, at the very least a place in which one goes about with a sense of caution that one must protect one's private space. These visible environmental cues clearly affect both public and private behavior leading to fear and flight; it may empty the streets so as to leave them to predators (Lewis and Salem, 1985; Reiss, 1983; Taub et al., 1981; Taub and Taylor, 1984; Wilson and Kelling, 1983).

Environments not only abound with physical cues that tell whether one's private space is threatened but with behavioral cues that lead people to see their fellow human beings as menacing and threatening. Loitering youth and adult males, intoxicated persons, the mentally ill, bag ladies, and panhandlers invade one's private space (Skogan and Maxfield, 1981; Taub et al., 1981; Reiss, 1985: 6-8). Some, like panhandlers, street prostitutes, the mentally ill, and the intoxicated, threaten by actual contact. Others, like loitering youths and "street people," menace because they may make lewd comments or in other ways harass passersby. Whenever people perceived as threatening concentrate in large numbers, they may create for one a climate of fear to go about in the streets. Such congregation is reportedly one of the reasons for the daytime depopulation of the central business districts of our cities (Reiss, 1985: 6-8). Correlatively, greater control by the public police of the population regarded as threatening and a reduction in the visible signs of a threatening environment in the central business district of Oakland by private developers and municipal departments have led to a repopulation of their streets during the daytime and some reductions in street crime (Reiss, 1985: 37-45).

People and organizations can misread cues as well. That which is familiar, whether or not it actually threatens one's private space, is more likely to be perceived as benign than that which is alien. The strange and unfamiliar are easily misread as threats to the integrity of one's private space. Correlatively, people may misread cues as benign when they are actually more threatening. The friendly person met at the bar may be contemplating a sexual assault, the excused jostle may hide a picked pocket, and the child's assist in helping with the groceries a ruse for a purse snatching. Perhaps even more to the point, the places and people we think of as safest—our homes and family members—are in reality among the most substantial threats to personal safety. The experience of being a victim of misread cues may well lead to hypercautionary behavior and even to withdrawal from the outside environment.

Efforts at self-protection and the confidence placed in others to protect one are critical to one's sense of personal safety. Perhaps especially important is the sense one develops about personal risk when going about in public places. Most people view their environment in terms of the risk it poses to their personal safety and seek cues that their private space will not be violated. Possibly one of the reasons why people place such high confidence in the job that the public police are doing, despite their concern for their own welfare when going about in policed areas, is that they rely upon their protection. A visible presence of public and private security, but especially of the former, is reassuring for it makes safety predictable.

What makes terrorism so devastating to ordinary citizens is that it strikes at the very core of protecting private space by defining the limits of protection. Terrorist incidents lack any sense of predictability, while at the same time shaking confidence in the ability of the police or anyone to afford any protection from being its victim. Terrorists are well aware that its major impact is that threat it poses to private space. It is intended to shake confidence in protectors, especially in the power of the state to provide it. Analogously, the poisoning of ordinary products, such as that of candy in Japan and Tylenol® in the United States, are highly threatening because of the seeming powerlessness of investigators to protect from mad or criminal persons. The ordinary cues about risk and personal safety cannot be trusted under these circumstances.

Cues as Clues to Protection

Ordinarily we search not only for the cues that may threaten our private space or assure us that the environment is benign but for cues about what is being done to protect it. We search for signs of protection and protectors as clues to what is being done to ensure the integrity of our private world.

Sometimes clues to our protection take the form of warning signs or announcements. "Proceed with Caution," "Travel at Your Own Risk," "Watch Out for Pickpockets," "Dial 911 in an Emergency," "Trespassers Will Be Prosecuted," and "Neighborhood Watch" all have a double meaning. They warn of possible harm. Some also suggest protection. Others have at least an aura of reassurance. "Only Authorized Personnel Are Admitted," "Members Only Admitted to These Premises," "Please Buckle Your Seatbelts and Stow All Packages Under The Seat In Front of You," and "These Premises Guarded By Ace Security" all have the reassuring quality that someone is concerned about our protection, even if the claim is misrepresented.

We are more likely to be reassured by *visible* signs of authority and particularly the visibility of persons who have some authority to ensure that we will be protected from intrusions into our private space. Visible uniformed public police are perhaps the most reassuring in democratic societies. We found in Oakland, California, that foot-patrol officers, officers on motorbike, and mounted uniformed police all were reassuring but that the mounted police were most reassuring because they were visible from the office tower as well as when going about on the street (Reiss, 1985: 14). Many office workers reported they were unafraid to leave their protected office space if they looked out the window and saw the mounted officers; one large office building had a sharp drop in patrons for its cafeteria once the police became highly visible on the streets of downtown Oakland (Reiss, 1985: 14). A mounted patrol has the additional advantage of reassuring the public. Horses reassure when their officers permit the public to talk to them, to stroke them, and even to serve as a perch for the kid's picture. Such public relations assure that the police are not only protectors but friendly ones who can be trusted.

More seems to be required than just a uniform, for what the uniform symbolizes as a protective resource seems more important. This is brought out when the visibility of uniformed private security forces are compared with those of the public police. Not only are private security personnel more likely to be regarded as instrumental rather than moral protectors, but as Shearing et al. (1985: 1) nicely show, "private security has not established itself as a stereotypic cultural object." They do not fit a general social category of protectors. Private police are seen in terms of personal characteristics rather than general social categories (Shearing et al., 1985: 6). Most of the public questioned by Shearing et al. felt they could rate police work but a third thought they could not do so for private security. To the degree that there was a core to their views of public and private police, the public—like their police—viewed security personnel as "low level inept persons" (Shearing et al., 1985: 7), hardly an image of a protector. Most could perceive a difference in their visibility on the basis of their uniforms, but that visible distinction is overlaid with a very weak image—if one exists at all— that they are there to protect. If anything, they are there to protect someone else's interests.

Cues as Clues to Intrusion

Although each of us seeks to protect our private space, to demand that others respect it, and to ensure that there are collective guarantees for its protection, each of us also invites or permits intrusion. Permission to intrude upon our private space is always conditional on its use for a specific purpose that is for our benefit. We may report our income to secure a loan for a home, a scholarship for our child, or as a legal obligation. The conditional nature of permissive intrusion is a signal that we regard it as a private or confidential matter and that we seek protection from any harm coming from disclosure.

Not all cues are voluntarily given, however. Each of us continually gives off cues and our possessions are cues to others. How we are dressed, what we are carrying, how we comport ourselves, and the state of our property, including ourself, all are cues to those who would invade as well as to those whose invasion we invite. Offenders and law enforcement agents are especially sensitive to our cues. But almost all occupations that deal with persons such as professionals and business or salespeople look for them. Some are more sensitive to physical behavior or condition and others to social and psychological states, but all of these cues potentially are keys to intrusion into private space. In that sense, the surgeon or salesperson is no less an invader than the assaulter or thief.

We ordinarily give signals to others that we are receptive to intrusion into our private domain. There are several different types of cues that indicate different degrees of openness, ranging from those that signal intimacy to those that signal cooperation.

Intimacy and intrusion. At the core of *personal* trust is an invitation to share one's private space with others. The most protected space is the private self—that which establishes one's unique identity and that has as its foundation the secret and nonsharable self. Just as a rape is a violent intrusion into the intimate self so is the consummation of love a merging of private selves. Trust is an invitation to explore one's private domain and love is an open invitation to do so. Even so, all of us tuck away some part that is unsharable and hide a part of it even from ourselves. It is that which makes psychoanalysis one of the most intensive of human experiences, for one must come to share with the analyst that which one ordinarily cannot share with oneself. Openness to intrusion into the inner self can be among the most painful as well as rewarding of human experiences.

The sharing of intimacy is for a limited few, however. What sets prostitution apart from intimate love is precisely that the turning of sex into a commodity or object relationship makes it a transaction in which the private self is protected. And, what sets friendship apart from a business or professional relationship is that the domains open are circumscribed by cues as to how far and how much intrusion into private space is possible. The rules of professional conduct and training in professional practice foster personal disengagement and asymmetry or lack of reciprocity. Professionals do not share equally with their clients in the exchange. Professional expertise is exchanged for private information. Still, when the cost or consequences of intrusion are perceived as low risk, considerable intrusion is possible, thereby making for disclosure of intimate content between strangers (Simmel, 1950: 127, 404).

Normally, adults are more open to intrusion by children than by adults. Adults more often interpret children's behavior as cues for assistance or are disarmed by the seeming openness of children. Yet, adults often mistake the cues of children as an absence of private space only to learn how quickly the child retreats from a lack of respect for his or her privacy. One notes, correspondingly, how quick adults are to take offense from the seeming lack of respect adolescents and teenagers display for their private space!

Public etiquette and intrusion. There is a public etiquette of intrusion into privacy. The rules of intrusion often differ for intimates, acquaintances, and strangers. The more intimate and parochial the setting, the more often one must allow intrusion, even though it may be stylized. The conventional greeting of "Gruss Gott" on meeting anyone in provincial Bavaria applies to intimates and strangers alike. In rural America one need not give advance notice of a visit to one's neighbors or even knock before entering. One must be reasonably accessible to others, even if it requires "putting on a face."

By contrast, as Simmel (1950), Wirth (1938), and others observed, the metropolis is not only a place of anonynmity but one of impersonality. We treat one another with at most courtesy and at the very least, suspicion. Intrusion is limited largely to seeking information, and the person who provides it is not expected to inquire as to why one wants that information. That is perhaps why it is so easy these days to substitute computers and their screens for people when providing information in public places.

Little is known about cues inviting intrusion in public behavior. Still, all of us search for cues as to when and where to intrude upon another's private space. If we wish information, such as to be given directions, we may be quite selective about whom we ask, lest we be rebuffed. Some years ago I had my students do random stops of strangers on the streets of New Haven, asking for directions in different forms to see what might be the response to their intrusion. Rebuffs were fairly common in random stops. They were far less so when each student was allowed to choose the person from whom to acquire the information. The student could not always articulate well the basis for making that choice or to specify why there was a failure when rebuffed. Not surprisingly, the cues they were most likely to look for when searching to request information of strangers in public places were those associated primarily with intimate cueing, such as friendly and smiling faces and "looking like they were not in a hurry." They were also more likely to seek information of persons who were like them—of the same race, age, sex, and social status or from "officials" who it seems likely will be able to provide that information.

Quite clearly, people search for strangers in positions of authority when intruding to request information. Observations of police in public places disclose that they are frequently asked to provide information. In a recently completed study on foot patrol in Boston, Massachusetts (Reiss and Miller, 1985), it was found, not surprisingly, that the composition of the beat affected considerably the rate of contact with strangers, casual acquaintances, and persons known by name. Where the beat included a large number of transient strangers, especially tourists and shoppers, such requests were unusually high. Three central area beats, for example, had recorded 40, 65, and 39 requests by strangers for information of foot-beat officers on one observed daily tour of duty (Reiss and Miller, 1985: 28). These requests were highly stylized with polite forms of address and request. There appears, then, to be an implied presumption that the officer is a public rather than a private self; yet, the form of the requests has an etiquette used when intruding into private space.

Cues for Police Intrusion

Policing is necessarily an intrusive activity and police officers must be trained in skills of how to intrude into private space and how to legitimate those intrusions. They must be sensitized both as to when intrusion is required of them and how to do so with a minimum of risk to the officer and usually, but not always, with a minimum of harm to the person or organization intruded upon. In deciding when to intrude, they must be alert to cues that private activity is being made invisible to intrusion. Detectives, for example, must develop interrogation skills to seek information and officers must be alert to suspicious persons and activities. Informants will be cultivated for their knowledge. Officers must learn to recognize cues of potentially harmful persons and activity if that harm is to be prevented. The very notion of "suspicion" carries with it sensitivity to such cues.

Similarly, when intruding, police officers must be sensitive to cues as to how people will respond. Responses can be cues not only of how an officer must deal with the person but they also serve to screen the law abiding from the law breaking. Research on policing of juveniles and adults emphasizes the importance of demeanor of the person stopped or apprehended by the police. Demeanor is consequential for disposition by the officer. Much depends upon how one responds to authority. Deference is more likely to bring lenient treatment or outright release, whereas challenges to authority— even subtle ones—are more likely to lead to an arrest in any kind of incident (Piliavin and Briar, 1964; Black and Reiss, 1970: 74-75). Moreover, failure to give cues of deference and cooperation with the police, especially cues that an effort is being made to control the officer's behavior or to resist the intervention, is more likely to lead to violence (Westley, 1953, 1970; Reiss, 1968: 18; 1970: 57-62).

Police are ever mindful that the most important cues they give are their visible presence as uniformed police. Their presumption is that police presence is a cue to deter unlawful and improper conduct—indeed, to control public etiquette. But, the cue of visibility is constraining for intrusion into private space and thus requires plainclothes rather than uniformed police. Spying, for example, requires very special training and skills because one must be sure that no cue is given off that will lead to exposure.

Cues for Offender Intrusion

A corollary of police intrusion into private space is prevention by offenders against police intrusion. Offenders ordinarily seek to cloak their behavior from being suspected. This means not only that they must avoid giving *cues* as to their intent and behavior but that they must avoid leaving the evidence of wrongdoing.

Stealthy offenders must be sensitive to cues in two senses. Not only must they cloak detection but they must be alert to cues that will permit intrusion without detection. It is surprising how little is known in criminology about how offenders search for and select potential victims or targets on the basis of cues. There are only commonsense notions about whether a residence is lighted and gives signs of occupancy, knowledge of the private space, the characteristics and behavior of persons, and particulars of the situation itself.

There are some rather substantial differences between public and private policing in the ways that they intrude upon private space and the cues that intrusion provides to both law abiders and law breakers. One way in which they differ substantially is the greater reliance that private police or security agents place upon technology or hardware to intrude upon people's privacy. Audio and visual equipment have the advantage that those whose privacy is intruded upon are unaware of it. Consequently, the private police do not face the same problems as do the public police when they intrude into the same matters. Awareness of the public police officer's intrusion is more likely to invite complaint about behavior and even physical attack threatening the officer's safety. Moreover, offender awareness of police presence leads to cloaking behavior that is more readily detected under technological surveillance.

Technological surveillance may also have a greater deterrent capability when the public is made aware of its use. Ordinarily its presence can be ubiquitous and continuous, something not as easily affordable with personal presence.

A PRISONER'S DILEMMA
AND DILEMMAS OF PROTECTION

Almost paradoxically, although we are sensitive to cues we are often unaware of being so. It is as if these cues operate subliminally. Moreover, we do not always translate our knowledge of variation in social and environmental cues into practical guides for our behavior. Most of us are certainly aware of how much risk varies in our real worlds. We know, for example, that some areas have higher crime rates than others or that we are more likely to be killed in an automobile than an airplane. And, we may actually choose what to do by weighing such risks. We make decisions about when risk is acceptable and when it is not. Similarly, we make judgments about how much protection exists to protect our private space against intrusion. Thus, we may decide to go out at night in our automobile rather than walk the streets and we will avoid going into some areas altogether, especially when alone.

We cannot, of course, know all of those risks and take them into account, especially those that threaten our private space. Much of the time most of us fail to comprehend how much those risks change from hour to hour and day to day—even minute to minute. The risks of intrusion into our private space change substantially as we move, for example, from our homes into the streets or from there into cars and highways, parking at the office or shopping center, on entering it, and again upon leaving it to go out into the streets. Under these circumstances self-protection is difficult because variation in risk is so considerable and each risk may require a different form of protection. The burden of self-protection is ameliorated to some degree by both public and private forms of police protection. The public police have a legal obligation for our protection and private police a legal liability when they assume it. Although both are legally obliged to *foresee* when others intrude into our private space, the consequences of such intrusions, and within reason, to prevent such intrusions, the private police are more likely to be held legally liable for failures to do so.

In the modern metropolis under all too many circumstances the public police are seen as failing to provide sufficient protection for intrusion into private space. They risk losing legitimacy as protectors against intrusions. This accounts in large part for the enormous growth of the private policing and the private security industry for large corporate and industrial facilities (Shearing and Stenning, 1981: 229). Government buildings, railway and airport terminals, courthouses, shopping centers, office buildings, and banks are privately protected. Although the private sector thus provides protection against intrusion and loss of corporate and governmental property (Shearing and Stenning, 1981: 212) as well as protection of persons within such domains, private persons are left essentially unprotected going between those places.

A dilemma for the citizen in a modern metropolis is that of becoming a prisoner of privately protected places when public places are viewed as essentially unprotected by the public police. Many citizens resort to moving among such privately protected spaces. They move from their self-protected domicile and motor vehicle to privately protected parking lots, office buildings, and shopping centers, for example. But in each case they are prisoners of such spaces and can move safely only *within* them and not *between* them. Perhaps one of the reasons for the rapid growth of arcades, plazas, and underground private byways is that they extend the size of one's "prison." Much public recreational or other space nevertheless is off limits. Each individual must assume the risk of going about publicly policed areas largely with only self-protection.

The extent to which people seek to be protected against intrusion into their private space, even when in privately protected places, is illustrated well by a growing body of case law in the United States. Many state constitutions, as well as the First Amendment to the U.S. Constitution, afford protection for free speech. In recent decades there have been broad interpretations of free speech coverage, especially where it involves matters of influencing others. Often the form of influencing others is regarded as an intrusion into private space, such as the use of amplification equipment that intrudes into one's private thoughts and speech, the distribution of leaflets as one walks about, and the seemingly endless interruption to sign some petition. Nowhere has controversy over this "right" generated more conflict in the United States than in privately owned and protected public places such as shopping malls. Both because their owners often have to deal with littering, noise, congregation within, and unwanted occupancy of their space as well as the complaints of their clients and customers who resent such intrusions into their private space, private owners have increasingly challenged whether access to their space is protected by constitutional guarantees of free speech. They have sought relief in the courts to exclude or restrict such use.

Although conflict over these forms of intrusion into private space is not resolved by the U.S. Supreme Court, a recent decision of the highest appellate court in New York State—the New York Court of Appeals—held that shopping malls are not public places where citizens are free to distribute politically related pamphlets as they choose. The ruling came in response to a case brought by an anti-nuclear protest group that was prohibited from distributing its literature by the Smithhaven Mall, a complex of 126 stores, walkways, and public areas in Lake Grove, Long Island, the largest retail center in Suffolk County, New York. The mall had enforced a blanket policy prohibiting handbilling. In a 5-to-2 opinion, the majority held that the free-speech provisions of the 1821 New York Constitution protected citizens only against governmental action and not restrictions imposed by private property owners. In the language of the opinion,

> While the drafters of the 1821 free-speech clause may not have envisioned shopping malls, there can be no question that they intended the State Constitution to govern the rights of citizens with respect to their government and not the rights of private individual against private individuals. [New York Times, 1985: B-11].

As much as case law may extend protections against intrusion into private space in privately owned public places, it does not solve the dilemma of the prisoner of private space. For inevitably one must move between public and private domains if one is to escape imprisonment.

Although there are only approximate solutions to dilemmas, it is to such approximations that U.S. cities faced with stemming the decline of its central cities have been turning. The public police, with their limited resources and priorities for allocating officers to police the central district, and the private police, with only limited jurisdiction that imprisons its public, are usually insufficient for the task. This is especially so because many persons fear to move beyond the confines of their self-protected and privately protected islands. Yet, often they have to do so, whether in going from a parking lot to some privately protected place or simply because their work or other activities require doing so. The suburb often seems a more attractive option for going about between privately protected places.

One rather ingenious approximation for resolving this dilemma has taken place in Oakland, California, where under the organizing genius of a Canadian developer of the downtown district and the cooperative interest of an Oakland police captain, the private sector agreed to a private assessment to provide funds for adding, by contract, public police officers to police the central area (Reiss, 1985: 16-18). The results have been most encouraging with not only evidence of decreased crime rates in the central district but of increased use of the public streets and increased commerce within the area, especially by its daytime occupants (Reiss, 1985: 39-45).

Yet, manpower is not enough to deal with the fears of intrusion into private space. For it turns out that persons are as concerned about "soft" as "hard" crime and other intrusions into their space as they move about the central district. They do not wish to be importuned, feel menaced by congregating youths, and by lack of conformity to public etiquette. To meet those fears, the Oakland Police Department has changed quite markedly its strategy of policing, reinstituting a diversity of peace-keeping strategies and enforcing the laws for soft crime and violations of ordinances. In cases when ordinances did not exist to cover an activity, they were successful in having them passed, such as a sack-sucking ordinance (prohibiting drinking any beverage cloaked by a paper bag) and restrictions on noise pollution (Reiss, 1985: 32).

There have been other approximations in other cities. In the Canadian city of Edmonton, Alberta, the Edmonton Police developed the Cooperative Policing Program for working with businesses and their private security agencies. A major part of this program is the joint monitoring of occurrences in malls by the police and security forces (*Liaison,* 19XX: 10-11). The most common has been an increase in the "rent-a-cop" industry. Many cities permit their sworn officers to do private duty with the full powers of their authority; some permit direct hiring by private corpora-

tions from the municipality whereas others leave it to a private contract. These officers are typically assigned to police the street areas
around a privately owned public place to exercise both compliance
and deterrence police roles.

Although each of these approximations raise important policy
issues about public policing authority and the allocation of public
policing resources, they are symptomatic of a demand by private
citizens that their private space be respected and protected in public as well as private places. They suggest, also, that protection
against intrusion cannot be left solely to public or private police
objectives. Employers of private police, therefore, may be shifting
from their major focus of protecting corporate property against
loss to protecting their employees and clients. The public police,
correlatively, may need to shift from major reliance on reactive
policing in response to citizen complaints of intrusions to proactive
compliance policing. Both appear to be shifting toward compliance
policing, especially as they seek to resolve the dilemma of the prisoner of private places. As they currently operate, private police
appear to have greater legal and practical opportunities to engage
in compliance policing, but the public police may rediscover that
police in the nineteenth century had many practical opportunities
to do so as well.

CONCLUDING REFLECTIONS

Modern citizens perhaps demand more protection against intrusion into their private space than did their predecessors. They
appear also to have expanded the scope of their private space. They
may even have increased the range of self-protection with technology such as the private automobile. Increasingly they have
demanded and received private protection as well, especially as
their belief in the capacity of the public police to afford protection
of their private space eroded. Yet, these protections may only have
exacerbated their situation. To ward off intrusions into their private space they have become its prisoners.

Perhaps our very strategies of policing have contributed to this
condition of modern cliff dwellers. The belief that the law centers
either upon deterring citizens from intrusions into private space or
litigating their consequences seems inadequate. Arresting offenders and tort litigation deal with harms that have occurred. Harm is
necessary to make private and criminal law systems work. Perhaps
that is not enough. Compliance models, based as they are histori-

cally in peace-keeping models of policing and in modern administrative law, may have more to offer as protections. Compliance seeks to prevent intrusions.

REFERENCES

BITTNER, E. (1967a) "The police on skid-row: a study of peace keeping." *American Sociological Review* 32: 699-714.
——(1967b) "Police discretion in emergency apprehension of mentally ill persons." *Social Problems* 14: 278-291.
BLACK, D. J. and A. J. REISS, Jr. (1970) "Police control of juveniles," *American Sociological Review* 34: 63-77.
ERICSON, R. V. and C. D. SHEARING (1986) "The scientification of police work," in G. Bohme and N. Stehr (eds.) *The Impact of Scientific Knowledge on Social Structures: Sociology of the Sciences Yearbook, vol. 10.* Dordrecht, West Germany: Riedel.
LEWIS, D. and G. SALEM (1985) *Fear of Crime: Incivility and the Production of a Social Problem.* New Brunswick, NJ: Transaction Books.
Liaison (19XX) "Cooperative policing: the way of the future?" Volume 9, pp. 9-12.
New York Times (1985a) "Albany high court lets malls restrict leafleting." (December 10: A-1, B-11.
——(1985b) "Excerpts from Court of Appeals Opinion." (December 10): B-11.
PILIAVIN, I. M. and S. BRIAR (1964) "Police encounters with juveniles," *American Journal of Sociology* 70: 206-214.
REISS, A. J., Jr. (1968) "Police brutality: answers to key questions," *Trans-Action* 5: 10-19.
——(1970) *The Police and the Public.* New Haven, CT: Yale University Press.
——(1983) "Crime control and the quality of life," *American Behavioral Scientist* 27: 43-58.
——(1984a) "Selecting strategies of social control over organizational life," in K. Hawkins and J. Thomas (eds.) *Enforcing Regulation.* Boston: Kluwer-Nijoff.
——(1984b) "Consequences of compliance and deterrence models of law enforcement for the exercise of police discretion," *Law and Contemporary Problems* 47: 83-122.
——(1985) *Policing a City's Central District: The Oakland Story.* Washington, DC: National Institute of Justice.
——and G. I. MILLER (1985) "An observational study of foot patrol in Boston, Massachusetts." New Haven, CT: Institution for Social and Policy Studies, Yale University.
SHEARING, C. D. and P. C. STENNING (1981) "Modern private security: its growth and implications," pp. 193-246 in N. Morris and M. Tonry (eds.) *Crime and Justice: An Annual Review of Research, vol. 3.* Chicago: University of Chicago Press.
——(1984) "From the Panopticon to Disney World: The development of discipline" pp. 335-349 in A. N. Doob and E. L. Greenspan (eds.) *Perspectives in Criminal Law:* Essays in Honour of John U.J. Edwards: Toronto: Canada Law Book.

————and S. M. ADDARIO (1985) "Public perceptions of private security,"
   Canadian Police College Journal 9: 225-253.
SIMMEL, G. (1950) The Sociology of George Simmel [Kurt Wolff, trans., ed.].
   New York: Free Press.
SKOGAN, W. and M. G. MAXFIELD (1981) Coping with Crime: Individual
   and Neighborhood Reactions. Beverly Hills, CA: Sage.
TAUB, R. P. and D. G. TAYLOR (1984) Patterns of Neighborhood Change:
   Race and Crime in Urban America. Chicago: University of Chicago Press.
————and J. D. DUNHAM (1981) "Neighborhoods and safety," in D. Lewis
   (ed.) Reactions to Crime. Beverly Hills, CA: Sage.
WESTLEY, W. A. (1953) "Violence and the police." American Journal of Soci-
   ology 59: 34-41.
————(1970) Violence and the Police: A Study of Law, Custom and Morality.
   Cambridge, MA: MIT Press.
WILSON, J. Q. and G. KELLING (1983) "Broken windows." Atlantic Monthly
   27, 4: 492-504.
WIRTH, L. (1938) "Urbanism as a way of life." American Journal of Sociology
   44: 1-24.

Chapter 2

PRIVATE JUSTICE AND THE POLICING OF LABOR:
The Dialectics of Industrial Discipline

STUART HENRY

In order to understand the actual state of the law we must institute an investigation as to the contribution that is being made by society itself as well as by state law, and also as to the actual influence of the state upon social law [Ehrlich, 1912: 504].

The factory is an establishment with its own code with all the characteristics of a legal code. It contains norms of every description, not excluding criminal law, and it establishes special organs and jurisdiction. Labor regulations and the conventions valid within economic enterprises deserve just as well to be treated as legal institutions as the manorial law of the feudal epoch. This too was based upon private rule, upon the will of a Lord. . . . No exposition of our legal order can be complete without it, it regulates the relations of a large part of the population [Renner, 1949: 114-115].

The recent flurry of work that recognizes private policing's contribution to the overall system of social control (Bowden, 1977, 1978; Bunyan, 1977; Draper, 1978; Shearing and Stenning, 1981, 1983; South, 1983, 1984; Spitzer and Scull, 1977; Stenning and Shearing, 1979) has given more attention to private security than to the broader phenomenon of private justice (Henry, 1978a, 1983). By private justice I mean the localized nonstate systems of admin-

AUTHOR'S NOTE: In its various stages this chapter has benefited from the comments and criticisms of a number of scholars to whom I am grateful. Most notably, these include Richard Abel, Peter Fitzpatrick, Elizabeth Morrissey, Clifford Shearing, and Timothy Carter. I also with to thank the British Economic and Social Research Council for funding the research on which the chapter was based with grant HR5907/2.

istering and sanctioning individuals accused of rulebreaking or
disputing within groups or organizations.[1]

Clearly, the range of institutions of private justice is as varied as
their source of generation. This can span from subadministrative
units within the wider system of state law, as evidenced by police
discretion, plea bargaining, and informal prison discipline, through
public, industrial, and commercial organizations with their ostensibly self-contained internal disciplinary bodies, boards, and pan-
els, to the relatively amorphous voluntary associations such as
self-help and mutual aid groups, whose members may impose
strict sanctions on their fellows. Nor should such a list exclude the
less obvious personal morality that one individual may generate
and impose on another or many others.

Any framework that is to grasp the totality of law and justice
must be sufficiently comprehensive to take account of these possibilities but not so broad as to be meaningless, as has become the
case for the overused and abused notion of "social control." The
framework I shall adopt here is a version of legal pluralism. This is
not the legal pluralism of Gierke (1900), who saw each institution
as the source of its own autonomous legal order, which was ultimately subordinate to state law. Ehrlich's (1912) insightful vision
of legal pluralism, wherein law was seen as a surface crust beneath
which was a series of layers of law-like rules and controls reaching
down to a dynamic source, the "living law" of the association, hints
at the right direction. But attention also needs to be paid to Gurvitch's (1947) contribution to this debate, which recognized that
while although there are numerous different sources of law with
their supporting systems of justice existing in a horizontal conceptual plane, each of these could also operate at different vertical
levels of formality, from fixed written law and procedures to spontaneous informal controls. Modern legal pluralists such as Pospisil
(1971) have certainly captured the essence of horizontal plurality
with the notion that "any human society . . . does not possess a
single legal system, but as many such systems as there are func-
tioning groups" (Pospisil, 1971: 98), and that the multiplicity of
these systems forms a mosaic of contradictory controls that simultaneously bear on an individual. But he arbitrarily talks of these
systems operating at various "levels" without recognizing Gurvitch's insight that each system is rooted in its own social form and
each can operate at a variety of levels of formality or informality.

More recently there has been a recognition that any notion of
legal pluralism must be simultaneously sensitive to the following:

the multitude of diffuse sources of power; the ways these generate their own forms of law and private justice, themselves operable at various levels of formality/informality; the substructures of power within any institutional form, ranging through factions to the individual human agent; the hierarchical ranking of substructures of power and their associated legal or normative orders and institutions of justice; the relations between each of these forms and state power; and crucially important, the notion that each institutional substructure of power and its form of law and justice can both penetrate and be penetrated by any other substructure and its associated form of law and justice, from the whole society at one level to the human agent at another (Abel, 1982; Fitzpatrick, 1983a, 1983b, 1984; Foucault, 1977; Henry, 1985; Santos, 1984). It is the central argument of this chapter that the nature of these relationships is best captured by a dialectical concept of legal pluralism.

A recent attempt at analysis from this perspective is Abel's (1981, 1982) notion of an endless cyclical relationship between formal and informal law in which first the formal, then the informal is expansive, with the movement between the two serving to legitimate the wider capitalist structure. Another attempt to formulate a dialectical concept is that by Galanter (1981), who argues that formal justice moves outward influencing indigenous orders of justice that exist in a variety of group and organizational settings where disputes are actually resolved; simultaneously this "legal shadow" provides "many rooms" of justice to handle the overflow from the formal state system.

However, I share Santos's view that the dialectical concept of "integral plurality" formulated by Peter Fitzpatrick (1983a, 1983b, 1984) is "so far the most stimulating and successful attempt to develop a social theory of legal pluralism" (Santos, 1984: 53). Fitzpatrick shows how state law is in part shaped by the plurality of other social forms, which includes substructures, such as the family, and their normative orders and how these other forms are simultaneously shaped by state law. He shows that this shaping is not so much external cause and effect but internal, such that some of the relations of state law *are* some of the relations of the social form and vice versa and that these relations exist in a dialectical, codetermining way.

In this chapter I have two aims. The substantive aim is to draw on my recent study of private justice in the workplace (Henry, 1979, 1982, 1983)[2] in order to illustrate Fitzpatrick's (1984) notion of integral plurality.[3] The more theoretical aim is to develop Fitzpat-

rick's dialectical concept of legal pluralism in order to suggest
how integral plurality operates not just between state law and other
social forms, but crucially, also *between* social forms. Finally, I
suggest that if modified to include the crucial dimension of human
agency, the resulting dialectical theory offers us the most promising framework for grasping the totality of law and private justice.

The chapter begins by briefly and critically reviewing the contribution of those who have looked at workplace discipline from a
perspective that gives priority either to the totality of social structure or to micro interaction, and argues that each of these approaches
assumes a far too mechanical relationship between components
constituting the totality of justice, in this case law and discipline.

TOTALIZING THEORY

Structural theorizing about private justice in the workplace examines changes in the form of private justice and relates the different
forms identified to structural changes in the society. Irrespective
of their political position these theorists agree that a change has
taken place in the form of discipline at work from "authoritarian-
punitive," which is characterized by harsh, rigid, irregularly applied
sanctions meted out to workers whose rule breaking is perceived as
willful and defiant acts, to a "representative-corrective" model that
uses "the co-operation of employees" to promote "self-discipline"
(Ashdown and Baker, 1973: 6). According to Jones (1961: 3-4):
"Although the individual is still penalized for his improper behavior, the action taken against him is . . . for changing his attitudes
and behavior so that in future he will meet expected standards."
Under this model those subject to discipline are accorded the rights
of natural justice, "notably a right to a fair hearing, a right to be
represented and a right of appeal" (Anderman, 1972: 57-58) and
"because discipline becomes impersonal and is meted out evenly
when someone violates these standards, it is accepted as fair that
such individuals should be disciplined" (Jones, 1961: 166).

Radical structural theorists (Kinsey, 1979; Lea, 1979; South and
Scraton, 1981) are concerned to associate changes from the "des-
potic rule" of early factory owners to the "man-management" of
the corrective representative model with changes in the wider society, arguing that this is simply a way for labor to be subordinated to
capital without the need for direct coercion (Henry, 1982). Under
the "contract of employment" the worker is ideologically manipu-

lated by organization of the production process and through his or her apparently voluntary acceptance of a contract to work. Worker participation in the administration of private justice is seen as little different from the nineteenth-century paternalism that, as South and Scraton (1981: 58-9) argue, "was not genuine participation, for the very form of traditional authority thereby legitimated was immutably based on a stable hierarchy."

Thus, both the consensus and radical structural theorists reduce discipline at work to a dependent aspect of developing capitalism. But little attempt is made to go beyond the notion that the emerging forms, incorporating participation, and corrective sanctions that function to legitimate the capitalist mode of production might also shape the wider structure and its system of law. Structural theory denies that private justice can be shaped in significant ways by the meaningful relations among constituent social forms, unless that meaning is preconstituted as functional to the wider capitalist structure. But it is not the case that private justice functions merely to support the capitalist relations of production, generating assent to the totality of social control and thereby reproducing the existing class-based social order. The relations of private justice exist actively and creatively as some of the relations of the total structure and cannot be reduced to or subordinated to that structure; they can and do give it new shape and direction. Nor is the possibility explored that what are ostensibly heralded as new developments in disciplinary form are no more than partial selections from the totality of interactive relations of private justice and themselves represent part of the ideological struggle of competing groups. If this were so, then what flourished as the disciplinary policy at any historical period would be merely a political construction, selected and rendered significant by pronouncement from the sum total of competing private justice forms that are actually operating at any given point in time and that have as their sources the myriad social forms that make up the workplace and the wider societal context in which it is set.

PLURALIST INTERACTIONISM

Those taking a micro pluralist approach (Gouldner, 1954; Mellish and Collis-Squires, 1976) argue that discipline at work is and always has been constituted through negotiated relationships between managers and unions whose conflicting interests are manifest both formally and informally. For example, Mellish and Collis-Squires (1976: 172) argue:

> What is a disciplinary issue depends in part on what management care to treat as such . . . on the interests they have in controlling any particular aspect of employee behavior and on their use, habitual or otherwise of disciplinary rules to control behavior. *But it will also depend on whether employees collectively allow an issue to be treated as an individual one.* This in turn will depend in part on their bargaining interests, strength and history [italics my emphasis].

Rather than seeing discipline at work as a reified product of social structure, these theorists show it to be a resource in the calculus between competing interest groups where "procedures may be operated or ignored for motives other than the settlement of issues technically falling within their scope . . . [and] 'sticking to the rules' or 'applying the procedure' can be a tactic used by either management or employees during disputes" (Mellish and Collis-Squires, 1976: 168).

But this is not to say that private justice has an autonomy that is independent of the social structure in which it is set. Nor are social actors completely free to pick and choose which elements of structure they shall use as resources in local power struggles. It is not enough to dismiss those recent changes in disciplinary technology (Henry, 1982) that have state legislation as their midwife, simply in terms of what management and workers find necessary for their local battles. These laws have real implications for the interpretative structure that is placed on particular disputes and that penetrate their nature, rendering some forms more credible than others, some more likely, and yet others more possible. Similarly, it is not enough to assume that participation by employees in discipline will occur whether formally granted or informally claimed, and as such mitigate sanctions that might otherwise have been harsher. State law can and does make a difference to the real power employee groups are able to exercise, just as the penetration of unions by organized crime has a real effect on whose interests are served by informal practices. Any perspective that does not attend to such incursions into workplace relations by the structure of the wider society must ultimately fail in its analysis.

In short, then, neither totalizing structural theory nor pluralist interactionism provide an adequate analysis for grasping the whole complexity of private justice. Instead we need a perspective that recognizes much more of a mutual interconnectedness between the wider social structure and the social relations between constituent parts constituting that structure; one that recognizes that social structure relies on the "semiautonomous" nature of private justice, just as private justice draws on the wider structure for support. But as we shall see later, acknowledging its semiautonomous nature means that some of the relations of private justice diverge from and are in opposition to those of the wider structure as are those of the wider structure in relation to them. It is in this sense that private justice, in its integral relations of support and opposition to the wider structure, is capable of transforming and penetrating that structure and its system of state law. It is the argument of this chapter that any framework that is to grasp adequately the relations between private justice and the totality of social structure must be grounded in a theory of integrative relations between social forms and social structure. It is the failure of previous attempts to develop fully such a theory that has starved their analysis of the capacity to capture the mutuality of constitutive relations between wider structure and component forms. By basing the analysis that follows in a dialectical perspective I hope to overcome this limitation and illustrate how such a position enables us to transcend the impasse that theorizing on private justice in the policing of labor has reached.

ON THE DIALECTICAL MUTUALLY CONSTITUTIVE RELATIONS BETWEEN STATE LAW AND PRIVATE JUSTICE

From his study of the impact of colonial law on the customs of developing nations Fitzpatrick (1980, 1981, 1983a, 1983b, 1984) has crafted a more sensitive version of structural Marxism than has hitherto been discussed. He rejects the totalizing theory of structural Marxists, arguing that these approaches are unable to grasp how social forms develop semiautonomously and in ways that are not wholly explainable in terms of functions served for the wider structure. But his celebration of the particular is also at odds with pluralism as "it does not seek to deny overarching and integrating structures of domination" (Fitzpatrick, 1984: 118). Taking the example of the family as one social form, Fitzpatrick (1983a: 159) argues that this is not ultimately subordinate to the overarching state legal order but exists in a mutually constitutive relationship with it such that the state legal order itself is profoundly affected by the family and its legal order. There is a constituent interaction of legal orders and of their framing social fields. One side of the interaction cannot be reduced to the other. Nor can both sides be reduced to some third element such as the capitalist mode of production.

As he argues elsewhere,

> It is not . . . so much that family relations function in support of relations of reproduction within the totality; family relations are some of those relations or reproduction . . . the family cannot be reduced to this totality or seen as only subordinate to it. [Fitzpatrick, 1983b: 8].

In his latest statement Fitzpatrick (1984: 115) offers us a sophisticated elaboration of this approach through his dialectical concept of "integral plurality." Here, "state law is integrally constituted in relation to a plurality of social forms" (Fitzpatrick, 1984: 115). From this perspective private justice institutions cannot be separated from the total society—for they are integral to it—such that some of the relations of private justice are some of the relations of the totality and vice versa. Nor can private justice be separated from state law, for each exists in a mutually constitutive relationship with the other. In this sense there is a constant movement between the parts and the whole that they constitute and both parts and whole change with a change in the other such that the parts and the whole may be described as "codetermining" (Swingewood, 1975; Lewontin et al., 1984).

An outcome of this dialectical relationship is that the shape or form of institutions of private justice may in part reflect the shape of the wider system of state law, but they may also diverge from it, as they are imbued with both the character of the societal structure in which they are rooted and with the uniqueness of the diverse individuals whose action constitutes their form.[4] Of particular interest here is the way in which larger structures such as state law, co-opt private justice forms of both similar and different shape, even when these forms exist in opposing relations to the totality. But equally important is the way this co-optation implies mutual penetration such that "bourgeois legality depends on social forms that tend to undermine it" (Fitzpatrick, 1984: 118).

Drawing on an interpretation of Hegel's concept of dialectic Fitzpatrick (1984: 117) argues that "social forms are constituted in contradictory relations of support and opposition with a plurality of other social forms" and that "the more social forms stand in relation of integral support, the sharper is the opposition between them."[5] He argues that state legal order (capitalist or bourgeois law) tends to converge with and diverge from, or maintain a distance from, other social forms. Relations with state law tend to converge not so much because of external influence but because "elements of law are elements of the other social form and vice versa" (Fitzpatrick, 1984: 122). For example, custom and law can have the same imperatives for behavior because law has incorporated custom into its codes and derives support from such incorporation. During incorporation, argues Fitzpatrick, "law transforms the elements of custom that it appropriates into its own image and likeness" (Fitzpatrick, 1984: 122). An excellent illustration of this is provided by the attempt in England to introduce a formalized and standardized code of discipline into industrial companies' disciplinary policy. The state legal order was brought into this arena amid a welter of other industrial labor legislation during the late 1960s for the purpose of reducing the growing number of strikes, one of the causes of which was identified as the arbitrary, custom-and-practice use of disciplinary and dismissals procedures. The belief was held, among government and industrialists, that if a formalized and standardized set of procedures could be adopted this would reduce the number of grievances and in its turn the number of strikes. I have documented elsewhere (Henry, 1982, 1983) how in England a succession of legislation based on survey data of industrial practice had by 1979 led to the industrywide adoption of the Code of Practice. The avoidance of this code could lead a company toward formal legal prosecution in the courts for the "unfair dismissal" of an employee, and result in subsequent fining as "compensation." The mutually constitutive relations of convergence wherein law and private justice were blended by a process of selection and sifting from existing custom-and-practice arrangements is captured in the following interview taken from my study:

> The form our discipline takes is that adopted in the Code of Practice (1977) . . . since going about these things in a different way might lead towards an industrial tribunal . . . The Code of Practice does in fact reflect the practices of industry. In drawing up the Code, ACAS, and the NJAC [advisory bodies to government] before them, did consult extensively with industry to find out what the practice was for discipline. They

have to some extent brought all these agreements, practices and customs together and said this appears to be what industry does and finds acceptable and therefore this is what we will recommend in the Code of Practice. We had disciplinary procedures for some years which predated the Code, but the Code certainly raised questions which we had to consider and we had to adopt similar provisions in our agreements.

The incorporation and transformation of private justice occurs in a variety of ways, from direct legislation commanding changes in rules and customary practices, through the employment of personnel such as security officers, who have experience in state legal systems, to the use of legal discourse in administering private justice. All of these shape the practice and form of private justice such that it can appear as a microcosm of the state legal system. For example, one manager I interviewed described his company's system of private justice as "comparable to court procedure:"

> The individual will be taken through the alleged offense. If the manager feels satisfied that there is a serious misdemeanor committed he will issue formal charges as we call them . . . at a formal interview he gives his defense. The formal interview then, takes the appearance, as it were, of a Magistrates' Court in that the man will come before the manager on an appointed date to answer the charges. The group manager will act as the prosecution and the person has the facilities for bringing with him a trade union appointed person as a spokesman or advocate. . . . Usually the group manager will have a note-taker, taking down the exchange of evidence. . . . The group manager will have to weigh up the evidence on both sides, whether or not he'll find the person guilty or not guilty and then decide on the punishment. The individual has got the right to lodge an appeal.

Moreover, it is not only that mutual appropriation and transformation occur in cases where private justice already closely approximates the shape of state law and the wider structure. Take the case of the joint misconduct committee of a tire company that I studied. The courts, in the form of an industrial tribunal (labor court), became enmeshed with this private justice form and in the process the overall shape changed; but the misconduct committee emerged from the case endorsed and strengthened. The company's industrial relations manager explained how, following the establishment of employment protection legislation, an employee took the company before an industrial tribunal on the grounds that its "misconduct committee was not right—the trade unions had no right to sit in judgment of their fellow workers":

> The chairman of the industrial tribunal ruled that if a trade union mutually agreed to a system of tribunal and one in which the man's trade union can say "We don't agree" and therefore you've got a hung jury—you have to adjourn it and let the man go back to work, then it was fair. He said ours was clearly written up in an agreement which everybody had put their signature to.

At the same time, however, the chairman of the court suggested that the company's joint participatory approach might be modified:

> He said, "I would like to point out that I think you should inform your employee of the offense he has committed in writing. You should spell out his rights under the law and his rights to appeal. He should have his shop steward with him." So we accepted all that. "And having done that I think your system is very good."

Notice then, that by accepting some due process modifications a tribunal of essentially different shape and practices to the formal legal system was given a degree of autonomy.

Indeed, as Fitzpatrick (1984: 122) points out, the process of appropriation and transformation is not one way but mutual, such that "law in turn supports other social forms but becomes in the process part of the other forms." This means that in supporting private justice, state law grants it a certain autonomy in decision making. In doing so, there is no guarantee that the definitions and practices used by private justice will conform to those of the state law. As we can see further on, forms of private justice generate their own criteria of what counts as rule breaking and what should be done about this. It is in this sense then that state law becomes transformed; its rule overall is not all of its rule in practice. One shop steward at a food manufacturing company, operating a joint management disciplinary tribunal, said:

> Petty pilfering—everybody does it right from the top to the bottom. All they say is "it's a bit of bad luck they caught me." It's something different to stealing—where somebody decides

they are going to have something and try to get it through the gate—or the clock fiddle. . . . It's different doing a quick pilfer as you go through—that's just temptation.

Similarly, a trade union representative in that company's disciplinary tribunal explained:

There's a difference in someone intentionally going to steal and succumbing to temptation. No way would I ever defend anybody that's walking out with half a dozen packets of it.

As another union representative to the tribunal demonstrated, his view of what counts as theft is not without consequences for the sanctions taken by the tribunal toward an offender:

The question is the volume and the value of the goods stolen. If it's say minor, one packet, we very often say to the management "Give him a good ticking off and tell him not to do it again," because it's not worthy of anything more. Then as the volume increases . . . you will go from say a day's suspension up, depending on the value of the goods stolen, to as much as two weeks suspension, if the offense is very grave.

Nor does management necessarily share the view of the formal courts of law on what counts as theft. As one factory manager on the tribunal explained:

Our understanding of what is a "fair cop," as opposed to what the outside courts might say, is totally different. We would understand that it is relatively easy to pilfer but that someone would have to go out of their way to amass a large bed-wrapper full of different sorts of them. Whereas to the courts a bag full of one sort would be indistinguishable from a bag full of another sort . . . I think you do actually temper what goes on by your knowledge of the site and . . . of the working conditions.

At a general level, then, we can see how state law and other social forms, in this case private justice at work, are dialectically and constitutively related. In considering "the operative modes taken by the contradictory relations of opposition and support" Fitzpatrick (1984: 118) begins a more systematic mapping of the "complex of contradictions" that is "founded on the dichotomy of

convergence and separation between law and other social forms."
He says constitutive relations of convergence have both positive
and negative aspects as do constitutive relations of separation or
divergence.

Relations of mutual support in a positive aspect can be seen in
the case of the following manager who explained how law supports
his company's system of private justice:

> I think we are better with the Code. . . . It enables the man-
> ager to manage more effectively in the secure knowledge that
> he is behaving in a way which is regarded as reasonable. I
> constantly argue with managers who say "Oh the tribunals
> [labor courts] mean we can't sack anybody" and I say on the
> contrary what the legislation has given us is the means by
> which we can dismiss someone fairly as a result of his own
> misconduct.

Although labor courts might appear to support individual employees in opposition to the internal system of private justice, they also
can constitute it positively.

The reverse mutuality in which private justice supports state law
is perhaps at its most obvious in its "prosecution" of employees for
theft and their punishment with fines or dismissal. The severity of
such punishment and the concomitant degree of support for formal
law will, as we have just seen, be dependent upon a number of factors, not least the other prevailing orders of private justice in a
workplace. It should already be clear, though, that private justice,
in spite of its relative autonomy from state law, can also be seen as
supportive of that law. As a union official said:

> I can remember a woman working here who was caught shop-
> lifting outside. Now as a result of that the police visited her
> home and found there some of our roller towels. So then the
> police came to the company and asked, "Had she got authority
> for these towels?" "No, she'd been stealing them." A tribu-
> nal met and decided on a week's suspension so she lost a
> week's pay. For the shoplifting offense the court gave her a
> suspended sentence—which means nothing.

Although it might be thought that relations of mutual support
occur more readily when the form of private justice is similar to state
law, this is not so. The last example was in fact taken from a joint
disciplinary system where the tribunal was made up of workers and

management and together these groups made a collective consensual decision about the cases before them. Moreover, I have also shown how this same relationship holds for forms of justice very different from state law, themselves rooted in untypical and oppositional social forms such as worker cooperatives (Henry, 1985).

Relations of mutual support also have their negative aspect because since by displacing some of the functions of law, convergence has a "tendency towards dissolution" (Fitzpatrick, 1984: 123). In reverse mutuality supportive relations exercised by the state law for private justice take away some of the power and authority that might have remained the prerogative of the local normative order, in this case workplace discipline.

> Dismissal is the ultimate power that we've got and even that is, of course, very very much restricted by the legislation in recent years—the Employment Protection Act. Everything is now dealt with, with the view that it might go to one of these tribunals [industrial courts].

Yet the support can again swing positive as the same manager acknowledges:

> To be fair, I understand that if this is dealt with properly through our own procedures, a tribunal will not throw it out.

Next Fitzpatrick considers relations of divergence or separation between state law and social forms. He argues that law relates positively to social forms by its very separation from the law. As he says:

> Law is separated from other social forms. It assumes some separate and autonomous identity in positive constitutive relations to other social forms. These are the relations of separation in their positive aspect. Law would not be what it is if related social forms were not what they are [Fitzpatrick, 1984: 123].

This is not as tautological as it sounds because it carries the same sense as Durkheim's famous dictum on the functional role of crime: "Crime brings together upright consciences and concentrates them" (Durkheim, 1893: 102), by which Durkheim meant that crime provides an occasion for the celebration and maintenance of law by invoking collective shock and cohesion against those activities that it defines as unacceptable. We might say, to paraphrase Durkheim, that in the divergent mode, private justice brings together capitalist legality and concentrates it. Thus, in the case earlier of the tire company, the industrial labor court makes it clear that the joint system of justice, though acceptable for those who agreed to it, is not *its* system of justice. In this distancing law is constituted positively.

Simultaneously, by the distance it maintains from state law, private justice can draw legitimacy from those over whom it has jurisdiction and is thereby also positively supported in its divergence. For example, employees in the food manufacturing company who were subject to a joint disciplinary tribunal argued the following:

> It's better than prosecution in a court. The management consider your work record, how long you've been here, or if you've done it before. In court they've got too much to do to consider all that. They just take you as another case.

> If they hadn't got the tribunal they'd have outside police in wouldn't they? And then your name and everything's gone. Here you might get two or three days suspension . . . which is surely better than having it plastered in all the papers.

> When the law becomes involved it's different because the judiciary don't really understand the feelings on the shop floor, what motivates people. But that chairman, those three union fellows, that manager who had come up through the shop floor himself, knew what it was like out there, what could have aggravated the situation.

Finally, Fitzpatrick (1984: 123) describes relations of separation or divergence in their negative aspect. Here "identity is asserted or maintained in the rejection of other social forms." Fitzpatrick identifies two ways in which rejection and opposition occur. The first and more obvious way is "outright rejection." As was argued before, state law is shaped in part by the distinctions that are made between it and other forms of justice. The distinctions may be made directly, as in those cases where laws are passed that are designed to control the activities of institutions of private justice, enforcing them to bring their disciplinary actions in line with the Code of Practice, and fining them by compensation payments to individual workers who bring unfair dismissal cases against their former employers. But this rejection of the private system by the courts need not eliminate the practices so much as sharpen the separation between these courts and factory tribunals. This may result in the system of private justice disregarding the law, just as law is disregarding private justice, and retaining its identity in rejecting state law. As one manager said:

> If we have got a bad apple in the barrel and we discipline him and he chooses to take us to a tribunal and they find against us and order us to—not to reinstate—but to pay compensation of 3,000 or 4,000, then the company is still better off to be rid of that individual . . . losing the case . . . would not deter us from taking precisely the same kind of action in a repeat case. Because we do what we think is right and if we are unlucky and trip up at the tribunal or get caught on the technicalities, or they think otherwise, then we will foot the bill. Because otherwise you put yourself in blackmail situations and I think once you start asking "What will happen if we did take it to a tribunal?" then you've lost your objectivity which is essential to remain.

Similarly, the refusal of an employer to enforce the sanctions specified in the company's legally constituted disciplinary code, perhaps because to do so would invoke problems of labor relations, means that theft law is not being enforced. It means too that the notion of private property ownership embodied in theft law is rendered malleable, just as it is in custom, such that there is never a clear line around the rightful owner. Who this owner is deemed to be depends upon time, place, interests, and whim. Thus, in relations of separation, law is shown neither to maintain completely its own form, nor always to be certain of relations of support.

We can see here, too, a further irony revealed by this perspective: Private justice, while opposing state law in the interests of its own social form (the factory enterprise), is simultaneously supporting the wider social structure, because industrial relations are maintained and industrial production continues to flow. Indeed, this same support for the wider social structure occurs when state law opposes private justice by granting an employee the right of compensation for unfair dismissal. Here the law is seen to work in the interests of the individual over the corporation, promoting a sense of justice that in turn confers legitimacy on the existing capitalist social structure. This illustrates too the importance of considering the dialectical relations between organizational forms and legal orders as well as those between legal and normative orders rooted in different organizational forms.

Finally, the distinction between law and other normative orders might be made less directly, as is the case when legal norms accept the validity of other norms within their own sphere without seeking to generalize them by incorporation:

> Law sets and maintains an autonomy for opposing social forms keeping them apart from itself and purporting to exercise an overall control. Yet this control is merely occasional and marginal. . . . In the limited nature of its involvement with other social forms, law accepts the integrity of that which it "controls." Its penetration is bounded by the integrity of the opposing social form [Fitzpatrick, 1984: 126-27].

Thus, Fitzpatrick concludes that "law is the unsettled product of relations with a plurality of social forms. As such, law's identity is constantly and inherently subject to challenge and change" (Fitzpatrick, 1984: 138). We might observe that the same is true of private justice with respect to its relations with state law.

Fitzpatrick's contribution to dialectical or integrated theorizing in his series of well-crafted expositions contributes to our understanding of law by enabling us to grasp the complexity of the relations between the law of society and the private justice of the social forms that make up a society. However, I should like to point to a number of areas where Fitzpatrick's theory of integral plurality might be developed and to suggest how these developments might be used to expand our framework for examining the relations between law and private justice.

ON THE MUTUALLY CONSTITUTIVE RELATIONS BETWEEN FORMS OF PRIVATE JUSTICE

Although Fitzpatrick's theory of integral plurality takes us further than other approaches to an understanding of the relations between state law and other social forms, there are certain limitations that need to be overcome if the theory is to be fully comprehensive. The first issue to be resolved in developing Fitzpatrick's theory is to distinguish clearly between forms of private justice and the social forms in which they are rooted. I have indicated earlier that insofar as each is constituted in fact in relation to the other, there is an element of artificial separation here. Nonetheless, I believe it is helpful for the analysis to conceive of the broader social form as the organization or collectivity of people sharing some common enterprise and interaction, whereas the form of private justice is the specific arrangements whereby members of a social form organize efforts to control one or more of its members or one or more members of another social form. Clearly, there are as many forms of private justice as there are social forms and an infinite number of these is possible.

A second, related issue that is not addressed by Fitzpatrick is whether there are different levels of social form and associated private justice. I am not suggesting that we should conceive of relations in terms of hierarchical superiority and subordination, which would negate the pluralist element. Nor am I talking here about levels of formality or informality. Rather, I am arguing that we need to tie what is taken to be a social form to the method of analysis. If we start with the notion of society as the all-inclusive social form (obviously a larger form could be postulated such as the world system) then it is possible to abstract parts from this whole such that the original part becomes the new whole. An industrial enterprise, therefore, might be one abstracted part from a capitalist society. It is possible to then further abstract from the industrial enterprise to its own constituent parts—say, management, trade unions, employees, and so on. Similarly, once formulated, it is possible to further abstract from these parts that are themselves each treated as new parent wholes. For example, a group of employees is made up of numerous subgroups or factions. One could continue in this fashion until the level of constituent individuals is reached.

It is of crucial importance here to retain the notion that any one of these parts is a part of something larger such that it exists not only in mutually supportive and opposing relations with that from which it is extracted, but also with the original whole and with the other parts. As Swingewood (1975: 44-45) says:

> The part, then, cannot be abstracted from the whole and sociologically examined apart from it and then mechanically inserted again after analysis. . . . For the fundamental principle of dialectical theory is that empirical facts must be integrated into a whole or they remain abstract and theoretically misleading.

This raises a third issue. How far should one abstract parts from wholes, or to put it another way, how many stages or levels of abstraction should there be? I take the view that this should be guided by two principles. First the number of stages of abstraction should not be so great as to make impossible a meaningful and intelligible framework for understanding the myriad mutually supportive and opposing relations between parts and wholes at different levels of abstraction. Second, and of crucial importance, is to abstract from the totality until we reach the level of the individual. Just as any characterization of a social form would be misleading without relating it to the widest totality (that is, the character of the whole society) so it would be equally misleading if characterizations of a society or the parts thereof were not related both to other social forms and ultimately to the human agency of the individuals that constitute these forms.

Fitzpatrick does not address these issues, although he recognizes their possibility. His solution is to stop at the first stage. However, this fails to consider the ways social forms are constituted by their mutual relations both with other social forms and with private justice systems. Second, and of crucial importance, it is imperative to address the contribution of human agency, not merely as another social form, but as both the spirit and medium of human creativity wherein interrelations between social forms and systems of justice are constituted. However, we need to go even further than this second dimension of analysis as both social forms and the wider structure that they constitute are themselves constituted by human agents. Because Fitzpatrick leaves out the individual agent he "reifies" the parts and wholes with which he deals. By "reify," I mean that he cuts out the very essence, the lifeblood of dialectical movement, which is human agency. He commits what Whitehead (1926) called the "fallacy of misplaced concreteness," and what for Marx was the error that made the social relations between men assume the form of a relation between things. Thus, in discussing the dialectical relations between law and social forms, Fitzpatrick talks of law maintaining an identity, having an autonomy, and so on. But it is only through human agents' interaction that law and other social forms are constituted; people make laws even though not in circumstances of their own choosing. It is only through human interaction that law relates to private justice, and Fitzpatrick does not consider this in his analysis. The omitted element is crucial to a full understanding of the totality of law and private justice because not only does law relate dialectically to private justice and to social forms at different levels of abstraction, but it does so through human agency. All exist in mutually constitutive relations. Without incorporating the agency-structure dialectic it is too easy to *assume* the character that social forms take, that is, "capitalistic," or "socialistic," and moreover to impose on them a character that in reality is derived from their roots in *both* agency and structure.

A number of theorists have been addressing the agency structure dialectic (see Giddens, 1979, 1982; Collins, 1981; KnorrCetina, 1981; Archer, 1982). Giddens, for example, argues that any examination of structure without reference to human agency or to agency without reference to structure is essentially misleading because action and structure presuppose one another in a mutually dependent relationship. Giddens argues that the structural properties of societies are both the medium and the outcome of the practices that constitute these societies and that structure thereby both enables and constrains actions that can change it. Each action, on the other hand, is at once new and performed in a historical context that without barring or mandating the action is involved in its production as a resource or a means through which the relationship between the particular action and the total social structure expresses itself. Thus, Giddens says, "Institutions do not just work behind the backs of the social actors who produce and reproduce them;" rather, "all social actors, no matter how lowly have some degree of penetration of the social forms which oppress them" (Giddens, 1979: 72). For Giddens (1982: 197-199),

> to be a human agent is to have power to be able to "make a difference" in the world. . . . In any relationship which may be involved in a social system, the most seemingly "powerless" individuals are able to mobilize resources whereby they carve out "spaces of control" in respect of their day-to-day lives and in respect of the activities of the more powerful. . . . There are many ways in which the seemingly powerless, in particular contexts, may be able to influence the activities of those who appear to hold complete power over them; or in which the weak are able to mobilize resources against the strong. . . . Anyone who participates in a social relationship . . . necessarily sustains some control over the character of that relationship or system . . . actors in subordinate positions are never wholly dependent, and are often very adept in converting whatever resources they possess into some degree of control over the conditions of reproduction of the system. In all social systems there is a dialectic of control, such that there are normally continually shifting balances of resources altering the overall distribution of power . . . an agent who does not participate in the dialectic of control *ipso facto* ceases to *be* an agent.

What is required, then, is a modification of Fitzpatrick's theory of integral plurality to include, first, the dimension of multiple dialectical relations of support and opposition between the range of social forms, and, second, the dimension of human agency.

Just as mutually supportive and opposing relations were possible between state law and private justice, so to is this possible between the private justice of different social forms. I have already described, for example, how management as a social form may form an alliance with other social forms, such as a union of workers, and in so doing undermine its own private justice system. This occurs when to invoke private justice in the form of the company disciplinary code may cause a disruption of production through strike action that would work against the interests of the enterprise. Here, then, social forms can be seen working in opposition to both their own system of justice and state law.

Similarly, insofar as employees as a group constitute another social form we can see that they are also capable of generating their own forms of private justice. Peer groups of employees who sanction their fellows could be seen as the informal operation of a worker-based system of private justice, whereas union labor disciplinary bodies would constitute a more formalized manifestation. In some instances the private justice of employees exists in supportive relations with the private justice of the factory, although they may simultaneously exist in relations of opposition with state law. An example of supportive relations at this level is given where a group of workers engaged in petty pilfering from their employer sanction a fellow for stealing too much. As Mars's (1974) study of pilfering by longshoremen showed, workers place limits on the amount of cargo that it is felt acceptable to take from a ship. A worker taking more than this value is seen as engaging in theft. Similarly, Horning (1970: 62) in a study of factory pilfering, found a view that "pilfering should be limited to that which is needed for personal use. To exceed these limits was viewed as a threat to the entire system." As one of Horning's subjects told him, "The workers frown on people who do it on a large scale because they're afraid the company will crack down on everyone!" They might exert friendly social control, such as "a word in their ear," or more collectively, as Horning (1970: 62) has shown, support of the work group might be withdrawn, "which includes the right to neutralize one's feelings and deny oneself the definition of one's acts as theft."

This example also illustrates the point that relations of support can operate between forms of private justice having a different shape and rooted in different social forms. Thus, by controlling the individual rule breaker who goes too far, the worker's private justice is maintaining theft losses to a controllable level and one that is acceptable to management as "shrinkage," "waste," and "write-offs." But at the same time the employee's justice in collusion with the social form (the business), is actually opposing state law as its action serves to preserve a general level of theft.

There are occasions, however, when the private justice of one social form is in opposing relations with that of another and with the state law. Take again the case of an individual disciplined for theft by a company's disciplinary machinery. The employee's private justice—that is, worker peer group sanctions—may lend support to the individual in a way that opposes, indeed, negates the effect of the company's disciplinary sanctions:

> All they said was "stupid bugger. Fancy getting caught with that. Why didn't you take a bigger piece?" . . . It would be a one day talking point then that's it. He'd get two day's suspension and when he comes back somebody would say, "Have you enjoyed your holiday?"

Conversely, state law can be aligned with one social form in opposition to that form's own system of private justice. Take as illustrative the case of an employee whom management wishes to sanction, but cannot because of its own disciplinary procedures. It is possible to draw on state law and undermine its own system of private justice. As a senior union representative I interviewed explained:

> They'd done a shop steward and they sacked him. Had he been an ordinary employee he would have had to go through the tribunal system and I'm ninety nine percent certain he would have still been working here. But they had fixed opinions of this guy. That was it—instant dismissal. Now when I walked in the room with the management, there in front of me was an open copy of the ACAS Code of Practice which says "a union representative can be seen in front of the senior shop steward and dealt with by the company." It stinks to me. The firm is now saying "Well we'll now put before the tribunal who we want to and those that we don't we'll see to ourselves because we will use outside words . . . the legislation." In other words, the company will use ACAS when it suits their purpose, which completely invalidates a local factory tribunal.

These examples should suffice to demonstrate the ways in which different social forms and their systems of private justice exist in mutually interconnected ways and so underline the complexity of the different relations of support and opposition.

CONCLUSION

I began this chapter by suggesting that private policing was one component of the wider phenomenon of private justice, and, further, that private justice was itself part of the totality of social control. I argued that it is necessary to develop a framework that is capable of grasping the totality of law and justice rather than limiting discussion to its more formalized and overt components. In locating the search for such a framework within one substantive area, private justice in the policing of labor, it has been possible to review perspectives that attempt to explain private justice in terms of both macro-structuralist and micro-interactionist accounts. These were rejected as both partial and mechanistic in accounting for the relations between forms of private justice and state law. A significant advance in understanding was made through the use of Fitzpatrick's dialectical theory of integral plurality and this was shown to be illuminating when applied to specific examples drawn from empirical evidence on workplace discipline.

The central theme to emerge from this analysis is that state systems of law and social control are constituted through mutually constitutive relations with a variety of forms of private justice; and that in the mutually penetrating relations state law gains identity and support through the co-optation of private justice, *but simultaneously* loses identity and generates opposition through fostering the semiautonomy of the private forms. This is not to say that law and formal justice dominates and subordinates but that it incorporates and in doing so is itself transformed. But this transformational capacity is mutual, such that while law is changed in its constitutive relations with private justice, so private justice is changed from what it would be were there no law.

Nor was the dialectical process found to be limited to relations between law and private justice. In addition, private justice was demonstrated to be mutually constituted in its relations with other forms of private justice, each simultaneously opposing and supporting those forms with which they have relations.

However, a central question remains unanswered. Why do social forms such as state law and the varieties of private justice exist in mutually interpenetrating relations at all? In one sense this is because society is a dialectically constituted totality. But this glib answer evades the issue. So far in this chapter I have only sign-posted a possible explanation; the evidence I have presented affords nothing more. Besides, it was necessary to establish the credibility of dialectical explanations of relations between forms before moving to the next stage of analysis. It is that in spite of a tendency to reification, human agency in its construction of social forms embodies dialectical process: movement between forms, separation and convergence of an apparent whole into its constituent parts, undercutting that which it creates, creating anew, destroying as it builds to destroy what it is, building through denial and contradiction. How else do we explain why every construction has an alternative emerging from within it, why every formalized system has its informalities and "hidden" forms, why even informal forms have their informalities? These are not dismissable as anomalies, exceptions, marginal cases, and so forth, but are evidence of the centrality of the internal dialectic of human agency projected into apparently objectifiable forms that bob and weave to the insecurity of their constitution and to the dismay of anyone attempting comprehensive constructions. This is why all typologies have their dustbin categories, all frameworks their exceptions. In short, although an attempt to capture the totality of law, policing, and justice by incorporating private and informal forms is an advance over partial approaches that seek to continue the ideological mystification that feigns at reality, it should be reassuring to know that even this must fail.

NOTES

1. As such, private justice forms one of a variety of "informal institutions" that are operative in all those areas that we have come to consider the province of societywide formal systems. For overviews of this broader area, see Henry (1981).

2. The research on which this chapter is based, reported in detail in Henry (1983), involved postal questionnaires, interviews with management, unionists, and employees and limited observation of disciplinary hearings. In all, 40 companies were sampled by questionnaire and from a further 10 companies, 21 managers, 5 unionists, and 18 employees were interviewed using tape-recorded interviews producing 800 pages of transcript material. The data was gathered in England in 1979 and 1980.

3. Any arena could have been chosen for the examination of institutions of private justice in their relations with state law. Fisher (1975), for example, looks at universities, labor unions, and prisons, whereas MacCallum (1967) looks at the shopping mall, and elsewhere I have addressed the phenomenon in the con-

text of self-help groups (Henry, 1978b). A distinction needs to be made between those institutions of private justice that occur "naturally" as part of any structured setting, such as discipline at work, in prisons, and in universities, and those institutions that are artificially constructed by bodies external to the organizational or community setting for the purpose of administering control, such as neighborhood justice centers.

4. The issue of what counts as human agency and how this generates dialectical movement between and within social forms is only touched on in the conclusion of this chapter; for a more thorough treatment, see Henry (1987).

5. Unfortunately, the term "social form" in Fitzpatrick's analysis is used to refer to both the legal order and the social organization or organizations in which it is rooted. Although it would be clearer to separate social form from legal form or normative order, Fitzpatrick is also aware that such separation would itself be artificial and necessitate a discussion of the dialectical integrally constitutive relations between legal orders and their parent social structures, because from his perspective each is a part of the other. But his purpose is not to address the whole complex of contradictory dialectical relations but to limit discussion to state law as a social form, showing how other social forms, which may include private justice rooted in subcollectives of the totality, are conditions of its existence. Nor does he consider (though he is aware of the issue) how other social forms exist in dependent constitutive relations with state law.

REFERENCES

ABEL, R. (1981) "Conservative conflict and the reproduction of capitalism: the role of informal justice." *International Journal of the Sociology of Law 9:* 245-267.

———(1982) *The Politics of Informal Justice, vol. 1.* New York: Academic Press.

ANDERMAN, S. D. (1972) *Voluntary Dismissals Procedure and the Industrial Relations Act.* London: PEP.

ARCHER, M. S. (1982) "Morphogenesis versus structuration: on combining structure and action." *British Journal of Sociology 33:* 445-483.

ASHDOWN, R. and K. BAKER (1973) *In Working Order: A Study of Industrial Discipline.* Report, Dept. of Employment, London.

BOWDEN, T. (1977) "Who is guarding the guards?" *Political Quarterly 48:* 347-53.

———(1978) *Beyond the Limits of the Law,* Harmondsworth, England: Penguin.

BUNYAN, T. (1977) *The Political Police in Britain,* London: Quartet.

COLLINS, R. (1981) "On the micro foundations of macro-sociology." *American Journal of Sociology 86:* 984-1014.

DRAPER, H. (1978) *Private Police.* Harmondsworth, England: Penguin.

DURKHEIM, E. (1893) *The Division of Labor in Society.* Chicago: Free Press.

EHRLICH, E. (1912) *Fundamental Principles of the Sociology of Law.* Cambridge, MA: Harvard University Press.

FISHER, E. (1975) "Community courts: an alternative to conventional criminal adjudication." *American University Law Review 24:* 1253-1291.

FITZPATRICK, P. (1980) *Law and State in Papua New Guinea.* London: Academic Press.

——(1981) "The Political Economy of Dispute Settlement in Papua New Guinea," in S. Spitzer (ed.) *Research in Law and Sociology. A Research Annual, vol 3.* Greenwich, CT: JAI Press.
——(1983a) "Law plurality and underdevelopment," pp. 159-182 in D. Sugarman (ed.) *Legality, Ideology and the State.* London: Academic Press.
——(1983b) "Marxism and legal pluralism." *Australian Journal of Law and Society 1:* 45-59.
——(1984) "Law and societies." *Osgood Hall Law Journal 22:* 115-138.
FOUCAULT, M. (1977) *Discipline and Punish.* Harmondsworth, England: Allen Lane.
GALANTER, M. (1981) "Justice in many rooms: courts, private ordering and indigenous law." *Journal of Legal Pluralism 19:* 1-47.
GIDDENS, A. (1979) *Central Problems in Social Theory: Action, Structure and Contradiction in Social Analysis.* London: Macmillan.
——(1982) *Profiles and Critiques in Social Theory.* London: Macmillan.
GIERKE, O. (1900) *Political Theories of the Middle Age.* Cambridge, England: Cambridge University Press.
GOULDNER, A. (1954) *Patterns of Industrial Bureaucracy.* New York: Free Press.
GURVITCH, G. (1947) *The Sociology of Law.* London: Routledge & Kegan Paul.
HENRY, S. (1978a) *The Hidden Economy.* Oxford, England: Martin Robertson.
——(1978b) "The dangers of self-help groups." *New Society 44:* 654-656.
——(1979) "Controlling the hidden economy." *Employee Relations 1:* 17-22.
——[ed.] (1981) *Informal Institutions.* New York: St. Martin's Press.
——(1982) "Factory law: the changing disciplinary technology of industrial social control." *International Journal of the Sociology of Law 10:* 365-384.
——(1983) *Private Justice: Towards Integrated Theorising in The Sociology of Law.* London: Routledge & Kegan Paul.
——(1985) "Community justice, capitalist society and human agency: the dialectics of collective law in the Co-operative." *Law and Society Review 19:* 301-325.
——(1987) "The construction and deconstruction of social control," in Lowman et al. (eds.) *Transcarceration: Essays in the Sociology of Social Control.* Farnborough, England: Gower.
HORNING, D. (1970) "Blue collar theft: conceptions of property. Attitudes toward pilfering and work group norms in a "modern plant," pp 46-64 in E. Smigel and H. Ross (eds.) *Crimes Against Bureaucracy.* New York: Van Nostrand Reinhold.
JONES, D. L. (1961) *Arbitration and Industrial Discipline.* Ann Arbor: University of Michigan Press.
KINSEY, R. (1979) "Despotism and legality" pp. 46-64 in Fine et al. (eds.) *Capitalism and the Rule of Law.* London: Hutchinson.
KNORR-CETINA, K. (1981) "Introduction: the micro sociological challenge of macro sociology: toward a reconstruction of social theory and methodology," in K. Knorr-Cetina and A. Cicourel (eds.) *Advances in Social Theory and Methodology: Toward an Integration of Micro- and Macro-Sociologies.* London: Routledge & Kegan Paul.
LEA, J. (1979) "Discipline and capitalist development," pp. 76-89 in Fine et al. (eds.) *Capitalism and the Rule of Law.* London: Hutchinson.

LEWONTIN, R., S. ROSE, and L. KAMIN (1984) *Not in our Genes: Biology, Ideology and Human Nature*. New York: Pantheon.

MacCALLUM, S. (1967) "Dispute settlement in an American shopping center," pp. 291-299 in P. Bohannon (ed.) *Law and Warfare*. New York: Natural History Press.

MARS, G. (1974) "Dock pilferage" pp. 209-228 in P. Rock and M. McIntosh (eds.) *Deviance and Social Control*. London: Tavistock.

MELLISH, M. and N. COLLIS-SQUIRES (1976) "Legal and social norms in discipline and dismissal." *Industrial Law Journal* 5: 164-177.

POSPISIL, L. (1971) *Anthropology of Law*. New York: Harper & Row.

RENNER, K. (1949) *The Institutions of Private Law and Their Social Functions*. London: Routledge & Kegan-Paul.

SANTOS, B. (1984) "On modes of production of social power and law." *Working Paper of Institution of Legal Studies, University of Wisconsin*, Madison.

SHEARING, C. and P. STENNING (1981) "Modern private security: its growth and implications," in M. Tonry and N. Morris (eds.) *Crime and Justice: An Annual Review of Research 3*. Chicago: University of Chicago Press.

———(1983) "Private security: implications for social control." *Social Problems* 31: 493-506.

SOUTH, N. (1983) "The corruption of commercial justice: the case of the private security sector," in M. Clarke (eds.) *Corruption: Causes, Consequences and Control*. London: Frances Pinter.

———(1984) "Private security, the division of policing labor and the commercial compromise of the state," pp. 171-198 in S. Spitzer and A. Scull (eds.) *Research in Law, Deviance and Social Control*. Greenwich, CT: JAI Press.

———and P. SCRATON (1981) "Capitalist discipline, private justice and the hidden economy." Middlesex Polytechnic, Enfield, England. (mimeo)

SPITZER, S. and A. SCULL (1977) "Privatisation and capitalist development: the case of private police." *Social Problems* 25: 18-29.

STENNING, P. and C. SHEARING (1979) "Private security and private justice." *British Journal of Law and Society* 6: 261-271.

SWINGEWOOD, A. (1975) *Marx and Modern Social Theory*. London: Macmillan.

WHITEHEAD, A. (1926) *Science and the Modern World*. New York: Macmillan.

Chapter 3

LAW, PROFIT, AND "PRIVATE PERSONS": Private and Public Policing In English History

NIGEL SOUTH

> Lawgivers have many times fortified their Laws with Penal-
> ties wherein Private Persons may have Profit, thereby to stir
> up the People to put the Laws in Execution [Davenant, "The
> Balance of Trade," 1699: 55; quoted in Beresford, 1958:
> 221].

To understand the importance and significance of modern private security policing we must make some attempt to understand
the historical roots and manifestations of earlier forms of private
law enforcement and social regulation. The modern police are
indeed a "new police" and in some important respects it is they and
not the modern phenomena of agencies within the private security
sector[1] that are out of step with the historical lineage of policing
forms. To regain this proper perspective on the contemporary division of policing labor it is necessary to be mindful of its anteced-
ents. For the purposes of this essay we must therefore consider the
historical importance of private prosecution, the onus on the private individual to gather "informations" and evidence, and the
necessity of private arrangements for ensuring the security and
protection of life and property.

In the forms of policing that pre-date nineteenth century state
intervention in the form of the development and organization of the
new police, we can clearly see the *differential* application of justice. We find differing social bases and sources of acknowledgment
for social order; cultural conflicts, adaptations, and resistances;
and popular movements in conflict, suppressed and celebrated. We

do *not* find organizations that are necessarily immediately recognizable as the police, or even as private police—nor should we (see Rock, 1983: 192). However, if we take Cain's direction that "police *must be defined in terms of their key practice,*" being "appointed with the task of maintaining the order which those who sustain them define as proper" (Cain, 1979: 158), then this necessarily broadens our view of those who qualify as police or agents of order. As Cain goes on to point out, having such a definition "means that organisations and individuals do not have to call themselves police in order for the sociologist to consider them as such," and she offers the work of Hay (1975a) as one example.

Adopting a perspective that focuses upon defining police by virtue of their practice and their historically specific function, this chapter briefly sketches some early examples of policing arrangements organized to operate in a private or quasi-private capacity, looks at the extension of policing across the community and locality, at divisions generated by differences in rural and urban development, and takes us up to those conditions that saw the emergence of a clearly and recognizably modern interventionist state and a public police system.

One point to note is that the following discussion limits itself to England. It should also be noted that the discussion makes no claims about history explaining modern forms of private policing. However, it certainly diminishes the sense of novelty attached to the phenomenon, and, of course, we can identify common, recurrent themes in practice and function as well as in the needs and directives of those who employ and sustain forms of policing. Clearly, policing within the modern state and developed capitalism is crucially different from forms under earlier social, political, and economic organization, but present-day forms of social, political, and economic organization, but forms of social control have developed out of antecedent forces and circumstances and we narrow our purchase on understanding—as well as our power of explanation—if we ignore this.

THE DETERIORATION OF FORMAL SOCIAL CONTROL IN THE LATE SEVENTEENTH AND EARLY EIGHTEENTH CENTURIES

As the end of the seventeenth century approached, its old formal system of policing arrangements was in a state of decline. Irregular and uneven policing followed from the "peculiar geometry" (Rock, 1983: 192) of the distribution of the population and its administration. Centralized direction was severely limited (Rock, 1983) and the deterioration of more localized, systematic direction well established.

Critchley (1967: 18) dates this deterioration from about 1689 onwards and identifies three markers that are worth noting by way of introduction and background to the period and the changes that are the subject of this essay. First, the system under which the supposedly voluntary, unpaid, and rotating office of constable was filled had been corrupted by, in essence, privatizing it and paying others to take up the often onerous position when it fell upon those of means. Exemption from the office was also conferred by the Tyburn ticket, granted to those who had successfully prosecuted a felon to conviction.

Second, the office of justice of the peace was diminished in respect, and in a substantive and demonstrable degree of legal fairness, by widespread corruption and private trading in justice. Essentially the system was debased, as the very administration of justice came to depend upon the payment of fees for it to be put in motion (see Critchley, 1967: 19). A familiar temptation arises here. If a system profits from encouraging business—even if the business is bad business—then there is a likelihood that such bad business will be found, and paradoxically, in the case of the search for *crime* in order to *prevent* it, it will instead apparently thrive. The "justice of mean degree" could not make a living out of law that was not exercised. "To fall into the clutches of such men," writes Critchley (1967: 19), "meant ruin to honest citizens, and the cupidity of the justices and their notorious relationship with known criminals brought the law into the utmost contempt." Indeed, corruption was so endemic that immunity from prosecution could be bought with relative ease. Not surprisingly, criminal activity adapted well to this state of affairs.

A system of thieving developed that derived its profit out of extortion and blackmail. Thieves and fences would return stolen goods for payment from its original owners, and in return for other payment could be "encouraged" not to rob from certain businesses in the first place, a principal target for such extortion being the banks. The notorious Jonathon Wild, self-styled "Thief-Taker General," offers a career in point. Wild pioneered the fencing practice of negotiating with the original owner of the goods, making "compromise" agreements (Parks, 1970: 78) to return all or, more usually, part of the stolen goods in exchange for the withdrawal of prosecution, amnesty, and any share in a reward (see Henry, 1977; McIntosh, 1976).

Finally, and third in Critchley's assessment of the breakdown of the old system, the expansion of the urban centers, the growth of population, and the generation of new wealth with the early stages of the Industrial Revolution, all multiplied the opportunities for crime (see Critchley, 1967: 18). The traditional social order and understandings were shaken and fading, and with them "the universal obligation to serve as constable on which the only available means of maintaining law and order still relied" (Critchley, 1967: 18).

Critchley's administrative history (see Phillips, 1983: 53) points to useful but highly conventional staging posts in the history of policing.[2] This is clearly evident in his evocation of the principle by which the office of constable was supposed to be filled and his assertion that it was on the preservation of this principle that the maintenance of law and order hinged. In fact, although public and private arrangements were both undoubtedly corrupted, private "principles" of self-interest were already well established in promoting various aspects of law and order maintenance. As the formal system declined, provision by private self-interest flourished, strongly encouraged by legislation that, from 1691, had offered substantial rewards to those who brought the prosecutions of certain offenses (Rock, 1983: 201). A whole range of crimes of theft and robbery was encompassed by this system of prosecution as private enterprise. The sources of rewards reflected the nature of this mixed economy coming from the state, as with the courts and the excise, as well as insurance companies and voluntary associations (Rock, 1983).

As the eighteenth century began, past arrangements for policing society, maintaining order, and imposing discipline were increasingly inappropriate or ineffective in the forms that they had traditionally taken, or else, as in the case of gearing and disciplining an *industrial* workforce, they were simply absent in any established form. Private and semiprivate defense organizations sprang up, private individuals assumed new claims to authority—sometimes legitimately, often spuriously—and odious professions trading in the provision of a strong-arm or secret information flourished. Although those of wealth and privilege were obvious targets of major and minor crime, violence, and damage, theirs was also the power and ability to pay for a variety of forms of private protection.

Arching over this transition in the modes of social control was a grander one as the momentum of industrialization gathered pace. Yet the emergence of industrial discipline must be set alongside agrarian paternalism and its means of social control for the two to be viewed in proper perspective. Similarly, the slow emergence and slower acceptance of the idea of the new police must be considered in the light of those sixteenth- and seventeenth-century peculiarities of the English prosecution system, relying on informers, prosecution societies, thieftakers, and so on, which persisted, to varying degrees, well into the nineteenth century.

RATIONALIZATION, DISCIPLINE, AND SOCIAL CONTROL IN THE EIGHTEENTH CENTURY

By the year 1700 disciplined industrial capitalism was already becoming familiar in certain parts of England, "with the time sheet, the time keeper, the informers and the fines" (Thompson, 1967: 82). For example, the *Law Book of Crowley's Iron Works* represented "an entire civil and penal code, running to more than 100,000 words, to govern and regulate [the] refractory labor force" (Thompson, 1967: 81). To implement and supervise such a regime, Crowley employed a "Warden at the Mill" and a "Monitor" to be the precise keeper of the time. In addition their charge was, as Thompson puts it, that of "morally righteous invigilation." They were to detect and report upon all breaches of workplace discipline, upon deviations from the required "thirteen hours and a half neat service" and on the "cheating" of time (Thompson, 1967: 81). The parallels with the tasks of modern private security are evident (see Shearing and Stenning, 1981, 1983; South, 1984, 1985).

Later, less autocratic masters sought visibly to impress workers with their own responsibility for their punctuality or tardiness. Faced with strong traditions of an irregular workpace—and, indeed, irregular work weeks—from his potters, Josiah Wedgwood established at Etruria the first recorded system of clocking in (Thompson, 1967: 83). Such clocks were known as "tell-tale" clocks, an expression still in colloquial use today. Interestingly, the early versions of such clocks (manufactured, according to Thompson, from about 1750 by John Whitehurst of Derby) "served only to ensure the regular patrol and attendance of night-watchmen, etc" (Thompson, 1967), a device still employed throughout the security guarding industry, often thought to be a relatively recent innovation.

The peculiar and new crime problems generated in the expansion of commercial enterprise stimulated the legal basis for another significant precursor of modern private security—the bonded courier and express delivery services. Their development was cradled in the eighteenth-century legal position by which

> the common law recognized no criminality in a person who came legally into possession of property and later converted it. Apparently it was thought that the owner should have protected himself by selecting a trustworthy person. Since, presumably, this could readily be done, the owner must have been negligent if he delivered his property to a person who absconded with it [Hall, 1935: 31-32].

Such a legal context basically offered a gamble on the trustworthiness of carriers and conveyors of the property owners' goods. Thus a need

> for regulation and for raising the standards of honesty resulted from the increasing necessity of the merchants to rely upon professional carriers rather than upon their own servants [Hall, 1935: 30; see Ditton, 1982: 67-68].

The same legal context, inadequate and inappropriate where invoked (Ditton, 1982: 68), therefore brought early forms of private, professional carrying and conveying of property into "the metaphoric growth of commerce to the point where" they became middlemen, and as such, "became a vital link in the chain of profit . . ." (Ditton, 1982: 68):

> It was thus a combination of the ineffectiveness and inappropriateness of existing law, which drove the control of embezzlement from the public to the private sphere [Ditton, 1982: 69].

In other ways, too, even within the agrarian economy, the eighteenth century measures of economic rationalization were of a recognizable and indeed a familiar form, emerging from within the changing nature of the old dialectic of deference to paternalism.

Thompson (1974) offers an account of a conflict arising out of such change resulting from the zealous actions of the Steward of Sir Jonathon Trelawny, Bishop of Winchester, in 1707. Of particular

interest is the justification offered by the Steward and its resonance
with modern managerial philosophy and private security programs
addressed to loss prevention (see South, 1982: 60-61; 1984).

Tenants and lower officials of the Bishop's Courts complained
of the Steward:

> "He breakes old Customes . . . in Minute and Small mat-
> ters, which are of Small value to your Lordshipp . . . he has
> denied to Allow five Shillings at Waltham to the Jury at the
> Court . . . to drinke your Lordshipps health, a Custome that
> has beene used time out of Mind . . . he denied your Lord-
> shipps Tenants Timber for the repaire of Severall Bridges and
> Common pounds [Thompson, 1974: 385].

The erosion of use rights and customary access to property
continued throughout the eighteenth and nineteenth centuries, of
course, though the legacy of such traditional understandings is still
with us today (see Ditton, 1977; Scraton and South, 1981, 1984).
But perhaps even more clearly with us, in the practice of modern
private security and managerial rationalization, is the spirit of the
steward's reply to his employer:

> I own, I affect sometimes to Intermit those minute Customs
> as he calls them because I observe that your Predecessor's
> favours are prescribed for against your Lordship and insis-
> ted on as Rights, and then your Lordship is not thanked for
> them; Besides though they are Minute, yet many Minute Ex-
> pences . . . amount to a Sume at the end [Thompson, 1974:
> 385].

Such emerging conflicts could also assume more serious proportions of course, especially in times of food shortage. Thus, there
was often the need for organized physical protection of mills, warehouses, and the like, against the very real threat of violence by riot.
In 1765, Thompson records that "a group of London merchants
had found it necessary to seek the protection of the military for their
cheese warehouses along the river Trent," where they were threatened by "riotous colliers" (Thompson, 1971: 100-1). The vagaries
of seasonal production and the intentions of profiteering merchants
often conspired to withdraw goods from the open market, resulting
in popular protest specifically directed against the more tractable
cause—the manipulators of the new political economy, the new
bourgeois merchants (see Thompson, 1971).

Just as many justices often faced a difficult set of decisions about how to deal with local public disturbance, so too, when called in, could the militia itself. First, they could often find themselves denied much comfort or support from those local magistrates who, born of their particular background as part of the traditional landed gentry, retained the paternalistic regard for the "fair," traditional arrangements of the local market and whose sympathy for greedy and unscrupulous merchants might be minimal. Second, of course, they repeatedly faced an angry crowd with whom they probably had as much in common as not. Not surprisingly, the militia were not predictable in their actions, on occasion apparently joining the crowd to supervise a fairer sale of goods seized from the merchants by the mob (Thompson, 1971: 112-113).

The point to be emphasized here is that any employment of private forces, agents, and intermediaries did not necessarily follow a sinister logic of the need of the state to have its own private army. Rather, necessity and logic often emerged piecemeal and halfheartedly out of the inadequacy of options available. Civil forces were by and large ill suited and ineffective for many of the situations they might face, and calling in the military was a step generally contemplated with reluctance. The latter in any case were quite capable of demonstrating their own reluctance to participate in the "odious service" of intervening in civil affrays (see Thompson, 1971: 121).

In a variety of circumstances, some degree of resorting to privately employed agents and privately raised forces could clearly offer the attraction of some surer direction of their actions. Yet, in the case of public protest it would be mistaken to suppose that massive resort to private force naturally followed. Such a response remained tempered by the legacy and legitimacy of traditional relations of deference and paternalism (see Newby et al., 1978). Only toward the close of the century did such strands of paternalism and common approval of the moral justice of the crowd's sentiment begin to diminish fully. As it did so a new paramilitary policing force of volunteers was raised in response to the fear of invasion from without and sedition from within (Thompson, 1971: 129). An acute anti-Jacobinism among the gentry eroded its traditional paternalism and encouraged a powerful antagonism against popular protest and activity. The new primacy of market relations legitimated such a response at the levels of both central and local authority.

In this state of fear and tension the public order problem and the need for social control demanded solutions but continued to meet with hesitancy and self-interest with regard to the proposals put forward. It was not until the 1770s-1780s that the very concept of policing as the more familiar notion of a force of civil intervention, rather than private watch and other initiatives or military suppression, began to gain even a minimum of public acceptance.

Instead, in the early years of the eighteenth century the private middlemen embraced the commercial compromises and opportunities that the state was prepared to offer in the promotion of law enforcement without the provision of a public police force. This transitional marketplace is neatly described by Rock (1983: 213) in the following summary:

> [T]he contingencies of social control forced the state to recruit the deviant as its own agent. Diffusely, such recruitment took the guise of the specific and temporary contracts which marked the employment of the reward and pardon system. Accused men became temporary instruments of government. More particularly, that tendency to recruitment led official institutions to hire pirates as pirate-catchers, smugglers as revenue officers, thieves as thieftakers and poachers as gamekeepers. . . .

In this section I have introduced the principal arenas in which private sponsorship or initiation of discipline, security, and control might be found in eighteenth-century England—the spheres of industrial, commercial, and agrarian change. I have briefly offered examples of industrial discipline, precursors of security services for commerce, the loss prevention philosophy that even in the early eighteenth century challenged traditional understandings about customary prerequisites, and noted the difficult and ambiguous nature of the series of options that waxed and waned as they revolved around the problems of maintaining legal regulation, public order, and social control.

In the next section I shall discuss the emergence of the police idea in this context and in relation to other private and public responses to problems of crime and disorder in eighteenth-centuryLondon.

THE "POLICE IDEA"

Where rewards, pardons, contracts, and the privileges of rather peculiar official (and private) authorizations were the principal underpinnings of the enforcement of law, mercenary and predatory entrepreneurs in criminal justice thrived. Prominent among these were the essentially private agents called thieftakers, who flourished as never before. Although their principal pursuit was profit, crime control and the apprehension of criminals were the by-products. In this sense, for all their corruption and other inadequacies, the thieftakers constituted something of a model—albeit a dishonorable one—that contributed to the slowly emerging idea of a public police force (see Rock, 1983: 215).

The work of the Fielding brothers, Henry and John, as the Magistrates at Bow Street had included the formation in 1750 of a body of constables bearing the authority of the court, who came to be known as the Bow Street Runners. In essence, the Runners themselves were perhaps closer to being a private police force than the noble precursor to the Metropolitan Police. Somewhat contrary to their portrayal in popular myth, Radzinowicz (1956a: 263) offers the incisive description of them as

a closely knit cast of speculators in the detection of crime, self-seeking and unscrupulous, but also daring and efficient when daring and efficiency coincided with their private interests.

The persistence of policing paid as piecework, for example, by prosecutions and convictions that resulted in a reward, meant it was similarly profitable to offer selective "protection" to certain parties. In particular, Saunders Welch, a well-known Runner, and most other high constables were also coal merchants and dealt in the course of their business with the local brothels and inns to whom, in return for good custom, they could offer protection from police harrassment (Bowden, 1978: 250). Though John Fielding had repeatedly emphasized the need for "a regular body of real thief-takers" (Bowden, 1978: 249), the Bow Street Runners lacked such organization, financing, or legitimacy.

Popular acceptance—and hence a source of legitimacy, for the "police idea" was still hard sought. The government of the day was impressed enough with the Fielding brothers' experiment, the "Beak Runners" as they were also called, to contribute £200 out of the secret fund for the continuation of the scheme. Yet despite the *apparent* success of the enterprise little further enthusiasm or organized support could be mustered.

Rock (1983: 208) describes the general scenario, persisting as it did despite piecemeal reform, as follows:

The policing, administration and jurisdiction of London were splintered and stratified in an extraordinarily complex fashion . . . Burgesses' courts, manorial courts, magistrates' courts, the courts of the City Companies, sheriffs' courts and aldermanic courts vied with one another. Separate police agencies patrolled their several districts and precincts. Beadles, javelin men, constables, watchmen, sheriffs' officers, the train bands, City Marshalls, magistrates' assistants and King's Messengers attempted to impose some order but their work was not co-ordinated. It lacked central direction or even a precise demarcation of tasks.

By 1780 a series of parliamentary committees had reported on the state of the watch in generally unfavorable terms. Yet, it seemed nothing could jar the apparent complacency of the lawmakers, or the populace, about the basic adequacy of traditional arrangements for policing. I shall explore further aspects of such traditional arrangements later and suggest some reasons why apparent complacency did not so much indicate a lack of interest as disguise the concern of interests already well served. Nevertheless, the contribution in that year of one anti-Catholic zealot by the name of Lord George Gordon, leader of the Protestant Association, a private group, was a significant jolt to both Parliamentarians and the general populace of London.

Gordon and his association were violently opposed to an Act of Parliament that had lifted certain sanctions and prohibitions that had applied to the Catholic population. (Their new "rights" included their eligibility to join the army at a time when the British were suffering heavily in the American war of independence!) Gordon led a massed force to Westminster, trapping Members within the House, and was only dispersed with the intervention of the cavalry (Fowler, 1979: 18). The route, however, was but the beginning of riots that saw the death or wounding of over 300 people, and the destruction of homes, Catholic chapels, and public buildings across London. Four prisons were stormed and 300 prisoners freed from Newgate. The Old Bailey received the attentions of the rioters, and John Fielding, one of the few magistrates to attempt to intervene, was attacked at his home and the Fieldings' manuscripts burned. The Bank of England demanded army protection, and eventually the army was used in force to dispel the rioters.

The army was, however, as often before, a somewhat unpopular agency of the last resort—the unwelcome intervention of the state in the business of the people. As Rudé (1952: 312) observes:

In the Gordon riots we find yet another form of [the] assertion of an Englishman's liberties—this time, by the property owners and householders of the City of London. They demanded the right to set up voluntary associations commanded by their own officers in order to protect their rights and properties both against the depredations of the rioters and the encroachment of government—a sort of citizens' militia, or *milice bourgeois*, nine years before the siege of the Bastille!

As a footnote, Rudé observes here that a parallel but socially superior organization, the St. Marylebone Associates, numbering among them 7 noblemen and 57 gentlemen and esquires, were more in the nature of a *milice aristocratique*. But in other ways also, the temper—and pockets—of traditional aristocracy *and* emerging capital, can be seen as ill-disposed toward the extension of the forces of the state to too proximate a location. Rudé continues:

> [A] similar spirit of sturdy independence and hostility to the executive was shown in the flat refusal of a majority of the City companies to contribute financially to the upkeep of troops quartered in the City during the (Gordon) disturbance [Rudé, 1952: 312].

The wealthy merchants of the city were more likely to hire their own patrols and guards, armed with staves, pistols, and, occasionally, muskets (Draper, 1978: 18); such a *preferred* practice as to constitute a very significant "incidental civil force," indeed (Radzinowicz, 1956b: 507-533).

Nevertheless, it did seem possible that in response to the rioting Parliament might enter into serious debate, in particular about how the French system might be adapted without all its feared iniquities. As Lord Shelburne put it, if the House were to study the Parisian system of policing, members "would find its construction excellent: its use and direction abominable. Let them embrace one and shun the other" (Parliamentary History, 1780-1781). However, such a plea for reasoned evaluation of the alternatives to the watch drew only temporary attention and the issue once again subsided until 1785, when Pitt introduced his London and Westminster Police Bill.

Pitt conceived of the police as a deterrent force, organized and therefore sure and more effective than the various watch arrangements employed throughout London. In this respect it was a recognition that although, as Solicitor-General Sir Archibald MacDonald put it, "the gallows groaned," crimes against person and property seemed to increase (Fowler, 1979: 19). Major resistance to the bill developed, more out of a conflict of threatened vested interests than simply over the idea of a patrolling police *per se,* though such a conflict was probably a welcome sabotage of the bill for others wary of such a precedent. It was proposals for the drawing of divisional boundaries of jurisdiction that proved contentious, for under the divisional system the prominent and influential city fathers found themselves threatened with the loss of the independence of the city, which became merely another police division.

The reaction was the familiar law and order backlash against liberal proposals for dealing with crime, though this was tempered at the time by an abiding unease with the idea of the establishment of the police—for both ideologically grand reasons pertaining to English traditions of individual liberty, and for the kind of local, selfish reasons that the spokesmen of the city were fighting for. The proposed police were viewed with some hostility as potential misusers of extraordinary and dangerous powers. But in the "reasoned" argument that accompanied the hysteria it was repeatedly (and familiarly) argued that the rise in crimes of property were directly attributable to the inadequacy of the punishments available. As one Alderman Townsend put it in the presentation of the case for the City,

> So strangely are men's feelings directed that thieves and robbers alone appeared to be fit objects of compassion in modern times [Parliamentary History, 1785-1786].

In the face of considerable opposition, the bill was lost and Pitt withdrew it, stepping down over the issue with the uncharacteristic admission that he was not "perfectly master of the subject" (Fowler, 1979: 20). The draft of the bill did, however, contribute to the Dublin Police Act of 1786 (Fowler, 1979: 20) and the Act of 1787 introduced for Ireland "for the better execution of the law and the preservation of the peace within the counties at large" (Bowden, 1978: 167).

In describing here the establishment of the Bow Street Runners as an experiment in public policing I have sought to make it clear that this development still reflected the perpetuation of a system of payment that maintained the privatization of its policing and services. Within the highly fragmented division of policing and judicial authority, however, the Runners played but a relatively small part. Mention must also be made of developments beyond London and of the private associations and other privately sponsored, semi-formal and informal civil groups and forces that were raised periodically while Parliament continued to debate the issue of a public police. It is to these matters that I turn next.

BEYOND LONDON

The development of arrangements for policing the metropolitan area—a task to unite the city, Westminster, and Southwark under a single system—differed significantly from the slower transformation of "old" policing in the rest of the country. In large part, the indifference of London-centered justices—from the Fieldings until Peel—of the "principled" participants in the policing debate—from utilitarians to constitutionalists—and of government itself toward local affairs outside the capital (see Critchley, 1967: 23), all pushed for innovation and reform of a more ambitious nature in London than outside the city. Thus, the potential for community, paternalistic, and privatized forms of social ordering remained strong, not only in traditional and slow-changing rural areas, but also in the new communities of industrial development outside London. Critchley (1967: 23) makes the following perfunctory observation:

> Elsewhere, the new race of iron masters, mill-owners and other industrial aristocrats who were sapping the authority of the justices, were concerned less with philosophy than with value for money in getting things done.

It would be wrong, however, to suggest that ideas of value and timely expediency did not find their own philosophical expression. Indeed, many of the new industrialists seemed a new and enlightened breed. Their backgrounds were typically "Quaker or Unitarian in religion, moderate or radical Whig in politics, scientific in their enthusiasms, and philanthropic in their avocations" (Ignatieff, 1978: 62). As reformers they were involved in the campaigns to abolish slavery, provide hospitals and dispensaries, and improve primary and technical education. However, the names of men like Boulton, Darby, Strutt, and Wedgwood are more strongly, and appropriately, associated with the foundation of the factory system and scientific management. As Ignatieff (1978: 62) notes,

> besides introducing mechanisation, extended division of labor, and systematic routing of the work process, they also devised

the new disciplines of industrial labor: punch clocks, bells, rules and fines. . . . Like the hospital and prison reformers these early industrialists rationalised their new discipline as an attempt to reform the morals and manners of their workers.

Such reformist principles echo through the debate about the need (or lack thereof) for a national, centralized or, at very least, organized police force. They present a point of convergence between new private interests, or more accurately, private concerns (in both moral and commercial senses), and a slow shuffling movement occurring around the traditional staples of parliamentary preoccupation, such as the extent of representation and concerns to control a testy populace. In the construction of the new penitentiary system, beginning with Horsham in 1778 (Ignatieff, 1978: 63), and the eventual formation of the new police, the administrative interests of the state were married with those private principles of the new industrial life, which demanded order, discipline, and respect for the workplace regimen. Silver (1967) neatly summarizes the divergent inclinations of the old agrarian paternalism and the new industrial disciplinarianism. But if the position of the latter seems in hindsight a crude support of cheap self-interest, then this does disservice to the subtlety of its argument and the acute understanding of the changing demands of social control relations upon which it was based. Not incidentally, their argument resonated strongly with utilitarian currents in political thinking and government debates and, in the invocation of the *constitutional obligations* of good government, could even flatter, or provide a point for concession to, even the unconverted.

Thus, at a time when the agrarian rich often sought to multiply and reconstruct the traditional means of self-defense against violent uprising and attack, those who sprang from the newer sources of wealth turned toward a bureaucratic system that insulated them from popular violence, drew attack and animosity upon itself, and seemed to separate the assertion of "constitutional" authority from that of social and economic dominance [Silver, 1967: 12].

Enlightenment, however, spreads thinly in English history, and although those whom Hay (1980: 58) observes have been rather "unsatisfactorily characterized" as reformers continued to debate and disagree among themselves, others were overwhelmingly opposed to the idea of the establishment of a police force. Hay (1980: 58) observes that the deep Whig prejudices against executive coercion by a political police continued well into the 19th century, while a precarious order was maintained by parish constables, troops, private watchmen and the yeomanry. The property of the rich was guarded by their servants. And a radical working class movement harassed by government spies and informers in the first three decades of the century denounced all proposals for a new police as an extension of those methods.

Even the most reasoned arguments about injustice and ineffectiveness were dismissed by many as irrelevant. Reformers such as Romilly argued that the certainty of detection of crime followed with inevitability by appropriate punishment would have more deterrent effect than sole reliance on the rituals of the courts and capital punishment. But such a position had limited attraction, particularly for the gentry and aristocracy (Hay, 1975b: 59). For them, power, privilege, and patronage offered the resources to guard against intrusion from without. Their problem, as Hay (1975b) observed, was rather more that of disaffection and disloyalty *within* their houses and estates: "No code of laws or police force would protect them there." As members of Parliament and justices of the peace, this class was well placed to pass legislation and sentence on the common offenders of the village and the countryside. Further, as I have indicated, despite the momentum of social and economic change that was gathering pace, both the customary authority of paternalism and the new managerial enthusiasms maintained the basis for private, informal means of imposing order and sustaining control and discipline within its accepted boundaries.

Clearly, there were important differences in practices and political philosophies, and new and significant alliances were being forged, but the stage for the acceptable entrance of a public police was still being set.

SELF-HELP AND SOCIAL
ORDER OUTSIDE LONDON

With archaic and ineffectual local government, the boroughs and the new industrial townships faced the breakdown of their inherited systems of decaying and confused parish vestries and court leets. It was no longer appropriate to contemplate total reliance upon regulation by custom and common law, and the persistence of the ancient obligations of individuals to render unpaid service as watch and constable was clearly unworkable as the eighteenth century unfolded.

Communities sought to improve this situation. First, by virtue of the proliferation of voluntary societies, funded by private subscription to pay for the organization of a local system to capture and prosecute felons under what was otherwise a highly expensive system (see Shubert, 1981), and second, under a series of improvement acts by which towns sought power from Parliament to police their locality.

The concept of police covered, in this respect, a wide range of local government service and administrative functions, and provision was thereby made for funding the watch as well as lighting, cleaning, and maintaining the streets. The significance of these changes lies in two directions. First, the improvement acts were a move toward formalizing and regularizing the payment of policing officials by clearly vested public authorities. Second, the acts laid the groundwork throughout the country upon which the Municipal Corporations Act of 1835 was finally to build a national body of municipal police forces. Such developments also illustrate the intimate connection between policing and broader social policy and politics. Rural life, however, was not so amenable to such radical change. Here, as Critchley (1967: 27) eloquently observes,

> Incentive to reform was totally lacking . . . the vestiges of court leet and presentment and the ghost of frankpledge slumbered on in a seemingly undying sunset, unclouded by the Industrial Revolution and the Napoleonic Wars. Lords of the Manor and Justices of the Peace held unchallenged and unchallengeable sway over parish constables, and the race of borsholders and tythingmen was not yet wholly extinct.

Through the eighteenth century rural crime rose, directly related to changes in the economic infrastructure and the designation of new statutory offenses: the Enclosures, the expansion of communications, the increase in legally defined vagrancy, and so on. The pattern of response was familiar, and according to some accounts, fairly simple:

> The wealthy paid gamekeepers to protect their property and slept with arms near to hand, and the middle-class tradesmen formed voluntary protection societies. The poor simply managed as best they could until the reform of rural police was at last put in hand [Critchley, 1967: 28].

But of course, the picture was not really quite so simple. There was much more to the complexity of the organization of social control than Critchley's account allows. Centrally, we need first to consider the influence of law and the power of property. Second, in the absence of a public rural police, we also need to examine more closely the forms of community, paternalistic, and privatized social control familiar to the period. These are the concerns addressed in the following sections.

FEAR AND RESPECT FOR THE LAW

The criminal justice system of the Tudors and early Stuarts was characterized by severity. As Hay (1975b: 57) observes:

> At that period and earlier, the gentry and the great houses usually had small armies of their own with which local disaffection could be crushed when necessary. But from the later 17th century the importance of managing opinion had made nuance, discretion and less obvious coercion a necessary part of the art of ruling. . . .

Timothy Nourse writing in 1706 clearly saw the criminal law as still much concerned with authority and property, and urged that the common people, being often "stubborn, cross-grain'd rogues" be sternly dealt with by such as the "Beadles, Catchpoles, Gaolers, Hangmen; such like Engines of Humanity are the fittest Tools in the World for a magistrate to work with in the reformation of an obdurate rogue" (quoted in Hay, 1975b: 25). However, the stern dealing recommended by commentators such as Mr. Nourse came to reflect a strange tension. The art of ruling and the reform of rogues discovered the coercion of consent, or perhaps more accurately, refined the dialectic of paternalism and deference within the framework of law.

From the end of the seventeenth century and into the eighteenth, the range of capital statutes multiplied dramatically, yet the administration of the law institutionalized the far less rigorous implementation of such legislation in practice. In short, the number of hangings were enough to breed fear and the proper respect for the law, yet few enough to instill a regard for the justice and humanity of the law's administration. Despite the success of this delicate compromise of justice there existed a cogent and convincing case for reform of the capital statutes in law, advanced by a vocal and fairly powerful group of reformers. Once again a major stumbling block in the passage of reform seems to have been the idea of creating a publicly accountable, national, or at least, city police force. The reformers were much inspired by plans for the administration of social order advocated by Cesare Beccaria. In 1769 Beccaria had assumed the Chair of Political Economy and Science of Police created for him by Marie Terese of Austria, and his ideas concerning the concept of policing as a blueprint for the "good order," a science of happiness and a science of government, were beginning to spread among thinkers influenced by the Enlightenment. For Beccaria, "the sciences, education, good order, security and public tranquility - objects all comprehended under the name of police . . . [constitute] the fifth and last object of public economy" (Beccaria cited in Pasquino, 1978: 45).

To deal with criminality Beccaria recommended a fixed code of laws with appropriate and commensurate punishments that must be observed to the letter; however, his plan made no provision for dealing with the needs and interests of government. "The Conservative gentlemen of England" observed Hay (1975b: 57):

> balked not only at the "unconstitutional" police that such plans required; they instinctively rejected rational plans as pernicious.

Regardless of the constitutional standing of any police force or fears about the creation of an agency of spies for the government, it also occurred to the gentry that such rational plans threatened to create a policing force less amenable to their own local control than standing arrangements. But there is a further clear connection to note.

Changes in legality and its administration were directly linked to changes surrounding the institution of private property. Locke's natural rights theory had been rendered more amenable to the *new* heirs to the contemporary concentration and maldistribution of property by the principles set out by Hume and developed by new utilitarians like Bentham and Mill. The notion of the present distribution of property and, more significantly, the ways in which *changes* in the ownership of wealth and property were occurring, as being something that was right and inevitable because it was history's answer to the state of the *needs* of society, was obviously a satisfying and attractive explanation of property distribution. The marshalling of the work force, which was the new "generator" (to use the mechanistic language of the utilitarians) of industrial wealth and property, and support for proposals to provide the means to secure that property, were obviously activities to be pursued seriously. Landed interests, however, saw in the utilitarian philosophy of property something new and fearful.

In opposition to such a principle the conservative political philosopher Edmund Burke invoked ideas such as experience and tradition. As Newby et al. (1978: 23) summarize Burke's argument, landed property was to be conceived of

> in terms of stewardship . . . in the context of the historical "process of nature" man's transitory and fleeting existence reduced him to the status of a steward serving and caring for the landed estate which transcended the generations. . . . The "steward" therefore served rather than owned his property. Consequently, Burke emphasized the obligations as much as the rights of property ownership. He feared the transfer of political power from land to the new industrial capitalists, since their utilitarian denial of moral obligation and duty as guides to action represented a threat to the continuation of a stable social order.

In Burke's conception of the stewardship of property we find the invocation of right by virtue of lineage, ownership, or eligibility by virtue of keeping that lineage unbroken. The traditional means of securing property and the allegiance of the propertyless were sound, whereas the devolution of such powers as a police force might have seemed distinctly unsound.

It was in the nature of such traditional and personalized views of property rights and the law that the privatization of legal responsibility and prosecution of the law should have held sway. Yet, if not quite moribund, the deficiencies of these arrangements had long been evident. As Brewer (1980: 25) asserts, "private initiative" was "crucial to the workings of the law. . . . [But] this permissive system was easily abused . . . legal profiteers exploited . . . both the absence of *salaried* officials and the incentives for private action."

Here Brewer highlights two key themes with which this essay is concerned and that, as fundamental features of the system of the administration of justice, inevitably flawed its fairness and effectiveness. Without the public provision of payment for official service and corresponding expectations of public accountability, private sources of remuneration were inevitably encouraged and institutionalized. Thus, for example, legal fees and charges for the food and lodging of prisoners were levied on those prosecuted and gaoled. Equally, common problems of crime and dispute were able to seek resolution through the courts, but public channels for the bringing of a prosecution, such as a public police, were absent and hence the incentives of compensation and rewards had to be invoked to encourage private prosecutions (see Brewer, 1980).

In short, this system rendered the administration of justice a matter of private enterprise; a procedure set in motion not merely by the demand for justice but also by the prospect of profit. Although inherent weaknesses of such a scheme of things are and were evident, the persistence of such privatization is more explicable if we understand the ways in which it served many different interests. In the following sections I shall briefly outline the acceptance by the state of the unsavory role played by the paid, private informer in the encouragement of voluntary policing, the activities of the reformation societies, and the employment of private agents by factory and landed interests.

"INFORMATIONS" AND PROVOCATIONS: THE TRADE OF THE INFORMER

The institutionalization of the use of informers as a force for what was seen at the time as voluntary policing offers an early example of what I have referred to as the commercial compromise of the state (see South, 1984, 1985). Beresford (1958: 221) succinctly describes the history of the early reliance on informers, their eventual discrediting, and the degradation of the pursuit and its very name.

When innocent and guilty alike were put in peril of a fine, some discredit was bound to fall on the principle of economic regulation, and the Crown could not avoid some share of unpopularity since its own share in the penalties made it a slow convert to schemes of reform. Economic offenses were those most zealously pursued, so that the informations provide details of an immense number of transactions in manufacture and trade in the period when the informers were most active, from 1550 to 1624; they were then a chief instrument for the enforcement of economic legislation and the indirect taxation of the kingdom; after 1624, virtually exiled from the courts at Westminster they remained at Assizes and the Quarter sessions as semi-official guardians of good order, with a tawdry bag of poaching, bastardy and theft . . . [Beresford, 1958: 221].

An examination of the type of offence alleged in informations . . . demonstrates the wide range of economic transactions which Parliament consented to leave vulnerable to the attentions of a common informer [Beresford, 1958: 226].[3]

The business of the informer did not, however, end in the seventeenth century, but continued to find its economic reward in the obligation of the offending party in any particular case to pay a forfeiture, this being payable to the successful prosecutor of an action. Such actions might be brought by any member of the public and the informer could thus make a remunerative, if parasitic, living from reporting and prosecuting, or alternatively blackmailing, offenders against the myriad statutes. Though legally termed "popular actions," common opinion held informers in little esteem. Radzinowicz notes one commentator describing them as "viperous vermin," who under the mantle of law "did vex and depauperize the subject . . . for malice or private ends." "In the 19th century they were called "unprincipled pettifoggers," whose office was a nuisance and an instrument of individual extortion, caprice and tyranny" (Radzinowicz, 1956b: 139). Although, as Beresford (1958: 228) warns us, it is sometimes difficult to distinguish between official and semiofficial informers involved in certain classes of prosecution and it is therefore important not to exaggerate the activity of the freelance, at the same time it is apparent that for a considerable number of years and even after their seventeenth-century decline common informers acted as a form of voluntary police that the state and many of its critics, both reactionaries and reformers, saw as a necessary evil and occasionally a positive good. The importance of this literally private pursuit of justice for private reward should not be forgotten or minimized in assessing the evolution of the British policing system. If nothing else the failure of the informer system was an important spur to the reform of policing and prosecution. As Beresford (1958: 231) notes,

while the very range and quality of informations laid between 1550 and 1616 might seem reason enough for the popular dislike of informers . . . the reforming proposals did not come solely from chastened sinners fresh from an appearance in

Exchequer. The notorious abuses of dishonest informers were sufficient to people a whole season of Johnsonian comedies.

Knowledge of the pernicious character of the practice was commonplace, yet the informer still enjoyed some peculiar position of legal standing. Lawmakers were increasingly faced with the uncomfortable recognition "that the intended policemen, guardians of the commonweal, had dissolved into first-class members of the criminal classes, as in a Kafka nightmare" (Beresford, 1958: 231).

The informers were elevated to their strongest position of legal authority and mandate under the early seventeenth-century system of patents whereby the informer could become a commissioned representative of the Crown. The patent gave an individual or group of informers (and their appointed deputies) a monopolistic right "to lay informations" as related to particular statutes or in certain areas. The scope for abuse of this monopolization of patentee's privileges was vast. Without competition in the information business, the informer had much greater leverage to exert for purposes of blackmail. Under the Crown's aegis they could also undertake searching and supervision functions. The common informer found a ready trade "by keeping an antiquarian's eye on unrepealed absurdities" (Beresford, 1958: 236): "Many of the said statutes through the alteration of tymes and change of mens manners are att this Day very hard to kept," wrote a contemporary compiler of a book on penal statutes (cited in Beresford, 1958).

Though the trade of the informer suffered little setback in the long term, as early as 1621 with the reading of a "Bill for the ease of the Subject concerning the Informacions upon the Penall Statutes" it was clear that resentment and public odium were finding some legislative expression. Beresford (1958) describes a "powerful triple alliance" forming against the informers' practice. "Critics of obsolete laws, . . . those who had lost faith in statutory restrictions" (as remedies for economic ills) "and those whose liberalism was more elemental, an antipathy to customs officers and the wish to do what one liked with one's own," came to view with some disdain a justice system allowing the thriving of the informer.

Indeed, throughout the seventeenth century an increasing degree of moral and social opprobrium became attached to the practice, while at the very same time the enforcement of laws continued to rely on it. A case in point is the passage of the Highwayman Act of 1692. For the arrest and prosecution to conviction of any highwayman the considerable sum of £40 was offered as a reward. As such successful prosecution usually depended upon possession of information normally available only to those actually involved in the perpetration of such crimes, this reward came to be known as "blood money."

Agents provocateurs were a logical product of a system that from the seventeenth century to the early nineteenth century allowed a criminal "to gain immunity from prosecution by the conviction of two or more accomplices (or supposed accomplices)" (State Research, 1980-1981: 47).

Exploring the contemporary persistence of the informant role, Gary Marx (1974: 404) suggests that a distinction may be drawn in theory "between the informant who merely plays an information gathering role and the agent-provocateur who more assertively seeks to influence the actions taken by the group" informed on. Empirically, however, this distinction seems a little more difficult to draw. "There are pressures inherent in the role that push the informant toward provocation" (Marx, 1974: 404). The simple influence of an informant's presence may be of some significance, and their behavior, no matter how apparently restrained, may in some measure contribute to provoking the kind of information that is being sought. The agent-provocateur, of course, will actively seek to have some influence upon the actions of the group or individual concerned, endorsing them, provoking them, or fabricating a story about the nature of their actions (Marx, 1974: 404).

All in all, despite widespread and common knowledge that the system was inefficient and corrupt, throughout the eighteenth century and into the early years of the nineteenth, statutes continued to be passed "which so widened the activity of common informers that an important section of criminal law came to depend upon them for its enforcement" (Radzinowicz, 1956b: 142). With unintended irony, informers could make profits of up to 200 pounds by reporting "Offences leading to Corruption of Morals" (Radzinowicz, 1956b: 142).

PRIVATE INITIATIVE AND
THE REFORMATION OF MORALITY

The scope for the trade of the informers also allowed for the flourishing of morally higher-intentioned bodies of social watchdogs. The Societies for the Reformation of Manners established themselves as private, voluntary organizations with branches across the country, riding on a crest of righteous vigilante zeal between the

1690s and dying out in the 1730s. Concerned over the way those laws meant to bring about the "Prevention and Punishment of Immorality and Profaneness" were ignored or not enforced, the members of these societies, drawn mainly from the respectable middle-class ranks of society, recruited judges and politicians in seeking to bring pressure to bear on the legal system. They condemned the immorality, laxity, and ungodliness of both upper and lower class and employed the system of private initiative and prosecution, hiring informers and "laying informations" to bring legal action against vice and sin (see Hall and McLennan, 1982).

The reformation societies may have died by the midpoint of the eighteenth century, but they left a legacy of evangelical zeal that was to be taken up and their cause and methods emulated by the Proclamation Society established by Wilberforce in the 1780s. The revival of the Evangelical movement saw a vigilante society founded in the West Riding by Hey, a campaigner for the eradication of venereal disease, and the more successful following of this lead by Wilberforce and others of the so-called Clapham Sect. Described by Radzinowicz (1956b) as a substitute "Evangelical Police," employing organized informers and drawing support from influential members of the church, the judiciary and Parliament, the society was able to pressure magistrates to impose harsh penalties for offences against morality. Indeed, such was their influence that in 1787 King George III was persuaded to support their enterprise with a "Proclamation for the Encouragement of Piety and Virtue and for the Preventing and Punishing of Vice, Profaneness and Immorality."

Not surprisingly, we begin to see that a system of law enforcement so dependent upon private initiative reflected a variety of private concerns, but these are principally the concerns of either the powerful and influential or those who sought personal gain. Rhetoric of equality and justice could sit oddly with the realities of the law's direction. That the less powerful and the poor could nonetheless make some effective use of the law is not disputed, but this was despite bias and disadvantage rather than because of equality and justice. Such bias is illustrated in the case of the enforcement of factory legislation.

PRIVATE SPIES AND
THE FACTORY INTERESTS

Carson (1979) notes how the early factory enactments were largely ineffectual, their supervision and enforcement being the responsibility of local justices of the peace before the establishment of a formal inspectorate. The justices rarely fulfilled this duty, and when they did, did so in only the most cursory manner. Many justices shared, after all, the pious regard for strong discipline and hard work that the Factory Acts were intended to curb when carried to excess. An interesting development in this situation is the use once again of private informers, often hired by rival manufacturers to bring a case against an overworking competitor. Though even here, notes Carson, "difficulties in persuading operatives to give evidence against their employers rendered the process fairly futile" (Carson, 1979: 41). Nonetheless, by the time that the Factory Act of 1819 was passed, resort to private informants had become a central resource in the enforcement process. Peel, attempting to secure new legislation on factory regulation, proposed certain concessions to the factory interest, one of which was that inspectors should only be empowered following complaint to a magistrate. Thus, only through the agency of the informer could an investigation commence (Bartrip and Fenn, 1980: 177). That private spies were also used on a regular basis by employers to warn of troublemakers and agitators is beyond doubt. What seems a little more doubtful in retrospect is their efficacy and reliability.

Reviewing the historical dispute surrounding the revolutionary nature of the Luddite disturbance of 1812, Bythell (1969: 209) contends that the argument is probably "incapable of final resolution," principally because, as Dinwiddy (1979: 34) also notes, "the validity of the evidence on which it turns—especially the reports of spies—cannot be definitely tested." As such reports were largely written for those who wanted to hear a particular message, one way or another, Bythell (1969:209) is perhaps not wholly unreasonable in suggesting that

> in the last resort, those who want to believe that England came near to revolution at this time will find support for their belief in these papers, whereas those who do not wish to believe this will find little difficulty in discounting the records.

This may be a somewhat bleak and pessimistic idea about historiography, but the point is well taken when considering sources of information, such as private spies, who face temptation to manufacture their raison d'etre and contrive satisfaction with their services. Both Thompson (1968: 535) and Cobb (1970: 6-7), among others, have noted such tendencies, with Thompson describing the informer as having an "occupational bias towards sensationalising his reports. The more mercenary his motives, the more he was at pains to provide the kind of information his employers wished to buy." The trade of the informer, whether on behalf of the Crown or a private employer, tended to be of a highly disreputable and mercenary nature. Thompson (1968: 532) suggests such informers were drawn from two groups. First,

> those who had fallen foul of authority in some way, and who purchased their immunity from prosecution (or secured their release from gaol) by taking up the trade. . . . The second group of informers comprises turncoats who, having been active reformers, became spies to save their own skins or for money; or, more simply, of casual mercenary volunteers attempting to sell information by the "piece."

A political and criminal tradition that has endorsed the employment of spies is, as Thompson observes, "an ancient part of British statecraft as well as of police practice" (Thompson, 1968: 532).

In the period 1780 to 1830 when the inadequacy of any regular police initiatives had led, as Thompson characterizes it, to a system of "payment by results," the reliance of state and capital on this privatized network of intrusive and untrustworthy informants continued to grow. The resistance of the English to a nationally organized policing system lay partly in fears of "the continental spy system," yet it is clear that the employment of spies intruding into political and work life was common anyway. Thompson (1968: 533-534) would also seem to be right in his assertion that the

> great majority of informers . . . belong . . . to the tradition of blood money mercenaries. Recent attempts to lift some of the odium traditionally placed upon such men . . . by representing them as "detectives" performing a dangerous but honorable part, according to their lights, are misplaced.

Where the utility of informers was minimized by the absence of actions to inform about, agents might be employed to provoke such actions. There is, indeed, little honor in such employment.

PRIVATE GUARDS AND THE LANDED INTERESTS

On a somewhat grander scale, Thompson's (1975) meticulous study of the history of the Black Acts analyzes a case of legislative provocation and provides several examples of the use of forms of community justice and private policing, which were employed in a bitter and intense struggle between local foresters and the officers of the landed and the monarchy, the forest officers.

A fall in prosecutions at the Windsor Swanimote courts in the late seventeenth century as, for example, forest officers performed their duties with less diligence, was reacted to by the landed in the early years of the eighteenth century with considerable vigor. An intensification of physical patrolling of the increasingly privatized property of the forest was to be followed, in the wake of a Royal visit to Windsor forest in 1717, by the notorious Black Act of 1723 increasing the compass of the rural statutes manifold. The enclosed lands and expanded estates created and protected under such laws were policed and patrolled by organized, and often relatively powerful, private security or police functionaries.

As Thompson's study illustrates, such functionaries cannot be dismissed as simply traditional manorial servants. Represented here is the relatively complex organization of sometimes private, sometimes semiprivate, semi-Crown policing of lands. For example,

> The effective duties of the forest were performed by thirteen or fourteen under-keepers, four gamekeepers, a vermin-killer and their servants. [There was also a parallel organization, staffed by some of the same personnel, of royal huntsmen—a Master of Buckhounds, a Chief Huntsman, yeoman prickers, and servants]. These posts carried small salaries—for under-keepers £20 per annum—and if not supplemented from other sources would scarcely have constituted a livelihood. But the best posts were in fact lavishly supplemented by perquisites [Thompson, 1975: 34].

Similarly, describing the vast estates of the Paget family in the 1780s, Hay (1975a: 193) notes a small-scale system of private, local social control:

> While the stewards gathered evidence, prepared informations and informed local magistrates of the wishes of the Pagets, seven warreners and keepers patrolled the chase and deer walks, assisted by their sons and servants.

As Hay observes, considering the size of the estate and the large quantity of game on the chase, the number of servants protecting it was "relatively few" (1975a: 207). But however meagre their number and whatever their private allegiance, they had the law of the state on their side. In the hands of anyone but keepers and landlords, the tools of the poaching trade, referred to as "engines of destruction" by the game laws, were illegal. The keepers could also use search warrants in their duties, and employed this power, sometimes acting with the local constable, on a regular basis—an exercise sometimes confounded by community support, which could forewarn those threatened of a search warrant having been obtained and, on other occasions, by a "wall of silence" in the face of enquiries" (Hay, 1975a: 198). Keepers and stewards could be completely ostracized by the local community and were often the subjects of long-term personal vendettas and conspiracies. Informers, too, were much despised, so in addition to providing alibis for one another, poachers would also lay false charges against informers and could organize "testimony" to support such charges (see Hay, 1975a: 196-198).

When the propertied class of farmers who did not enjoy game rights themselves took to poaching, they too could be arrested and fined. Thus, as Hay argues,

the game laws not only smoothed relations between two classes of men whose interests were often sharply opposed; they helped to obscure the law as an instrument of class power.

Further,

the power which the threat of an information gave to a poor man over his master helped partially to redress the balance of power between propertied and propertyless [Hay, 1975a: 212].

Here at least all were equal in the eyes of the law and in the sights of the gamekeeper's gun. The power that the gamekeepers possessed was

a necessary but vexatious aspect of the game laws for sporting gentlemen. They could not protect their own game without them, but they had to stay on good terms with those of their neighbors [Hay, 1975a: 215].

The keepers could be arrogant and vindictive, and certainly possessed a wide range of powers granted by statute, including the right to destroy poachers' dogs. The discretionary aspect of their statutory powers and the latitude afforded by the instructions of absentee landlords in practice gave them an even greater authority despite the fact that they remained *private* guards.

The notion of equality in the eyes of the law and the sight of the gamekeepers is not however, *simply* a matter of obscuring class power. As Thompson (1975: 259-261) notes, to say that

> the rule of law is only another mask for the rule of a class . . . is not the same thing as to say that the rulers had need of law in order to oppress the ruled while those who were ruled had need of none. What was often at issue was not property, supported by law, against no property; it was alternative definitions of property rights. . . .

I shall take up some elements of Thompson's point in my conclusion. Here I have described the varied roles of informers, agents-provocateurs, private reformation societies, the use of private spies by competing factory interests, and the conflict between local foresters and private forest officers. Thematically, familiar policing practices of surveillance, undercover work, patrolling, and gathering of evidence leading to arrest are represented here. But these were private—or at best, semiprivate—policing initiatives. To put these practices into perspective I turn finally to examine the broader context in which they played their parts.

LAW, PROPERTY, AND PRIVATE POLICING

During the transition from enclosure to the period of more substantial capital accumulation and developing industrialization, new and more subtle forms of social control had to be developed to maintain stability yet sustain a dramatic shift to a new world of production. For owners of capital in the new mode of production the simple problem that emerged was one of the transmission of surplus value from labor to these owners. Under feudalism this conveyancing had been direct, sanctioned by ideology, principle, and customary law. The problems of transmission were a relatively simple mixture of physical enforcement and ideological principles of tradition. In feudal society the landlord had an authority of almost total dominance over the land and its produce.

Less overt social control depends for its viability much more directly on popular perception of the legitimacy of the social order.

As the nature and very dimensions of production change historically over time, so too does the nature of the social order and the basis of its legitimacy. As successful social order can only find its roots in the popular acceptance of its legitimacy, so too must the enforcement of law and the power of coercion. In feudal society, administrative functions and legal definitions found their expression within a localized social framework, based on traditional economic relationships and the more direct means of social control that held sway.

However, such localization and tradition, when coupled with the degree of individual autonomy workers had over their labor, meant that the system of customary rights and privileges with regard to the fruits of labor and the incidental bounty of the land (such as firewood, wild vegetation, and so on) were not easily disturbed. Their erosion and transformation—alongside that of forms of community, privatized and paternalistic arrangements for policing, and social control—came with industrialization and the development of the market for labor power. These changes meant that the capitalist now purchased the labor time of the workers, who must therefore be coordinated and disciplined. The process produced punctuality, removed the dignity of any past familiar autonomy, and eroded, in the name of private property, all sense of common rights. Pearson (1978: 123) offers a necessary caution when he observes that although

> under the pre-industrial systems of production men had been much more in control of the rhythms of their lives . . . one should not romanticize this state of affairs—as if every man had been an independent, unalienated and free man—but one should recognize nevertheless, what was involved in the changes in production systems.

The system of law enforcement so reliant on private entrepreneurial initiative depended strongly upon forms of deference, first under an agrarian and then under a new industrial economy (see Little and Sheffield, 1983: 801). But the private agents, the semiprivate/semipublic mediators, and the public officials all played out their parts against a grander backdrop.

The law, whether wholeheartedly supported, entrepreneurially exploited, or cynically abused, nonetheless stood—terrible yet judicious—as the hegemonic framework that sustained the fractured system of social control. As Hay (1975b: 56) has persuasively argued,

[T]he criminal law, more than any other social institution made
it possible to govern 18th century England without a police
force and without a large army.

The power of law was such that it retained the appearance of neutrality, as if it mattered not who owned property and who did not.
Much was made, especially in the eighteenth century, of equality
before the law and stress was laid on the fact that contrary to standard practice on the continent, the accused in the English courts
had a relatively extensive body of rights. Law was characterized,
as much as anything, by the narrow and formal style of its interpretation, particularly in offences against capital statutes. This severe
formalism, sometimes carried to the point of apparent absurdity,
often led to the failure of prosecutions on grounds of minor technicalities and errors. However, it was precisely such a degree of falli-
bility that contributed to popular belief in and reification of the law
into "The Law" as something above all men and women. Quite
naturally, the occasional sentencing to death of a person of property served as a further deep and powerful promoter of the belief
that no one was exempt from the full justice of the law (see Hay,
1975b: 33). As Rock (1983: 202-3) puts it,

> Government accordingly was involved in the generation of two
> distinct planes of regulation. On one plane, law and policing
> agencies tried to manufacture a moral universe whose con-
> tours and consequences were clear. There was a lucid drama-
> tization of the properties of social order. A great number of
> offences were made capital. . . . On the other plane, how-
> ever, everyday control practices systematically made those
> margins ambiguous and murky. The consequences of law
> were eminently negotiable. Legal penalties and inducements
> combined to create an equivocal, malleable and complex
> scheme which could be exploited by the knowing.

The maintenance of this new balance was not, of course, achieved
solely by ideological assertion and consensus about the justice (or
mighty terror) of the law. As I have tried to indicate, Parliament's
law as well as private interest and authority *were* policed in a real,
active fashion. A modern acceptance of what policing is and should
look like should not diminish our awareness of the range of manifestations of the policing forms—private and public—that have historically served the differing interests of the few and the majority.

CONCLUSION

In this chapter I have dealt with some aspects of various arrangements for policing and social control up to the eve of the emergence and development of the new police. The exercise has been pursued in order to indicate that the lineage of policing and social control is erratic, that forms of private policing have a long, complex, and rich history, and to suggest that being mindful of this can help to illuminate our modern commonsense conceptions of what policing is for and how it works.

As Cain (1979) points out, the overwhelming majority of studies of the police take the object of their analysis completely for granted; it is assumed "that we 'know' what the police, as an institution, really is. This unscientific myopia precludes, of course, the raising of questions about what the police might be" (Cain, 1979: 143). It also tends to neglect the question of what the police *have been*.

In common, the motives and foundations for the various individual and collective actions described here turned upon the need for private initiative in order to make the rather fragmented and variegated system of law enforcement and policing effective. Such private action was, of course, also keenly stimulated by its profitability, either insofar as private prosecution societies could collectively support the great expense of prosecution in an economical manner not available to the sole individual (see Little and Sheffield, 1983) or else, as for example in the case of the thieftakers and informers, it was a profitable source of income.

But the variegated nature of this system persisted. For example, for the private prosecution societies "neither the concept of the law nor its content were in question" (Little and Sheffield, 1983: 798). Yet, for the informers and the thieftakers there was clearly a far more questionable and ambiguous attitude and relationship to law and crime. As Rock (1977: 214) observes:

> The thieftakers relied on an intimate acquaintance with deviance, and because their stake in it was principally financial, they often husbanded and encouraged crime in order to develop a flow of useful and manageable cases.

The trade of the informers persisted on similar lines. To the gamekeepers and their like accrued a significant degree of semi-private and semiofficial power. A host of private voluntary associations and societies proliferated, sometimes for the promotion of high principles, more often protecting private interests.

But if the history of private policing and initiatives is apparently confused when viewed from the stance of traditional historiography, it can also be perceived as developing with a functionalist logic when interpreted from the stance of the new revisionist historians (see Cohen and Scull, 1983). To be brief, neither viewpoint would be very satisfactory. Undoubtedly, confusion and contradiction were consistent accompaniments of changing developments in private arrangements made for policing and social control. At the same time, it was undeniably those of wealth and power who could best afford to instigate and hire the private services and agents that proliferated.

It would be crude, however, to suggest that the *ways* in which privately paid persons actually provided their many and varied services can be simply characterized as chaotic, or mechanistically regulated by a market, or directed by the conspiratorial hands of capital and state.

Realistically, the private provision of services of order maintenance and social control, of information gathering, thieftaking, and prosecution were part of a more complex framework of social life. They and their activities were part of the fundamental features of life in town and country, city and community.

Private militia could renege on their tasks, foresters fought back against the gamekeepers employing similar tactics, and those who despised the informers were nonetheless caught in a legal system that might require similar actions from them if they sought to bring a prosecution. Furthermore, despite its bias the law *was* embraced by the working class as a means of remedying injustice perpetrated by others of the working class (see Phillips, 1977). Within a changing political economy in which both the powerful and the powerless were actors, specific conditions of law and economy, culture and politics, and tradition and innovation all shaped the nature of the responses to the absence of any centrally initiated and organized policing system.

Such an absence of central direction was itself a reflection of fracture and fragmentation, not merely amongst parliamentary and other powerful interest groups, but across England as a whole and throughout its changing class structure. Crime and riot, profiteering, and property rivalry reflected in their particular ways the changes occurring and the opportunities for social protest and selfish gain that followed. Nor should it be forgotten that the crime and violence that can be so casually and loosely embraced by a reference to social protest actually involved real hurt, rape, and murder.

Idealism about such matters does a disservice to those who lived
this history and if we tend to pay less attention to how the poor
sought their own private or popular justice in a more localized and
less dramatic form than riot, machine breaking, and so on, then
this is a failure that we should seek to remedy. In the meantime we
should certainly not imagine that privately organized and informally sanctioned initiatives were the prerogative solely of the well-
to-do. It is likely that in the England of this period *all* private persons
of all classes were seriously concerned about the crime affecting
them and their families.

Thus, private provision in the sphere of law or rule enforcement,
regulation, and order had some serious degree of acceptance and
ideological legitimacy, founded substantially upon the recognition
of the necessity of some mode of response to crime. Of course, serious conflict and strong opposition were generated in response to
the overbearing private justice of landlords and factory owners. As
with the acceptance of the rule of law, the parameters of private justice were to be negotiated, avoided, or resisted where necessary, but
in the absence of an acceptable alternative the system was accorded
legitimacy both ideologically and in practice.

Private direction of the means to pursue private justice sows fer-
tile seeds of injustice. But the history of the breadth of private policing initiatives prior to the establishment of the new public police
must also acknowledge that their instigation and acceptance also
followed from the need to respond to those crimes that claimed "a
moral consensus that knew no class lines" (Langbein, 1983: 108).
With regard to the rule of law, "that is why men of the non-elite
could predominate [as prosecutors and jurors] in convicting persons who committed property crimes" (Langbein, 1983). With
regard to private policing, that is why it was generally acceptable—
if unsatisfactory—that "Private Persons may have Profit, thereby
to stir up the People to put the Laws in Execution" (Davenant, 1699,
cited in Beresford, 1958: 221).

NOTES

1. This volume represents a significant contribution to the literature on private security policing and key references to other work in this area are provided in
other essays here. However, for work on this subject that is informed by historical
precedent, see Shearing and Stenning (1981, 1983), South (1984, 1985), Spitzer
and Scull (1977a, 1977b), and Weiss (1978, 1981, 1986).

For the obvious reason of space limitation there are several private ventures in
policing that are omitted from discussion here but that are well represented in the

general literature on the history of policing. My intention here is to draw together a picture of developments that is less evident in standard histories. Special mention should perhaps be made of one omission, this being the work of Patrick Colquhoun and the privately sponsored Port of London police. In this essay I have had to subsume the Port police within general references to the diversity of private arrangements for policing in London, but for an interesting case study of their work and development see Radzinowicz (1956a, chap. 12).

2. In this particular history Critchley largely misses the significance of a number of developments arising out of shifts in law and economy.

3. The role of the informer in the execution of the criminal justice system in the United Kingdom has been a long and wide-ranging one. It was not until 1951 that the final 48 common informers statutes were repealed after the reading of the Common Informer Bill (Parliamentary debates, 1950-1951). "It is not a flattering testimony to the adequacy of our law enforcement," wrote Sir Carleton Kemp-Allen, "that for over five hundred years we have felt it necessary to set the law in motion by this means" (Kemp-Allen, 1953, quoted in Radzinowicz, 1956b: 155).

REFERENCES

BARTRIP, P. and P. FENN (1980) "The conventionalisation of factory crime: a re-assessment." *International Journal of the Sociology of Law* 8: 175-86.

BERESFORD, M. (1958) "The common informers, the penal statutes and economic regulation." *Economic History Review* 2, 2: 221-238.

BOWDEN, T. (1978) *Beyond the Limits of the Law.* Harmondsworth, England: Penguin.

BREWER, J. (1980) "Law and disorder in Stuart and Hanoverian England." *History Today* 30: 22-26.

BYTHELL, D. (1969) *The Handloom Weavers.* Cambridge, England: Cambridge University Press.

CAIN, M. (1979) "Trends in the sociology of police work." *International Journal of the Sociology of Law* 7: 143-167.

CARSON, W. (1979) "The conventionalisation of early factory crime." *International Journal of the Sociology of Law* 7, 1: 37-60.

COBB, R. (1970) *The Police and the People: French Popular Protest 1789-1820.* Oxford, England: Oxford University Press.

COHEN, S. and A. SCULL [eds.] (1983) *Social Control and the State.* Oxford, England: Martin Robertson.

CRITCHLEY, T. (1967) *A History of Police in England and Wales, 900-1966.* London: Constable.

DINWIDDY, J. (1979) "Luddism and politics in the northern countries." *Social History* 4, 1: 39-63.

DITTON, J. (1977) "Perks, pilferage and the fiddle: the historical structure of invisible wages." *Theory and Society* 4: 39-71.

———(1982) "Natural sociology: a sociological method for analysing an historical etymological paradox." *Working Papers in Sociology,* no. 2, Department of Sociology, University of Glasglow, Scotland.

DRAPER, H. (1978) *Private Police.* Harmondsworth, England: Penguin.

FOWLER, N. (1979) *After the Riots: The Police in Europe.* London: Davis-Poynter.

HALL, J. (1935) *Theft, Law and Society.* Indianapolis, IN: Bobbs-Merrill.
HALL, S., and G. McLENNAN (1982) "Customs and law: law and crime as historical processes," in *Issues in Crime and Society.* Milton Keynes, England: Open University Publications.
HAY, D. (1975a) "Poaching and the game laws on Cannock Chase," pp. 189-253 in D. Hay et al. (eds.) Albion's Fatal Tree: Crime and Society in 18th Century England. London: Allen & Unwin.
——— (1975b) "Property, authority and the criminal law," pp. 17-63 in D. Hay et al. (eds.) Albion's Fatal Tree: Crime and Society in 18th Century England. London: Allen & Unwin.
——— (1980) "Crime and justice in 18th and 19th century England," pp. 45-84 in N. Morris and M. Tonry (eds.) *Crime and Justice: An Annual Review of Research, vol. 2.* Chicago: University of Chicago Press.
———P. LINEBAUGH, and E. THOMPSON (1975) *Albion's Fatal Tree: Crime and Society in 18th Century England.* London: Allen & Unwin.
HENRY, S. (1979) "On the fence." *British Journal of Law and Society* 4: 124-133.
IGNATIEFF, M. (1978) *A Just Measure of Pain.* London: Macmillan.
LANGBEIN, J. (1983) "Albion's Fatal Flaws." *Past and Present* 98: 96-120.
LITTLE, C. and C. SHEFFIELD (1983) "Frontiers and criminal justice: English private prosecution societies and American vigilantism in the 18th and 19th centuries." *American Sociological Review* 48: 796-808.
MARX, G. (1974) "Thoughts on a neglected category of social movement participant: the agent provocateur and the informant." *American Journal of Sociology* 80, 2: 402-442.
McINTOSH, M. (1976) "Thieves and fences: markets and power in professional crime." *British Journal of Criminology* 16, 3: 257-266.
NEWBY, H., C. BELL, D. ROSE, and P. SAUNDERS (1978) *Property, Paternalism and Power: Class and Control in Rural England.* London: Hutchinson.
PARKS, E. (1970) "From constabulary to police society: implications for social control." *Catalyst* (Summer): 76-97.
Parliamentary History (1780-1781) "Debate on the Gordon riots." *Parliamentary History of England* volume 21.
——— (1785-1786) "Debates on London and Westminister police bill." *Parliamentary History of England* volume 25.
PASQUINO, P. (1978) "Theatrum politicum: the genealogy of capital, police and the state of prosperity." *Ideology and Consciousness* 4: 41-54.
PEARSON, G. (1978) "Goths and vandals: crime in history." *Contemporary Crises* 2, 2: 119-139.
PHILIPS, D. (1977) *Crime in Victorian England.* London: Croom Helm.
——— (1983) "A just measure of crime, authority, hunters and blue locusts: the 'revisionist' social history of crime and the law in Britain, 1780-1850," pp. 50-79 in S. Cohen and A. Scull (eds.) Social Control and the State. Oxford, England: Martin Robertson.
RADZINOWICZ, L. (1956a) *A History of English Criminal Law and its Administration from 1750, vol. 2.* London: Stevens and Son.
——— (1956b) *A History of English Criminal Law and its Administration from 1750, vol. 3.* London: Stevens and Son.
ROCK, P. (1983) "Law, order and power in late 17th and early 18th century England," pp. 191-222 in S. Cohen and A. Scull (eds.) Social Control and the State. Oxford, England: Martin Robertson.

RUDÉ, G. (1952) *Paris and London in the 18th Century.* London: Fontana.
SCRATON, P. and N. SOUTH (1981) *Capitalist Discipline, Private Justice and the Hidden Economy.* Occasional Papers in Deviance and Social Policy 2. Enfield: Middlesex Polytechnic.
———(1984) "The ideological construction of the hidden economy: private justice and work-related crime." *Contemporary Crises* 8: 1-18.
SHEARING, C. and P. STENNING (1981) "Modern private security: its growth and implications," pp. 193-245 in M. Tonry and N. Morris (eds.) *Crime and Justice: An Annual Review of Research, vol. 3.* Chicago: University of Chicago Press.
——— (1983) "Private security: implications for social control." *Social Problems* 30, 5: 493-506.
SHUBERT, A. (1981) "Private initiative in law enforcement: associations for the prosecution of felons, 1744-1856," pp. 25-41 in V. Bailey (ed.) *Policing and Punishment in the 19th Century.* London: Croom Helm.
SILVER, A. (1967) "The demand for order in civil society: a review of some themes in the history of urban crime, police and riot," pp. 1-24 in D. Bordua (ed.) *The Police: Six Sociological Essays.* New York: John Wiley.
SOUTH, N. (1982) "The informal economy and local labour Markets," in J. Laite (ed.) *Bibliographies on Local Labour Markets and the Informal Economies.* London: Social Science Research Council.
———(1984) "Private security, the division of policing labor and the commercial compromise of the state," pp. 171-198 in S. Spitzer and A. Scull (eds.) *Research in Law, Deviance and Social Control, vol. 6.* Greenwich, CT: JAI.
———(1985) "Private security and social control: the private security sector in the UK, its commercial functions and public accountability." Doctoral dissertation, Centre for Occupational and Community Research, Middlesex Polytechnic, London.
SPITZER, S. and A. SCULL (1977a) "Social control in historical perspective: from private to public responses to crime," pp. 265-286 in D. Greenberg (ed.) *Corrections and Punishment.* Beverly Hills, CA: Sage.
———(1977b) "Privatization and capitalist development: the case of the private police." *Social Problems* 25, 1: 18-29.
State Research (1980-1981) "Supergrass policing." *State Research* 4, 21: 46-57.
THOMPSON, E. (1967) "Time, work discipline and industrial capitalism." *Past and Present* 38: 56-97.
———(1968) *The Making of the English Working Class.* Harmondsworth, England: Penguin.
———(1971) "The moral economy of the English crowd in the 18th century." *Past and Present* 50: 76-136.
———(1974) "Patrician society, plebian culture." *Journal of Social History* 7: 382-405.
———(1975) *Whigs and Hunters.* London: Allen Lane.
WEISS, R. (1978) "The emergence and transformation of private detective industrial policing in the United States, 1850-1940." *Crime and Social Justice* (Spring/Summer): 35-48.
———(1981) "The private detective agency in the development of policing forms in the rural and frontier United States." *Insurgent Sociologist* 10, 4: 7, 21.
———(1986) "Private detective agencies and labour discipline in the United States: 1855-1946." *The Historical Journal* 29, 1: 87-107.

Chapter 4

FROM "SLUGGING DETECTIVES" TO "LABOR RELATIONS": Policing Labor At Ford, 1930-1947

ROBERT P. WEISS

His [Bugas's] methods were in strong contrast to those of the hard-hitting Bennett. It was the difference between the slugging detective who was just switched from a uniform to plainclothes, and a Sherlock Holmes who adorns his deductions with intellectual overtones [Business Week, 1946b].

This chapter examines an aspect of private policing history: labor discipline during the years from 1930 to 1947. This was an important period in private policing history, a time during which private industrial policing went from its highest level of activity to a dramatic decline. By 1947 a new discipline in the form of conservative trade unions was securely established in many industries. Throughout the years of the Great Depression the Ford Motor Company was perhaps the most notorious employer in its resistance to collective bargaining. Then, suddenly, during World War II Ford made an abrupt turnaround in corporate philosophy and policy regarding labor, and become a leader in the new approach. The case of Ford thus provides us with sharp lines of change. Ford is also valuable as a case study because of the light it sheds on the *definitional* problem of private policing, and on the relation of private agencies to the state and state power. After discussing changes in the nation's political economy that facilitated this transformation in labor discipline, we will focus on the Ford Motor Company as a case study.

AUTHOR'S NOTE: This is a revised version of a paper presented at the 37th Annual Meeting of the American Society of Criminology, November 1985, San Diego. I wish to thank Anne Rowland for her editorial comments.

DEVELOPMENTS ON THE LABOR FRONT

Labor historians often have noted that the American labor movement has as its central feature a paradox. Although American workers were among the most militant, displaying a degree of solidarity that was never achieved in Western Europe, they left no radical institutional legacy. There were, of course, many reasons for the failure of workers to build lasting and comprehensive union structures. The tendency of American workers to be localistic and parochial has been noted by Lichtenstein (1982: 9) in his study of the Congress of Industrial Organizations (CIO) during World War II. But a not insignificant reason for the failure of worker organizations has been that workers who went out on strike were confronted by an oligopolistic industry that according to the Interchurch World Movement Commission of Inquiry (1920, 1921: 15) reports on the 1919 steel strike, was simply too big and too wealthy, holding too much influence with press and pulpit, and enjoying the support of local and Federal authorities.[1]

Corporations in the extractive and heavy manufacturing industries especially had the financial wherewithal to withstand the scattered resistance of strikers while they were supported by a state that declared strike activity illegitimate. Courts issued strike injunctions, the National Guard and the U.S. Army were called out to break strikes and, most important, for 85 years the federal government tolerated the operation of a vast private army of spies and strikebreakers. Nearly every one of the findings in 29 Congressional investigations (from 1882 to 1925)[2] into the use of private police during strikes shared Weber's (1972) insight that the power of coercion belongs to the state's representatives, and therefore private policing was a "usurpation of state power by private interests." Yet, Congress repeatedly claimed that it lacked constitutional authority to regulate the policing business. For their part, the individual states and many local officials commissioned private police. In the case of Pennsylvania, officials sold for $1.00 its police power (Shalloo, 1933). Corporations enjoyed this favorable treatment by the state until the 1930s, when the federal legislature and judiciary did an about-face and gave legal support to unionization.

Throughout the 1920s unionism had little influence. Fueled by the patriotic fervor of World War I and a war-swollen federal bureaucracy (including a vastly strengthened Federal Bureau of Investigation), events of the postwar red scare dealt a severe blow to radical organizations such as the Industrial Workers of the World. Conservative trade unionism all but disappeared by the late 1920s as well (Auerbach, 1966; Dubofsky, 1969). Even as popular discontent rose during the early years of the depression, unions like the AFL failed to resist wage cuts and layoffs. Then, suddenly, in 1933 and 1934 there was a great surge of rank-and-file militancy and political radicalism (Brecher, 1972; Lichtenstein, 1982: 9). Encouraged by a federal government that appeared sympathetic to labor, hundreds of thousands of workers forged a powerful movement of protest and self-organization. To help deal with the depression crisis, Franklin Roosevelt established the National Recovery Act of 1933, which contained a provision (Section 7A) granting workers the right to organize and bargain collectively, free from employer interference or coercion. A rush to unionization followed, and labor war resumed full force. The 1934 battles included the bloody conflicts in the Southern and New England textile industry, at Akron rubber plants, between police and the Teamsters in Minneapolis, and at the Auto-Lite Plant in Toledo (Lipsitz, 1982).

Although the upsurge in rank-and-file militancy did not last long into 1935, according to Lichtenstein (1982) the upheaval was enough to frighten the left wing of the New Deal into fighting for passage of the Wagner Act in 1935, which gave legal force, backed by fines, to labor's right to organize. After the Wagner Act, unionization efforts surged: from 1936 to 1944 membership increased from 4 million to 14 million, and in the face of employer opposition to union recognition, there were 4000 strikes in 1937 alone (Brecher, 1972). Companies in the competitive sector, as well as the giant manufacturers Ford Motor Company and Bethlehem Steel, resisted the unionizing drive with all their strength. Private labor policing reached a peak of intensity and sophistication with thousands of spies and sluggers working for hundreds of labor detective agencies. It was in this context that early in 1936 the American Civil Liberties Union (ACLU) approached Senator Robert M. La Follette, Jr., to inquire about launching a congressional investigation of the private police business and its infringement on civil liberties (Auerbach, 1966: 61).[3] For the first time in 20 years, Senators were inclined to investigate, not unmindful of the labor vote prospects in the 1936 election.

Despite the additional pressure of the Senate investigation, many corporations continued to resist unionization, no doubt in the belief that the Wagner Act would be ruled unconstitutional. However, between 1933 and 1937 the bulk of workers in basic industries were organized by the CIO or the American Federation of Labor (AFL)

(Aronowitz, 1967: 234). General Motors (GM) succumbed to the union drive of 1936-1937, and a week after the sitdown drive at GM, U.S. Steel concluded an agreement recognizing the Steelworkers Organizing Committee. The conservative "brass hat" entrepreneurs like Ford and those steel companies organized in the National Association of Manufacturers held out until the 1941 CIO militant organizing drive. The strike wave, in combination with an upturn in the economy and pressure from the Roosevelt administration for uninterrupted war production, contributed to a turnaround in management philosophy and strategy. The most remarkable example of the "new attitude" toward unions occurred at Ford Motor Company, and events there serve as a case study in the suppression of the private labor policing business. Suddenly and dramatically, Ford Motor officials abandoned their robber baron approach to industrial relations and embraced the New Deal attitude toward unions. Ford, in fact, became a leader among automakers and maintained that lead through the 1940s.

In this chapter we will examine some of the legal and political forces, economic conditions, and the changes in corporate philosophy and strategy that marked the demise of the "slugging detective" and the ascent of the "labor relations department" as front lines in dealing with organized labor at Ford. This transformation was accomplished with the immediate involvement of three groups whose roles are examined: (a) trade union leaders, (b) gangsters, and (c) "labor relations" executives, many of whom were former FBI agents. We conclude with a consideration of these events in terms of various conceptions of the exercise of state power.

FORD SERVICE

Henry Ford: "an industrial fascist—the Mussolini of Detroit" [New York Times, January 8, 1928, quoted in Sward, 1968: 369].

For introducing the flywheel magneto moving assembly line in 1913, Henry Ford has been known popularly as a great innovator. Among labor he was also known as a tyrant who demanded from his workers absolute obedience and machinelike behavior to complement his technocratic vision of the ideal factory. At the 1100-acre River Rouge plant, 80,000 workers toiled at the various

productive operations for Ford's industrial empire. Some worked
the 950-foot main assembly line. There, especially, Ford expected
absolute regimentation, with chatting and fraternizing among workers forbidden even in the lunchroom. That grim scene was poi-
gnantly captured by John McCarten (1940: 7):

> They do not whistle while they work; they do not even whis-
> per. Only the tools they use make any sound as they demon-
> strate the efficiency of mass production. Their silence is a
> tribute to the Machine-Age Pavlovs who determine from week
> to week just how much men can stand before running amok.

From the 1920s to the postwar period "Ford discipline" went
through three distinct stages: (1) a brief period of *benevolent paternalism* lasting from 1914 to the early 1920s; (2) *brutal repression*
during the 1920s and 1930s; and (3) *"Human Engineering"* of the
1940s. The last phase, reflecting a management liberalism that recognized the "human factor" (including union membership), was
accomplished only after an initial period (1941-1945) when the
company attempted to manipulate the United Auto Workers (UAW)
and intimidate the rank and file while promoting company or
"mock" unions. The final transformation at Ford came only when
Henry II took over control of the company from the elder Ford.

Henry Ford flirted briefly with progressive notions, as when in
1914 he introduced the Five Dollar Day. That startling notion specified shorter work hours and doubled the prevailing wage in the
auto industry. However, Ford's proposition to share profits with his
workers was highly conditional, and only those workers who con-
formed to Mr. Ford's own puritanical notions of moral behavior
qualified. "Living unworthy of a profit-sharer" included alcohol
use, separation or divorce, promiscuity, and "spending foolishly"
(Sward, 1968/1948: 60-62). The new "profit sharing" incentive
system was administered by the "Ford Sociology Department,"
which was responsible for investigating the personal lives and home
situations of his workers.

Impatient with the insufficiency of mere social controls, Ford
abandoned the paternalism of the Five Dollar Day by 1920 and insti-
tuted a system of undisguised brutality. This happened as Mr. Ford
became increasingly isolated and hardened in his prejudices, and
after 1921 his company lost most of its former innovative energies.
To lower prices and increase flagging sales of his Model T, Ford
ordered "speed-ups." Soon his factories had the worst reputation

for driving workers. In 1921, the head of the Sociological Department, Reverend Samuel Marquis, resigned. As competition intensified during the 1920s, Ford resorted increasingly to the rule of fear to run his machine-age nightmare. Finally, the 1930s depression economy saw the disappearance of the last pretense of benevolence at Ford. As production dropped, workers were laid off without relief.

By 1932, from 30% to 50% of Detroit's wage earners were unemployed, including 50,000 to 60,000 Ford employees (Sward, 1968/ 1948: 233). The manner in which the automaker dealt with the Ford Hunger Marchers provides a dramatic example of the brutal repression period at Ford. In a protest organized by a communist group, several hundred jobless workers, carrying handbills listing demands for reform of Ford policy, participated in the 1932 march to the Rouge plant. The group proceeded unmolested while in Detroit (which had a reform mayor at the time), but once they crossed the city line into Dearborn they were met by 30 or 40 Dearborn police who tried to disperse them with tear gas. A melee resulted; at the point when the violent give-and-take centered around Gate 3, the main entrance to the Rouge plant, Ford company police joined the fray with high-pressure fire hoses. When, moments later, Ford's police chief was seriously injured by a flying brick, another Ford police official directed: "Get your gats out and let them have it" (Sward, 1968/1948: 235). Dearborn officers and Ford's private police opened with machine gun fire point-blank at the crowd. When the smoke cleared, four hunger marchers lay dead and a score were wounded.

Unlike the other automakers, Henry Ford developed his own in-house police system. At its peak, the Ford Service Department, as the police force was called, consisted of 3500 roughnecks— football players, wrestlers, ex-convicts, gangsters, and broken-down cops. They were led by an elite Service Squad. Ford Service was augmented at various times by an assortment of community groups acting as auxiliaries, including legionnaires, the middle-class vigilante Knights of Dearborn, and American Nazis (Sward, 1968/1948: 297, 317). Sward (1968/1948: 293) tells us:

This instrument, stamped by Ford's temperament and molded by Bennett's genius, was twenty years in the making. It constituted, when fully spun, a web of spies and private police which the *New York Times* designated in 1937 as the largest private quasi-military organization in existence.

Its effect on workers was known as "Ford neurosis."

In an extension of the nineteenth-century company town, Ford's servicemen permeated nearly every sphere of workers' lives, employing everyone from shop-floor spies to men who checked on the family life of disgruntled workers. Ford Service also patrolled taverns, stores, restaurants, and hotel lobbies. This produced around the Detroit and Flint areas what Sward identified as "community neurosis." This awesome police force was headed from 1919 by Harry H. Bennett, a former Navy boxer. But he was by no means a mere glorified private detective. Bennett was given sole authority over company labor policy; only Mr. Ford himself could rescind Bennett's orders. He controlled the company purse strings and jobs. With this power, he bought political influence by "padding the payroll," and used it to threaten workers (conservatively estimated, according to Sward, Bennett fired 4000 people between 1937 and 1941 alone).

Bennett's position at Ford made him a power in Michigan politics. He was respected among the state's influential citizens, and thus Bennett's use of police power had the trappings of legitimacy. But, although force was available, he did not always have to use it. At times corruption could serve his purposes. Political power and tactical control of his policemen gave Bennett a flexibility largely denied the commercial private detective agency.

Most corporations and employers' associations of the time hired men through private detective agencies to do their police work. In doing so, management surrendered a significant measure of control over labor policy.[4] The antagonism these businesses generated usually precluded a negotiated settlement. All private detective agencies were involved in a central paradox: they had a strong interest in prolonging the very strikes that they were hired to suppress (Huberman, 1937). This was the case especially with fly-by-night agencies, which were in essence simple shakedown operations (U.S. Senate, 1939b: 29).

The La Follette Committee (1939a: 29) observed that over time private detective agencies that provided strike services sorted themselves into a distinct hierarchy. This stratification was based on the kinds of tactics particular agencies were willing to employ, as well as their proclivity to prolong confrontations. According to the committee (1939b: 98), "in the case of the more permanent and well-established agencies this interest is counter-balanced to some extent by the desire of the agency to establish a reputation with employers and to build up a substantial clientele."

This is true of the Burns agency, and also of the Pinkerton agency, as its order book indicates. In the smaller agencies, however, or in an agency such as Bergoff's, the pecuniary motive for prolonging the strike or increasing its bitterness knows no such limits.[5]

The activities of those individuals and businesses near the bottom of the heap merged imperceptibly with gangland racketeering. Known as "regular finks," men were drawn from the ranks of "exconvicts, thieves, gangsters," according to the deposition given by one agency veteran (1939b: 103). The committee helped document that assertion through its examination of the arrest or conviction records for theft, robbery, violence, and fraud among a selected group of 150 "detectives."

Harry Bennett's tactics, in contrast, were not designed to prolong open battle and thus endanger production. Because he personified the totality of Ford's interests, the activities of Bennett's Service Department did not always reflect the worst aspect of Mr. Ford's temperament. McCarten (1940: 11) has observed this as well. "He indulges in such crude displays of power [as threatening shutdowns] only when all else fails, and he would rather patch up a truce with the union leaders than endanger production so drastically." But, when negotiations proved unsatisfactory, Bennett readily applied physical force. And in those instances when extra muscle was needed, Bennett also used gangsters. He could rely on his Detroit underworld friend, Chester La Mare (Beynon, 1973: 21-31; Sward, 1968/1948: 300, 371) for support. In exchange for operating shop-floor rackets and receiving monopolistic business concessions (Whittey, 1970; Sward, 1968/1948: 299), Detroit mobsters would perform labor-policing services for employers throughout the city. But Bennett seems to have kept gangsters under his control; his Service Squad tolerated no crimes "that might endanger the Ford family or its property," McCarten (1940: 202) observes. Michigan criminals not only feared him for his willingness to use force, but also respected him because of his connections with the Michigan State Prison Commission.[6] A former commissioner himself, Bennett had friends on both sides of the law. Unlike most other corporate security chiefs, "Bennett's field of action was state-wide and political, as well as plant-wide and industrial" (Sward, 1968/1948: 326).

Bennett's knowledge of the Michigan underworld and his work in solving area crimes placed him in a good relationship with the

city police of Dearborn and Detroit, and with the Michigan State
Police. McCarten (1940: 201) observed:

> They are indebted to him for innumerable favors. He has saved
> official scalps by helping solve crimes all over northern Michi-
> gan, which he regards as a kind of cordon sanitaire attached
> to his industrial bailiwick.

There were additional bases for favorable relationships between
Bennett and government officials. For instance, the Dearborn safety
commissioner and its chief of police were former Ford servicemen. And many former politicians and area police officials found
jobs at Ford. One of Bennett's most strategic allies was Municipal
Judge Leo J. Schaeffer, a 15-year veteran of the local bench. Sward
(1968/1948: 317) observes:

> By virtue of his office Schaeffer could act, all this while, as
> one of the city's final arbiters of free speech and free assem-
> bly. He represented, consequently, the judicial arm of the
> police power of the city, the authority who was entrusted with
> the enforcement of any and all municipal ordinances.

A close friend of Henry Ford, the judge held a very profitable cater-
ing concession at the Ford plants. Politicians benefited from Ford
largess at election time. Supporters of the Ford slate were "put on
the payroll" during municipal elections. This political influence
helped ensure that Bennett would have little interference from the
constituted authorities of law and order. To the extent to which it
possessed de facto state power, the Ford service was probably
unique in the history of private police systems.

Bennett's police force occupied a structural space between the
gangland and the official police, enjoying the best of both worlds in
its exercise of police power without public accountability. "Bennett usually acts as a middleman between the underworld and the
police. In that capacity, he is hedged with protection both from
above and from below," observed McCarten (1940: 203). This system served well enough during the worst of the depression, but in
the end, the strong-arm police approach was limited in value to
Ford.

By the late 1930s, legal and organizing pressure was mounting
on the few holdout employers who did not yet recognize unions.
Bennett, sensing something serious, tried to display his flexibility.

In 1938 and 1939, he held secret talks with CIO international president, Homer Martin, agreeing to allow the CIO to organize Ford unmolested. After all, he once said, "When I can't lick the CIO, I'll join it" (quoted in McCarten, 1940: 208). But, no doubt, in his negotiations with Martin, Bennett was confident that the union association would remain under Ford's control (Sward, 1968: 380-384). When Martin was ousted from the CIO in 1939, Bennett backed out of the agreement. He believed that the United Autoworkers (UAW) was so weakened by factionalism that it would be easy prey to force and intimidation. By the winter of 1940, however, the UAW was able to devote all of its organizing resources to the last company holdout. Official or not, police power would prove insufficient to hold back the "Ford drive." And although Bennett could display a degree of tolerance for organized labor when it was strong, Ford Service qua police was not flexible enough to encompass genuine union-negotiated agreements.

Changing times were leaving Bennett behind, and although he was Ford's representative at the signing of the 1941 contract with the UAW, his days as personnel director were clearly numbered. The important action in the future would no longer be on the shop floor or at the factory gate.

FORD GOES "THE WHOLE WAY" FOR UNION PROTECTION

When the autocrat Henry Ford authorized Harry Bennett to sign a union shop and dues checkoff contract with Philip Murray, president of the UAW, an executive of a rival company exclaimed that Bennett had made him "a present of the whole goddamn industry" (Business Week, 1941). CIO officials had asked for a contract that contained seven demands, including wage increases, abolition of the Service Department, and time-and-a-half for overtime. The octogenarian Mr. Ford was not mellowing: after 38 years of implacable opposition, the company "decided to go the whole way" with the union, but not without the union's pledge of no labor trouble. *Business Week* discussed other ways in which the automaker could benefit from the new contract, including union sniping at Ford's competitors and preferential treatment in the awarding of government contracts. But the primary benefit, in the words of the magazine, was "union protection, a kind of plant policing by the union for the company." In effect, Ford was giving responsibility for disciplining the rank-and-file to the union leadership, which, in exchange, would have a guaranteed membership; union membership would henceforth be a condition for employment. This worked to the advantage of both interests. Without the checkoff, *Business Week* observed from management's viewpoint, "a labor organization must ever be active if it is to anchor the loyalty of employees and keep them convinced that it is to their interest to pay their dues. To achieve this, it constantly seeks 'grievances,' and where they cannot be found it often manufactures them." But once a company gets a union checkoff, "the pressure for demonstrating its value to members and possible recruits is lifted." As an example, the magazine cited the dispute at Brewster Aeronautical Corporation, which had a closed shop contract with the UAW and whose workers in one department went out on a six-hour strike (Business Week, 1941):

> The union summoned up before it 10 men who were reputed to be the ringleaders in the stoppage. In a quick trial before the union's executive board, they were accused and convicted of being "Communist obstructionists."

> The company was notified that the men had been expelled from the union and, under the agreement providing the company would employ only union members, must be discharged. *The union was policing that plant as the employer never could* . . . [italics added].

After the 1941 contract, the UAW and Ford were "in business together" as "partners." There were some wrinkles, however. For one, gangsters had infiltrated union ranks; in the ensuing struggle for control, Walter and Victor Reuther were shot. Another potentially more threatening problem involved left- and right-wing factional disputes within the union. Top officials "found it impossible to crack down on troublesome local leaders," *Business Week* (1941) noted:

> The only way Ford is going to get union protection in his plants, without which his union shop contract can mean complete chaos, is to have U.A.W. transformed into a strongly centralized organization exerting iron discipline over its constituent locals and over its rank and file. For the Ford-U.A.W. partnership to be profitable, U.A.W. must first put its house in order.

But World War II was to test severely the ability of the union leadership to discipline its membership. By the start of the war, unions were recognized by nearly all large industrial corporations. As in World War I, big union bosses once again pledged no strikes or walkouts, and the leadership of the AFL and the CIO got busy disciplining their rapidly increasing membership. As a consequence, during a time of labor scarcity and burgeoning profits, those unions failed to make wage gains. Communist-led unions were no exception, and according to *Business Week,* they had "perhaps the best no-strike record of any section of organized labor," and were "the most vigorous proponents of labor-management cooperation" (Business Week, 1944). Wartime working conditions were so bad, however, that despite the union and management cooperative effort to discipline workers and prevent "wildcat" strikes, there were more strikes "than during any period of comparable length of United States history" (Brecher, 1972: 226).

Midway through the war, management and the rank and file were in a struggle over shop control. There followed a wave of unauthorized strikes, protests, slowdowns, and work stoppages protesting production standards and discipline. From the beginning to the end of the American war presence, there were "14,471 strikes involving 6,744,000 strikers" (Brecher, 1977: 226), most "quickie" stoppages protesting managerial toughness (Lichtenstein, 1982: 121).

In 1945 union leaders were preparing for their worst crisis since recognition—the end of the war. Without government-supported "maintenance-of-membership" provisions, unions faced large defections and a bitter struggle for survival. Additionally, "reconversion" was expected to result in the layoff of millions, with millions of discharged military personnel joining them on unemployment. For those still working, the end of the war also would end overtime and incentive pay. "At the end of the first World War," *Business Week* (1945a) observed, "unions were smashed by industry after wartime growth to then-record highs. This time labor is watching suspiciously." And in contrast to the 1918-1920 postwar rise in wages, weekly earnings in 1946 were expected to experience a 20% decrease because of the reduction of work hours alone (Business Week, 1945). With the prospect of such a drop in income in 1945, combined with continually rising prices, strikes were certain. The question was, would they be "wildcat" or union led?

There followed a rash of union-backed demands for higher wages, with a 30% increase being the CIO standard (Business

Week, 1945b). How was management to deal with this? Try to repeat its post-World War I strategy of smashing unions? (Business Week, 1945a). Ford Motor Company again provides an instructive example. Ford officials reasserted progressive leadership and maintained it throughout the 1940s. In 1945, Ford leadership turned decidedly liberal in its attitude toward unions. This dramatic shift coincided with the transfer of leadership from Henry Ford to his grandson, Henry II, who put forth a new labor philosophy and strategy.

FORD EMPLOYS NEW STRATEGY

Henry Ford II, grandson of the 88-year-old founder, took over as president in September of 1945. Within a week of assuming office, he made major executive changes that announced an important shift in corporate philosophy. The first top official to go was Harry Bennett. A variety of Bennett's confidants and assistants promptly resigned or were transferred—a signal that "Ford Runs Ford," in the words of *Business Week*. To help him wrest control of the company from Bennett and his gangsters, Ford solicited the help of James J. Bugas, Bennett's recently appointed assistant. He promoted Bugas to head of "industrial relations," a new Ford title (Business Week, 1945d, 1945e).

Mr. Bugas came to his job well prepared to deal with the new labor situation. He had come to the attention of Ford officials when he was chief of the Detroit office of the Federal Bureau of Investigation, one of the nation's "hot spots," and where recently he had supervised raids against "communists."[7] According to *Business Week*, Bugas joined Ford in 1944 only "on the company's plea to Edgar Hoover that his experience concentrated at Ford would help win the war" (Business Week, 1945b). The changing of the guard at Ford, from gangsters to ex-G-men, brought a "new style" to Ford's labor relations effort, involving "subtle" tactics rather than the slugging offensive of Bennett. "J. Edgar Hoover boasts that under his technique the G-men never have to use rubber-hose or other physical persuaders" (Business Week, 1945b). Bugas's approach was not timid, but direct and "frank," a strategy designed to control the situation. Unions would be recognized, but their leadership would be put on the defensive and held accountable to the *company's* demands.

Bugas's assistant, Mel B. Lindquest, also came to the job well prepared. His position as superintendent of labor relations put him on "the direct firing line in the Ford relationship to labor." An ex-boxer? No, Lindquest came from the "labor relations" department of the Murray Corporation, where the "company evolved its program for training union members as time study experts, so the union would have its own advocates in any dispute on timing of operations" (Business Week, 1942, 1945f). This fitted in well with Ford's new strategy, which, succinctly put by Henry II, was "company security" should equal "union security." The company was willing to grant generous wage and hour concessions, but insisted on rank-and-file discipline.

At the start of the 1945 contract negotiations Bugas advanced 31 demands of the union in exchange for the "union security" of a union shop and dues checkoff. Bugas put the UAW on the defensive with these counterproposals to ensure worker efficiency and continuity, and suggested fines of $5.00 a day per worker on the local treasury for wildcat strikes. Moreover, there were certain matters that were off limits; the company would not consider negotiation over profits, for one. Another company demand excluded from UAW membership certain classes of personnel, such as supervisors and clerical workers. Corporate leaders, Lichtenstein (1982: 242) observes, "emerged from World War II with new strength, determined to curb informal, localistic power unionized workers had won during the previous decade." Management wanted to regain control over production on the shop floor, and they followed Ford's lead in demanding company security antistrike clauses. In 1946, however, the United States witnessed a strike wave of unprecedented proportions.

STRIKING AGAINST THE GOVERNMENT

I think the men are more radical than their leaders in most cases [Senator Robert A. Taft, in *U.S. Senate*, 1947: 574].

Labor's postwar struggle over control of the work process and over wages intensified capital's determination to regain traditional managerial controls. In 1946 there were more strikes than in any one-year period of American history (Lipsitz, 1982: 37); these included simultaneous nationwide work stoppages in steel, auto, and electronics. Unable to prevent the strikes, union leaders reluctantly led them for fear of losing their memberships and in hope of gaining some control over them. At this point, Congress stepped in with new legislation designed to restrain the rank and file by strengthening the institutional power of trade unions.

Among the provisions of the 1947 Taft-Hartley Act were sanctions against unions for mass picketing, walkouts, wildcat strikes, sympathy strikes, and secondary boycotts. The law also mandated a "cooling off" period. Penalties included heavy fines and imprisonment of union officials (Aronowitz, 1967: 253). National Labor Relations Board (NLRB) sanctions against labor's tactics in the 1946 general strikes "made the institutional survival of the unions dependent upon their control over the rank-and-file," Lipsitz (1982: 127) observes. Many of these labor practices were already in violation of numerous local and state laws, and laws in at least half of the states "go well beyond the curbs provided by the Taft-Hartley measure," observed *Business Week* (1946a). And, as the magazine points out, the language of the Taft-Hartley bill "specifically provides for the sanctity of state legislation more stringent than the federal law." Why, then, did Congress bother? Lipsitz (1982: 127) argues that by federalizing the offenses the law "allowed for multiple penalties for the same act while lessening the likelihood that popular pressure could provide license for illegal measures." With its legislative attack on rank-and-file militance, Congress signaled a new partnership, one between government and business. The previous partnership between government and labor as embodied in the Wagner Act had spilled out of control; by the late 1940s it had become evident to corporate liberals that union leaders were having difficulty keeping labor demands "reasonable." Lipsitz (1982: 127) observes that the "Taft-Hartley Act, by increasing union powers to police their own members—transformed union leaders into not only agents of labor peace, *but agents of the state as well*" (italics added). On the other hand, "government efforts to put the power of law behind strike-breaking gave millions of workers a shared experience of defying the law and striking against the government," Lipsitz (1982: 52) concludes.

Business Week's 1941 argument that the centralization of union power was an essential element in the new partnership between unions and business reappeared as a principal feature of Taft-Hartley. Following its passage, Lichtenstein (1982: 243) observes that

> the transformation of the foreman into a simple disciplinarian and grievance buck passer necessarily diminished the independent leadership role of his counterpart, the union stew-

ard, who became at best a referral agent frequently bypassed in the actual working grievance procedure. Once shop disputes were reduced to written form and began to make their way up the grievance ladder, they were out of the steward's control and subject to a lockstep body of umpire-made "law" that defended managerial prerogatives regarding the work process and harshly penalized extracontractual pressure by the union.

Under the act, local officials were held directly responsible for slowdowns or work stoppages, thus transforming "plant committeemen and other local officers into contract policemen." Beginning with the New Deal's Wagner Act and ending with Taft-Hartley, the federal government helped facilitate a "new discipline" of labor in the form of business unionism.

CONCLUSION: EXTENDING THE CONTINUUM OF POLICING ORGANIZATION

The Wagner Act marked the end of laissez-faire policy toward labor. This legislation "embodied a radical exercise of state power on behalf of unionization," according to Lichtenstein (1982: 33).

By politicizing so much of the nation's economic life, the New Deal had undercut the old voluntarist ideology and located the battleground for labor's struggles as much within the apparatus of state policy formulation and administration in Washington as on the factory picket line [Lichtenstein, 1982: 33].

Representatives of business and labor entered a political relation, and the slugging-detective style of labor discipline became inappropriate and dangerous. Under the new system, as long as union bosses limited contract demands to wage and hour considerations, negotiations could be "reasonable." Developments in the mode of production since the turn of the century, including automation, "scientific management," and monopolization have permitted industries in the oligopolistic sector to pass the price of increased wage demands on to consumers. In this way, Habermas (1973: 38) argues, "the monopolistic sector can, as it were, externalize class conflict." The reformist nature of labor and management has made them "wage scale partners," concerned with middle-range demands on the state. And, for the most part they have been able to find broad areas of compromise. On those occasions when the rank and file have resisted agreements, union bosses have employed many of the same measures as did the old private "labor detectives" and company police, including the use of strikebreakers to combat "wildcat" strikes, the imposition of fines, and red-baiting.

Federal support for private labor detective policing arrangements ended with the Great Depression. After 60 years of cooperation with management on the labor issue, the state exercised its "relative autonomy" from business in order to act on behalf of the *capitalist class as a whole.* Concerning the Wagner Act, Lichtenstein (1982: 82) argues:

> State action opposed to the immediate interests of the major corporations was sometimes necessary to ensure the maintenance of social peace and an ideological consensus that would placate, if not incorporate, the most important elements of a sometimes estranged liberal and labor Left.

Union activity has been given legal support since the New Deal, but only within certain limits. Workers unwilling to play by the rules of the wage-and-hour game have been labeled "subversives," and have become enemies of the Department of Justice. In addition to its campaign against radical political organizations, the federal government has assisted capital directly in its dealings with union leadership. Former FBI agents migrated into labor relations work in the years immediately following World War II. The FBI functioned as a sort of Academy of Scientific Labor Discipline, with its alumni continuing on to personnel and labor relations departments of major corporations or private detective agencies. "The FBI training and practice develop unusual qualities that are being sought by various business concerns," *Business Week* observed in a July 20, 1946, article discussing the elevation of Bugas to director of personnel at Ford. The area of labor discipline was "natural" for old grads, *Business Week* continues. "FBI experience has taught them not only how to handle personnel but to know what is going on within groups, with special reference to communistic and other subversive activities." The social mechanism facilitating the exchange of personnel was the Society of Former Special Agents of the Federal Bureau of Investigation, Inc. This organization helps to "keep alive the old bonds," *Business Week* (1946b) continues, and a "special committee keeps track of employment possibilities and passes information along. Relations with the old chief are cordial, almost reverent."

The dramatic change in policing approaches—from the use of slugging detectives to labor relations executives—obscures an underlying *continuity* in labor discipline. The diminution of the private labor detective business after the depression did not mean an end to labor policing; union officials came to assume a similar disciplinary function. And in incidents when rank-and-file action threatened the national union leadership, union bosses resorted to many of the same tactics used by the old private police. What is more, union officials enjoyed police power that was supported at the highest level of government. The Taft-Hartley Act put federal law behind the strike-breaking efforts of union leaders.

To clarify the position of various "formal" and "informal" institutions of rule enforcement and discipline in relation to the state, Nigel South (1984: 173) has suggested the usefulness of employing "a model of a *continuum* of policing organization in society in which both the public and private contributors exchange expertise, key personnel, and, importantly, accommodate each other's shifting parameters of operation and priorities in action." Shearing et al. (1980: 14) also have advanced the notion of a continuum in understanding modern private security, with those organizations possessing special powers and public accountability at one pole, and those with no special powers and accountable only to private interests at the other pole. They observe (1980: 14) the following:

> Where on this continuum any given security employee should be placed depends, we believe, not only on who his immediate employer is but also on what legal powers he possesses and to whom he is accountable for the exercise of those powers.

Our investigation in this chapter supports the usefulness of the continuum model of social control. In the course of our research we have seen that, in terms of legal powers and accountability, labor policing during the years 1930-1947 extended along a continuum. At one end or pole we can place vigilantes and the slugging gangsters who masqueraded as "detectives," whereas the various official police occupy the other. Private detectives and company police can be found somewhere in the middle of the continuum. Intervention of the federal government in labor affairs, mainly through the Wagner Act and the Taft-Hartley Act—but also through the FBI's involvement in ferreting out of radicals from union ranks—helps extend that continuum beyond the customary notion of police to include labor union officials as well. Perhaps the most remarkable police organization in the labor discipline business was the Ford Service Department: a single institution that, in its varied operations, extended almost the entire continuum, reaching from gangland rackets at one pole to the police activity of the servicemen—supported by corrupt local and state officials—at the other.

NOTES

1. The Commission of Inquiry, Interchurch World Commission's Report on the Steel Strike of 1919 (1920: 220-248) presented data on local magistrates and police authorities in and around Pittsburgh and throughout western Pennsylvania, Indiana, and Illinois, who "were frequently steel mill officials or relatives of mill officials" (p. 239). More disquieting, the report documents the widespread intimate connection between corporations' "secret service" systems and Federal authorities (pp. 226, 240), especially the Department of Justice, "whose connection with steel company "under-cover" men . . . dealt with raids in search of "reds" in the steel strike" (p. 240).

2. For a summary of these congressional investigations, see U.S. Senate (1939), report no. 6, Part I, pp. 139-148.

3. Auerbach (1966: 25) points out, however, that although the ACLU promoted the investigation, civil libertarians were wary of the centralization of power that the New Deal represented. The New Deal had not at that time restricted the rights of any group, as Auerbach points out, but "the absence of wholesale suppression offered slight cause for rejoicing, *'because there is as yet no significant opposition to suppress.'*" As we will see, that was forthcoming later in the decade and the response of FDR was to reestablish in 1939 the General Intelligence Division of the FBI.

4. This was especially the case when companies belonged to employers's associations. The National Metal Trades Association (NMTA), for example, with nearly a thousand members in 1937, was one of the most steadfast of antiunion employer groups. Membership funds collected by the whole association were often devoted to a single strike. Member employers surrendered control of their own labor policy to the governing body of the association: "The association assumed complete control and direction of the strike situation," the La Follette Committee observed (U.S. Senate, Committee on Education and Labor, 1939: 31). Any settlement not approved by the association resulted in suspension or expulsion and the repayment to the association of all money spent on the strike.

5. The La Follette Committee's (U.S. Senate, Committee on Education and Labor, 1939b: 19-29) research revealed that the large and more established agencies were themselves graded or stratified. For instance, among the five largest businesses that were selected for detailed investigation, Pinkerton (since 1892) and Burns (in operation at the time of the Senate investigation) refused to provide strikebreakers; but there was evidence that Railway Audit & Inspection Company did (evidence gathered despite the refusal of railway officials to appear and

testify, and their destruction of subpoenaed records). Fearing bad publicity and personal lawsuits (p. 107), Pinkerton abandoned even the strikeguard business by 1935. But the Burns agency took up the slack and provided industrial guards at 100% profit. However, even Burns was occasionally reluctant to provide the level of guard violence desired by some employers.

6. In 1934 Henry Ford was quoted in the Detroit *Times* as saying that his company employed as many as 8000 former prison inmates.

7. In 1939, by executive order, FDR reestablished the General Intelligence Division within the FBI, and "domestic intelligence provided the Bureau with a new source of appropriations and a unique source of power within the federal government" (Poveda, 1982: 196). According to evidence gathered by a 1940 Senate committee investigating the Department of Justice, "the FBI had, in 1939 and 1940, engaged in many illegalities suggestive of the years 1919 to 1924" (Lowenthal, 1950: 321). So, just as recognition of conservative trade unionism was being facilitated by the FDR administration, there was a resurgence of a spy system employing illegal practices over "factory employees who are under investigation, not for any criminal action, but only by reason of their views and activities in regard to labor unions and other economic movements" (quoted in Lowenthal, 1950: 322).

REFERENCES

ARONOWITZ, S. (1967) False Promises. New York: McGraw-Hill.
AUERBACH, J. S. (1966) Labor and Liberty: The La Follette Committee and the New Deal. Indianapolis, IN: Bobbs-Merrill.
BEYNON, H. (1973) Working for Ford. London: Allen Lane.
BRECHER, J. (1972) Strike! San Francisco: Straight Arrow Books.
Business Week (1941) June 28, p. 41.
———(1942) August 29, p. 42.
———(1944) March 18, p. 44.
———(1945a) August 18, p. 98-99.
———(1945b) September 22, pp. 99-100.
———(1945c) August 25.
———(1945d) September 29.
———(1945e) October 8, pp. 18-19.
———(1945f) December 8.
———(1946a) June 14, pp. 19-20; p. 90.
———(1946b) July 20, pp. 96-98.
DUBOFSKY, M. (1969) We Shall Be All. New York: Quadrangle.
HABERMAS, J. (1973) Legitimation Crisis. Boston: Beacon.
HUBERMAN, L. (1937) The Labor Spy Racket. New York: Modern Age Books.
Interchurch World Movement, Commission of Inquiry (1920) Report on the Steel Strike of 1919. New York: Harcourt, Brace.
———(1921) Public Opinion and The Steel Strike: Supplementary Reports. New York: Harcourt, Brace.
KOLKO, G. (1963) The Triumph of Conservatism. Chicago: Quadrangle.
LICHTENSTEIN, N. (1982) Labor's War at Home: The CIO in World War II. New York: Cambridge University Press.

LIPSITZ, G. (1982) Class and Culture in Cold War America. South Hadley, MA: J. F. Bergin.

LOWENTHAL, M. (1950) The Federal Bureau of Investigation. New York: Sloane.

McCARTEN, J. (1940) "The little man in Henry Ford's basement." The American Mercury 1, 197: 7-15 and 1, 198: 200-208.

POVEDA, T. G. (1982) "The FBI and domestic intelligence: technocratic or public relations triumph?" Crime and Delinquency 28, 2: 194-210.

SHALLOO, J. P. (1933) "The private police of Pennsylvania." Annals of the American Academy 146: 55-62.

SHEARING, C., M. FARNELL, and P. STENNING (1980) Contract Security in Ontario. Centre for Criminology, University of Toronto.

SOUTH, N. (1984) "Private security, the division of policing labor and the commercial compromise of the state," in A. Scull and S. Spitzer (eds.) Research in Law, Deviance and Social Control, vol 6. Greenwich, CT: JAI Press.

SWARD, K. (1968) The Legend of Henry Ford. New York: Russell & Russell. (originally published in 1948)

U. S. Senate, Committee on Education and Labor (1941) Labor Policies of Employers' Associations. Report no. 151, 77th Congress, 1st Session. Washington: Government Printing Office.

———(1939a) Strikebreaking Services. Report no. 6, part 7, 7th Congress, 1st Session. Washington: Government Printing Office.

———(1939b) Private Police Systems. Report no. 6, part 2, 76th Congress, 1st Session. Washington: Government Printing Office.

———(1939c) Labor Policies and Employers' Associations. Report no. 6, parts 4-6, 76th Congress, 1st Session. Washington: Government Printing Office.

U. S. Senate (1947) Hearing Before the Committee on Labor and Public Welfare (February 7). Washington: Government Printing Office.

WEBER, M. (1972) "Politics as a vocation," in H. Gerth and C. W. Mills (eds.) From Max Weber: Essays in Sociology. New York: Oxford University Press.

WEINSTEIN, J. (1968) The Corporate Ideal in the Liberal State: 1900-1918. Boston: Beacon.

WHITTEY, M. D. (1970) "The United Auto Workers face Detroit underworld." Criminology 8, 2: 129-144.

WOLFE, A. (1973) The Seamy Side of Democracy: Repression in America. New York. David McKay.

Chapter 5

POPULAR JUSTICE AND THE POLITICS OF INFORMALISM

AUSTIN T. TURK

With varying degrees of enthusiasm, many social theorists predict the imminent or inevitable collapse of the international structure of capitalist "liberal democratic" political economies. Several focus upon the declining legitimacy and efficiency of control institutions. At the extreme, Habermas (1975) sees a "crisis of legitimation"; Unger (1976: 192) observes the "disintegration of the rule of law"; and Black (1976: 132-137) anticipates "the return of anarchy." Whether established legal control institutions have the adaptive capacity to control crime and preserve order under changing conditions is at issue. One focus of the debate is the contemporary "popular justice" movement in Western Europe and the Americas.

This chapter presents a working paper from the Toronto popular justice research project that (1) summarizes current theorizing and evidence from prior studies, (2) briefly describes the project, (3) offers some first-stage observations about the rhetorics and realities of the politics of informalism, and (4) ventures a few conclusions regarding theoretical and policy implications for both "conventionals" and "radicals."

THE MEANING OF POPULAR JUSTICE: ALTERNATIVE VIEWS

There are two contrasting views regarding the political significance of citizens' organizing to deal with local crime problems. The "radical" interpretation is that such efforts reflect the public's growing distrust and rejection of an intrinsically unfair and ineffective criminal justice apparatus. The "conventional" view is that popular justice efforts show the public's growing understanding that official crime control efforts should and must be actively, not merely tacitly, supported. Among as well as between radical and conventional analysts, opinions vary considerably on matters such as the relative merits of independence versus cooperation between popular justice organizations and governmental agencies, and of limited, specifically focused approaches versus broad multipurpose strategies.

The Radical Perspective

Agreeing upon the premise of an unfair, ineffectual, and deteriorating governmental crime control system, radicals look to premodern and/or postrevolutionary experiences, and to anarchist and other communitarian theories, for guides in constructing alternative nongovernmental crime control programs. In addition, radical interpretations are derived in part from, and addressed to, experiences of those directly involved in the creation and work of popular justice alternatives.

"The politics of informal justice" has been analyzed most thoroughly in the two volumes of original papers brought together by Abel (1982). Detailed reviews of historical and comparative cases and research literatures sustain the general conclusion that although informalism is not a panacea, formalism is worse. Informalism is considered on the evidence to be especially likely to promote injustice when imposed externally from the top down, simply as an extension of state power (for example, diversion, legal aid, small claims courts, collective bargaining tribunals, community corrections), or when communities are characterized by gross inequalities in power and privilege. State interventionism is seen as destructive or overly constricting in its impact upon efforts to develop effective community-based programs of crime prevention and control. The best hope is found to lie in the autonomous creation, from the bottom up, of community-based egalitarian and independent organizations. It is questionable how far this is possible under capitalism, and analyses subsequently turn mainly on the goals and tactics of organizing popular justice so as to help in "the transition to socialism." The views of Brady and Santos are representative.

Brady (1981a, 1981b, 1982a, 1982b) is very clear in rejecting both "auxiliary" and "vigilante" activities in favor of a truly "popular" justice—characterized by explicit opposition to fascist and racist vigilantism as well as governmental repression. However, the tactical option of working within auxiliary (cooperative) popular justice organizations is acceptable as long as there is insufficient support for genuine alternatives. Whether directly through true popular justice initiatives or indirectly through influencing auxiliary programs, the political goal is to deal with crime "on terms and through means that will advance class consciousness and working-class organization" (Brady, 1981b: 185). Conscious of the problematics of trying to develop alternatives to state controls and authority, Brady nonetheless sees in the popular justice movement a means of promoting democratic socialism against both capitalist and socialist state interventionism. Highly critical of post-Mao legalism and pragmatism in China, he finds in postrevolutionary Cuba a model of how popular justice can under democratic socialism become the basis for an effective governmental system for preventing and controlling crime (Brady, 1981c, 1981d, 1982a).

Santos (1979, 1982a, 1982b) uses Brazilian, Portuguese, Russian, and other Western historical and contemporary materials to delineate the "central contradiction" between the reality of capitalist state domination and the legitimating rhetoric of popular support. Because "even state-controlled community justice requires a certain amount of popular participation," he sees "a potentially liberating element" to be "unleashed and made effective only through an autonomous political movement of the dominated classes" (Santos, 1982a: 264). Yet, the recent Portuguese experience in particular leads Santos to caution against too hasty and sweeping a rejection of politico-legal restraints upon the vagaries of an undisciplined ad hoc popular justice movement—that is, the petty bourgeoisie especially may carry things too far (Santos, 1982b: 277-279).

The Conventional Perspective

Conventionals accept existing capitalist democratic legal control systems as basically just and viable, but are concerned with perceived declining respect for public order and authority and rising crime rates. Moreover, in their view, the police and other agencies charged with protecting and assisting the public face the prospect of a growing disparity between their responsibilities and their resources. Despite widespread concern about potential vigilantism and skepticism regarding the efficacy of nonprofessional crime control efforts, many conventionals (including numerous police and other control agents, governmental and community leaders, law reformers, criminologists, and other influentials) see in the popular justice movement a potential solution to all three problems; that is, deteriorating order and authority, increasing crime rates, and inadequate resources for official crime control efforts. In this regard, some evidence has been found in American and British studies that popular justice activities may contribute to decreasing fear of crime, increased community pride and concern for others, better police-community relations, and lower crime rates (Newton, 1978; U.S. Department of Justice, 1980; Moore and Brown, 1981). Unfortunately, most of the studies are so methodologically questionable that the evidence for popular justice effectiveness must be regarded as still inconclusive. The following studies are representative.

Washnis (1976) surveyed popular justice organizations in the 100 largest American cities, followed up by on-site reviews of 36 projects in 17 cities. The study focused upon groups in close cooperation with the police, and involved detailed questioning of hundreds of police officials, neighborhood block leaders, and residents in Philadelphia, Oakland, and Compton (California). In general, it was found that block leaders were more likely than the police to believe that popular justice activities helped to reduce crime; and residents in neighborhoods with active organizations tended to be approving. Sampling, data collection, and analytic procedures were not clearly specified in this report, nor were the results systematically presented. The author seems to have been mildly favorable but cautious in discussing popular justice options suggested by the research.

Yin et al. (1977) estimated at the time of their research that over 800 resident patrols were active in American urban areas. The patrols were classified as building, neighborhood, social service, and community protection according to function and location. Observations were made of 226 patrols operating in 16 cities. Building patrols "seemed to be effective in preventing crime and increasing residents' sense of security" (Yin et al., 1977: 30). The effectiveness of the neighborhood patrols was unclear, and there were more residents' complaints about this kind of patrol. The evidence was insufficient to judge the effectiveness of the social service and community protection types. "Vigilante-like behavior" was rare, mostly involving occasional harassment of teenagers—particularly by some members of neighborhood patrols. There was some indication that public housing patrols may help improve police-community relations in low-income projects. Admittedly exploratory, the Rand study regrettably failed to differentiate direct citizen participation from the hiring of guards for the patrols.

Moore and Brown (1981) provide a description and largely interpretative analysis of the Crime Prevention Support Unit (CPSU) of the Devon and Cornwall Constabulary. Cases such as St. Louis' ill-fated Pruitt-Igoe housing project and Liverpool's "Piggeries" are presented as illustrative proof that "neighborhoods with weakening informal control systems will suffer from increasing levels of crime" (Moore and Brown, 1981: 26). After detailed examination of interview and other materials, the authors conclude that "the most important crime control forces in society are those in its informal control systems" (Moore and Brown, 1981: 115). Accordingly, the "Devon-Cornwall model" is advocated, which emphasizes minimizing distance between police and community, seeking ties and coordination with other agencies and community groups, supporting community institutions and development, and balancing preventive and reactive approaches to policing. Given that the senior author was a detective with 17 years of experience and head of the CPSU, it is hardly surprising that his doctoral study found value in his program—but the objectivity of the research needs demonstrating far beyond what this report offers.

Lavrakas and Herz (1982) report one of the few methodologically sophisticated efforts to learn why citizens participate in popular justice activities. They note that people may respond to the threat of crime in three basic ways—by restricting their own behavior, creating physical and psychological barriers to potential offenders, or by joining others in active efforts to prevent crime. Responses of the third, or popular justice, type were investigated in a telephone survey of Chicago area residents that produced 1803 completed interviews (a response rate of two-thirds), yielding a weighted sample of 1656 after correcting for multiple-phone households. Respondents were questioned about their awareness, participation, and attitudes regarding various types of neighborhood crime prevention activities. Among the major findings were the following: (1) popular justice activities were more often reported for urban center low-income and disproportionately non-white areas; (2) proactive activities—perceived "potential" problems—characterize suburban areas, whereas reactive activities—perceived "present" problems—characterize the city; (3) the higher the level of involvement an activity requires, the lower the level of participation; (4) most citizens aware of popular justice activities do not participate, usually citing lack of time as the reason; (5) participants tended to be males in their thirties or forties, with some college education, disproportionately non-white (primarily black), and more involved generally in community organizations; and (6) "territorial attitude" and greater community involvement of active participants (especially in patrols and escorts) clearly outweighed fear of crime and perceived risk of victimization in motivating participation in popular justice activities, although participants (27%) were somewhat more likely than nonparticipants (21%) to have been a crime victim in the past few years.

Despite its methodological strengths and substantive importance, the Lavrakas-Herz study is limited by its use of telephone surveying as the only data collection method and reliance upon respondents' perceptions as the sole data source—particularly for indicators of the availability of popular justice activities and of their proactive or reactive nature. Moreover, no effort was made to obtain data bearing upon the effectiveness or the political significance of the popular justice movement.

Differences between radical and conventional interpretations tend to be reflected in conceptual and methodological differences in research. Radicals base their views not only upon theoretical assumptions and political goals, but also upon experiences in attempts to organize and influence popular justice activities to be alternatives to official crime control institutions. Their reports typically emphasize the insights gained from participant observation and political interpretation. The conventional perspective tends to generate and reflect largely technocratic and more quantitative assessments of the extent and effectiveness of popular justice activities.

To determine the political significance and efficacy of the popular justice movement, it is clear that both radical and conventional research strategies are necessary. The observations and impressions of observers need to be supplemented and verified by quantitative data on both the views of participants and nonparticipants and the factual contexts and effects of popular justice activities. Conversely, surveys of *individuals* have to be augmented by longitudinal case studies of *organizations,* given that the significance and impact of popular justice programs depend upon how—and how well—they are organized.

THE TORONTO PROJECT

An effort is being made in the Toronto project to address the conceptual issues and methodological concerns outlined above. The pilot study begun in 1984 is preliminary to a contemplated larger study with the following general aims:

- to determine the extent to which the popular justice movement in Canada reflects citizen support or rejection of existing legal institutions for controlling crime and maintaining public order;
- to compare the Canadian proactive pattern with the reactive pattern generally found elsewhere, especially in urban centers; and
- to measure the effects of popular justice activities upon crime rates, public attitudes and perceptions regarding crime and law, and police-community relations.

The objectives of the pilot study are to develop data collection instruments and strategies for use in a multicity and possibly cross-national comparative study, and to generate a limited set of findings useful mainly for designing the larger and more definitive study.

Using a modification of the random-digit-dialing procedure (see Tuchfarber and Klecka, 1976), a telephone survey of Toronto adult residents (N = 200) was completed in the fall of 1984. Respondents were questioned regarding (1) awareness and experience with respect to specified kinds of crime-prevention activities, (2) perceptions and views about crime in general and in terms of specific forms, (3) concern and fear regarding neighborhood safety, (4) attitudes and beliefs regarding official crime-control agencies and practices, (5) victimization and reporting, and (6) relevant social and demographic background characteristics. Follow-up field interviews were conducted with respondents having prior or current crime-prevention experience. Because of the small number of such respondents, 38 additional interviews were completed with key persons in various popular justice organizations (mostly neighborhood watch committees). The solicited interviewees were also asked to respond to the telephone interview schedule. Combining the initial telephone sample and the supplementary field interviews, 244 usable "telephone interviews" and 49 usable "field interviews" were obtained.

Apart from the survey, exploratory case studies of nine popular justice organizations were carried out from January to April, 1985. These included four neighborhood watch committees, a block parents organization, an "action committee for street improvement," a club heavily involved in a child indentification and "streetproofing" program, the Toronto Gay patrol, and the Guardian Angels. The next phase of the preparatory work is to develop indicators for assessing the effectiveness of popular justice activities. In the literature there is no consensus on either the definition or the measurement of effectiveness (Abel, 1982; Lavrakas and Herz, 1982; Lavrakas and Bennett, 1984; Newton, 1978; Skogan and Maxfield, 1981; Tomasic and Feeley, 1982). The main issues may be summarized as follows:

(1) Is effectiveness to be defined as the deterrence of crime or as the elimination of sources of crime?
   (a) Is deterrence adequately measured by reductions in reported crime? Can the effects of popular justice activities be separated from the effects of official crime-control activities?
   (b) Assuming the sources of crime are primarily environmental, should effectiveness be measured in terms of decreases in such environmental variables as fear of crime, inadequate security consciousness, lack of a sense of community, and poor relationships between police and public?
(2) To what extent should indirect as well as direct effects be taken into account? For instance, how far should or can one go in trying to determine the relative contributions of overall community improvement programs, media reporting practices, citizen-participant crime prevention activities, and policing policies to changes in whatever measures of effectiveness are used?
(3) How much time should be allowed for effects to occur? To what extent is effectiveness to be measured in the short term or the long term?
   (a) If a decrease in reported crime is the measure, how soon should or can it be expected?
   (b) If reducing an environmental source of crime is the measure, how soon are such effects expected? How soon before they should produce a decrease in crime?
(4) What is the relevant "social space" for assessing effectiveness? How are displacement effects to be treated? For in-

stance, in what sense can a neighborhood program aimed at reducing crime be considered effective if increased crime in other (especially adjacent) neighborhoods results in no reduction or an increase in crime for the city as a whole?

Formal analysis of the survey and case data is in progress. However, the admonitions of "reflexive" methodologists such as Schatzman and Strauss (1973) suggest that it is useful—even essential—to think about one's observations throughout the research process rather than only at its beginning and end. Impressions have, of course, been gained from several months' collective experience, inspection and discussion of completed interview schedules and case reports, and examination of basic frequency distributions. On the whole, those impressions are consistent with the more critical literature on popular justice.

INFORMALISM: RHETORICS AND REALITIES

Informalism is an ideology of resentment—at complexity, organization, procedure, impersonality, and change. The desire for simplicity and the personalized attention of others has roots in both experience and myth. Values and expectations acquired in interpersonal and intimate settings, or believed to characterize small-scale community life, are used as yardsticks for measuring the quality of life in today's vastly different world. Conventional or radical, the rhetorics of informalism offer some kind of hope or outlet for the frustrated and fearful as well as the sensitive and concerned.

Nostalgia and individualism are salient in conventional rhetorics (especially as articulated by "New Right" politicians and ideologues): The clock should be turned back to a time when "everyone" was free to pursue and enjoy personal success without fear or interference. Radical rhetorics (especially as articulated by anarchosocialists and communists) feature liberation and communalism: The clock should be turned forward to a time when "everyone" is free to share in the pursuit and enjoyment of collective success. Both kinds of rhetoric assume that people "left alone" will naturally relate to one another in respectful and mutually beneficial ways. The considerable experience and evidence to the contrary are discounted by alluding to the distorting effects of whatever presumptively alien, "unnatural" forces (capitalism, socialism, and so on) are blamed for "dehumanizing" life.

Irrespective of their factual basis, the insecurities and resentments echoed in and fostered by the rhetorics of informalism do constitute a political resource. Demogogues seeking votes, liberals criticizing bureaucratic insensitivities, conservatives attacking governmental inefficiencies, and radicals promoting resistance to state and corporate ordering of social life—all hope to mobilize support by informalist appeals. The common message is that the complex can be simplified, formalities and technicalities abolished, accountability and sensitivity ensured, and uncertainties ended if their program is accepted and their leadership followed.

Responding to a widely shared fear, political activists from both the Right and the Left have focused much of their rhetoric on the problem of crime. Citizens are called upon to participate in all sorts of more or less informal programs to prevent crime and reduce its costs to society. Whether the activists' enthusiasm for popular justice is genuine or merely tactical, there is mounting evidence that they may be overestimating citizen receptiveness to the linking of informalism and crime control.

Despite the enthusiasms of activists, academics, and the media, citizen interest in popular justice appears to be quite limited. For instance, in their three-city survey Skogan and Maxfield (1981) found that only 17% of Chicagoans, 12% of Philadelphians, and 11% of San Franciscans had ever been involved with an anticrime group effort. Even though these cities "are all at the top of the scale" in comparison with other areas, fear of crime was rated as "moderate" on the basis of the survey results (Skogan and Maxfield, 1981: 53). Moreover, and surprisingly,

> Those who were *less* fearful and who thought that conditions in their locale were getting *better* were more likely to report being involved in a group that was doing something concerning crime, while measures of crime-related conditions were otherwise unrelated to crime [Skogan and Maxfield, 1981: 233].

In the Toronto survey, respondents were questioned in more detail about the type of participation, which ranged from a high of 26% (neighborhood or block watch program) to a low of only one individual who had ever participated in a citizen patrol. A total of 21% had at some time attended a meeting on crime prevention in the neighborhood. The great majority (86%) felt very safe in the daytime, and more than half (57.4%) felt safe at night walking in their neighborhood. Only about one-third (34%) thought crime is a serious problem in Toronto. Although most (78%) believed crime is increasing in the city, only 37.3% perceived an increase in crime in their neighborhood. These data suggest that most Toronto residents have relatively little awareness or concern about crime as a serious problem, and that few of them do anything in particular to prevent crime. There is some awareness of popular justice activities, but little experience or interest in participation. Furthermore, the case studies indicate that even the initiators and most active tend to feel they have little support, and with rare exceptions tend to "burn out" after a year or so even in the most active organizations.

Lack of citizen interest and involvement in popular justice programs has also been noted in European socialist as well as capitalist settings. For instance, among the findings reported in Cain and Kulcsár (1983) are observations of Bulgarian villagers' preference for alternatives to Comrades' Courts (pp. 175-182), the limited success of Yugoslavian efforts to decentralize and informalize the judicial system (pp. 183-202), and Danish lack of awareness and use of the Consumer Tribunal (pp. 203-219). Further, even where the most determined postrevolutionary efforts have been made to establish popular justice mechanisms (for example, China, Cuba), they have eventually withered in the face of centralized political controls, emerging professionalism, and a general inclination to give priority to one's own affairs instead of popular justice activities (see Brady, 1981d, 1982a; Hipkin, 1985; Salas, 1983).

Barring dramatic new and contradictory evidence, the observed reality is that both conventional and radical rhetorics of informalism presuppose too much. People may like to grumble in informalist terms, but the likelihood of their actually being galvanized by such ideologies into sustained and politically consequential action seems small.

POLITICS AND POLICIES: INTERIM NOTES

Conventional or radical, enthusiasts and activists on behalf of popular justice face the strong likelihood that informalism is far more rhetoric than reality. From the evidence so far available, the great majority of people will not voluntarily participate in popular justice activities. Moreover, it appears that among those who do, the level of participation tends to decline fairly soon. Leaders are prone to burn out as their followers lag and drop out. Turnover of members is generally high, and the life expectancy of organizations is generally low. Spontaneous controls arising from ethnic homogeneity and/or residential stability seem to be much more enduring and effective than the planned control efforts generated by "artificial insemination"—that is, efforts resulting from police sponsorship, initiatives of self-appointed organizers, or other actions not originating in regular interactions among locals. All this indicates that the theoretical and policy assumptions of popular justice advocacy are faulty. Among the most questionable assumptions are the following:

(1) Crime is at or near the top on the scale of popular concern.
(2) Informal controls can be deliberately created.
(3) Local or "private" control sectors can be autonomous.
(4) Popular justice (informal control) is more effective at less cost than official justice (formal control).
(5) Popular justice is more legitimate or "just" than official justice.

On Crime as a Priority

Evidence of popular concern about crime has come mainly from general surveys. Indicators of fear, rankings of crime as a social problem, and related quantitative measures of concern have rarely been grounded or verified in systematic qualitative field research. Even though the statistical evidence may be reliable, it may well be misleading because of the necessarily superficial data collection techniques characteristic of routine survey research. Survey questioning seems more likely to elicit abstracted reactions to media stimulation or gossip than to identify personally meaningful concerns. Real concern about crime (or anything else) is more likely to be reflected in how people develop and qualify initial responses, discuss their concerns informally and in private, and invest their time and resources. Though qualitative evidence is badly needed, the degree of popular concern about crime would seem to have been greatly exaggerated.

On Creating Informal Controls

Popular justice advocates have in several respects seriously misunderstood the nature of social organization and control. First, social aggregates have often been treated as if they were groups—for instance, in assuming that a neighborhood can be defined in terms of residential propinquity within some arbitrary boundary (block, building, ward, police district, and so on). Second, even if the existence of a group was not taken for granted, advocates have rather incongruously assumed that informal networks can be created by special organizing. Third, organizing campaigns have typically proceeded as though groups have no controls until something like a watch committee or patrol is organized. Against such notions, social scientists have long since established that the construction of social bonds can only be accomplished by actors themselves, that relationships are built through recurring interactions over time, and that control is present insofar as a relationship exists.

On Local Autonomy

The ideology of informalism has too sharply differentiated community from society and society from state. Advocates have romanticized informal social relations, ignoring or minimizing the extent to which they are embedded in larger contexts. In addition, informalism has fostered blindness to the oppressiveness and exploitativeness so often found in close relationships, to the fact that intimacy does not necessarily preclude inequality, coercion, or insensitivity and even hatred. Most critically, the interpenetration of official (formal, central) and unofficial (informal, local) controls has been surprising to those who took the analytical distinction to be an empirical reality (see Henry, 1983).

On the Impact of Popular Justice

Whether informal controls are more effective than formal ones is debatable; they are certainly not cheaper. Insofar as informal controls arise spontaneously in the development of close relationships, participants must indeed take them seriously into account. Although conformity is by no means automatic (as against much now obsolete social science lore), individuals must be unusually strong or perverse to resist the demands of close associates. What is not at all clear is that individuals are any less (or more) vulnerable to formal controls. The arsenal of legal and extralegal controls available to governments and other corporate entities is formidable. In any case, both informal and formal controls are costly, in time, money, and/or relationships. Although the time-consuming and expensive procedures of formal control are more often emphasized, informal justice proceedings in traditional and revolutionary settings tend to involve even more people in sometimes interminable open-ended deliberations. And in neither formal nor informal proceedings are cases always settled without damage to the social fabric. Regardless of effectiveness and cost, there is so far no reason to believe that genuinely informal alternatives to formal controls are even possible in an established modern polity.

On Justice and Legitimacy

Justice is not necessarily popular, nor does informality guarantee legitimacy. Informal and popular (majority?) control efforts typically are ad hoc reactions to particular incidents, not tactical moves aimed at a generalized class of acts. Ad hoc controls are intrinsically arbitrary, and unrestrained by provisions for appellate review. Arbitrariness and nonreviewable sanctions—that is, vigilantism—challenge any image of justice as an enduring and transcendent standard of right. At the more concrete level of legitimacy, there is an inevitable tension (or "contradiction") between whatever is popular at the moment and the ongoing mechanisms of political organization. Vigilantism implies weakness in the apparatus of official, formal control, and is thus potentially disturbing to those whose life chances depend upon political might and state-defined right. Political stability depends less upon popularity than upon power, which means that social controls must above all be exerted so as to convince enough of the politically consequential (relatively powerful) that the needs for stability and change, security and adaptation, are being properly balanced. This is the empirical meaning of legitimacy, whether or not "justice" is done.

CONCLUSION

Efforts to create "popular" alternatives, much less rivals, to official control institutions have little if any chance of success. The assumptions of informalism are too much at odds with the realities of social control, especially in large-scale technologically advanced societies. Even where innovative adjuncts to established institutions have had some success, their legitimacy has been shaky and their scope limited to relatively minor disputes. Frequently they have been effectively captured by more powerful "players" such as creditors and landlords. As for vigilantism, it has as a rule been tolerated (or encouraged) only as long as short-term goals of formal control were advanced. Because it undermines whatever legal basis is claimed for the state, vigilantism has tended to be soon repressed in the interest of long-term legitimacy. Political realism, for conventionals and radicals alike, would seem to begin in understanding that formal and informal controls are increasingly fused in modern societies, and that the formal increasingly outweighs the informal as local social orders (communities?) are incorporated into ever more complex higher-orders of social organization. Instead of dreaming of their destruction, or of escaping them, activists are better advised to seek ways to make complex orders and formal controls more sensitive and responsive to human diversity.

REFERENCES

ABEL, R. L. [ed.] (1982) The Politics of Informal Justice, vols. 1 and 2. New York: Academic Press.

BLACK, D. (1976) The Behavior of Law. New York: Academic Press.

BRADY, J. P. (1981a) "Sorting out the exile's confusion: or dialogue on popular justice." Contemporary Crises 5: 31-38.

——(1981b) "Towards a popular justice in the United States: the dialectics of community action." Contemporary Crises 5: 155-192.

——(1981c) "Fresh winds on rotted sails: Spanish legal reforms, American parallels, and the Cuban socialist alternative—a reply to Antonio Beristain." International Journal of the Sociology of Law 9: 177-200.

——(1981d) "A season of startling alliance: Chinese law and justice in the new order." International Journal of the Sociology of Law 9: 41-67.

——(1982a) Justice and Politics in People's China: Legal Order or Continuing Revolution? New York: Academic Press.

——(1982b) "Arson, fiscal crises, and community action: dialectics of an urban crime and popular response." Crime and Delinquency (April): 247-270.

CAIN, M. and K. KULCSÁR [eds.] (1983) Disputes and the Law. Budapest, Hungary: Akademiai Kiado.

HABERMAS, J. (1975) Legitimation Crisis. Boston: Beacon Press.

HENRY, S. (1983) Private Justice: Towards Integrated Theorising in the Sociology of Law. London: Routledge & Kegan Paul.

HIPKIN, B. (1985) "Looking for justice: the search for socialist legality and popular justice." International Journal of the Sociology of Law 13: 117-132.

LAVRAKAS, P. J. and S. F. BENNETT (1984) "Evaluating the Eisenhower Foundation's neighborhood anti-crime self-help program." Presented at the annual meetings of the American Society of Criminology, Cincinnati, November 7-11.

LAVRAKAS, P. J. and E. J. HERZ (1982) "Citizen participation in neighborhood crime prevention." Criminology 20: 479-498.

MOORE, C. and J. BROWN (1981) Community Versus Crime. London: Bedford Square Press, National Council for Voluntary Organizations.

NEWTON, A. M. (1978) "Prevention of crime and delinquency." Criminal Justice Abstracts 10: 245-266.

SALAS, L. (1983) "The emergence and decline of the Cuban popular tribunals." Law and Society Review 17: 587-612.

SANTOS, B. de SOUSA (1979) "Popular justice, dual power and socialist strategy," pp. 151-163 in Bob Fine et al. (eds.) Capitalism and the Rule of Law: From Deviancy Theory to Marxism. London: Hutchinson.

——(1982a) "Law and community: the changing nature of state power in late capitalism," pp. 249-266 in Richard Abel (ed.) The Politics of Informal Justice, vol. 1. New York: Academic Press.

——(1982b) "Law and revolution in Portugal: the experience of popular justice after the 25th of April 1974," pp. 251-280 in Richard Abel (ed.) The Politics of Informal Justice, vol. 2. New York: Academic Press.

SCHATZMAN, L. and A. STRAUSS (1973) Field Research: Strategies for a Natural Sociology. Englewood Cliffs, NJ: Prentice-Hall.

SKOGAN, W. G. and M. G. MAXFIELD (1981) Coping with Crime: Individual and Neighborhood Reactions. Beverly Hills, CA: Sage.

TOMASIC, R. and M. FEELEY [eds.] (1982) Neighborhood Justice: Assessment of an Emerging Idea. New York: Longman.

TUCHFARBER, A. J. and W. R. KLECKA (1976) Random Digit Dialing. Washington, DC: The Police Foundation.

UNGER, R.M. (1976) Law in Modern Society. New York: Macmillan.

U.S. Department of Justice (1980) Citizen Crime Prevention Tactics: A Literature Review and Selected Bibliography. Washington, DC: National Institute of Justice.

WASHNIS, G. J. (1976) Citizen Involvement in Crime Prevention. Lexington, MA: D. C. Heath.

YIN, R. K. et al. (1977) Citizen Patrol Projects. National Evaluation Program: Phase 1 Summary Report. Washington, DC: National Institute of Law Enforcement and Criminal Justice.

Chapter 6

VIGILANCIA REVOLUCIONARIA:
A Nicaraguan Resolution
To Public and Private Policing

W. GORDON WEST

Our cause will triumph because it is the cause of justice and of love.
—A. C. Sandino

In so many ways, Nicaragua impresses one as yet another poverty-stricken, dangerous, underdeveloped Third World country.

The late afternoon flight from Miami has dumped us onto the searing heat of the tarmac, where even my summer weight leisure suit leaves me dripping with sweat. Immigration officials are bureaucratically officious, regulations immediately relieve one of $60 US (the price of socialism?) and custom inspectors, while personally friendly, are meticulously thorough. Emerging from the airport doors, I'm met by a dozen barefoot urchins wearing only shorts, offering to carry my bags, get me a taxi, do anything to relieve me of my scarce professorial travel grant. I succumb, knowing I'm being conned, and climb into the beaten up cab. Jeez! What am I doing here? I cannot even speak Spanish properly.

AUTHOR'S NOTE: I would like to acknowledge particularly the help of Dra. Vilma Núñez de Escorcia, Peter Rivera, Rosa María Rodriquez, and Lillian Hurtado Cubillo of the Corte Suprema; Commandante Leticia Herrera of the CDS; Enrique Reynoso of the Instituto de Investigaciones Economicas y Sociales; Jim and Margaret Goff of the Centro Ecuménico Valdivieso; David Dye and Rosalyn Frank; Judy Butler and Carlos Vilas of El Centro de Investigaciones y Documentaciones de la Costa Atlantica; Joe Gunn and Jose García of El Fondo Canadiense Para la Niñez; Jock Young; Clifford Shearing for editing suggestions; Ken Reshaur for his instruction on the public-private distinction; and Vivian Ching-Ako and Gail Buckland for typing assistance.

We roar past poverty-stricken hovels with naked light bulbs and children, dirt floors and flies buzzing. The cabbie avoids various pedestrians on the unlit main highway to town, then swerves dramatically to miss an errant cow. The "city centre" is a pile of rubble, acres of deserted blocks with building skeletons left from the 1972 earthquake and the 1979 insurrection. We pull into a dark street at the edge of this no-man's land and I climb out, all my criminologically alerted senses of personal danger on red alert . . .

Fifteen minutes later, I'm amazed to find myself lured onto the street again. "No problem," my newly met fellow hotel guests incredibly claim, "we'll just walk 10 blocks to the restaurant." Through these unlit poverty-stricken slum streets, and walk back at midnight, probably half drunk, with more American dollars in our pockets than most of these people make in a year??? These are my new friends?? This has got to be crazy! I carefully walked in the middle of my two colleagues, encouraging us to keep to the center of the street, warily eyeing small groups of potential muggers on most corners . . . But nothing untoward happened [field notes, October 1983].

The cause of my safety became apparent a few nights later:

It's midnight. We're out on *vigilancia revolucionaria*—revolutionary vigilance, or, more comprehensibly, citizen's groups' security patrol. . . . We set off on patrol with the security coordinator—a strange lot of sociological tourists trailing a dozen interested local citizens, with the invaluably first-hand on-sight view but sometimes painful awkwardness of a prison tour. Our guide took us down various streets past the burning signal tires with their filthy black smoke, around corners, across a highway and back in a hour or so. We stopped and met some local volunteers, some of the most fervent and active welcoming us with little speeches and answering any questions about volunteers, hours, problems. We chatted more openly and directly with non-officials as the walk went on. At one corner there was a typical monument to a fallen hero/martyr; the matronly warm woman volunteer guard there was his mother, who gave us a blow-by-blow description of her son's assassination by the *Guardia Nacional* during the insurrection: "It was around suppertime. He had just finished eating, gave me a hug, picked up his rifle and told me not to worry, he'd be careful, when a boy lookout came running to tell him the *Guardia* was coming. He ran out the back to go down the sidestreet, but they were coming there too and shot. He ducked back but there were just too many of them. . . . He died here in my arms, and we buried him here; they want us to move his remains, but I want him to stay here, beside me always. . . . He helps me do my guard duty." There were guards on every block, on every streetcorner, sitting quietly chatting, often just outside their own houses [October 1983].

What I had taken that first night to be potential muggers were the citizen watchpersons. In a world with seemingly inevitably increasing street crime, where traditional criminology (for example, see Clinard and Abbott, 1973) would expect crime, the Nicaraguan experience of falling crime rates deserves attention.[1] Although there are doubtlessly many possible causes and explanations for the safety of Nicaraguan streets (see Núñez de Escorcia, 1984), I believe a large part of this unique success story is attributable to *vigilancia revolucionaria*, organized by the neighborhood *Comites de Defense Sandinista* (CDS—Sandinista Defense Committee).

But what is *vigilancia revolucionaria* under the CDS? Is it private or public policing? The distinction is admittedly difficult to apply even within the developed Western countries. Freedman and Stenning (1977) first define public police as:

(1) peace officers who have the right and duty to maintain the peace in all "public" places, and
(2) persons, such as law enforcement officers, special constables, and auxiliary police appointed in Police Acts who have as their sole function the assistance of persons in all public places.

They then define private security residually as:

All other persons involved in law enforcement, whether peace offices or private citizens, whether publicly or privately employed, whether they work on public or private property [Freedman and Stenning, 1977: 18-19].

Even more explicitly, Farnell and Shearing (1977) include under private security private citizens' groups:

Private citizens sometimes band together in groups with the express purpose of providing for their collective security through, for example, organized neighborhood patrols. While such groups are becoming more widespread in the US, to our knowledge, very few exist in Canada at present.

Initially, then, it would seem that the CDS volunteers would fit such definitions as private police; but closer examination will reveal that the *vigilancia revolucionaria* has some statutory status, and the CDS volunteers are in some senses more publicly accountable than are most Western public police. Indeed, using the CDS example, this article will argue that such public-private distinctions rest upon political concepts founded in and appropriate to narrowly Western, First World experiences of liberal democratic capitalism.[2]

To understand the CDS and *vigilancia revolucionaria,* however, it is essential to put them into the specific historical context of Nicaragua and the self-serving privatization of public policing by the *Guardia Nacional* under Somoza, to consider policing issues raised by the armed insurrection, and to contextualize them within some of the other main achievements and problems of crime and justice under the *Frente Sandinista* government.

PRIVATIZED POLICING UNDER THE SOMOZAS

It is better to die as rebels than to live as slaves [A. C. Sandino].

In contextualizing the neither public nor private nature of policing by the *vigilancia revolucionaria* under the direction of the CDS, it is necessary to understand that despite formal appearances Nicaragua never really had what the Western world regards as public policing, formally beholden to the rule of law interpreted by an independent judiciary without political party bias or private interest. Whereas most First World discussions of private policing either trace the historical move from private to public policing (for example, in England) or consider the recent corporate development of forms of private policing that are relatively independent of the state (see Farnell and Shearing, 1977), in examining the privatization of the mechanism for providing a service (and not the transformation of the objective from public to private interest), Nicaragua provides a perhaps prototypical Third World contrast. The high liberal ideals of the revolt in 1821 from Spanish rule seem never to have moved beyond a formal commitment to the ideal of the rule of law. The social reality of seigneurial latifundism, the demise of the United States of Central America in 1838, followed by Walker's filibusters' invasion in the 1850s (Booth, 1982) and the conservative Granada-based dictatorships followed by Zelaya's Léon-based dictatorship only gave birth to continuing internecine, interfamily rivalry and American occupation from 1911 to 1933. The Nicaraguan example reveals how the formally public police the Americans left was "privatized" de facto when the necessary economic and political conditions for liberalism were absent, as they tend to be outside of the industrialized First World.

In Nicaragua, as with so many other Latin American republics, the revolt from Spanish domination allowed only a short period of indigenous capitalist development in traditional import-export markets, followed by development of coffee exportation, sugar and cotton, and gold and meat in succession (Wheelock, 1974). The result of the development of this agroexport economy, dependent upon large numbers of seasonally employed migrant peasant laborers, produced a "classic" large landless or small-holding *campesino* class, continually driven by atrocious rural conditions to swell the cities' marginal economy ranks, and a tiny landlord and business elite dependent economically and culturally on the West (Barry et al., 1983).

With more than half the land units composing less than 4% of the total area, and less than 1% of the units making up 30% of the land area (Wheelock, 1974: 203), Nicaragua experienced the exponential population growth rates typical of Latin America (over 3%) resulting in half the population being under age 15, swollen cities, one of the world's lowest per capita income levels ($660 U.S. in 1979), a 20%-45% unemployment rate, a population more than half illiterate, a high infant mortality rate (130 per 1000), and a malnutrition rate of 50% of those under five. Half the homes lacked toilets, 20% lacked water, and there was a low life expectancy—56 years (Pearce, 1982).

Although these conditions spawned the traditional social problems and crime integrated into a marginal economy so often discussed in the literature (petty juvenile delinquency, drunkenness, prostitution, brawling, and minor theft; see Clinard and Abbott, 1973; Castro Rodriguez, 1945: 42), the more noteworthy and certainly more profitable activity had been the all but ignored upperclass crimes, most notably by the Somoza dictators. Starting from an unremarkable small-holding family in 1933, Anastasio Somoza García parlayed control of the American-established National Guard into Presidential power; for the next half century the family used every conceivable governmental and military perquisite and possibility for corruption, engaging in a truly remarkable criminal spree of rapacious and brutal greed. With the *Guardia* responsible for policing, defense, traffic control, vehicle registration, postal services, tax collection, health and sanitation inspection, and customs and immigration, the Somozas turned every opportunity into personal gain—granting themselves monopolies, insisting on bribes, selling favors, "patriotically" confiscating the not inconsequential German holdings during World War II, misappropriating funds and services, as well as relying upon the more usual types of enforced indebtedness and property confiscations of typical Latin American Latifundist systems (see Wheelock, 1974; Diederich, 1981). By the time of the third Somoza's exile in 1979, the U.S. government estimated his fortune at almost a billion dollars (Black, 1981: 34). The irony, of course, was that such rapacious family capitalism had finally alienated even the local bourgeoisie: The Somoza state finally failed to provide conditions for growth by "capital in general" (Jessop, 1983). The public state had become entirely controlled by private interests.

The Somozas' power base in the national police force had been endowed upon them by the United States in its classic "gun-boat diplomacy" attempts to prevent any challenge to its interoceanic canal interests by the incipient Nicaraguan bourgeoisie. Tired of the previous two decades of direct occupation, its draining guerrilla war against Sandino, and wanting to implement Roosevelt's good neighbor policy, in 1933 the Americans endowed "ungovernable" Nicaragua with a "professional nonpolitical" police force in the *Guardia Nacional,* under Somoza, to maintain "orderly economic development."

From the murder of Sandino in 1934 and the extermination of hundreds of his followers in the northern mountains, through the illegal confiscations and corruptions to the earthquake scandal of the 1970s, the formally public police—the *Guardia*—increasingly were not only actually the private police of the Somozas, but they also became the major criminal group in the country (see Diederich, 1982: 311; Booth, 1981: 67; CIERA, 1984: 12; Del Olmo, 1980: 17, 39, 78; Black, 1981: 34-6; Pearce, 1982).

Continuing American support for this regime (see especially Wheelock, 1974: 132) served to prevent the formation of a "normal" liberal-democratic capitalist state that might challenge American interests, and also prevented the autonomous development of the local bourgeoisie. Speaking to our concerns, it prevented the establishment of a Western-style public police under the liberal rule of law, which assumes an established separation of public and private spheres (see Arendt, 1959).

There were nonetheless always some oppositional groups. Besides the alternative centers of power available at least latently from family, business, and church organizations, every decade of the Somozas' reign experienced some political party challenge and armed rebellion, squelched by deceit and force. In addition, however, for our purposes it is worth noting that by the 1950s the church and some community agencies had begun drawing upon the local tradition of community self-help. Christian base communities, community organization projects, more politically explicit efforts by Leftist groups, and so on, gave differing ideologies to different community groups; further, their specific concerns ranged from gospel reading to health, sewage, installation of light and water systems, and so forth. Although a few of these committees can trace roots back almost 30 years to the 1950s, many more started in the 1960s and 1970s (CIERA, 1984: 28ff.).

Furthermore, as the 1970s progressed and the *Guardia* brutality became so widespread and well known that people could no longer rely upon the authorities to carry out even minimal security functions properly, such parallel structures began to provide an alternative to Somoza's resolution of public-private contraditions in policing through absorbing the public sphere as his own private domain, enforced by police terror.

THE INSURRECTIONAL COMMITTEE RESPONSE TO GENOCIDAL "PUBLIC" POLICE

With the murderers running free in the streets, the only alternative is an armed people.

Both liberal (for instance, Weber, 1964) and radical (for example, Gramsci, 1971) social theorists argue that a stable social order requires fundamental legitimacy, not simply force, for its maintenance. Similarly, theorists of policing have argued that effective policing requires citizen support for crime control and public order. Pre-1979 Nicaragua provides an "extreme case" (Becker, 1970) of a country without police legitimacy, and although it speaks eloquently to the possibility of the efficacy of the leadership of a revolutionary party (Turok, 1981), it even more eloquently acclaims the centrality of a mobilized populace.

As insurrectional opposition to the dictatorship continued and grew more widespread in terms of popular support in the last years of the 1970s, the social, economic, political, judicial, and military chaos became more extreme. The spontaneous urban uprisings that followed the January 1978 assassination of Chamorro, the major opposition figure, and the August 1978 capture of the National Palace signaled the coming end of the Somoza regime in headlines of the day: "A Holocaust," "Stories that Seem to Be from Vietnam," "Estelí Hour by Hour and Death by Death (*La Prensa*, Sept. 13, 1978); "Hundreds File before the Casket of the Child Leader, L. A. Valesquez, 9 years old," "Today It's a Crime To Be a Child" (*La Prensa*, March 4, 1979); "Estelí Has Not Known Such Horror"; "The Human Rights Commission Shouts the Nicaraguan Tragedy to the World" (*La Prensa*, April 17, 1979). The routine corruption and brutality of the previous decades gave away to fullblown police state terror with the states of siege (1974-1977; 1978-1979) in which all civil liberties were suspended, and death squads executed people as systematically as a garbage disposal disposes of garbage (Diederich, 1981: 300). As Somoza lost all support except the police, he ordered his air force to attempt systemically to bomb and machine gun the defenseless civilian population into submission. [See, for example, *Comisión Permanente de Derechos Humanos*, (CPDH), 1978: 116; *Comisión Interamericana de Derechos Humanos*, (CIDH), 1978: 35, 49, 51, 80.]

It is necessary to be on site to understand what Somoza did, with the military means which the United States and other western countries provided him with. It was a *war of extermination against his people* [Pax Christi, 1981: 6].

It wasn't until the military failure of the September 1978 spontaneous uprising that the need for more organization by the opposition became completely apparent (CIERA, 1984: 31; 55). Although in retrospect, the early guerrilla campaigns of the *Frente Sandinista de Liberación Nacional* (FSLN) can be seen as providing experience and growth, publicity, and some tactical successes, there were many zig-zags and near terminations, especially after the serious military defeats at Bocay and Pancasán. At such times the *Frente* returned to the cities and went underground, working with students, working-class communities, unions, and so on. Even after the success of the December 1974 Christmas party raid, the growing number of guerrilla actions in 1976 and 1977, and the

National Palace attack in 1978, the *Frente* was unprepared for the February and September 1978 popular uprisings. It could not abandon the spontaneous insurgencies in the cities, but with its few hundred armed militants alone, the FSLN was not yet militarily able to defeat the *Guardia*. The organization of the *Commites de Defensa Civil* through 1978-1979 became the missing link in the military strategy; without them, there would not have been a Sandinista revolution (Black, 1981: 137, 162-163, 167-168; EPICA, 1980: 59 ff; CDS, CEN, 1981: 1).

Growing from the Christian base communities, the neighborhood improvement associations, and the social work and union efforts, the CDCs were basically spontaneous organizations of neighbors who needed and trusted each other. They took immediate action where needed and possible (such as clearing blocked sewers and providing food to a needy elderly neighbor whose distant-living children could no longer visit). "Safe houses" had to be provided for guerrillas in need of immediate refuge from the *Guardia* patrols, medical supplies and weapons had to be stockpiled, pamphlets had to be runoff, and so on. Trustworthy escape routes had to be arranged for the combatants. Information sources regarding *Guardia* movements had to be identified and utilized.

Moreover, during the final offensive from April of 1979 onward, the CDCs were often the only "government" type of organization operating, as services were cut or abandoned, and factories and businesses were struck, bombed, and shut. What had been a corrupt and very personalized dictatorial state at best crumbled into chaotic anarchy as all of Somoza's efforts went into the *Guardia*'s desperate attempt to maintain power. Any pretense of professional policing was abandoned in the paranoia-generating uncertainty of unpredictable but ferocious house-to-house combat, irregular front lines, sniping, commando raids, indiscriminate air bombardment, stray mortars, rumors, and so forth (see Diederich, 1981: 234, 257). In this situation, the CDCs not only made the revolution possible, they suggested a possible new politics, a reformulation of public and private, and exemplified an alternative policing.

SOCIAL AND LEGAL JUSTICE IN THE GOVERNMENT OF NATIONAL RECONSTRUCTION

Sandino lives; the struggle continues.

When the insurrection triumphed on July 19, 1979, Nicaragua was a country jubilant, but in ruin, bleeding and grieving. Revolutionary Nicaragua inherited all the problems of underdevelopment, poverty, and dependency upon an agroexport economy. To these were added the disasters of the 1972 earthquake and the horrendous destruction inflicted by the *Guardia* in its dying moments: In a country of less than three million, half a billion dollars in damage, some 50,000 killed—almost all of whom were under age 25 (proportionately more than Britain lost in all of World War II)— 100,000 injured, 40,000 orphaned, 200,000 families homeless, and 750,000 dependent on food assistance. Somoza and his cronies had literally looted the national treasury in the last days, leaving only $3.5 million, while they had indebted the country with $1.6 billion (the highest per capita in Latin America), much of which they, of course, had also managed to siphon off personally (EPICA, 1980).

Relying upon popular enthusiasm and the local organization provided by the *Comites de Defensa Sandinista* (CDS, reconstructed from the Commites de Defensa Civil), a revolutionary coalition (of not only guerrillas, workers, and students, but also small-holding peasants, rural and urban bourgeoisie, and liberal professionals), international aid, and its nationalized inheritance of the Somozas' vast holdings, the Government of the National Reconstruction has reactivated the agroexport economy under a formally mixed model (with 60% of the economy still privately owned, although socially controlled. It has redistributed land (especially to cooperatives), maintained basic real incomes through food subsidies, inaugurated award-winning health and educational programs, and pursued a foreign policy of nonalignment. Although political dissent and tension over the new government's clear "option for the poor" have continued to be strong, and the *ex-Guarida contrarrevolucionarios* supported by the Reagan administration have waged a very draining terrorist guerrilla war (see West, 1986), Nicaragua has successfully managed to hold general elections while stimulating the development of alternative participatory power structures through mass organizations of all sorts (unions, professional associations, youth organizations, the CDS, and so on). It is against this social background of economic and military adversity, matched by political will and the reorganization of public and private property relations, that specifically legal developments must be seen.

Criminologically, one of the most striking achievements of the revolution has been the dramatic decline in the official rates for ordinary crimes (see Table 1).[3]

TABLE 1
Official Rates for Ordinary Crimes, 1980-1984

| | Criminal Occurrences | | | | |
	1980	1981	1982	1983	1984 (est.)
Total (all crimes)	38,781	22,554	10,439	8,402	7,500
Murder and homicide	864	390	313	320	
Robbery	10,497	4,147	1,435	1,986	

SOURCE: Núñez de Escorcia (1984).

Doubtlessly, the success of the revolutionary government in managing an economic recovery—with more just distribution, and under a government and society perceived as legitimate—has had some impact on these figures. Created and believed in most especially by youth (traditionally the most crime-prone group), the revolution has also scored spectacular successes in incorporating young people into its programs, in health, education, and political campaigns, expanded schooling opportunities, the armed forces, and mass organizations.

In addition, specifically legal measures likely have contributed to the lower crime rate. The *Gobierno de Reconstruccion Nacional* immediately declared adherence to international declarations of human rights, and maintained the 1974 Criminal Code (based on a continental system), subject to its being superseded by new decrees; on the other hand, with almost all the corrupt Somoza-appointed judges, officials and police having fled or being in custody, it had to appoint new officeholders, many untrained and inexperienced.

In general, despite the emergency war situation engendered by the U.S.-sponsored contra attacks (IHCA, 1984), complaints by the Right concerning the wartime emergency legislation (see, for example, CPDH, 1984), and the inevitable mistakes of a new system with previously inexperienced and untrained personnel (see Borge Martinez, 1982), the present formal legal system has maintained the independence of the judiciary, operated under the formal rule of law with progressive new legislation and programs, and focused on quite typical crimes. A number of progressive social welfare and family laws have followed. In addition, new types of crime have been identified, from government bureaucratic corruption and fraud to the exploitation of women's bodies in advertising, to decapitalization and Somozista counterrevolutionary activity. All these imply different styles and methods of policing. Nonetheless, most of the court and newspaper reports quite typically read as follows: "Sugar speculators jailed"; "Five workers steal Coca Cola equipment"; "Criminal neglect"; "Homocide and incest." (There are also some local incidents that sound especially exotic to First World ears, for example, "Drunken machete fight".)

In dealing with the 8500 *Guardia* prisoners and some 600 *contrarrevolucionarios* captured since 1983, special courts have been organized with speedier processing and relaxed rules of evidence; although these have drawn some human rights criticism, they have regularized the processing of the huge numbers of prisoners and cleared up the backlog. Furthermore, the clearance rates were higher than in normal courts, no death penalty was possible, and by 1983 only some 3000 *Guardia* remained in custody (Lopez, 1984). The prison system itself has been remarkably innovative and successful at rehabilitation (see Del Olmo, 1980, 1983; McCabe, 1984).

It must be noted that the Ministry of the Interior built a reasonably efficient, modern, and just public police force literally from nothing. The flight of Somoza led to the disintegration of the *Guardia,* his army/police.

> The transfer of power was done in the street. There was no legal institution. The maintenance of order had to be secured by the troops of the young guerrillas. The same desert existed in administration [Pax Christi, 1981: 8].

Although, as will be argued, the CDS (reconstituted from the CDCs) provided the substantive order, the FSLN guerrillas and the Popular Militias (organized by the CDS and FSLN) obviously possessed the most coordinated concentration of force, and it was from their ranks that the *Policía Sandinista* was developed, although not until a year had passed (Decree No. 485, August 9, 1980); this marked a decisive break with the Somozist past, when the army and police were one. Although extremely short of resources (for example, in 1983 one station covered a population of 100,000 with only one vehicle!), the force has become more efficient in clearance rates (Núñez de Escorcia, 1984: 30) as it has become more professional. It has operated in cooperation with both the uniformed *Policía Voluntaria* (since 1981) and the *Cuerpo de Protección Física* (since 1981). Though publicly paid, the latter resembles our private security guards as it mainly guards sites of economic activity whereas the former acts in direct support capacity to the regular *Policía Sandinista.*

In an attempt to derive substantive justice (see Pashukanis, 1978), there has been an emphasis on informal minor problem solving without formal charge; the local stations are literally beehives of complaints, discussions, and resolutions in comparison with Canadian stations. It is not unusual, for instance, for some 30 to 50 citizens to be milling around the front desk of the Eastern Market station (field notes, April 1985). Furthermore, the police have been very active working with juveniles (who since 1979 are not formally chargeable under age 16), both in community and "big brother" types of programs, and also in cooperating closely with the Social Service Ministry in running "Re-education Centres" (training schools).

Despite dramatically increased patrol hours (see Núñez de Escorcia, 1984), this new style of policing would doubtlessly lower most official rates whether or not criminal behavior was actually reduced; murder rates, however, would not be so affected, and they too have shown a dramatic decline. Furthermore, all anecdotal reports (interviews, newspapers, commentaries, and so on)—including even those of the highly critical Permanent Commission on Human Rights (CPDH)—attest to real reductions in ordinary street-crime behavior.

THE COMITES DE DEFENSA SANDINISTA AND VIGILANCIA REVOLUCIONARIA

All Arms to the People.

The eyes and ears of the Revolution.

Besides the deeper structural causes embodied in social reform and the public justice system changes previously noted, however, a more noteworthy reason for Nicaragua's lowered crime rate and safe streets lies in the operations of *vigilancia revolucionaria* by the Sandinista Defense Committees, which although private—not state—institutions, are publicly accountable.

It must be stressed that the committees are in many senses quintessential exemplars of the Sandinista Revolution (Serra, 1984: 1). They are the largest (with 600,000 members) and most powerful mass organization (others include youth movements, unions, the peasant movement, the women's movement), with the largest number of seats on the Council of State from 1980-1984. Organized territorially, they cover the country; they have been central in various

government campaigns, from real income maintenance, to education and health, and they retain their status as the crucial partners
(with the Sandinista Front guerrillas) in making the revolution.
There have been historical changes in the operations of the CDS
since the triumph, as the economy has been restored, governmental services began to operate, and policing became established.

The contradictory relation between the popular organization
and the state in the initial stage of the Sandinista revolution
has resulted in part from an indefinition of their respective
functions and also of power; in part from the character of both
as institutions supporting the same process of social transformation [Serra, 1984: 30].

In late 1979, early 1980, and again in March 1981, responding in
part to criticisms for acknowledged abuses (see further), the CDS
clarified and specified their specific objects and tasks in defending
the revolution politically, socially, economically, and militarily as
follows: organization maintenance, provision of information and
education, economic defense, community development, and social
defense (CIERA, 1984: 55; CDS/CEN, 1981; CDS/CEN, 1984).
(Although particular statements of objectives vary in their emphasis, the general direction is clear.) This clarification and organization was the particular task of the new National Executive
Committee (CDS/CEN, 1981, 1984).

There are over 15,000 committees in operation (Serra, 1984),
varying from a handful to dozens of members. Anyone regardless
of age (above 14), sex, race, religion, or politics can join as long as
they support the goals of the revolution: Some executive members
for instance, are members of the Independent Liberal Party (PLI).
In fact, however, activists tend to be young adults, female, working
class, "popular church" members, and FSLN supporters. They
meet approximately once a week; decisions of the groups are carried out by executive members in charge of the task areas, working
with citizen volunteers. Both incorporation to membership/parti-
cipation and decisions are made democratically by argument, discussion, and persuasion; the national office has explicitly rejected
use of coercion, favors, and so on (CDS/CEN, 1984). Each local
CDS elects representatives to the barrio or rural community committees, which in turn elect zonal, regional, and national committees in a democratic pyramid structure (CDS/CEN, 1984). The
original CDS representatives to the governmental Council of State

included a spectrum of students, accountants, peasants, and various small tradespersons (*Barricada,* May 4, 1980).

Suggesting, stimulating, administering, and criticizing almost the entire range of programs that are normally carried out by government agencies in the liberal-democratic West, the CDS has proposed new legislation, sent representatives to commissions, and worked closely with government ministries. In our topic area, for instance, the block and barrio security coordinators would cooperate with the *Policía Sandinista* and the *Ministerio del Interior* (MINT) concerning neighborhood issues of crime and delinquency. There may also occasionally be some contact with the courts, and education or social ministries.

Although social defense has always been a core activity of the CDS, it was in March 1981 that *vigilancia revolucionaria* was formally reorganized by the CDS, and protected by statute, the Ley de Protección del Vigilante Revolucionaria, in 1982.

Thus, operating formally within the law, and cooperating voluntarily with the *Policía* and MINT, control of the activities of the local *vigilancia* is worked out democratically by each neighborhood committee, under advice and general policy set by the national executive. Also formally independent of the *Frente Sandinista* Party, the CDS is increasingly controlled by persons who are *FSLN* members as one proceeds from the local neighborhood committee to the national executive.

Although firearms are not normally provided for *vigilancia revolucionaria,* many watchpersons actively carrying firearms elsewhere (for example, in the militia, police, army, and so on) bring them on patrol. Revolutionary guard duty is voluntarily carried out on almost every block throughout the country with shifts from 11-2 a.m. and from 2-5 a.m., or in 2-hour divisions supported by 2-person mobile patrols. Women make up a slight majority of the volunteers, which includes youngsters as young as age 14. In Managua's El Nicarao barrio, for example, there are 29 CDS's for 5,400 persons in the neighborhood, with 1,670 watchpersons. In a country of less than 3 million there are 300,000 watchpersons (USOCA, 1984: 116-117). In Managua alone there are about 72,000 watchpersons. They far outnumber the police, both in numbers of patrolpersons and hours logged. Given the number of volunteered hours, this amounts to an enormous saving for the public purse.

It is primarily preventive work, guaranteeing tranquillity to neighborhoods and workplaces: "We detect all the movements that happen on our block. When you entered with that car, one of us went to the other block to seek coordination in case there was any difficulty. Here, enemies and delinquents don't escape from us" (*Barricada,* September 20, 1984). Although they are authorized to make citizen's arrests, they normally try to involve the regular police as soon as possible if there is a serious offense. "For Socorro Navarro Alvarado, 45 years old, revolutionary vigilance has ended delinquents and scandals in the neighborhood. 'Now, nobody dares to show themselves to us drunk in the streets, because they know that they'll meet us. This care is rear-guard work because it allows the workers to sleep in peace and produce better at their jobs,' expounded Socorro, a housewife." (*Barricada,* September 21, 1984). Although the judicial functions exercised during and immediately after the insurrection have passed to the courts, there continues to be much informal "on-the-spot" resolution of minor disputes (assaults, domestic issues, morals offenses, juvenile offenses, and so on). According to an article in *Barricada,* (March 1, 1985) quoting the head of the CDS, in barrio Los Angeles

> with our patrol persons that number 400 and each day increase, we have not only captured delinquents, but one night we verified a fraud with the Sandinista Police. It happened that as we did the vigilance block by block, near here we stopped a truck from the Internal Commerce Ministry, from which was being unloaded 23 sacks of rice, which were doubtlessly contraband. The cargo was turned over to the police so they could deal with it. . . . That's how we are fighting delinquency and robbery that unscrupulous persons commit in the public sector, which deserves better. At the same time we can see that people now work more legally and where there were cantinas and whorehouses during the dictatorship, now one can see mechanics workshops, electric shops, cabinetmakers, bedmakers, and mattress factories. This increases production and also prepares young people in these trades, so that they can avoid delinquency.

In trying to implement the governmental and social mandate to stimulate production, they have been as active as the unions in their concern for economic crimes: prerevolution crimes of expropriation and seizure, crimes of hoarding and speculation, nonutilization of productive capacity, and most crucially of all, decapitalization (removal of investment capital). In rural Matagalpa: "In the past year there, watchpersons in different zones of the department detec-

ted 76 cases of counterrevolutionary activities, which were chan-
nelled to the appropriate authorities for the deserved application of
revolutionary justice" (*Barricada,* September 1, 1983). Although
cooperating with the police and operating within the law, the local
watch is particularly sensitive to neighborhood concerns, and tai-
lors its activities and responses accordingly. In this way, although
formally a private organization, it is very publicly accountable.

In a context of growing pains (see Consejo del Estado, July 1,
1981; Arguello Hurtado, 1982, 1983), extreme external aggres-
sion, the state of emergency, and remarkable candor regarding mistakes throughout the entire legal system (for example, see Borge
Martínez, 1982), a number of specific problems have arisen in the
operations of the CDS in *vigilancia revolucionaria.* The various
irregular patrol forces and courts operating under neighborhood
committees during and immediately after the insurrection not only
provided order and coordination as noted, but sometimes "ran
wild" in quite decentralized activities, occupying suspected Somozista properties, harassing suspected spies or informers, and even
assaulting some people (see Black, 1981: 168; *Barricada,* March
27, 1985).

> "People's" tribunals often tried the "ears" and "toads". For
> an informer who was convicted or found to have caused the
> deaths of Sandinistas whom he had informed against, the sen-
> tence was immediate execution. Then there were the loosely
> controlled "popular militia" and other undisciplined groups
> over which the Sandinistas often had a minimal influence.
> They were known to kill guard informers without the niceties
> of a popular trial and judgment [Diederich, 1981: 301].

In some remote areas, the CDS became involved in marriage cere-
monies, and charged money for local fiestas (Black, 1981: 241).
There were the initial "teething" problems of abuse of authority in
such areas as certification of local travel visas by petty officials
using their office to settle personal scores (Paredes, 1980; EPICA,
1980: 80). It was to control, regularize, and introduce justice to
such activities, of course, that the FSLN government established
the special courts, and regularized the *Policía Sandinista* and *vigilancia revolucionaria.* Early CDS functions as police and security
clearance authorizers for visas (needed originally to control *Guardia* remnants) were soon taken away (Booth, 1982: 193); the over-
zealous seizing of some properties and churches by some of the
CDS has been curtailed (Booth, 1984: 139).

The fiercest attacks on the CDS (echoed—or stimulated?—by the Reagan administration) have come from the political right-wing opposition (CPDH—*Comisión Permanente de Derechos Humanos; La Prensa; El Consejo Superior de Los Empresas Privadas*—all of which have now been revealed to be in receipt of U.S. government funds!).[4] For instance, the CPDH charges that the CDS exercises "political and military control of the population" (CPDH, 1984: 1) on orders from the National Directorate of the FSLN:

> The support of the CDS to the defense of the Sandinista revolutionary process consists in brazen spying of one neighbor on another, and is realized through house to house visits in which members of the community are pressured to watch (by turns) their house block and to pass daily reports to the police and the State Security. Houses which refuse to collaborate are marked "Here lives a counterrevolutionary, watch him" or "Contra, we are watching you" [CPDH, 1984: 3].

Although there is too much smoke to deny the likelihood of some fire, nonetheless almost all investigating commissions from without as well as within Nicaragua (such as Pax Christi, 1981; British Parliamentary Delegation, 1982; Nicaragua, Ministerio de Justicia, 1983; Americas Watch, 1985) have found such charges to be exaggerated, unsubstantiated, or relatively isolated cases (especially occurring immediately after the triumph) rather than systematic government or CDS policy (*Barricada,* June 11, 1984). Certainly there is much inefficiency (for instance, in record keeping and processing commands) typical of most Third World countries. I experienced this directly when reporting a simple theft took three visits over five days to two police stations, recounting the incident to some six officers, who made out three reports, the first of which was lost by the time of my third visit! The lack of substantiation, the political interconnectedness to local and foreign groups, and the fervor of the attacks against the CDS suggest other types of class motivations:

> These groups, which before arrested popular power together with the Somoza family, felt this growing process of organization and participation in the popular organizations as an inadmissable insubordination of the inferior classes. Church figures like the catholic bishops had prohibited the clergy and the faithful from participating in them, describing them as

communist mobs. . . . Five years after the triumph there were businessmen like Bolaños Geyer, president of COSEP (the Higher Council of Private Enterprise) who had the boldness to fire his workers for the simple fact of trying to organize a union in his company [Serra, 1984: 27].

In addition to these fierce attacks from Right-Wing reactionaries, the CDS have also suffered increasing self-doubts in the last year. Active membership and attendance at meetings has fallen, there have been charges of corruption, and some scandalous conduct by local functionaries revealed concerns over bureaucratization (see Herrera, in *Barricada,* September 11, 1985). Besides immediate, relatively isolated causes, many of these difficulties are attributable to organizational "growing pains." Many of their early, concrete, and visibly successful tasks have been accomplished: streets are cleaned, drains are cleared, housing is reallocated. Additionally, as government ministries (such as housing, education) and agencies (such as the police) become more efficient, they have satisfied demands that were previously met by the CDS. After a few years, all voluntary organizations experience similar difficulties in sustaining the founders' initial enthusiasm.

The increasing economic crisis engendered by the Reagan administration's economic sanctions has drained material resources. And the grinding horror of the "low-intensity" war with the American-sponsored contra has siphoned off many competent activists to the front. The organization has responded with improved internal policing, new training programs, and countrywide CDS elections November [1985]; only time will indicate the success of these self-renewal efforts.

The CDS developed under Somozista oppression, civil war shaped them, and the threat of imperialist invasion continues to animate them. In such a not impossible eventuality, intimate knowledge of friends and enemies of the revolution would be crucial to any orchestrated defense. It is also very clear that the committees have been very much "in process," that they have never been "standardized" (CIERA, 1984: 56). The CDS thus continue to exemplify the lively political debate within Nicaragua. The questions of how to reconcile the old (liberal-democratic) legal code with the current needs of the revolution for popular justice, responsive to the substantive priority needs of the people, are recognized. There are continuing discussions between the Ministry of the Interior and the *Policía Sandinista* in responding to the demands of the Supreme

Court that judicial orders must be immediately and unquestion-
ingly obeyed; that rules of evidence and proof beyond any reasonable doubt must be established (Consejo del Estado, July 1, 1981).

What type of relationship should exist between the mass organizations and the FSLN or the state? How will the newly-
introduced concept "popular power" be put into practice?
And how will the immediate needs of the masses be balanced
with the long term goals of the revolution? How will the working class be unified? The ultimate character of the revolution
will be determined by the way in which these questions are
answered, not just in terminology, but as real contradictions
emerge that must be dealt with [Burback and Draimin, 1980:
21].

CONCLUSION

Traveller, there is no road. The road is made by going forward. [Machado, quoted in Núñez de Escorcia, 1984]

In regard to private policing, a comparative, cross-cultural perspective is needed to correct ethnocentrism; a comparative perspective that moves beyond traditional "development" theory,
which assumes that the untutored natives in the rest of the world are
becoming more like us English, Americans, or Canadians, but are
unfortunately retarded, and hence need our technical assistance to
organize a truly modern and efficient police force. Spurred on by
the oil and debt problems within the current global economic crisis, development theory has increasingly been challenged by
"dependency" or "underdevelopment" theory, which argues that
the Third World has not been and is not independent of the First
and Second worlds but intimately linked; indeed the "retardation"
of its crime and policing problems are dialectically related to First
World development through imperialist exploitation (see Sumner,
1981). As argued previously, although the pre-revolutionary *Guardia Nacional* was a formally public police force, the extremely
exploitative imperial context of Nicaragua constituted it as a force
in reality privately accountable only to the Somozas, and, through
them, to the imperial power, the United States.

Such a comparative perspective, of course, is theoretically most
compatible with critical perspectives on crime, justice, and policing within the First World. Conflict theories (see Taylor et al., 1973;

Quinney, 1977; Chambliss, 1977) argue that societies are maintained by force (policing being a preeminent means) and ideological mystification, with continuous conflict between groups with
opposing goals and values. In capitalism, the fundamental conflict
occurs between labor and capital, grounded in contradictory, historically specific relations of production not only of material goods,
but also of labor power itself (primarily through gender relations),
and of culture, social institutions, and so on. This fundamental
conflict is crucially revealed in the increasingly social and public
organization of labor, contrasting with increasing private concentration of profit and wealth.

Although such conflicts get worked out in First World liberal-
democratic capitalism through the growth of private policing referred to in the definitions provided earlier and described in most
of the other chapters in this book, the more typical manifestations
in the underdeveloping Third World are the obscene privatization
of police and army in Somoza-type national security states, replete
with American-sponsored death squads (see Chomsky and Herman, 1979).

A central thrust of critical theories of crime and justice is the
claim that revolution or progressive social transformation could
provide a more just order and by implication, better policing, while
avoiding the dangers of orthodox communist totalitarianism (Thompson, 1978; CSE/NDC, 1979). Third World revolutions offer further historical test cases of these claims of critical criminology, and
this chapter argues that the Nicaraguan case is particularly interesting in suggesting a humane and progressive possibility.

The CDS exemplify the liberation and blossoming of a people's
organizational and creative potential in participatory democracy:
one of the most exciting aspects of Nicaragua's Sandinist Popular
Revolution is that although inspired by Sandino and led by the Sandinista Front, it has been made and continues to be made by the people. Furthermore, the committees exemplify a new type of power
locus, a new politics, a new form of state unrecognized (indeed suppressed) within more traditional Western capitalist-liberal democracies or Stalinist state-capitalist one-party communism. These
states, respectively, formally maintain the public-private split with
real private dominance, or attempt to eliminate the private (and
civil liberties) entirely.

When triumph is achieved, a state of the civil society emerges,
a state permeated by civil society—democratic, popular, and

progressive. The people, inserted into the state, are the state. The task of the people, more than commenting on the state, is to act within it in a way that serves both them and their functionaries. . . . a civilian society-state takes shape, a people-state in which society and people do not merely have opinions, do not merely vote and have representation; in addition, they become integrated into, joined with, and form part of that emergency state, that state-nation or that nation-state, in which curiously, one can find the extreme discipline implied by liberation combined with the most diverse moral, religious, popular and civilian currents of a war that involves the *entire* civil population [Gonzalez Casanova, 1984: 220-221].

This type of Left variant of social control through popular councils (Arendt, 1964) has been centrally concerned with the redrawing of boundaries between public and private, with balancing local control and central coordination, with equity versus substantive justice. Such a resolution of private and public contradictions most effectively replicates the Sandinist resolution of private ownership under public control in the economy.

The *Comites de Defensa Sandinista* have struggled desperately to survive against infiltration, death, invasion by imperialist powers allied with local capital that opposed the revolution, and the centralizing tendencies of an extremely threatened fledgling bureaucracy and governing party. To this point, at least, Nicaragua's brave experiment with popular power, exemplified in *vigilancia revolucionaria*, has survived—though battered—with its ideals intact. Doubtlessly, it is this very success in reformulating the relationship of private and public policing that has attracted such inordinate fear and outrage and such intemperate attacks from the centers and local representatives of capitalist-liberal democracy.

Vigilancia revolucionaria offers a model of community self-policing that, although privately organized, is a significant development of public accountability and effective security far beyond any policing experiments in the West.

NOTES

1. A more detailed account of my data collection techniques and sources will be given in a forthcoming monograph, tentatively entitled *"Just Revolution,"* but basically I have followed a participant observer style, combining direct on-site

experience with in-depth casual and formal interviews, records, and other documents. Although this chapter is in many ways theoretical and speculative, it draws upon research data from Nicaragua gathered in October 1983, December 1984, and March, April, and September 1985.

2. Methodologically, what the chapter attempts can be conceived as a critique of criminology patterned after Marx's critique of political economy, whereby a concept is analyzed to reveal the necessary presuppositions for its sensible use. To the extent that both the concept and its presuppositions are grounded in real historically specific experience, the analysis reveals necessary determinations of the phenomenon corresponding to the concept (see West, 1984, for a fuller discussion). In more general terms, I believe the evidence allows a claim that Nicaragua is a revealing "extreme-case" in terms of case-study logic (see Becker, 1970).

3. I have used here only postinsurrection statistics; although all official statistics are on methodological grounds somewhat suspect as indicators of criminal activity, the *Guardia's* style of policing renders their statistics literally incomparable; for instance, the Somozist Supreme Court even abandoned official reports entirely from 1974 to 1979! Needless to say, no self-report figures are available. Under the comparatively normal administration since the insurrection, the murder figures can be taken as relatively accurate, and their decline is so substantial as to almost certainly indicate behavior change. Besides giving some indication of behavior change on the part of citizens, of course, these figures more accurately indicate changes in policing behavior, a topic of equal interest to us here.

4. The CPDH figures have all too often been shown to be inaccurate (*El Nuevo Diaro,* June 27, 1983; January 8, 1983). They use press reports (especially from *La Prensa,* which systematically refuses to publish response letters from the "disappeared" person; see *El Nuevo Diaro,* June 12, 1983). Their own figures indicate falling numbers of incidents on the same pages of reports where they claim rising numbers (*CPDH,* Testimony, May 12, 1984: 2). The former director of CPDH has joined forces with the Contras (March 3, 1982, *Barricada*). *La Prensa* systematically also refuses to publish material on Contra atrocities against Nicaraguan civilians, and its editor recently was taped saying he supported the Contras and hoped they were successful (incredibly tolerant, the government has not charged him with treason nor sedition in what is a war situation!). The COSEP president has recently exercised his FSLN guaranteed freedom to refuse to recognize his employees' union (Serra, 1984: 27).

REFERENCES

America's Watch (1985) *With Friends Like These.* New York: Pantheon.
ARENDT, H. (1959) *The Human Condition.* New York: Vintage.
———(1964) *On Revolution.* Harmondsworth, England: Penguin.
ARGUELLO HURTADO, R. (1982) "Puntos de vista sobre la ley de reforma procesal penal." *Monexico* (November): 40.
———(1983) "Corte Suprema habla claro." *La Prensa* December 20.
BARRY, T., B. WOOD, and D. PREUSCH (1983) *Dollars and Dictators.* New York: Grove Press.
BECKER, H. S. (1970) *Sociological Work: Method and Substance.* Chicago: Aldine.

BLACK, G. (1981) *Triumph of the People: The Sandinista Revolution in Nicaragua*. London: Zed.
BOOTH, J. (1982) *The End and the Beginning: The Nicaragua Revolution*. Boulder, CO: Westview.
———(1984) "The revolution in Nicaragua: through a frontier of history," in D. E. Schultz and D. H. Graham (eds.) *Revolution and Counterrevolution in Central America and the Carribbean*. Boulder, CO: Westview.
BORGE MARTÍNEZ, T. (1982) "On human rights in Nicaragua," in T. Borge (ed.) *Sandinistas Speak*. New York: Pathfinder.
British Parliamentary Delegation (1982) *Good Neighbours? Nicaragua, Central America and the U.S.* London: CIIR 1.
BURBACK, R. and T. DRAIMIN (1980) "Nicaragua's revolution." *NACLA Report on the Americas* 14,3: 2-35.
CASTRO RODRIQUEZ, R. (1945) *"Sistemas carcelarios."* Doctoral dissertation, Universidad de Leon, Nicaragua.
CDS/CEN (*Comites de Defensa Sandinista/Comite de Ejecutivo Nacional*) (1981) "El Comites de Defensa Sandinista de mi cuadra." Unpublished manuscript.
———(1984) "Los CDS somos: poder popular." Unpublished manuscript, CDS National Headquarters, Managua.
CHAMBLISS, W. (1977) "Functional and conflict theories of crime," in W. Chambliss and R. Seidman (eds.) *Whose Law? What Order?* New York: John Wiley.
CHOMSKY, N. and E. HERMAN (1979) *The Washington Connection and Third World Fascism*. Montreal: Black Rose.
CIERA (Centro de Investigaciones y Estudios de la Reforma Agraria) (1984) *La Democracia Participativa en Nicaragua*. Managua: Author.
CLINARD, M. and D. J. ABBOTT (1973) *Crime in Developing Countries*. New York: John Wiley.
CIDA (Comisión Interamericana de Derechos Humanos) (1978) *Informe Sobre la Situacion de los Derechos Humanos en Nicaragua*. Organization of American States, document 16, Managua.
CPDH (Comisión Permanente de Derechos Humanos) (1978) *Los Derechos Humanos en Nicaragua*. Managua: Author.
———(1984) *Testimony of the Nicaragua Commission on Human Rights*. Managua: Author.
Consejo del Estado (1981) "Periode de Preguntas y Resquestos de la Expositión del Co. Pres. de la Corte Suprema de Justicia, Dr. R. Arguello Hurtado." Sesion Ordinaria #7, July 1. Managua: Author.
CSE/NDC (Conference of Socialist Economists/National Deviancy Conference) (1979) *Capitalism and the Rule of Law*. London: Hutchinson.
DEL OLMO, R. (1980) *Los Chiguines de Somoza*. Caracas. Edit: Atenéo.
———(1983) "Remaking criminal justice in revolutionary Nicaragua." *Crime and Social Justice* 18.
DIEDERICH, B. (1981) *Somoza and the Legacy of U.S. Involvement in Central America*. London: Junction.
EPICA (Ecumenical Program for Interamerican Communication and Action) (1980) *Nicaragua: A People's Revolution*. Washington, D.C.: Author.
FARNELL, M. B. and C. D. SHEARING (1977) *Private Security: An Examination of Canadian Statistics 1961-71*. Centre of Criminology, University of Toronto.

FREEDMAN, D. and P. STENNING (1977) *Private Security Police and the Law in Canada.* Centre of Criminology, University of Toronto.

GONZALEZ CASANOVA, P. (1984) "Intervention and negotiation in Central America," in *Nicaragua Under Siege,* in *Contemporary Marxism, #8.*

GRAMSCI, A. (1971) *Selections from the Prison Notebooks.* London: Lawrence & Wishart.

IHCA (Instituto Historico de Centro America) (1984) "Nicaragua 84: the human and material costs of the war." *Update* 4, 1.

JESSOP, B. (1982) *The Capitalist State.* Oxford: Martin Robertson.

LOPEZ AMANDO, S. J. (1984) "Los derechos humanos en Nicaragua." *Amanecer* (January): 22-23.

McCABE, B. (1984) "Las granjas abiertas." Unpublished manuscript. Managua: Comisión Nacional de Protección y Promocion de Derechos Humanos.

Nicaragua, Ministerio de Justicia (1983) *Nicaragua y los Derechos Humanos.* Managua: Author

NÚÑEZ DE ESCORCIA, V. (1984) "Transformación revolucionaria y control social de la delincuencia en Nicaragua." Published (1985) as "Justice and the control of crime: The Sandinista popular revolution," in *Crime and Social Justice, 23.*

PAREDES, O. (1980) cited in El Nuevo Diario, July 9.

Pax Christi (1981) *Derechos Humanos: Informe de la Misión.* Managua: Author.

PEARCE, J. (1982) *Under the Eagle.* London: Latin American Bureau.

QUINNEY, R. (1977) *Class, State, and Crime.* Boston: David MacKay.

USOCA (United States Out of Central America) (1984) "Vigilancia Revolucionaria: guarding the revolution." in *Nicaragua Under Siege, Contemporary Marxism #8.*

SERRA, L. (1984) "Las organisaciones populares en la Revolución Sandinista." Unpublished manuscript, Sociology Department, Universidad de Centroamerica, Managua.

SUMNER, C. [ed.] (1981) "Crime, justice and underdevelopment: beyond modernisation theory," in *Crime, Justice and Underdevelopment.* London: Heinemann.

TAYLOR, I., P. WALTON, and J. YOUNG (1973) *The New Criminology.* London: Routledge & Kegan Paul.

THOMPSON, E. P. (1978) *The Secret State.* London: State Research Pamphlet.

TUROK (1981) *Revolutionary Thought in the Twentieth Century.* London: Zed.

WEBER, M. (1964) *The Theory of Social and Economic Organization.* Glencoe, IL: Free Press.

WEST, W. G. (1986) "El Terrorismo Internacional en Nicaragua," *Capitulo Criminológico.* [Instituto de Criminologia Universidad de Zulia, Maracaibo, Venezuela] 13, 187-200.

———(1984) "Phenomenon and form in interactionist and neoMarxist qualitative research," in L. Barton and S. Walker (eds.) *Education, State, and Crisis.* London: Croom Helm.

WHEELOCK ROMAN, J. (1974/79) *Nicaragua: Imperialismo y Dictadura.* Havana: Editorial de Ciencias Sociales.

Chapter 7

THE INTERWEAVING OF PUBLIC AND PRIVATE POLICE IN UNDERCOVER WORK

GARY T. MARX

In documenting the important differences between private and public police Shearing and Stenning (1983) offer a needed corrective to traditional views of social control that ignored private police altogether, or simply saw them as adjuncts to public police. Yet our language and the social trends inspiring a topical issue such as this can result in the distinction between private and public police being drawn too cleanly. It is important to consider commonalities and interdependencies, as well as differences.

Historically it was easier to talk of public as against private police. In popular conceptions there was little doubt about who the Pinkertons and the G-men were. Yet today in many cases such distinctions are more difficult to make. Attention must be given to a number of dimensions that interweave the basic public-private distinction (for example, sponsorship, function, interest served, organizational form, and location).

There are interstitial areas where public and private police are functionally or organizationally linked, or even merge. Even when this is not the case, there is some convergence in behavior as a result of the movement of public police to the private sector and the carrying out of equivalent tasks using similar means.

In this work I illustrate these points and consider some of their implications for social theory and public policy. The data presented have been gathered as part of a broader study of undercover police in the United States.[1] Five forms of interdependence between public and private police are considered: (1) joint public/private inves-

AUTHOR'S NOTE: I am grateful to Nancy Reichman for critical comments.

tigations, (2) public agents hiring or delegating authority to private police, (3) private interests hiring public police, (4) new organizational forms in which the distinction between public and private is blurred, and (5) the circulation of personnel between the public and private sector. Although these five forms are described using examples of undercover investigations, they represent more generic forms of interdependence.

JOINT PUBLIC-PRIVATE INVESTIGATIONS

An example of a joint investigation can be seen in an FBI-IBM sting involving the sale of computer secrets in Silicon Valley. In perhaps the largest industrial espionage case ever in the United States, the two organizations participated in a fake consulting firm named "Glenmar Associates." An IBM security official posed as the firm's attorney. The firm offered to sell supposedly stolen IBM secrets to Hitachi and Mitsubishi.[2]

The sting emerged when a former IBM employee notified IBM that he had been approached by Hitachi about obtaining documents. The next day he was visited by IBM security officers. He later introduced sting participants to Hitachi officials. As a result of the sting, criminal charges were filed against 21 persons. IBM also filed a suit against Hitachi and several affiliated companies asking for unspecified damages for the alleged theft of its trade secrets.

FBI Director Webster commended IBM for "excellent assistance during this investigation" (New York Times, June 23, 1982). However, defense attorneys claimed that the sting was controlled by IBM and was undertaken as part of a struggle against international competition. The government refused to provide documents requested by the defense that would permit assessing this contention. This resulted in the dropping of charges against some defendants (San Jose Mercury, September 29, 1982).

Another sting carried out by private detectives working for National Semiconductor and Signetics corporations, in cooperation with police and federal agents, resulted in the arrest of two men for receiving supposedly stolen computer chips. Police were notified when several boxes of stolen chips were found in a Milpitas, California motel. These were traced to a suspect. Signetics and National Semiconductor then hired private investigators to pose as thieves. Over an eight-month period they approached the suspect and others and offered to sell stolen parts. Those arrested were thought to be key links in a network that used components made in Silicon Valley to manufacture counterfeit Apple computers in Asia (*San Jose Mercury News,* October 2, 1982).

The National Automobile Theft Bureau (a private organization supported by the insurance industry) carried out an undercover operation with the Tennessee Department of Revenue and the Metro Nashville Police Department. Concerned over the fact that vehicle theft and fraud in East Tennessee was escalating, the three agencies provided personnel and funding for a sting. It was coordinated by an assistant district attorney general.

The nine-month operation used an auto repair shop as a front. The operation made buys of stolen cars and sought intelligence. Its agents infiltrated auto auctions, salvage yards, and junk yards in the hope of encountering professional thieves. This resulted in the recovery of 72 stolen vehicles with a retail value of $475,000. In a joint statement, agency heads said, "The success of this operation shows what can be accomplished when the public and private sectors join forces against crime" (International Association of Chiefs of Police Newsletter, August 1982).

In another joint effort the Insurance Crime Prevention Institute (ICPI; an umbrella organization of 400 insurance companies) cooperated with the San Jose Police in a year-long property sting. The sting purchased nearly half a million dollars of property and 35 persons were arrested. While undercover public police ran the storefront purchasing stolen property, insurance investigators worked behind the scenes identifying the owners and insurers of stolen property and serving as liason between insurance companies and the San Jose police (*ICPI Reports,* January 1981).

STATE HIRING OR DELEGATION OF AUTHORITY TO PRIVATE POLICE

According to one estimate in 1984 approximately 36,000 of the nation's 1.1 million private security guards worked for government. The figures for federal, state, and local government were, respectively, 11,000, 9,000, and 16,000 (Cunningham and Taylor, 1984). For example, they serve as U.S. marshals in federal courthouses, and guard military bases, nuclear facilities, NASA, and various public buildings, including city halls and public housing projects. They also provide security at airports. But let us just consider some undercover examples.

A private detective agency called Multi-State Unit, Inc. specializes in providing contract undercover services. Among its clients are small towns and rural areas lacking skill in fields such as drug enforcement. It was founded by a former police chief and head of Ohio's bureau of criminal investigation. Its employees are all former police persons with narcotics experience. An incentive to solve cases (not available to public police doing equivalent work) is a share of the company's profits.

There are an unknown number of itinerant individual entrepreneurs who move from department to department selling their covert skills. For example, in a small Wisconsin county one such person was made a temporary deputy sheriff. He spent six months in an undercover capacity. When he surfaced, the prosecutor had 30 warrants. The agent testified. Highly recommended by his employer, he quickly located work through an informal law enforcement network and moved on to an equivalent job in another state.

Private individuals are often hired for vice work. As opposed to sworn agents they may pose as prostitutes or as their clients. It is much cheaper to hire a part-time employee for close to the minimum wage than a sworn agent. A strategic reason for using civilians, especially in smaller jurisdictions, is that regular officers are often well known, and hence can not do vice undercover work.

Informer Mel Weinberg and an ex-FBI agent he worked with on the Abscam case played a central role in what may be the first privately financed, court-sanctioned sting. Their private police organization approached businesses thought to be vulnerable to counterfeiting. Through use of the sting tactic they offered to gather evidence regarding trademark infringements.[3]

In operation "Bagscam" they were hired by Louis Vuitton, a manufacturer of *haute couture* handbags. The operation was directed against businessmen who allegedly sold counterfeit Vuitton handbags. The operation was overseen by an attorney for Vuitton who was appointed a special federal prosecutor and authorized to gather evidence by a U.S. district judge. The judge's order also authorized videotaping of meetings between Weinberg and the targets of the sting.

As in Abscam, Weinberg promised financing for a questionable venture as a lure and used an unwitting middleman to reach a suspect. The suspect was previously convicted of criminal contempt for violating an injunction that barred him from selling counterfeit Vuitton handbags. Weinberg offered to help the defendant obtain financing to establish a factory in Haiti to manufacture imitation Vuitton handbags.

In other cases Weinberg sought to purchase a small number of such bags (for example, 25 for $25 each) from what appear to be very small-time operators. According to a defense attorney Weinberg did and said things no government operative would have. In one such case he threatened to break the target's head open. In another he told the target that there was nothing wrong with such a sale and that it did not violate federal law. In a videotaped meeting he advised the target not to discuss the meeting with his lawyer (*National Law Journal,* May 21, 1984; *60 Minutes,* October 21, 1984).

The attorney for Vuitton, Joseph Bainton, has played a pioneering role as a special prosecutor in the development of such sting operations. He has set traps in a number of cities for those trading in bogus luggage. In the mid-1980s he was involved in an annual average of 40-50 prosecutions of counterfeiters and copyright pirates (Thompson, 1986).

These cases stand out because they involve a judge appointing a private attorney to carry out an undercover investigation on behalf of the private interest for whom the attorney is employed. When the individual appointed as a special prosecutor is paid by the direct beneficiary of the law enforcment activity there can be an obvious conflict of interest, or at least the appearance of one.

The justification for the above-described incident was that the U.S. attorney's staff was overworked and had higher priorities than the problem of counterfeit luggage. Other reasons for turning to private police are the belief by political authorities that public police lack skills and resources, are unreliable, incompetent, or even corrupt, or, contrarily, are *too* bound by the rules to take the actions deemed necessary. For example, in a controversial Florida effort, the governor "commissioned" private detectives from the Wackenhut Corporation to conduct investigations on behalf of his state. This was part of a war on crime program. The head of the program was the president of Wackenhut. Payment came from private donations. The investigators did not have the power of arrest, nor the privilege to carry arms. But law enforcement agencies were asked to cooperate with them and to surrender confidential police files. At the time Florida had no statewide law enforcment agency. Rather than trying to create one, and gain funding for it through an uncertain legislative process, the governor thought it more expeditious to simply hire Wackenhut and solicit donations from private citizens.[4]

Another example is former President Nixon's use of "the plumbers" to ferret out information on leaks and political intelligence and to damage political opponents. Nixon and his aides were apparently dissatisfied with the level and type of effort put forth by the CIA and FBI. A "national security" justification was used to serve highly partisan interests through illegal means.

Private police may be used in instances where public police have the resources and skill to carry out a task, but lack the will. It may appear unseemly for state agents to carry out a given enforcement action even though they are technically able to do so. For example in New York, private detectives from the Always Zon Guard agency visted the Hidden Desire massage parlor and paid for services. They then filed affidavits detailing their activities. This was the basis for forcing the business to close. (The private detectives were not themselves prosecuted for their illegal sexual acts.)

In another example that would probably not have been undertaken by state police for reasons of propriety and public relations, an attractive female private investigator parlayed a specious romantic involvement into a confession of a double murder. The private detective was hired by the three daughters of the deceased. Police had suspected her target but had been unable to gather sufficient evidence to solve the crime over a three-year period (*Boston Globe,* February 27, 1985).

The investigator contrived a meeting with the suspect and then dated him for several months. The suspect proposed marriage, but the agent said she first wanted to know what it was that he seemed to be hiding. With Houston public police listening through a transmitter in her purse, he subsequently confessed to the murder of two people.

PRIVATE-SECTOR HIRING OF PUBLIC POLICE

The private sector historically has made extensive use of undercover tactics. But, as with other forms of private policing, prosecution was usually not an important goal, relative to prevention, recovering property, denying a claim, gathering intelligence, or managing employees.[5] For example, it is far easier to pay criminals and go-betweens for the recovery of stolen property than to engage in successful prosecution.

However, in recent years segments of private-sector police have become more prosecution-oriented. With this has come increased cooperation with public agents and the provision of resources for undercover operations.

For example, four insurance companies operating through the ICPI contributed $20,000 to finance the first fencing sting in Connecticut. The companies write homeowner policies and had recently experienced a "major increase" in burglary claims. According to the attorney general one of the goals was "spending a minimum of tax dollars." The state did contribute $500 for the rent of a store-front, $500 for the purchase of narcotics, and two officers who posed as fences. An insurance company spokesman states,

> We didn't do it with the thought in mind of cost-benefit for our own companies. None of the goods recovered have so far been determined to be insured [by us]. It's a message to the people who are plaguing neighborhoods with burglaries that something can be done about it, and will be done about it [New York Times, May 14, 1981].

Trade associations and chambers of commerce have also financed sting operations. Thus, in operation "mod-sound" the recording industry contributed $100,000 to an FBI investigation of pirated records and tapes.

In an important Massachusetts arson case in which more than 30 individuals were indicted, private investigators played a major role. According to an assistant attorney general, the insurance industry gave the equivalent of a blank check to help finance it. Its money was used to provide protective custody for the government's chief witness, to pay overtime for state employees, and to supplement the attorney general's investigation through private efforts. Some private investigators worked directly as consultants to the state and were paid by it whereas others worked for insurance companies, but in conjunction with public authorities (Reichman, 1983: 359).

Among the institutional supports for the increased private-sector involvement in prosecution efforts are the ICPI founded in 1972, and the National Auto Theft Bureau, founded by insurance companies in 1912 as a voluntary organization to help recover and identify stolen vehicles and to prevent auto theft. However, in 1979 the latter organization underwent a series of changes supportive of prosecution. Its agents were authorized to sign criminal complaints. In 1979 its agents contributed to the prosecution of 949 persons on larceny, auto theft, and fraud charges; by 1981 this figure had increased to 1706. For the ICPI the number of arrests contributed to has increased steadily from an initial 221 in 1972 when it was founded, to 1229 in 1979-1980.

Of particular interest are the creation of state-run fraud bureaus to investigate and apprehend insurance fraud offenders. Five states now have these and others are considering them (Reichman, 1983). These are in large part financed by the insurance industry in the particular state. The National Association of Insurance Commissioners has drafted model legislation for creating fraud units with law enforcment powers in state departments of insurance. The legislation calls upon insurance companies to report suspected insurance fraud and grants them civil immunity for filing such reports.

NEW QUASI-PUBLIC OR QUASI-PRIVATE ORGANIZATIONS

The merging or blurring of the public/private distinction can also be seen in the appearance of new permanent organizational forms (rather than only in the temporary forms as with the joint FBI-IBM investigation). What can be called quasi-public or quasi-private permanent police organizations appear to have increased in prominence.

Consider for example the Law Enforcement Intelligence Unit (LEIU). This was founded as a private organization for local and state police to share intelligence files. Its membership is restricted to public police. The private nature of the organization apparently permits the exchange of information that would not otherwise be possible by agents acting strictly in a public capacity. Privacy and confidentiality protections regarding the collection and sharing of information are avoided. Because the files are held by a private organization they are exempt from the Freedom of Information Act and privacy laws that give people access to their own files. A former chairman of the organization told a senate subcommittee that the purpose of the LEIU is "the gathering, recording, investigating, and exchange of confidential information not available through regular police channels on individuals and organizations, involved, but not necessarily restricted to organized crime."[6]

The National Auto Theft Bureau, although a private non-profit organization, has public elements in its role as a clearinghouse for auto theft information. Its North American Auto Theft Information System is a unique data base that, beyond basic information such as when and where stolen and previous history, includes the hidden vehicle indentification number. Law enforcement officers and insurance agents in many states are legislatively required to report auto theft information to it. In some states its agents are granted immunity from civil prosecution when information is exchanged in the course of an investigation. This significantly increased communication among private insurance investigators and between them and state agents.[7]

There are also anomalous forms such as Anderson Security Consultants, Inc. of Virginia. They did standard security work for private interests. They also did work for the federal government including watching CIA and Pentagon employees whose loyalty was suspect, recruiting federal undercover drug agents, and infiltrating the peace movement through Project MERRIMAC. The private security firm was in fact a CIA front—created and staffed by agency members (O'Toole, 1978: 223). The CIA is under severe restraints with respect to domestic operations. Such proprietaries offer ideal covers for intruding into legally and politically sensitive areas.[8]

THE CIRCULATION OF PERSONNEL

Another form of interdependence can be seen in the circulation of personnel between the public and private sectors. Public-private exchanges of personnel and technology have gone on for over a century. After the Civil War as federal policing began and local policing rapidly expanded, the shift was most often from the private to the public sector (and sometimes back, as politics dictated). Private detectives such as Alan Pinkerton introduced covert tactics into the public sector, first as contract employees and later as direct agents.

But in recent years the flow has moved in the other direction.[9] The significant expansion of undercover tactics in the last decade has created a pool of experienced and well-known public agents who have taken their skills to the private sector. For example, the police lieutenant who was central to Washington DC's large, widely publicized stings (PFF Inc., Police FBI Fencing Incognito, and G.Y.A., Got Ya Again) retired and opened his own investigative agency, Sting Security, Inc. Mel Weinberg started his own private investigative agency, Abscam Incorporated, after the investigation he played a central role in. Gordon Liddy of Watergate infamy started an agency called "Gemstone," named after an aborted Watergate scheme. The IBM security agent who worked on the sting in the Silicon Valley obviously felt at ease working with federal agents, as he had previously been an FBI agent and had also worked for the Department of the Treasury and the Bureau of Narcotics and Dangerous Drugs.

More generally, the vast private security industry continues to expand. This industry, particularly at the more professional and leadership levels, is composed of thousands of former military, national security, and domestic police agents for whom public service was a revolving door.[10] Some federal agents leave when they face mandatory retirement at age 55, many local police retire at a relatively young age after 20 years of service. However, limited mobility opportunities and more lucrative private-sector offers attract many others long before retirement.

These agents were schooled and experienced in the latest control techniques while working for government, but are now much less subject to its control. They may also maintain their informal ties to those still in public policing. An insurance company executive, in explaining the rationale behind hiring former police officers for investigative work, notes that if the latter cannot gain direct access to the needed information, "there are their friends". This opens "up the doors for us so we can work both sides of the street" (Ghezzi, 1983).

Former public police, particularly at the federal level, often belong to organizations such as the Association of Federal Investigators (with membership open as well to exfederal and nonfederal investigators), the Society of Former Special Agents of the FBI, the Association of Retired Intelligence Officers, and the International Association of Chiefs of Police. These groups do not have explicit operational enforcement goals, but through their newsletters and conferences they create formal and informal networks that serve to integrate those in public and private enforcement. Through lobbying and other political activity they may condition the environment within which policing occurs.

Even in the absence of such networks, there is a transfer of technology and culture such that although they are organizationally distinct, the line between public and private police is increasingly blurred with respect to their attitudes, behavior, and style.

SOME IMPLICATIONS

This chapter has used the case of undercover investigations to illustrate five ways in which public and private police can be interdependent.[11] I will consider some of the implications of this for public policy and social theory.

There is need for increased public information about the extent to which state police agents are in effect hired to carry out inves-

tigations at the behest of private interests. There may also be a
need for clear policy statements and new forms of accountability.
Although private support and cooperation may be welcomed in
financially restrictive times, other issues are present. What limits
should be placed on the private sector's ability to hire public agencies? Equity questions are raised to the extent that well-placed high
bidders may be able to garner a share of public law enforcement
denied to those unable or unwilling to pay. Just what is being bought
with the private sector's contribution? If the money comes with no
strings attached and is for an investigation consistent with an agency's priorities and one that it would have been likely to carry out
anyway, there can be little problem. However, to the extent that law
enforcement priorities, discretion, tactics, confidential information, or prosecutorial actions are affected, then the tactic must be
closely examined.

Important questions are also raised when the public sector commissions private agents to act on its behalf. How cozy should this
relationship become? Although there are obvious advantages in
cooperation,[12] from a standpoint of accountability and the protection of privacy there may be drawbacks. The ability of public police
to regulate private police and to protect citizens from their abuses
may be compromised. Goals may conflict, for example, the private
sector's profit-making concerns and its lessened emphasis on use
of the criminal sanction.

The circulation of personnel also raises policy questions. Are
former government agents experienced in highly sensitive and intrusive operations able to neutralize or weaken investigations carried
out by the public agency for which they formerly worked? Do they
find it easy to cover illegal investigative activities because they
know how public police who might discover violations operate?
Should former government agents employed in an investigative
capacity by the private sector face greater restrictions and a registration requirement?

In spite of historic American concerns over centralized government and the importance granted checks and balances, elements
of a national police may be emerging in the United States. This is
based not on a centralized structure, but on a common occupational culture, informal networks, similar tasks, and the exchange
of personnel.

An important theoretical implication of this material is that public and private police may serve as functional alternatives for each
other. Although sources of conflict and competition can be identi-

fied,[13] public and private police may also be drawn together to supplement their respective weaknesses.

The case of private police using public police is the more obvious. Thus, through hiring off-duty public police, entering into exchange relationships, or participating in cooperative investigations they may benefit from the power of state agents to arrest, search, interrogate, carry weapons and use force and electronic surveillance, and gain access to otherwise protected information. Their legal liability may also be reduced or eliminated. The training, experience, skill, and backup support that public police can offer are other factors. The threat of using arrests and civil suits can be an important negotiating resource for private police. There are obvious advantages where a private interest's concerns can be defined as in the public interest and the responsibility of public law enforcement.

Perhaps less clear is what private police might offer public police. An important factor is information. Sworn agents cannot be everywhere and they face restrictions on access to private places and on the collection of many kinds of information, absent a warrant. But private agents, operating on private property and in contexts where persons appear voluntarily, are granted wide authority to carry out searches, to keep people under surveillance, and to collect and distribute extensive personal information. Citizens agree to cooperate as a condition for entering or staying on the property, or obtaining some desired benefit. Private police may also offer specialized skills and sophisticated equipment that local police departments lack (such as the ability to investigate computer crime or industrial espionage and advanced surveillance devices).

Private police vastly extend surveillance and reduce demands on public police. In addition, as the empirical examples considered earlier suggest, they may offer public police a way to get things done that the former are prohibited from doing.

There are two versions of this "dirty work" argument.[14] The first assumes that the actions in question are *illegal* no matter who does them. But it is less risky to have them done by private police. If discovered, public agents can simply deny that they requested the behavior. The second version of the argument is that private police can *legally* do things that pubic police cannot. This is a result of the historic development of American liberties (such as the Fourth And Fifth Amendments) which, as far as criminal justice went, protected citizens from government but not from each other. Private police, if not deputized, are constitutionaly treated as citizens.

For obvious reasons it is difficult to find evidence for the first version of this perspective (private police are used by public police to take actions that are illegal no matter who does them). We are dealing after all with specialists in the covert arts. Such evidence must come from accidents (as with the Watergate plumbers), court testimony, or first-person accounts.

Although it is hard to know if my sample is representative, most of the nonpolitical cases I have encountered do not involve anything as sinister as what has been described. What seems to be most often at stake in the public use of private police is either propriety, some strategic (but legal) advantage, or the addition of specialized skills or extra resources.

Thus a police sergeant observes, "a private investigator is able to do things the police can't do legally."[15] An organization such as the LEIU also seems to fit here (although it is merely an adjunct and does not have direct operational responsibility). The Constitution does not offer protection against unreasonable search and seizures by private persons (although persons engaging in such behavior may face civil liability or criminal charges). A department store detective (although generally having no right to conduct a search) can ask shoplifting suspects to come into an office and answer questions without advising them that they have the right to an attorney, to remain silent, or that what they say may be used against them.[16] There is no constitutional protection against self-incrimination in such cases. If a private person acting on his or her own suggests a crime to an otherwise nonpredisposed person and the crime is committed, there is no defense of entrapment. If this private person enters the house of an acquaintance and searches through drawers to find incriminating evidence, the exclusionary rule prohibiting it from being introduced as evidence in court does not apply. Unlike the case for public police, the results of an improper search by a private party *are* admissable.[17]

Yet this must be qualified. If the person engages in such behavior at the behest of police, then the same standards that apply to police are relevant. The key factor is the relation of the two prior to the behavior in question. Those to whom police delegate tasks are viewed as their agents, and are subject to the same legal standards.[18] Just what constitutes "agency" is open to interpretation. The courts do not always find agency where one might think they should. There are no doubt sometimes understandings between public and private police such that what is intended is well understood by both parties without an explicit verbal delegation.

It is ironic that the Bill of Rights and related protections emphasize restricting the behavior of government agents rather than also those operating on behalf of private interests. At the time it was written the major threat to liberty was perceived to be the state. The development and mass marketing of surveillance techniques that can be used by individuals, and the rise of powerful private organizations such as national and multinational corporations was hardly envisioned. There is need to broaden constitutional protections to take account of these new facts.[19] It is poor policy to permit citizens and private organizations to harm each other in ways that government may not.

Other private components of the criminal justice system such as process servers and bail bondsmen on occasion also serve equivalent functions. Pike (1980) suggests that bail bondsmen become unofficial court officers controlling traffic in the courtroom, doing errands and favors and acting as agents of social control. The power of the bondsman to bring to court those who have left the state is a good example:

> The bondsmen is largely immune from judicial control; his power over an accused may exceed the power of the state. . . . the bondsman may seize the accused in a foreign jurisdiction without the slightest compliance with extradition requirements in the foreign jurisdiction [*Yale Law Journal,* 1964].

Private police, like bail bondsmen, are removed from many of the ethical, organizational, and legal constraints that bind criminal justice system officials. Yet although they are outside of the system they are also a part of it. This marginal structural position, for better or worse, may help the system meet at least some of its goals and enhance its legitimacy.

To the extent that the functional alternative explanation helps explain the increased prominence of private policing and its connection to public police, we learn something about the complexities of reform. It is ironic that a factor in the recent growth of private policing may be efforts to limit the power of state police. The legal environment in which police work has changed in recent decades. Supreme Court interpretations, federal and state Legislation, and the internal policies of enforcement agencies have on balance restricted the conditions under which public police can gather and exchange information.

These changes may have come at a cost of increased reliance on private police. A hydraulic principle may be at work: Restrict the police's use of coercion and their use of deception increases via undercover investigations. Restrict police investigation after a crime occurs, and increased attention will be paid to anticipating crimes by the categorical collection of information. Restrict the conditions under which the police can carry out searches and seizures and undercover activities, coercive interrogation after arrest, or collect data on those who are not specific suspects, and police may make increased use of private detectives and informants who are less accountable and not as subject to such limitations. New private/public organizational forms will appear. This is certainly not an argument against reform. But it does suggest the need to be aware of displacement affects and to ask what the impact of a proposed change for public police will be on private police.[20]

There are also, of course, countering forces of a more intended variety, which operate to push enforcement from the private to the public sector. The history of policing can partly be read as the struggle over which private concerns will be made into public concerns. Some of the blurring and interdependence noted here is transitional and involves the process of redefining a private contract or wrong into a criminal matter within the province of public agents. In the case of insurance fraud, for example, what began as almost entirely a private or civil matter has now been criminalized. Through educational and lobbying efforts and financial contributions, the insurance industry is in the process of creating much stronger public enforcement support for what previously usually was tolerated as a cost of business or was handled privately. There are historical parallels in other areas to the insurance fraud units now being created in many states.[21]

Some of the activities of private police noted here are consistent with the basic ideas of the Anglo-American police system. This system values self-protection and citizen participation in law enforcement and police who are mobilized in response to complaints and evidence offered by citizens. But I think something more than this is involved.

There is need for new concepts to describe the cooperative investigations I have discussed and the hybrid organizational forms such as the Law Enforcement Intelligence Unit, the National Automobile Theft Bureau, and the Wackenhut organization's involvement in the War on Crime Program in Florida (where agents controlled by a private corporation and paid by private interests act on behalf of the state and carry out official functions).

In the past, in an organizationally simpler time, it was easier to talk of private as against public police. But today there seems to be an increasing number of cases where the distinction is difficult to draw, if seen in either/or terms. Rather than simply asking whether police are public or private, we might first ask a series of questions: (1) Where does the policing occur—in public, private, or mixed space? (2) Whose interest is served by the policing—the general public, a private interest, or both? (3) What is the function of the policing? (4) Who pays for, or sponsors, the policing—public or private interests, or both? (5) Who carries it out—regular sworn agents of the state with full police powers, special purpose deputies with more limited powers, or citizens with no official powers? (6) Who controls and directs the policing? (7) Where the policing involves data collection and investigation, who has access to the results?[22] (8) What popular and self-definitions characterizes those doing the policing? (9) What organizational form does the policing take? (10) To what extent are social control agents linked together in informal networks that transcend their nominal definition as public or private?

Of course, empirically determining answers to these questions may be difficult and observers may well disagree (for example, when is the public as against a private interest served?)[23] But using such distinctions in thinking about policing will take us farther than the simple public-private distinction of most popular and academic discourse. An elaborate multidimensional matrix could be constructed from answers to such questions. The number of empirical configurations probably almost matches the number of logical possibilities. The pattern today is certainly more varied than it was in 1860 or even 1960.

There is obviously no simple answer as to why this should be the case. As suggested previously some of it simply reflects Anglo-American law enforcement traditions. But in summary let us note that beyond this, it partly reflects

(1) the increased organizational complexity and interdependence found throughout contemporary society,
(2) the crisis or overextension of the welfare state, which is leading to the privatization of a number of government functions,
(3) legislation facilitating and even mandating public-private cooperation,[24]
(4) the appearance of new enforcement needs requiring joint or more cooperative ventures (such as highly specialized white-collar crimes, greater emphasis given to the enforcment of laws regarding civil violatons, and increased emphasis on

the maintenance of order in quasi-public places such as shopping malls),[25]

(5) a degree of convergence in functions (for example, private
police are becoming more prosecution-oriented and public
police are giving greater formal recognition to the use of discretion and to nonlaw enforcement activities),

(6) an unintended consequence of efforts to reform public police
and hold them to higher standards of accountability and
legality, and

(7) the emergence of a common police culture that transcends
the public/private distinction.

As blurring and convergence continue, in the future it may be
more difficult to speak of either the privatization of control, (Spitzer and Scull, 1977) or the expansion of the Leviathan state (Marx,
1986). What we are seeing is something in between. This may be
but one aspect of a more general blurring of the line between the
public and the private that can be seen in other areas such as space
(as with shopping malls), property (records of credit card or
telephone transactions held by third parties), corrections (state-
subsidized and state-regulated but profit-making half-way houses,
diversion programs, and even prisons), courts (neighborhood justice and mediation centers), and economic enterprise (for instance,
public corporations and joint public-private development efforts).

The growth of private policing and its increased interdependence
with public police, along with the increased use of undercover
tactics and ever more sophisticated and penetrating surveillance
techniques, means increased intrusion into private places and relationships. This has implications for the line between the public and
the private and for liberty. In a society concerned about the level of
crime and disorder these changes may be welcomed. Yet they are
not without costs and risks. They not only raise traditional concerns over encroachment upon liberty by the state and by the private sector (a more neglected topic), but the new issue of concern
over joint assaults. There is a danger that instead of serving to
check each other, public and private police may collude in ways
that are detrimental to the public good. Or the private may become
ever more powerful at the expense of the public.

Students of social control have generally ignored the role played
by private police. Fortunately, as this volume indicates, this appears
to be changing. Yet as this changes, it is important to look not only
at the distinctive roles played by private and public police, but at
the ways in which they may be intertwined.

The consequences of this blurring for law enforcement are mixed. In many societies an unclear line between the public and the private is associated with a weak and/or corrupt state. This is not the case in the contemporary United States. There are some obvious advantages of public-private cooperation. As Tom Sawyer knew, that the fence gets painted can be more important than who actually paints it. Such cooperation need not mean a new age of robber barons who run the state as a private preserve, nor need it mean a totalitarian society where the private sector is dominated by the state. Yet the need for research on these developments and for vigilance is clear.

NOTES

1. See G. T. Marx (forthcoming). This study focused on public police. But in the course of interviews and the analysis of documents, some information on private police was also gathered.

2. The secrets were not, of course, stolen, but were willingly supplied by IBM. This shows some parallel to selling sugar as heroin and to the "bait-sale" where supposedly "stolen" goods are offered for sale.

Indicative of the complexity of social control is that as one branch of the Justice Department was actively cooperating with IBM in action to protect its business interests, another was seeking to prosecute it for antitrust violations.

3. Such "enforcement entrepreneurs" who induce or facilitate others to break rules can be contrasted with "moral entrepreneurs" (Becker, 1963) who play a role in having certain behavior initially defined as illegal.

A private role here is, of course, not without risks. U.S. Attorney Rudolph Guiliani in Manhattan turned down the chance to get involved in this case and questions such operations: "how far do we want to go in using people to fool other people into committing crimes? You shouldn't use Mel Weinberg to try to catch someone who's engaged in minor or marginal criminality" (*60 Minutes,* Oct. 21, 1984).

4. T. Frankel (1969) describes this. Whatever its apparently modest impact on crime in Florida, the program appears to have been good for Wackenhut. The company president reported to shareholders in 1967 that the Governor's War On Crime "has drawn both national and international attention to the Wackenhut Corporation . . . [T]he Wackenhut name is now known from coast to coast." He goes on to report that dollar volume of private investigative work increased 63% during the first quarter, and when the War on Crime investiations are included the increase goes to 208%. The Quote is from an address by George Wackenhut, as cited in Frankel (1969: 655). At the local level, Wackenhut has provided full public safety services to several Florida communities.

5. This last is the most commonly used form of private sector undercover means. A frequent usage is to warn employees that they may be tested and subjected to covert quality control inspections. Thus, employees of firms serviced by one of the largest national agencies are given a form entitled "Responsibilities of

Sales Personnel," which states: "SYSTEMATIC CHECKINGS are made of every employee; you never know what day or hour you are being checked." The goal of such actions is prevention and intelligence—rarely arrest. A specialist in retail security reports that the use of undercover means is "not just for trouble. Undercover employees point out the good people, too." A presumed example of a "bad person" can be seen in the following:

> On Sept. 25, I was fired from my job as a cashier. . . . the management takes it upon itself to test its employees for their "honesty". . . . I was at my register when a man rushed up with a package of underwear costing $4.19. I was waiting on another customer when he handed me the price tag and a $5 bill. He said, "Keep the change" and then rushed for the exit. I tried to stop him and give him his change and receipt, but he paid no attention. Once back at my register, I rang up the sale, but kept the change. I was then told to go on a break. Upon returning, I discovered that my register was closed and a security guard was waiting for me. I was summoned before the head security agent and the store manager, who demanded the return of the 81 cents. The store manager told me I no longer had a job [Letter to the editor, *Providence Journal*, January 2, 1981].

Signs prominently displayed in FTD flower shops, meant to reassure customers and motivate shop keepers, proudly announce that quality and fair pricing are maintained by the use of secret shoppers. "Spy riders" who take flights to grade airline employees are another example.

6. As cited in O'Toole (1978: 133):

> The activities of Jay Paul, a detective assigned to the Los Angeles Police Department's Public Disorders Intelligence Division has some similiar elements. Stymied by a tight budget, PDID officials turned to Paul for help in obtaining funding for a computer. He went to Larry McDonald, a former chairman of the John Birch Society. The latter, in founding the Western Goals Foundation in 1979 wanted to computerize data on leftists. In exchange for a $100,000 computer installed in his wife's law office, Paul would develop an intelligence data base for both the private foundation and the police department. Later when senior police department officials requested that certain intelligence materials be destroyed, rather than complying Paul kept them in his garage and apparently passed them to private sources. Partly as a result of Paul's discrediting activities the intelligence unit has been restructured and renamed [*Los Angeles Times*, April 30, 1984].

7. See Reichman's article in this issue and Ghezzi (1983).

8. There are laws against the reverse—private persons and organizations formally posing as public police. However, private police often attempt to create the impression that they are public agents through their vehicles, uniforms, badges, and ambiguous business names such as "Community Protection Service Bureau," "Statewide Security," and "North Shore Protective Patrol Detectives," and through using titles such as "special investigator" and "special agent." Some states prohibit them from carrying badges or calling themselves detectives.

9. As the phenomena of moonlighting suggests, this circulation may also be temporal. During off-duty hours public police may serve as private police (in 1984 an estimated 150,000 were doing so). In many big city departments such

employment is a jealously protected perquisite. Some departments in effect run private businesses out of headquarters. While operating on behalf of private interests they have all the powers of sworn agents and may even drive official patrol cars. It would be useful to examine trend data to see if this has increased in recent decades. I would hypothesize that it has and also that the deputization, or otherwise formal granting of powers to private police, has also increased.

10. See, for example, Hougan (1978), O'Toole (1978), and Shearing and Stenning (1983)

11. This hardly exhausts the possibilities, particularly those of a subrosa nature.

12. Realization of this has led to calls for the closer integration of the types of control. See, for example, Cunningham and Taylor (1984).

13. For example, from the perspective of public police this may involve their greater focus on arrest and prosecution, authority conflicts, competition over off-duty jobs, the belief that private police are more concerned with serving their clients than with seeing justice done, and concern that the image of public police is damaged when less well-trained, chosen, and supervised private police act in a heavy-handed manner.

14. See Hughes (1962).

15. Similar exchanges go on between public police agencies having jurisdiction over different matters and with different powers. For example, local police may draw upon the power of alcohol beverage control officers to search places where liquor is sold without a warrant and agents often have an interest in learning what is on income tax files they have no legal right to see.

16. For example, a Supreme Court ruling in 1984 (*United States v. Jacobsen*) saw nothing unconstitutional in Federal Express employees opening a package they were to deliver. The Court held that once the package was opened and cocaine was in "plain view," police could seize it without a search warrant.

17. A more extreme example involving the admissability of a forced confession can be seen in a Boston case. Damaging statements made by a murder suspect to vigilantes who kidnapped him were allowed into evidence at the trial, where he was found guilty of murder. The suspect had previously been questioned by police, but released for lack of evidence. No body had been found. A year after the murder he was abducted. Through their own means his abductor's elicited a confession and the suspect led them to the body (*Boston Globe,* December 16, 1975).

18. See *U.S. v. Henry* (1980).

19. An example of this broadening is Title II of the 1968 Omnibus Crime Bill, which bans the use of electronic surveillance by private parties.

20. For example, the recent Supreme Court decision restricting certain police searches in schools is likely to mean that teachers will do some of the things police did before.

21. Thus, at first railroads and other forms of transportation were privately policed. But laws were eventually passed creating special public transit authorities. In the 1920s the enforcement of laws regulating dogs was often legislatively delegated to societies for the prevention of cruelty to animals. This was gradually taken over by public police. Whether something is seen as a public or private responsibility (or neither) can be dynamic. Responsibilities can also be taken away without concomitant delegation to some other policing unit. Thus, the National Labor Relations Act of 1935 severely curtailed the activities of both pri-

vate and public police in labor disputes. The Supreme Court's decision on abortions and the repeal of Prohibition also eliminated police responsibilities.

22. Brodeur (1983) argues that the legal distinction between what is public and private with respect to data has become obsolete as part of the expansion of a more absorbent style of "high" policing. As police data gathering becomes more intensive and extensive, the interstitial area between what is neither public nor private expands.

23. Becker (1974) notes limitations on using single criteria such as sponsorship or function as the basis for distinguishing public from private police.

24. These include reporting requirements and immunity protections for exchanging information noted earlier. Some states such as Massachusetts also offer immunity from civil or criminal liability should an insurance company seek to prosecute a case. In addition, federal legislation sets security standards that must be met by an increasing number of private groups (defense contractors, airports, nuclear power facilities, health-care institutions keeping controlled substances, banks). The Bank Protection Act, for example, mandates security measures involving vaults, alarms, cameras, guards, and employee screening. The Department of Energy and the Nuclear Regulatory Commission mandate standards for facilities where nuclear materials are used. This includes standards for security personnel and their coordination with public police, as well alarms, surveillance systems, reporting requirements, and inspections (Post, 1983).

25. Shearing and Stenning (1983) note that an increased proportion of public life takes place on property that is privately owned and likely to be privately policed. The protection of private property has thus increasingly come to involve maintaining public order.

REFERENCES

BECKER, H. (1963) Outsiders. Glencoe, 11: Free Press.

BECKER, T. (1974) "The place of private police in society: an area of research for the social sciences." Social Problems 21, 3.

BRODEUR, J. P. (1983) "High policing and low policing: remarks about the policing of political activities." Social Problems 30, 5.

CUNNINGHAM, W. and T. TAYLOR (1984) Crime and Protection in America: A Study of Private Security and Law Enforcement Resources and Relationships. Washington DC: National Institute of Justice.

FRANKEL, T. (1969) "The governor's private eyes." Boston Univ. Law Rev. 627: 627-657.

GHEZZI, S. (1983) "A private network of social control: insurance investigation units." Social Problems 30, 5: 521-531.

HOUGAN, J. (1978) Spooks: The Haunting of America: The Private Use of Secret Agents. New York: Bantam.

HUGHES, E. (1962) "Good people and dirty work." Social Problems 10, 1: 3-10.

International Association of Chiefs of Police Newsletter (1982) August.

Insurance Crime Prevention Institute Reports (1981) January.

MARX, G. T. (forthcoming) Undercover Police Work: The Paradoxes and Problems of a Necessary Evil. Twentieth Century Fund.

———(1986) "The iron fist in the velvet glove: totalitarian potentials within democratic structures," in J. Short (ed.) *The Social Fabric*. Beverly Hills, CA: Sage.

O'TOOLE, G. (1978) *The Private Sector: Rent-a-Cops, Private Spies and the Police Industrial Complex*. New York: W.W. Norton.

PIKE, D. (1980) "Bail bondsmen: unofficial court officers." Unpublished manuscript, Yale University, New Haven, CT.

POST, R. (1983) "Security, industrial," in Encyclopedia of Crime and Justice. New York: Free Press.

REICHMAN, N. (1983) "Ferreting out fraud: the manufacture and control of fraudulent insurance claims." Doctoral dissertation, M.I.T., Cambridge, MA.

REISS, A. and D. BORDUA (1967) "Environment and organization: a perspective on the police," in D. Bordua (ed.) The Police: Six Sociological Essays. New York: John Wiley.

SHEARING, C. and P. STENNING (1983) "Private security: implications for social control." *Social Problems* 10, 1: 493-506.

SPITZER, S. and A. SCULL (1977) "Privatization and capitalist development: the case of private police." *Social Problems* 25, 1: 18-29.

THOMPSON, M. (1986) "Who's minding the store?" *Student Lawyer* 14, 6: 24-29.

United States v. Jacobsen (1984) 104 S. Ct. 1652.

United States v. Henry (1980) 447 U.S. 264.

Yale Law Journal (1964) "Bailbondsmen and the fugitive accused—the need for formal removal procedures. 73; 1100.

Chapter 8

POLICING TRUST

SUSAN P. SHAPIRO

Crises and disasters have always held a special fascination for social scientists, at least in part, because they expose the fundamental assumptions, institutional arrangements, social linkages, and cleavages that are normally implicit in the social order. A truly dazzling and rather remarkable crisis interrupted the preparation of this chapter on the policing of impersonal trust. The chapter was to (1) provide an abstract overview of trust relationships, (2) examine the ways in which their social organization impedes traditional policing while opening opportunities for other kinds of penetration and normative constraint, and (3) inventory the repertoire of strategies mobilized in the social control of trust.

The palpable lessons of crisis insinuated themselves into this theoretical agenda. Not only did they breathe life into abstract categories, they also offered more dynamic variations on the original themes. These concerned, for example, the evolution of trust relationships, the interplay of competing social control strategies, the conflict between public and private policing, the symbolic role of social control arrangements in shoring up the appearance of trust, and the ramifications when trustees themselves have trust relationships and when trust policing organizations are also trustees.

These provocative lessons pose analytic problems, of course, both the matter of the generalizability of a case study (exacerbated by the fact that this crisis touched a rather distinctive set of trust institutions) and the risk of deviant case analysis. Crisis represents the failure of social control and therefore exposes the infrastructure of trust and policing organizations that may bear little similarity to those that escape notice because they function so smoothly. As an evocative device to question theoretical assumptions, generate new

AUTHOR'S NOTE: I am grateful to Beth Stevens and Clifford Shearing for their helpful comments and to the Russell Sage Foundation for its support.

hypotheses, and redirect empirical inquiry, analyses of crisis pose little danger, however.

This chapter offers a duet between the abstract sociological agenda and the palpable events of crisis. The urgent voice of crisis opens the composition.

CHRONOLOGY OF A CRISIS

Dutch and German immigrants began settling in the Cincinnati area 150 years ago. Between 1860 and 1900, immigrant families formed local building associations (*bauvereine*) into which they contributed their weekly savings. Members would draw lots or bid interest rates to determine who would borrow from the association. These cooperatives were organized as men's social clubs, housed in bars, saloons, cafes, barber shops, grocery stores, or bowling alleys. Members would meet once a week for several hours, make their deposits or mortgage payments, open the mail, process transactions, pass around a cigar box to raise extra capital, play cards, and have a few beers (Sloane, 1985; Eckberg, 1985; Wallace et al., 1985; Stricharchuk and Bussey, 1985).

Because the associations served tightly-knit ethnic communities, they experienced few problems of recruiting members or of ensuring that borrowers met their financial obligations. As one bank director observed, "You were expected to show up with your $5 mortgage payment. If you didn't, people wanted to know why" (Eckberg, 1985: 4). During the years of the Great Depression, Ohio had 334 bank failures; Cincinnati, with hundreds of these ethnically based neighborhood savings institutions, had only one. In the years that followed, the *bauvereine* avoided government regulation and eschewed federal deposit insurance, most contributing to a private insurance fund, a few forgoing insurance protection altogether.

The immigrants' conservatism, distrust of formal organizations, and opposition to government interference, expressed in these autonomous community banking institutions, were passed along in the financial organizations that served their children, grandchildren, and great-grandchildren. Even in the 1980s, one could find savings and loans that operated a few hours a week out of a single room, whose depositors, on a first-name basis with bank tellers, would leave their passbooks at the teller's window just as they stored their drinking mugs with the neighborhood bartender—a custom that apparently exasperated bank examiners because of the potential for fraud (Stricharchuk and Bussey, 1985; Amatos and Gates, 1985). A banking official explained, "They [the banks] had people who trusted them" (Sloane, 1985).

These quaint Cincinnati banks would seem the most unlikely candidates to be drawn into an international financial crisis that threatened millions of individuals, tens of billions of dollars, and the solvency of dozens of firms. But, in the spring of 1985, Ohio savings and loan institutions were swept into the eye of a tornado that whipped through seemingly unrelated financial institutions—from securities to banking to insurance to the dollar to commodities futures, and then back to securities and banking—causing exponentially increasing damage in its path. The following chronology traces its course.[1]

1977-1985: The managing partner of a major national accounting firm, charged with accepting $125,000 in bribes, provides unqualified opinions regarding the financial soundness of ESM Government Securities, Inc., a little-known Fort Lauderdale securities dealer. In fact, hundreds of millions of dollars in losses (of which the accountant was allegedly aware) were fraudulently concealed in the books of this insolvent firm. On the basis of the CPA reports, savings and loans and municipalities across the country did business with the firm, lending money or securities in relatively complex two-step cash-and-securities transactions, known as "repurchase" and "reverse repurchase agreements."[2] Because many of these lenders did not take delivery of the collateral involved in their deals, ESM was able to pledge the same collateral to several different lenders.[3]

March 4, 1985: A court orders ESM into receivership amid allegations of self-dealing, misappropriation, and fraud. The court-appointed receiver later estimates that some 13 local governments and 5 thrift institutions face losses totaling $315 million.

March 7,8: Worried depositors withdraw $90 million from the Cincinnati-based Home State Savings Bank, which will likely incur huge losses from its transactions with ESM.

March 9: Home State closes. Banking officials say its losses may exceed $150 million. The losses threaten the reserves of the state's privately financed deposit insurance fund (the Ohio Deposit Guarantee Fund, with assets of $136 million). The fund covers 71 other savings and loan associations (none of which had dealings with ESM). Together, these thrift institutions hold between $4 and $5 billion in savings of more than half a million "ordinary citizens."

March 13: A new $90 million fund—that cannot be touched by Home State—is authorized by Ohio legislators to shore up insurance protection for the other savings and loans covered by the Ohio Deposit Guarantee Fund. The move prompts considerable news coverage about the weakness of the private insurance fund.

March 14: Some of the 71 thrift units across the state face a flood of withdrawals, totaling $115 million in just the three previous days. In a classic run on the banks, depositors line up overnight (huddled in lawn chairs and armed with thermos bottles, kerosene heaters, sleeping bags, and portable television sets) to withdraw their funds the next morning. State banking officials hold an evening press conference to urge calm.

March 15: The Ohio governor orders the 71 thrift units closed for at least three days (the first bank holiday since the Great Depression). These actions send tremors through national and international financial markets. Reacting to fears about the stability of the banking system, investors worldwide make a "flight to quality," switching from bank certificates of deposit to the safety of short-term Treasury bills (driving up rates of the former, while those of the latter plummet). Meanwhile, an Ohio newspaper prints a front-page photograph of a local couple praying at their kitchen table and other papers detail the hardships of local depositors without funds for food, mortgage payments, college tuition, and so on.

March 19: Gold soars almost $36/ounce—a record percentage gain—and the dollar plunges dramatically against foreign currencies. International markets react with nervousness to the Ohio situation and the prospect that, because of the banking crisis, dollar investments would become less desirable as the Federal Reserve responds to the credit needs of the faltering banks.[4]

March 20: Critics actively begin to question the efficacy and integrity of Ohio banking regulation as well as the self-regulation exercised by the members of the private insurance fund. Public and private regulators apparently knew for some time that Home State had too many of its eggs in the ESM basket, but were largely unable to induce the bank to close out its position with the firm. Criticism of state regulation is fueled by the fact that the owner of Home State Savings Bank (who also had ties with ESM) was a large contributor to the Democratic Party with close connections to the Ohio governor.

March 21: For only the second time in the 51-year history of the Commodities Exchange of New York, a member firm collapses after it fails to meet $26 million in margin calls for customers in gold options. The firm was selling these options short and could not meet its obligations when the price of gold suddenly soared two days earlier amidst international fears regarding the Ohio banking crisis. [Two of the traders involved are seen with a suitcase full of securities trying (unsuccessfully) to leave the country.] Meanwhile, a prominent Republican Cincinnati lawyer is named special prosecutor to investigate the Home State Savings Bank failure and the role of state government in the collapse.

April 7: A New Jersey government securities firm (Bevill, Bresler, & Schulman—BBS) collapses, with estimated losses of over $240 million. In the wake of the ESM bankruptcy, clients of the New Jersey firm (mostly savings and loans, small banks, and municipalities) demand delivery of collateral—supposedly held in safekeeping by several transfer agents—for their loans to the firm. Their demands far exceed the amount of collateral actually being held. The amounts that some of the thrift institutions are owed are nearly as large or larger than their net worth, therefore threatening the viability of these institutions.

April 10: Amid rumors of new banking problems following the failure of the New Jersey securities firm, the dollar declines once again and prices of most major foreign currency futures rise sharply in international trading.

April 12: Two small securities firms, one in Chicago and another in Little Rock, close after sustaining losses in repurchase agreements directly or indirectly involving the New Jersey government securities firm that collapsed earlier in the week. The president of the Arkansas firm laments, "It's the darndest thing I've ever seen. It's like standing on a street corner and being hit by a stray bullet" (Kristoff, 1985a). More savings and loans and small banks doing business with these newly bankrupt securities firms stand to lose millions.

May 9-14: The *Baltimore Sun* publishes a front-page article enumerating management problems and possible irregularities at Maryland's second largest privately insured thrift institution. By the end of the day, 500-600 depositors have withdrawn funds from a suburban Baltimore branch; the next day, the run spreads to other branches; the third day, a second bank experiences heavy withdrawals of depositor funds. Within days, the run spreads to other privately insured Maryland savings and loans, with total withdrawals exceeding $600 million. Maryland's attorney general assesses the effect of the run on Ohio thrift institutions and the growing crisis of confidence in private insurance on his own state's banking problems: "the seismograph began to shake after Ohio"; the "Ohio experience clearly was a psychological jolt" (*McNeil/ Lehrer NewsHour,* transcript 1985: 7).[5]

In the short period of two months, American financial institutions experienced runs in the billions of dollars on bank deposits and CD investments, certain government securities transactions, and the dollar. A few of the runs, like those on Home State Savings Bank and several of the Maryland thrift institutions, reflected a crisis of confidence in a specific firm, sparked by tangible evidence of abuse or of incipient financial demise. These crises exposed much more than the unsoundness of particular organizations, however. They also dramatized the vulnerability of the institutional protections— insurance, collateral, government, and self-regulation—structured to ameliorate the risks of first-order trust relationships like securities and banking. The crises of confidence that drove thousands of individual and institutional depositors and investors to bail out of the other financial institutions pertained, not to the soundness of the institutions themselves, but rather to that of these second-order institutional protections. Most of the Ohio and Maryland savings bank depositors who queued up to close out their accounts and most of the municipalities and thrift institutions that tried to bail out of their repurchase agreements with the New Jersey securities firm responded to concern about the efficacy of deposit insurance, collateral, and regulation. When fears move from the particular to the universal—from unsound organizations to all organizations shored up by suspect institutional protections or systems of social control—the spread and velocity of a run can be considerable and the ability to contain crises of confidence rather limited. Indeed, these crises can become self-fulfilling prophesies.

AGENCY RELATIONSHIPS AND TRUST

The financial debacle precipitated by the ESM bankruptcy fraud and subsequent Ohio banking panic provides a metaphor for a more abstract set of social relationships whose evolution and impact are less easily identified or measured. These are "agency" relationships, in which individuals or organizations act on behalf of another.[6] The agents touched by the ripples of the crisis—bankers, insurance officials, securities and commodities traders, government and private regulators, and politicians—mostly process, invest, or protect other people's money. Other agents care for people's children or elderly relatives; repair, maintain, or provide custody for their property; type their manuscripts; gather, disseminate, and evaluate data, research findings, or news reports; heal their broken hearts or transplant or bypass their ailing hearts; fight their wars; police their streets and corporate suites; inspect their elevators, nuclear power plants, and nursing homes; and design and build their roads and their ballistic missiles. Although their job descriptions obviously vary considerably, they do share common elements. Like the financial intermediaries, these agents supply labor and expertise, exercise discretion, provide access to information beyond reach, mediate and broker relationships or transactions, and offer economies of scale and protection from risk by collectivizing and representing the interests of discrete actors (Shapiro, 1985; Mitnick, 1984).

Agency relationships are structurally precarious and vulnerable to abuse where agents have custody of property they do not own, discretion over the allocation of opportunity, and the ability to create and disseminate information that recipients cannot verify because they lack access or expertise. Moreover, agent roles present inherent temptations; one never knows whether agents will opt to act in the best interest of their beneficiaries (or "principals" in legal jargon) or exploit the power, access, and riches they hold in trust for their own benefit.

The early generations of Cincinnati immigrants coped easily with the potential vulnerabilities of their agency relationships. They coparticipated with agents, sharing or rotating among their male neighbors the tasks of bank teller, bookkeeper, or loan officer, often conducting bank business during social encounters in full view of all interested parties. Moreover, agency roles—from bank directors to the tradesmen chosen to construct building association homes—were filled from the membership of immediate social and ethnic networks. Agents were therefore selected for their reputations of integrity or competence. Their responsibilities and obligations were clearly specified by those for whom they acted. Their performance was readily subject to surveillance and evaluation and their misdeeds vulnerable to a potent array of informal sanctions that flowed from their ongoing ties with principals (Burns, 1977; Macaulay, 1963; Velez-Ibanez, 1983; Galanter, 1974: 124-35; Schwartz, 1954; Black, 1976). In short, Dutch and German settlers "personalized" agency relationships.

This personalized model of social control assumes that candidates for agency positions are recruited from the ranks of familiar social networks, that agent performance is accessible to principal scrutiny, and that ongoing relationships between principals and agents provide the mechanisms to deter and, if necessary, sanction unacceptable agent performance. These assumptions hardly apply to many agency relationships in complex societies where agents, in order to carry out their responsibilities, must be recruited from and located at some distance from their principals, individual agents are increasingly replaced by diffuse organizations with shifting composition and boundaries, agents offer esoteric skills and specialized expertise inaccessible to principal evaluation, principals have neither ongoing relationships with their agents nor particularly multiplex ones, and the balance of power in agency relationships tips toward the agents.[7]

The tentacles of informal social control therefore rarely reach these impersonal agents, these multinational banking corporations, union pension funds, international wire services, health maintenance organizations, insurance/baby food conglomerates, "Big Eight" accounting firms, census bureau data gatherers, department store legal clinic franchises, and Wall Street brokerage firms. Nor do contractual or pseudocontractual arrangements constrain impersonal agents, where principals lack not only the expertise and access to stipulate agent performance and then to monitor and evaluate it, but also the resources and power to induce their agents to enter into and then abide by contractual agreements in the first place (Shapiro, 1985; Galanter, 1974).

Unable to exploit personalized social control or to fashion or enforce substantive norms or contractual agreements to constrain these agents, we hold them instead to the norms of trust (Shapiro, 1985). These procedural norms respond to the generic opportunities for abuse embedded in the structure of agency relationships. Given agents' custody of and discretion over property and opportunity, we demand disinterestedness (that agents place the interests of those for whom they act over their own) and fiduciary behavior. Given their special access to information, we prescribe full and honest disclosure. And given their expertise, we require role competence (Shapiro, 1985; Barber, 1983; Stinchcombe, 1986; Mitnick, 1975). Moreover, we assemble an array of formal social control systems to ensure trustworthy behavior or to inspire confidence in the institution of trust.

POLICING TRUST

Ironically, the very conditions that impel principals to trust impersonal agents also pose the impediments to policing trust, to scrutinizing the activities of trustees and detecting and investigating their misdeeds (Shapiro, 1985). The social organization of trust creates unique social control problems for which traditional policing strategies are woefully inadequate.

There are few red flags when trust has been abused. Principals entrust agents to exercise discretion—to admit students to professional schools, disburse bank loans, make arrests, invest money, pay claims, allocate government largesse, give grants, and so on. The fact that trustees doled out all the money, positions, or contracts, filled the court docket, processed all applications—or, indeed, failed to do so—provides no indicator of whether agents abided by the norms of trust in their exercise of discretion. The output of discretionary activities betrays neither disinterestedness nor the possibility that self-dealing, bribery, or corruption influenced the process.

Moreover, principals often entrust agents to administer a process with contingent or uncertain outcomes (Deutsch, 1962: 303-304). Whether the outcomes are ultimately positive or negative—the value of securities goes up or down, the surgery is successful or the patient dies, the child prodigy is or is not admitted to Juilliard—is therefore only partly affected by the trustworthiness of these agents. Indeed, when the market is strong, the patient fundamentally healthy, and the offspring exceptionally talented, incompetent, corrupt, of self-interested trustees may undeservedly preside over positive outcomes, whereas their more trustworthy counterparts take the blame for loss, death, or shattered dreams when conditions are adverse. Disappointing outcomes of agency relationships cannot be construed as an indicator of abuse any more than can pleasant contingencies be taken as a sign of trustworthiness.

Furthermore, the organization of trust rarely yields conclusive signs of its abuse because few trustee misdeeds are "situationally specific." Jack Katz has observed that, unlike most street crime, crime in the suites "integrates acts widely dispersed over time and place . . . built up over a series of concrete events, each of which . . . would appear to be part of ordinary occupational routines" (1979b: 436). A single decision, conversation, memorandum, purchase, or sale rarely betrays the potential of illicit conduct as conclusively as does holding a gun to someone's head, picking a pocket, cracking a safe, or smashing and entering a window (see also Vaughan, 1983: 89-90). Because of the complex nature of most agency offerings, principals or other social control agents must analyze patterns of discrete situations or actions (often spanning years and considerable geographic and interpersonal distance) to even begin to suspect that compliance with the norms of trust is in question. Indeed, where discrete contributions to an illicit task are segregated and particularized, even individual coconspirators may be unaware of the larger misdeeds in which they participate, a fact with profound implications for both deterrence and whistle-blowing.

Penetrating abuses of trust is impeded further by the very nature of some agency relationships. Some trustees, like accountants, lawyers, journalists, or social scientists, act as a conduit, providing limited access to information protected by institutions of privacy, secrecy, or confidentiality. Lacking the privileged access of their agents, principals are unable to survey agent behavior and thereby assess the veracity of their disclosures. Other trustees provide expertise and specialized or esoteric skills to naive or unaccomplished principals who are therefore incapable of judicious scrutiny or evaluation of these agents.

And many trustees preside over "futures transactions"—insurance, investment, pensions, banking, credit, medical treatment—in which principals make an initial commitment in the expectation of or to protect themselves from a future outcome or return. Futures transactions therefore provide errant trustees an ample cushion of years and often decades in which to abuse their trust, recruit and exploit additional victims, cover up their misdeeds, hide or dissipate their profits, wait out the statute of limitations, and then disappear before principals expect any return on their commitment and thereby realize that their trust was misplaced.

For all these reasons, principals are likely to be unwitting victims of abuses of trust. One of the most timely and prolific sources of reactive intelligence and investigatory collaboration in traditional policing is therefore incapacitated in the control of trust. And many other traditional reactive and proactive policing techniques are subverted as well by the location of trust in private places; its subtle dissection and diffusion over time, space, situation, occupational routines, and roles; its complexity; and its contingent quality. Traditional social control strategies are at best too slow, awaiting the blatant failure of trustees to honor future commitments, and at worst forever blind to more subtle and complicated misdeeds.

In short, the social organization of trust tends to sabotage its control. Policing and sanctioning systems that attempt to respond to the unique organization of trust abuse are therefore supplemented by other social control arrangements that anticipate its sources, opportunities, and potential harm. These anticipatory strategies restrict entry to positions of trust, impose structural and normative constraints on the social organization of trust, and offer institutionalized "side bets" to cushion the impact of abuses of trust or of social control failures.

The impetus to undertake these social control measures comes from varied sources: the principals and potential victims of abuses of trust, the trustees themselves (who fear loss of business or reputation, litigation, disbarment or expulsion from positions of trust, or other sanctions), various trust "guarantors" who bear contingent risk or liability for abuses of trust (insurance companies, for example), and third parties such as government regulators, public interest groups, or private social control entrepreneurs. They variably seek to facilitate compliance with the trust norms, reduce the opportunities for abuse, deter potential violations, discover and abort ongoing misdeeds in a timely fashion, punish offenders, and provide protection or compensation to victimized principals. And many strive to enhance perceptions of institutional trustworthiness. Because principals are so unable to identify the signs of their own victimization, they look to other indicators that their trust is well-founded. The perception of vigorous policing can, therefore, be as important as the fact of trustworthy agency in maintaining confidence.

Policing and Sanctioning

Despite the impediments to traditional policing, the social organization of trust is not immune from other forms of penetration or surveillance. Trust relationships are typically ongoing; unlike many other forms of victimization, their abuses constitute continuing violations that are vulnerable to inspection and provide repeated opportunities for discovery. These relationships are frequently consummated, processed, and transmitted in recorded transactions, certificates, policies, quotations, accounts, shares, and the like that can be audited, inspected, or cross-matched long after the illicit activities have ceased. Because trust violators often require telephone lines, mail services, public access computer networks, credit cards, advertising, public transportation, or stock market quotations to recruit victims or facilitate their misdeeds, these ancillary— often public—pieces of their violations are vulnerable to surveillance. Because the delivery of trust usually requires the collaboration of numerous individuals and diverse organizations, agency relationships are ripe for sting operations, in which one set of conspirators provides illicit opportunities to "entrap" potential coconspirators. Moreover, the resulting diffusion of potentially incriminating information in widely participated interorganizational abuse facilitates whistle-blowing and other disclosure of potentially incriminating information.

Policing organizations are variably located in the world of trust, with differential access to trustees and ability to penetrate and scrutinize their activities. Social control departments within trustee organizations themselves,[8] industry or professional self-regulatory groups,[9] private independent regulators paid by the trustees,[10] insurance companies, and government regulators share some degree of legitimate access to trust organizations. Other policing organizations that serve principals typically do not. The latter group includes private social control entrepreneurs for hire (such as testing or research organizations like Consumers' Union, private detectives, corporate or consumer credit reporting services, polygraph outfits, or contingency-fee attorneys), public interest groups, and various organizational forms that collectivize principals for purposes of social control (for example, performing rights associations like ASCAP and BMI or class action suits; Ackerman and Zhito, 1969; Galanter, 1974).

These organizations use surveillance, audits, inspections, reviews, examinations, undercover investigations, sting operations, and the mobilization of informants, victims, and other complainants to draw inferences—however inconclusive—about possible abuses of trust, to investigate these suspicions, and to deter would-be violators. Their arsenal of sanctions is considerable. More informal penalties include firings and demotions, censure, public disclosures or unfavorable publicity, and boycotts. More formal sanctions include suspension or revocation of licenses, membership in self-regulatory organizations or of entitlement to hold trustee roles; disbarment; fines; injunctions or other civil litigation; administrative proceedings; and criminal prosecution. In addition, policing organizations sometimes impose orders to rescind illicit transactions, disgorge profits, make restitution, undertake remedial action, or alter firm organization and governance.

Entry Restrictions

The practice of assigning agency roles to trusted members of the social networks of principals represents the cornerstone of personalized agency. Where principals must entrust strangers, formal selection procedures and entry restrictions to positions of trust simulate the informal practice. Through different mechanisms, systems of licensing, registration, prior clearance, reference, accreditation, certification, or credentialism serve to vouch for or verify the honesty, disinterestedness, competence, and general trustworthiness of potential agents—both individuals and organizations—and to exclude those unlikely to abide by the norms of trust. Because principals lack access and expertise as well as the familiarity and personal knowledge necessary to select their trustees, they often entrust a second tier of agents—some familiar and others themselves strangers—to be the gatekeepers to positions of trust.

The most direct legacy of personalized social control is expressed in procedures that identify trustworthiness by association, selecting candidates according to nominations, references, recommendations, vetoes, or blackballs solicited from trusted familiar judges. Other formal gatekeepers—peer reviewers, bar or other professional associations, accreditation committees, licensing agencies, credit reporting firms like Dun & Bradstreet,[11] resumé sleuths, the Educational Testing Service, and so forth—offer expertise, access, or resources for surveillance rather than personal knowledge of trustee candidates. Some perform background checks; others scrutinize trustee performance, administer examinations or auditions, conduct audits or surprise inspections, or collect, verify, and disseminate standardized information concerning these candidates.

Requirements of formal education, training, apprenticeship, or internship as prerequisites to positions of trust represent a different and, in some ways, more powerful strategy to restrict entry. In addition to assuring trustee competence, these requirements also create an opportunity for resocialization[12] and provide an extra filter to remove undesirable candidates through restrictive entry requirements to educational programs and by failing, expelling, or terminating admitted students subsequently deemed unacceptable.[13]

Structural and Normative Constraints

Social control strategies that implement restrictions on entry to positions of trust assume that trustworthy behavior (or at least the perception that trust norms will be complied with) is a matter of who is selected to fill these positions. But, in complex societies, agency roles performed by solo trustees are overshadowed by those undertaken by corporations, partnerships, group practices, associations, franchises, foundations, municipalities, legislatures, and the like. And, therefore, ensuring trustworthy agency performance is far more complex than simply filling these organizations with presumptively trustworthy candidates.

A third group of social control arrangements looks beyond the individual variations in the social background and credentials of the candidates who seek to fill agency roles and identifies the sources of trustworthiness or deviance in the nature and organization of the roles themselves. They reflect assumptions that agent disinterestedness, honesty, and competence, on the one hand, and opportunities for self-dealing, blocking, distorting, or falsifying information, and committing or concealing incompetence, on the other, are at least in part functions of the normative climate, social structure, and organization of agency (Stone, 1975).

Social control activities directed to the normative climate of organizations develop procedural regulations and organizational routines that operationalize the trust norms and thereby limit agent discretion and subjective (mis)interpretation of role obligations. These regulations specify basic operating procedures or minimum standards of competent role performance, norms about collecting and disseminating information,[14] record-keeping requirements and controls, specific decision rules to be followed, the chain of and procedures for the exercise of supervision and accountability, circumstances under which individuals should not participate in agency activity (such as rules on conflict of interest), and procedures to maximize trustee role distance and minimize role conflict (requiring stock divestiture or blind trusts, restricting "revolving door" employment transitions, or mandating celibacy, for example).

The manipulation of organizational structure to impede opportunities for trust abuse institutionalizes a system of checks and balances and a curious tension between collectivization and segregation in the delivery of trust. Collectivization strategies mandate redundant, overlapping, or "triangulated" responsibilities and create interdependent social networks of performance, decision making, diffusion of information, supervision, and accountability within trustee organizations (Katz, 1979a). They assume that incompetent or self-interested behavior is more difficult to accomplish and cover up, and more vulnerable to exposure, when it is visible to and requires the participation or consent of large numbers of collaborators, who often have quite different abilities, agendas, constellations of interest, and degrees of and sensitivity to potential culpability (Simmel, 1950).

But, of course, periodic scandals of large-scale, long-term illicit conspiracies testify to the fact that the structural impediments to collectivizing lying, cheating, self-dealing, corruption, incompetence, and cover-up are not insurmountable.[15] In order to extinguish established conspiracies of wayward trustees and to maximize the costs of collaboration and reorganization, firms therefore rotate personnel; segment, separate, and insulate responsibilities; and institutionalize functional independence, even as they collectivize other responsibilities (see Katz, 1979a; Vaughan, 1983).

In the face of compelling organizational incentives to lie or to protect self-dealing or incompetence, however, functional segregation and manipulation of intraorganizational structure—regardless of their efficacy—may do little to create an appearance of trust. Trust organizations therefore often segment their offerings and delegate responsibilities to or purchase the symbolic independence of disinterested third parties to perform the tasks that would create blatant conflicts of interest if discharged within the organization. For example, they use independent appraisers to set the value of real estate, outside laboratories to perform clinical tests of new pharmaceuticals, or transfer agents to cancel old stock certificates and reissue and distribute new ones in securities transactions.

Side Bets

Finally, principals and trustees make side bets in case the vast scaffolding of social control arrangements collapses. These side bets take the form of insurance,[16] bonding (such as, fidelity bonds for employees or fiduciary bonds for guardians or conservators), collateral, minimum reserve or capital requirements, guarantees, or warranties. These insurance-like arrangements respond particularly to the riskiness implicit in the "futures" component of so many trust relationships, which require that principals make an "investment" long before the scheduled "payoff" and therefore trust that future commitments will be honored. Secured either by principals or trustees before they consummate agency relationships, side bets promise an independent source of restitution or compensation in the event of future trust violations (and sometimes protection for trustworthy but undesirable outcomes of agency relationships as well).

In addition to greasing the wheels of agency relationships by cushioning their risk, institutionalized side bets also make a contribution to the exercise of trust. The literature equivocates on whether this contribution is positive or negative, however. On the one hand, side bets are said to contribute to "morale hazard," a decline in vigilance once insurance-like protections are secured (Heimer, 1985: 29-30; Berton, 1985b). On the other hand, insurance providers can exercise considerable social control over trustees—setting standards, establishing organizational routines and standard operating procedures, implementing and supervising entry restrictions, fashioning deductibles and other arrangements to increase the incentives both for trustworthiness and internal social control, conducting inspections and audits, placing responsibility for control or other loss-prevention activity in disinterested third parties, and, if necessary, intervening directly in trustee business operations (Heimer, 1985; Walsh, 1985; Bardach and Kagan, 1982). Though easily overlooked, insurance providers occupy a unique control position unavailable (because of insufficient access, expertise, resources, investment, or clout) to many others concerned with preserving the integrity of trust.

THE OHIO BANKING CRISIS
AND THE POLICING OF TRUST

Many of the institutions that were nudged and rapidly collapsed like a string of dominoes during the Ohio banking crisis had been protected by some combination of these public and private social control arrangements. The two brokerage firms that failed amid charges of widespread fraud had been audited by certified public accounting firms. The accountants were themselves accountable to professional self-regulatory groups and ultimately the Securities and Exchange Commission. Collateral arrangements and independent transfer agents protected the repurchase and reverse repurchase agreements offered by the brokerage firms to banks and municipalities. State banking and private insurance regulators policed the Ohio and Maryland thrift institutions, and the Federal Reserve and private deposit insurance funds supported them. The bankrupt deposit insurance funds were self-regulated. The commodities firm that failed was protected by minimum reserve and margin requirements, industry self-regulatory organizations, and the Commodities Futures Trading Commission. And presumably all of these organizations operated with the benefit of entry restrictions, elaborate procedural norms, structural constraints, and internal systems of governance and accountability.

The Ohio experience illustrates the complicated matrix of strategies mobilized for policing and protecting trust. The exercise of trust—be it banking, insurance, science, or government—is often organizationally complex and ongoing, ever changing over the course of the agency relationship. Social control strategies therefore respond to different pieces of its organization, functions, sequences, or routines. Some oversee particular roles, others particular activities, records, and other artifacts they generate. Some scrutinize processes that occur at the inception of a trust relationship (the exercise of entry restrictions or recruitment of principals, for example); others direct their vision to the output of futures transactions (for example, payment of dividends or benefits). Some anticipate problems; others react to them. Some exploit their access to the private settings of trust; others, located outside of trust organizations, develop inferences about what goes on inside. Some pursue deterrence, some restitution or remediation, and others pursue punishment.

Because of the multiplicity of social control agents and agencies, of loci of penetration, and of temporal points of intervention, most trust organizations receive ongoing scrutiny and duplicative protection from competing sources. This rich, overlapping texture of social control arrangements would seemingly provide a safety net when one of them fails. But, in the Ohio crisis, one policing failure instead touched off a geometrically escalating chain reaction of associated failures of trust and social control among these interdependent institutions. Granted, not all the vulnerable institutions failed. Still, observers must wonder whether the strands of this social control safety net are woven like the rip-stop nylon of a parachute or rather like a nylon stocking, in which even a small catch will inevitably produce an enormous run.

It is unclear how much can be generalized from the Ohio experience to other kinds of trust relationships (especially nonmonetary ones) and policing strategies. But this dramatic scenario raises obvious questions about the efficacy of the social control arrangements—individually and collectively—that surround the institution of trust. Is it possible to predict with any degree of accuracy which individuals or organizations are most likely to be trustworthy agents and to develop selection criteria and entry restrictions accordingly?[17] Do structural constraints or procedural regulations maximize the opportunities for trustworthy agency or rather minimize the quality and effectiveness of agency services (by limiting trustee discretion, creating unnecessary redundancy, snarling performance in red tape, cutting lines of communication, and so on) while increasing their cost? How much abuse do these policing organizations miss? Indeed, is it possible to penetrate, in their early stages (if at all), subtle, complex, well-concealed misdeeds that victimize unwitting principals? And does the promise of surveillance, accountability, sanctions, or losses of insurance coverage pose a potent deterrent threat or merely induce would-be violators to be all the more clever and furtive in implementing their misdeeds?

Do the social control opportunities afforded by side bets and other insurance-like arrangements outweigh the problem of morale hazard and the incentives they provide for greater laxness or further abuse? Unlike other disasters, there are few natural barriers to contain the spread of crises of confidence. Is it, therefore, possible to ensure adequately against abuses of trust, particularly given the real and symbolic interdependence of trustee institutions that inflames distrust? Recent controversies surrounding astronomical rate inflation and the demise of certain lines of insurance coverage associated with trustee roles (professional malpractice, accountant liability, and officers' and directors' liability insurance) suggest that it might not be possible (Andresky et al., 1985; Berton, 1985a; Diamond, 1985; Hilder, 1985; Loomis, 1985). Indeed, as obstetricians stop delivering babies because they cannot afford malpractice insurance, unprotected directors resign from corporate boards, and municipalities stung by the Ohio bank crisis claim that they did not take possession of collateral in their repurchase agreements because the cost of safeguarding their investment cut significantly into the interest they would earn, one must also consider the cost of social control efforts (however effective they may be) relative to the demand for the trust relationships they protect.

Is it possible for institutionalized conflicts of interest—like self-regulation or social control entrepreneurs who are paid by the very trustees they investigate—to yield disinterested policing? Indeed, can any of these social control agents and arrangements be trusted? After all, the policing of trust is simply a second-order trust relationship. Principals entrust agents to select and train their trustees, monitor and evaluate their conduct, investigate and sanction their misdeeds, develop and enforce procedural regulations that facilitate trustworthy agency, and provide compensation at some point down the road if their trust is nonetheless abused. Principals expect social control trustees, like the first-order trustees they oversee, to be disinterested, honest, and competent. And, like the latter, the former have considerable opportunities to abuse their trust—to allocate positions of trust to friends and relatives, to accept bribes or lucrative contracts in exchange for disregarding detected trust abuse, to accept liability or deposit insurance premiums with no intention of compensating legitimate claims, and so forth. Does the policing of trust shore up this vulnerable institution or simply create new opportunities for trust abuse?

Finally, do the lessons of crisis expose the inadequacy of the inherent coverage and capacity of the matrix of policing strategies and their associated side bets? Or, rather, do they suggest erroneous pre-crisis assumptions about institutional vulnerability to trust abuse, the level of risk associated with the implementation of these social control strategies, or the amount of risk principals are willing to tolerate? For example, is it that bank audits cannot anticipate, uncover, or deter abuse or, rather, that these examinations must be more frequent and more comprehensive to have this effect? Is it that deposit insurance cannot protect against a significant bank failure or run on the banking system or, rather, that annual premiums of one-twelfth of 1% of deposits do not generate sufficient reserves and that insurance funds with a narrow customer base and inability to diversify or spread risk are particularly vulnerable to crisis?

Unfortunately, these questions about the efficacy, timeliness, reach, degree of penetration, deterrent capacity, or fundamental trustworthiness of the various social control arrangements have received far more anecdotal speculation and ideological assertion than systematic and comparative empirical inquiry. Moreover, the lessons of the Ohio banking crisis raise troubling questions about the relevance of considerations of efficacy at all when mere perceptions incite crises of confidence that topple or severely threaten even healthy institutions.

PUBLIC VERSUS PRIVATE POLICING

The financial debacle of the spring of 1985 tolled the death knell for Cincinnati's *bauvereine*. The Ohio phase of the crisis was eventually contained after the state legislature passed a law permitting savings and loan institutions to reopen after they applied for insurance from the Federal Savings and Loan Insurance Corporation (FSLIC). Unfortunately, the informal community banks, many of which were financially sound and had experienced neither a run on their deposits nor any crises of confidence, were too small to qualify for FSLIC insurance. They were either closed or merged into larger institutions.

The banking crisis also hammered a nail in the coffin of private deposit insurance. Maryland legislators followed the lead of their Ohio counterparts, responding to their state's even costlier bank panic, by ordering privately insured thrift institutions to apply for federal coverage. Within weeks of the Maryland crisis, privately insured savings and loans in Massachusetts and North Carolina (two of the three remaining states with sizable private funds), prodded by state officials, had applied to the FSLIC as well. Voices from the U.S. House and Senate, the Federal Home Loan Bank Board, and the editorial boards of major newspapers called for federal insurance coverage for all depository institutions (Tolchin, 1985; *Washington Post,* 1985; *Baltimore Sun,* 1985; *New York Times,* 1985).

Cries for federal intervention in institutions touched by the Ohio banking crisis went beyond private deposit insurance. Several other major actors in the debacle enjoyed relative immunity from government regulation. ESM and BBS, the two government securities dealers whose collapse contributed to bank and other failures, were counted among roughly 100 small secondary dealers that flourished in a regulatory vacuum.[18] Within a month of the ESM failure, a House bill with bipartisan sponsorship, calling for federal regulation of the government securities market, had been introduced. Despite fears that regulatory intervention might hamper what one regulator described as "a super mechanism [that] . . . handles trillions of dollars in financings without incident" (Ingersoll, 1985), drive up interest rates on government securities, and thereby increase the national debt, consensus in Congress (and even among officials who traditionally support deregulation) for federal control grew.[19]

Accounting firms, like the one that precipitated the chain reaction (by fraudulently distorting the financial condition of ESM), also enjoy little public oversight. Their official public watchdog, the Securities and Exchange Commission, has traditionally delegated most of its rule-making and enforcement responsibilities to professional self-regulatory organizations. Congress, which had already begun investigating the accounting profession before the ESM failure, stepped up its critical scrutiny as events unfolded. A House committee chairman warned the accounting profession that it is facing "what may be its last opportunity to regulate itself instead of having somebody else do it" (Klott, 1985).

The fallout from the banking, government securities, and accounting crises incited or fueled preexisting demands for public intervention in these vulnerable institutions. Ironically, while government officials tout deregulation, they simultaneously clamor for ways by which public agencies can bail out the failures of their private counterparts.

Given the dearth of empirical data, it would be foolhardy to comment on proposals for either renewed or unprecedented regulation or for deregulation. But some demystification is possible. The fact of the matter is that the public sector has—and exercises— the same repertoire of social control options as the private sector. Government agencies perform their own policing, inspections, surveillance, investigation, litigation, and sanctioning; restrict entry to positions of trust (with registration, licensing, and prior clearance requirements); define elaborate role-specific procedural norms for trustees; mandate forms of organizational structure, governance, and internal social control (through regulatory requirements and rules of incorporation); and either offer insurance-like protections or require that trustees themselves undertake various institutional side bets (collateral, margin or minimum reserve requirements, bonding, or mandatory insurance rules). Moreover, public police are no different from private ones in the considerable variation in the efficacy and trustworthiness of their social control initiatives—the vigilance of policing, degree of access to the loci of trustee misdeeds, ability to anticipate abuse, timeliness of intervention, capacity to restore or compensate victimized principals, deterrent threat, and so forth—and in the level of acceptable risk to which these policing standards aspire.

But, at a time of crisis, government intervention does have some unique symbolic virtues. First, unlike private agencies, federally backed ones have potentially bottomless pockets that continue to come up with funds when those of their counterparts have been long depleted—a particularly desirable quality during a "run." An FSLIC television commercial, aired on major networks during the banking crisis, reminded viewers—with pictures of the Capitol and other imagery that evoked security and integrity—of that very fact. Second, unlike most private social control arrangements that are undertaken by trustees themselves, industry representatives, or outside policing entrepreneurs on trustee payrolls, government represents an independent third party. During crises of confidence and epidemics of distrust, public police are uniquely positioned to renegotiate the level of acceptable risk, to offer disinterested social control, and thereby to restore trust.

Of course, when the storm clouds have passed and trustee business is restored, politicians rediscover their disinclination to pay for public policing, trustees their unwillingness to stand for the regulation and scrutiny, principals their skepticism about the disinterestedness, diligence, and competence of their civil servants, and regulatory critics their conviction that public social control monopolies with deep pockets are less vigilant, less flexible, more expensive, and ultimately less effective than free market controls.

The symbolic rationale that creates sudden cravings for public policing and propels policy on a dizzying roller coaster between episodes of regulation and deregulation is not entirely inappropriate in the policing of trust given the power, velocity, and devastating impact of even unfounded crises of confidence. With trillions of dollars and a fundamental strand of the social fabric of complex societies in the balance, a little empirical elucidation of the tradeoffs between various strategies of public and private policing does not seem unreasonable.

NOTES

1. This account is based on coverage of the Ohio and Maryland banking crises in the *Wall Street Journal, New York Times, Financial Times, Washington Post, Cleveland Plain Dealer, Cincinnati Enquirer, Columbus Post Dispatch, Baltimore Sun, Barron's,* and *Business Week.*

2. In a repurchase agreement ("repo"), a dealer like ESM puts up government securities as collateral for short-term cash loans from customers (municipalities with idle cash, for example), with the agreement to buy back the securities at a specified time and at a higher price. In a reverse repurchase agree-

ment ("reverse repo"), a customer (usually a financial institution) puts up the securities and borrows against them, agreeing to buy back the securities at a specified time and price. The risk that the market value of the securities might decline during the course of the transaction is borne by the initial owner of the securities.

3. Some lenders falsely believed that the collateral was in the possession of the transfer agent. Others were unwilling to forgo the slightly higher interest rates offered to those who do not take delivery. And others chose not to incur the costs of additional paperwork or of establishing a safekeeping account with a Federal Reserve bank in order to take delivery of collateral.

4. A foreign exchange dealer explains, "The Europeans tend not to be very familiar with the American banking system. They look at their own system, which has a small number of very large banks, as opposed to the large number of very small banks in the United States. So that makes them nervous when they read about difficulties in American institutions, even if they are small ones" (Kristoff, 1985b: D1).

5. The ripples of the Ohio banking crisis did not end here, of course. In order to stem the crisis of confidence in Maryland, the state ordered all privately insured banks to apply for federal insurance. In the months that followed, one Bethesda savings bank was informed that, to qualify for FSLIC coverage, it must divest and discontinue extending loans to its troubled real estate subsidiary. In mid-August, the now cash-starved subsidiary missed a $15 million interest payment due on over $1 billion in mortgages and mortgage-backed securities. As word spread that the subsidiary could not meet its obligations, depositors staged a run on the bank, beginning on August 16. On September 5, the subsidiary filed for bankruptcy, threatening both the investors in its real estate partnerships and the private insurers that covered them. The bankruptcy ignited fears of yet another crisis of confidence, this time in the $350 billion mortgage-backed securities market. That same day, the private insurer with the greatest liability for the mortgage default announced that it would discontinue issuing new policies, amid rumors that the firm would begin laying off employees and closing branch offices. And so it goes.

6. For discussions of the concept and implications of "agency," see the work of Jensen and Meckling (1976), Mitnick (1975, 1976, 1984), Stinchcombe (1986), and American Law Institute (1983).

7. On this last point, see Marc Galanter's (1974) discussion of the advantages of "repeat players" over "one-shotters." As agents play the role of collectivizing principals' interests and assets (into insurance companies, publicly traded corporations, pension funds, charities, mutual funds, and the like), they amass power and autonomy that generally protect them from the demands of discrete principals.

8. Examples of intraorganizational social control include internal affairs departments, inspectors general, audit committees, compliance officers, quality assurance reviews, morbidity and mortality committees, newspaper and magazine fact checkers, and grievance committees.

9. Examples of self-regulatory groups include bar associations, the American Institute of Certified Public Accountants, and the National Association of Securities Dealers.

10. Examples of paid independent regulators include bond-rating firms like Standard and Poors or Moody's, certified public accountants that validate corporate financial statements to investors or creditors, the Audit Bureau of Circulation

that verifies newspaper circulation claims to advertisers, and kashruth inspectors who certify that meat was slaughtered and other food products prepared according to Jewish law (Ubinas, 1984; Jones, 1983; Gastwirt, 1974). The history of kashruth inspection illustrates the transition from personalized agency to formal social control in eliciting the trust of strangers. "Jacob Horowitz arrived in New York from Hungary in January, 1883. In response to the concern of the Hungarian Jews over *kashrut* of Passover matzo then being produced in New York by non-Hungarian bakers, Horowitz rented a bakery and make it ritually fit." For five years, the Horowitz family was "able to sell their matzo without any rabbinical supervision because their *landsleit* [fellow countrymen] trusted them. Only after they had decided to expand and to attract more than a local clientele did they feel compelled to retain rabbinical supervision" (Gastwirt, 1974: 6).

11. The history of credit reporting in the United States illustrates the transition from personalized agency to reliance on impersonal gatekeepers. Norris (1978: 8), in a fascinating history of R. G. Dun & Co., reports that credit reporting firms developed as creditors and merchants sought to expand their clientele beyond local circles of known business associates:

> The booming economy of the late 1820s and early 1830s persuaded most merchants, when faced with the alternative of granting credit on the basis of inadequate information or losing sales to more liberal competitors, to extend the credit and hope for the best. The panic of 1837 and the subsequent depression convinced many hard-pressed merchants who survived of the need for more accurate information upon which to base credit decisions . . .

So the practice developed of paying local lawyers to check on the credit worthiness of these strangers.

12. For example, through strategies for the "mortification of self" (Goffman, 1961: 14-48), total institutions can erode the self-interest of agents in training and thereby maximize their capacity for disinterestedness.

13. Many gatekeeping techniques—from nomination and apprenticeship to requirements of extended and costly higher education—tend to replicate the social backgrounds of the gatekeepers and to perpetuate existing patterns of stratification or exclusion (Auerbach, 1976). These discriminatory entry restrictions represent remnants of personalized agency. Unable to install familiar agents into positions of trust, principals and their agents exercise formal selection criteria that limit trustee candidacy according to similar social background or connections, class, race, religion, ethnicity, or gender.

14. For example, for "intelligence" roles like those of scientist, journalist, accountant, or investigator, the disclosure norm is embellished with rules about standards of proof (corroboration or replication), accuracy, record keeping, sampling, randomization, surprise or spontaneity, control groups, statistical inference (or other assessments of validity, reliability, or alternative interpretations), confidentiality or the proprietary nature of information, and the threshold (what is "material," what must be disclosed, and what can be omitted) and timing of disclosure.

15. See, for example, Sherman (1978; police corruption); Loeffler (1974; massive corporate fraud); Boffey (1985; organized medical incompetence); Broad and Wade (1982; fraud in scientific laboratories); and Vandivier (1972; fraud in defense contracting).

16. For example, FDIC, FSLIC, or private deposit insurance, Securities Investor Protection Corporation (SIPC) brokerage firm insurance, insurance policies for municipal bonds, mortgage-backed securities, or money market funds, officers' and directors' liability insurance, malpractice insurance.

17. Research, at least with respect to predictions of recidivism among common criminals, suggests that social science cannot do so (von Hirsch, 1976).

18. The Federal Reserve monitors the daily trading activity of the 36 primary government securities dealers (firms like Salomon Brothers, First Boston Corporation, Goldman Sachs & Co., and Citicorp). Another 300-odd secondary dealers also perform banking or corporate stock brokerage services that subject them to oversight by bank regulators or the SEC. But the remaining 100 firms that deal exclusively in government securities had been ignored by public watchdogs.

19. Final legislation would most likely require that government securities dealers register (with either the Treasury Department, Federal Reserve, or SEC) and subject them to inspection, collateral requirements, and rules about minimum capital, margins, auditing, bookkeeping, and periodic disclosure.

REFERENCES

ACKERMAN, P. and L. ZHITO [eds.] (1969) *The Complete Report of the First International Music Industry Conference*. New York: Billboard.

AMATOS, C. A. and A. GATES (1985) "Little S&Ls caught up in big problems." *Columbus Post Dispatch* (March 24): H1.

ANDRESKY, J., M. KUNTZ, and B. KALLEN (1985) "A world without insurance." *Forbes* (July 15): 40-43.

American Law Institute (1983) *Restatement of the Law, Agency*. Philadelphia: Author.

AUERBACH, J. S. (1976) *Unequal Justice: Lawyers and Social Change in Modern America*. London: Oxford University Press.

Baltimore Sun (1985) "Insuring the S&Ls." (May 17): 14A.

BARBER, B. (1983) *The Logic and Limits of Trust*. New Brunswick, NJ: Rutgers University Press.

BARDACH, E. and R. A. KAGAN (1982) *Going By the Book: The Problem of Regulatory Unreasonableness*. Philadelphia: Temple University Press.

BERTON, L. (1985a) "As accounting firms' premiums soar, some might drop liability insurance." *Wall Street Journal* (May 30): 17.

———(1985b) "Investors call CPAs to account." *Wall Street Journal* (January 28): 30.

BLACK, D. J. (1976) *The Behavior of Law*. New York: Academic Press.

BOFFEY, P. M. (1985) "Two Navy inquiries failed to fault doctor who was later dismissed." *New York Times* (June 23): 18.

BROAD, W. and N. WADE (1982) *Betrayers of the Truth: Fraud and Deceit in the Halls of Science*. New York: Simon & Schuster.

BURNS, J. J. (1977) "The management of risk: social factors in the development of exchange relations among the rubber traders of North Sumatra." Doctoral dissertation, Yale University.

DEUTSCH, M. (1962) "Cooperation and trust: some theoretical notes," pp. 275-319 in *Nebraska Symposium on Motivation*. Lincoln: University of Nebraska Press.

DIAMOND, S. (1985) "Sweeping insurance changes may increase business costs." *New York Times* (June 11): A1, D5.

ECKBERG, J. (1985) "S&L crisis threatens neighborhood tradition." *Cincinnati Enquirer* (March 24): A1, A4.

GALANTER, M. (1974) "Why the 'haves' come out ahead: speculations on the limits of legal change." *Law and Society Review* 9: 95-160.

GASTWIRT, H. P. (1974) *Fraud, Corruption, and Holiness: The Controversy Over the Supervision of Jewish Dietary Practice in New York City 1881-1940.* Port Washington, NY: Kennikat Press.

GOFFMAN, E. (1961) *Asylums: Essays on the Social Situation of Mental Patients and Other Inmates.* Garden City, NY: Doubleday.

HEIMER, C. A. (1985) *Reactive Risk and Rational Action: Managing Moral Hazard in Insurance Contracts.* Berkeley: University of California Press.

HILDER, D. B. (1985) "Risky business: liability insurance is difficult to find now for directors, officers." *Wall Street Journal* (July 10): 1, 21.

INGERSOLL, B. (1985) "SEC, Fed disagree on which agency would register treasury bond dealers." *Wall Street Journal* (June 19): 46.

JENSEN, M. C. and W. M. MECKLING (1976) "Theory of the firm: managerial behavior, agency costs and ownership structure." *Journal of Financial Economics* 3: 305-360.

JONES, A. S. (1983) "Circulation bureau under fire." *New York Times* (December 27): D1, D2.

KATZ, J. (1979a) "Concerted ignorance: the social construction of cover-up." *Urban Life* 8: 295-316.

———(1979b) "Legality and equality: plea bargaining in the prosecution of white-collar and common crimes." *Law and Society Review* 13: 431-459.

KLOTT, G. (1985) "Accounting role seen in jeopardy." *New York Times* (February 21): 22.

KRISTOFF, N. D. (1985a) "Closed firm cites Bevill." *New York Times* (April 17): D26.

———(1985b) "Gold soars on worries about Ohio." *New York Times* (March 20): D1, D17.

LOEFFLER, R. M. (1974) "Report of the trustee of Equity Funding Corporation of America." Los Angeles: U.S. District Court for the Central District of California.

LOOMIS, C. J. (1985) "Naked came the insurance buyer." *Fortune* (June 10): 67-72.

MACAULAY, S. (1963) "Non-contractual relations in business: a preliminary study." *American Sociological Review* 28: 55-67.

McNeil/Lehrer NewsHour (1985) "Shaky finance." May 15 (transcript).

MITNICK, B. M. (1975) "The theory of agency: the fiduciary norm." Presented at the annual meeting of the American Sociological Association, San Francisco, (August).

———(1976) "The theory of agency: a framework." Presented at the annual meeting of the American Sociological Association, New York (August).

———(1984) "Agency problems and political institutions." Presented at the annual meeting of the Midwest Political Science Association, Chicago (April).

New York Times (1985) "Let's cancel private bank insurance." (May 15): A22.

NORRIS, J. D. (1978) *R. G. Dun & Co. 1841-1900: The Development of Credit-Reporting in the Nineteenth Century.* Westport, CT: Greenwood Press.

SCHWARTZ, R. D. (1954) "Social factors in the development of legal control: a case study of two Israeli settlements." *Yale Law Journal* 63: 471-491.
SHAPIRO, S. P. (1985) "The social control of trust." Unpublished manuscript, New York University.
SHERMAN, L. W. (1978) *Scandal and Reform: Controlling Police Corruption*. Berkeley: University of California Press.
SIMMEL, G. (1950) *The Sociology of Georg Simmel* [Kurt H. Wolff, trans., ed.]. New York: Free Press.
SLOANE, L. (1985) "Ohio thrift units paid high rates." *New York Times* (March 23): 30.
STINCHCOMBE, A. L. (1986) "Norms of exchange," in *Stratification and Organization: Selected Papers*. Cambridge: Cambridge University Press.
STONE, C. D. (1975) *Where the Law Ends: The Social Control of Corporate Behavior*. New York: Harper & Row.
STRICHARCHUK, G. and J. BUSSEY (1985) "Cincinnati thrifts seem about to lose old German flavor." *Wall Street Journal* (March 26): 1, 27.
TOLCHIN, M. (1985) "Private insurance for banks debated." *New York Times* (June 11): D15.
UBINAS, L. (1984) "Small bond rating firms are competing aggressively for a bigger share of market." *Wall Street Journal* (September 7): 29.
VANDIVIER, K. (1972) "Why should my conscience bother me?" pp. 3-31 in R. L. Heilbroner et al. (eds.) *In the Name of Profit*. New York: Doubleday.
VAUGHAN, D. (1983) *Controlling Unlawful Organizational Behavior: Social Structure and Corporate Misconduct*. Chicago: University of Chicago Press.
VELEZ-IBANEZ, C. G. (1983) *Bonds of Mutual Trust: The Cultural Systems of Rotating Credit Associations Among Urban Mexicans and Chicanos*. New Brunswick, NJ: Rutgers University Press.
von HIRSCH, A. (1976) *Doing Justice: The Choice of Punishments*. New York: Hill & Wang.
WALLACE, G. D., Z. SCHILLER, K. DEVENY, D. COOK, and B. RIEMER (1985) "Tremors from Ohio's bank run." *Business Week* (April 1): 28-30.
WALSH, M. W. (1985) "Risky business: insurers are shunning coverage of chemical and other pollution." *Wall Street Journal* (March 19): 1,18.
Washington Post (1985) "Another S&L run." (May 11): A22.

Chapter 9

SELF-REGULATION AND THE CONTROL OF CORPORATE CRIME

JOHN BRAITHWAITE
BRENT FISSE

Much has been written in recent years on the sheer volume of corporate crime and on the very slim enforcement resources available to control it (Geis, 1973, 1982; Reiman, 1979; Clinard and Yeager, 1980; Grabosky, 1984; Wickman and Bailey, 1982). What this literature shows us is that corporate crime is responsible for more property loss and more injuries to persons than is crime in the streets. Yet we know it is politically and fiscally unrealistic to expect that our generation will see the public resources devoted to corporate crime control approach anywhere near those expended on crime in the streets. Thus, the relevance of assessing how much private enforcement might contribute to corporate crime control.

Corporate crime is defined here as conduct of a corporation, or of individuals acting on behalf of a corporation, that is proscribed and punishable by law (Fisse and Braithwaite, 1983: 317). It is not difficult to understand how private policing by corporations can have an important role in protecting corporations from being victims of crime. Indeed the editors of this volume have been the leaders in fostering such an understanding (Shearing and Stenning, 1981). But why should corporations spend resources on private policing programs to stop offences when they are the offenders and the intended beneficiaries of the wrongdoing?

There are many reasons why they do. First, the question assumes an overly economically rational view of corporate behavior: Corporations are at times moral actors that are concerned to obey the law because to do so is ethically right, even if costly (Stone, 1985). Second, corporations are in many ways even more concerned about their reputations than are individuals; individuals often subjugate economic rationality to preservation of their good name and self-respect, and so too do corporations (Fisse and Braithwaite, 1983). Third, corporations often invest in self-regulation to pre-empt the less palatable alternative of government regulation (Cranston, 1984: 59). Indeed, governments sometimes enter into a tacit social contract with business: unless business makes self-regulation work, public intervention will be the result. There are other reasons as well, but we need not devote time to them. The simple fact is that companies do spend considerable resources on self-regulation, so that the study of how effective self-regulation can be is an important topic. Self-regulation is defined broadly to include social control against corporate crime engaged in by both individual corporations and trade associations. It includes private enforcement of the law and private enforcement of corporate policies designed to prevent corporate offences (such as accounting policies designed to prevent slush funds and bribes).

Over the past decade we have been involved in three empirical studies of how corporations regulate themselves (Fisse and Braithwaite, 1983; Braithwaite, 1984, 1985). The illustrations in this chapter are drawn from these studies, though much of the material did not appear in any of the three books. The case studies used describe the situation as it existed in the companies discussed at the time that the fieldwork was conducted between 1978 and 1983.

THE VIRTUES OF SELF-REGULATION

Clinard and Yeager (1980: 95-97), among others, have documented the abysmally ineffective coverage of workplaces by occupational health and safety inspectors, pollution outlets by environmental inspectors, consumer product safety lapses by consumer protection officers, and so on. A program of self-regulation has the potential to expand coverage dramatically. Under the terms of Section 15A of the Securities and Exchange Act of 1934, for example, the National Association of Securities Dealers (NASD) inspects offices, books, and records of its members for violations of SEC regulations. In 1968, 45% of NASD members were inspected under this program (Katz, 1976: 161, 167). In 1969, by way of contrast, SEC inspectors surveyed only 5 1/2% of dealers who were not members of the NASD (Securities and Exchange Commission, 1969).

In addition to a capacity to achieve wider coverage, self-regulation can achieve greater inspectorial depth. In the international pharmaceutical industry, for example, a number of the more reputable companies have corporate compliance groups that send teams of scientists to audit subsidiaries' compliance with production quality codes. In one Australian subsidiary of an American firm visited, inspections by the headquarters compliance group were conducted twice yearly and were normally undertaken by three inspectors who spent over a week in the plant. The government health department inspection, on the other hand, consisted of an annual one-day visit by a single inspector. Although employees had advance warning of the government inspection, the corporate compliance group arrived unannounced.

Corporate inspectors also tend, at least in the pharmaceutical industry, to be better trained than their government counterparts. It is commonplace for corporate inspectors to have doctorates. Corporate inspectors' specialized knowledge of their employer's product lines also make them more effective probers than the government inspectors, who are forced to be generalists. Their greater technical capacity to spot problems is enhanced by a greater social capacity to do so. Corporate compliance personnel are more likely than government inspectors to know where "the bodies were buried," and to be able to detect cover-ups. One American pharmaceutical executive explained in part why this is so:

> Our instructions to officers when dealing with FDA inspectors is to only answer the questions asked, not to provide any extra information, not to volunteer anything, and not to answer any questions outside your area of competence. On the other hand we [the corporate compliance staff] can ask anyone anything and expect an answer. They are told that we are part of the same family, and unlike the government, we are working for the same final objectives.

Perhaps this statement exaggerates the goodwill between company employees and internal compliance inspectors. The production manager of the Guatemalan subsidiary of another company was asked: "Do you think of the internal quality auditors from headquarters as part of the same team as you?" His answer probably grasped the reality: "I think of them as a pain in the ass."

The power of corporate inspectors to trap suspected wrongdoers is often greater than that possessed by government investigators. One quality assurance manager told of an instance where this power was used. His assay staff was routinely obtaining test results showing the product to be at full strength. The manager suspected that when they found a result of 80% strength, the laboratory staff would assume that the assay was erroneous, simply mark the strength at 100%, and not recalculate the test. The manager's solution was periodically to "spike" the samples with understrength product to see whether his staff would pick out the defects. If not, they could be dismissed or sanctioned in some other way. Government inspectors do not have the legal authority to enter a plant and entrap employees with a spiked production run.

Another example of the greater effectiveness of internal inspectors concerns a medical director who suspected that one of his scientists was "graphiting" safety testing data. His hunch was that the scientist, whose job was to run 100 trials on a drug, instead ran 10 and fabricated the other 90 so they would be consistent with the first 10. The medical director possessed investigative abilities that would have been practically impossible for a government investigator. He could verify the number of animals taken from the animal store, the amount of drug substance that had been used, the number of samples that had been tested, as well as other facts. His familiarity with the laboratory made this easy. As an insider, he could probe quietly without raising the kind of alarm that might lead the criminal to pour an appropriate amount of drug substance down the sink.

We have seen that corporations may be more capable than the government of regulating their business acitvities. But if they are more capable, they are not necessarily more willing to regulate more effectively. Although self-regulation can be potent in theory, all too often in practice it is little more than a symbolic activity. Our comments earlier about corporations being concerned about much more than profit maximization do not mean that economic rationality does not place an enormous constraint on self-regulation in practice.

This is why elsewhere we have developed the idea of enforced self-regulation—a proposal for exploiting the superior breadth and depth of self-regulatory surveillance by forcing it upon industry, as it were (Braithwaite, 1982; Braithwaite and Fisse, 1985). This is also why sophisticated regulatory agencies often effectively compel self-regulation by threatening draconian government intervention unless industry produces solid evidence that self-regulation is working well. Moreover, one of the best ways of securing industry commitment to making corporate compliance systems work is by prosecutions of senior executives: executives—particularly chief executives—who are afraid of conviction will impose much greater demands on their self-regulatory systems.

This chapter is not about how to force industry to self-regulate; it is about how to make self-regulation effective, given a commitment to this approach. But this does not imply any naive assumption that we need rely only on the goodwill of business to secure these achievements.

THE ESSENTIAL REQUIREMENTS OF AN EFFECTIVE SELF-REGULATORY SYSTEM

One of the authors examined, largely on the basis of interviews with executives, the characteristics of the internal compliance systems of the five American coal mining companies with the lowest accident rates for the industry in the early 1980s. He also reviewed other empirical work on the organizational characteristics associated with safety in mines (Braithwaite, 1985: 41-71). A characteristic that consistently emerged was that companies with good safety records had detailed plans of attack to deal with identifiable hazards. This may be a characteristic that is not as relevant to determining the effectiveness of other kinds of internal compliance functions as it is for occupational health and safety. However, the other features that emerged from this empirical work seem to us of likely general relevance. Companies that effectively self-regulate share the following characteristics:

(1) a great deal of informal clout and top management backing is given to their compliance personnel (safety inspectors in the case of mine safety);
(2) accountability for compliance performance is clearly defined and placed on line managers;
(3) that performance is monitored carefully and managers are told when it is not up to standard;
(4) compliance problems are effectively communicated to those capable of acting on them; and
(5) training and supervision (especially by front-line supervisors) for compliance are not neglected.

These characteristics of successfully self-regulated corporations will be considered in turn.

CLOUT FOR INTERNAL COMPLIANCE GROUPS

At a recent seminar on laws to control animal experimentation one of the authors asked the animal welfare officer from a very large Australian research institution how she dealt with researchers who refused to comply with Australia's voluntary code on the use of animals in experiments. "Easy," she said, "If they don't do what I ask, I don't give them any more animals." Her role encompassed the ordering and delivery of animals to experimenters. This gave her organizational clout in dealing with researchers. Most fundamentally, then, clout for internal compliance groups comes from their control of resources that are important to those who must be made to comply.

Clout is central in the same way to the success of government regulators. Health departments find it easier to control drug companies than food outlets, and find it much less necessary to resort to law enforcement to do so because health departments hold sway over so many decisions that affect the success of pharmaceutical companies. They decide whether new drugs will be allowed on the market, and if so, with what promotional claims, at what price, and with what quality-control requirements during manufacture. Organizational actors are more compliant with requests from actors who control vital resources (such as approvals and licences) for the organization.

Often it is organizationally difficult to give compliance staff control over contingencies that matter to those regulated. In these circumstances, it is important for top management clearly to communicate the message to the organization that in any dispute it is likely to stand behind its compliance staff. Regrettably, in most organizations the opposite message is part of the folklore of the corporate culture—that when the crunch comes, management will stand behind its production people and allow them to push aside that which impedes output. In contrast, with the coal mining safety leaders visited, when a company inspector recommended that a section of a mine be closed down because it was unsafe, in all five companies it was considered inadvisable for line managers to ignore the recommendation because of the substantial risk that top management would back the safety staff rather than themselves.

Quality-control directors in many pharmaceutical companies are given clout by quite formal requirements that their decisions can only be overruled by a written directive of the chief executive of the corporation. This gives quality control unusual authority because not many chief executives want to risk their career by overruling their technical people for the sake of a single batch of drugs, when the danger—however remote—is that this batch could kill someone.

CLEARLY DEFINED ACCOUNTABILITY

A senior pharmaceutical company executive once explained, "There's a Murphy's Law of a kind: If someone else can be blamed, they will." Active policies to resist this tendency are needed for companies to be effectively self-regulating. At all five coal mining safety leaders, the line manager, not the safety staff, was held accountable for the safety of his work force. A universal feature was also clear definition of the level of the hierarchy that would be held responsible for different types of safety breakdowns. They were all companies that avoided the problem of diffused accountability: People knew where the buck stopped for different kinds of failures.

In contrast, companies with little will to comply sometimes draw lines of accountability with a view to creating a picture of diffused responsibility so that no one can be called to account should a court look into the affairs of the company. Everyone is given a credible organizational alibi for blaming someone else. Perhaps worse, other non-self-regulating companies calculatedly set out to pass blame onto others. Thus, some pharmaceutical and pesticide companies have some of their most dicey toxicological testing done by contract laboratories that survive by telling large companies what they want to hear. They get results indicating the safety of their products without risking the consequences of a conviction for the presentation of fraudulent data. The use of sales agents to pay bribes is perhaps the best-documented device of this sort in the corporate crime literature (Reisman, 1979; Boulton, 1978; Coffee, 1977).

At three of the large American pharmaceutical companies visited it was revealed that there was a "vice-president responsible for going to jail," and two of these were interviewed. Lines of accountability had been drawn in these organizations such that if there were a problem and "someone's head had to go on the chopping block," it would be that of the "vice-president responsible for going to jail." These executives probably would not have been promoted to vice-president had they not been willing to act as scapegoats. If they performed well, presumably they would be shifted sideways to a safer vice-presidency. Corporations can pay someone to be their fall-guy in many ways. Exceptionally generous severance pay is the simplest method. In summary, most companies make little effort clearly to define lines of responsibility for compliance: The result is that when something does go wrong the complexity of the organization is usually sufficient to make it difficult to convict any individual. Calculatedly noncompliant companies sometimes create lines of accountability that will point the finger of responsibility away from their top managers. And effectively self-regulating companies have principles of responsibility that make it clear in advance which line managers will be held responsible should certain types of noncompliance occur. However, a number of the pharmaceutical companies visited had an each-way bet: They had clearly defined lines of accountability for their internal disciplinary purposes, while contrivng to portray a picture of confused accountability to the outside world. The fact that the latter does occur is one reason why "private police" can be more effective than "public police," and why self-regulation has the potential more effectively to punish individuals than government regulation.

MONITORING COMPLIANCE PERFORMANCE

Two of the surprising findings from the survey of the organizational characteristics of coal mining safety leaders were that the size of the safety staffs of these companies varied enormously, as did the punitiveness of their approach to disciplining individuals who breached safety rules. It was expected that among the defining characteristics of companies that were leaders in safety would be that they would spend a great deal on safety staff and would be very tough on safety offenders. Although a large safety staff is not necessarily a characteristic of safety leaders, putting enormous accountability pressures for safety on line managers is. Although a policy of sacking or fining safety offenders on the spot is not typical, communication of the message that higher management is deeply concerned when individuals break the rules is universal for safety leaders.

There is no magic formula for how this is achieved, because, as Bethlehem Steel's Director of Safety pointed out, "You can't cookbook safety." Each company must find a solution appropriate to its corporate culture. But to illustrate how one company monitors safety performance and communicates the message that top management cares about safety, we will use U.S. Steel. This will be followed by case studies of Exxon and IBM.

U.S. Steel

U.S. Steel leaves no ambiguity in its official communications about where safety stands in the hierarchy of priorities. For example, the corporate "Safety Program" document states the following:

It is doubtful that any company ever made significant safety progress just by being "interested in" or "concerned about" safety, as it is so often expressed. Rather, management—top management—must have strong convictions on the necessity for placing safety first, above all other business considerations (p. 4).

On the monitoring side, foremen, departments, and entire plants must all produce summary safety activity reports either weekly or monthly. These indicate how many safety contacts, observations, injuries, disciplinary actions, job safety analysis conferences, unsafe conditions, and inspections there have been during each week. These reports ensure the accountability of foremen, department heads, and superintendents for the safety performance of their units.

The accountability mechanism for general superintendents of mining districts is more interesting. The general superintendents attend a monthly meeting with the president of the mining company and other senior executives at corporate headquarters. Each general superintendent, in turn, makes a presentation on his or her district's performance during the previous month—first, on safety performance (that is, accident rates) and, second, on productive performance (tons of coal mined). After the safety presentation, the corporate chief inspector of mines has the first opportunity to ask questions. If the accident rate has worsened in comparison to previous months, or to other districts, the question invariably asked is, Why? The 24 or 25 senior people who attend these meetings exert a powerful peer-group pressure on general superintendents whose safety performance is poor. It is an extreme embarrassment for general superintendents to have to come back month after month and report safety performances falling behind those of other districts.

These meetings, incidentally, also fulfill the function of regulatory innovation. Each mining district, rather than the corporation as a whole, writes its own rule book. General superintendents who have introduced new rules or technologies that have worked well in reducing accidents will score points by mentioning these successes in their reports. Other districts will then adopt these controls. An advantage of the combination of decentralized rule making and centralized performance assessment is that creative approaches to reducing accidents may be more likely to emerge than under the stultifying influence of a corporate book of rules.

Exxon

A different example of how a large corporation can monitor the compliance performance of its far-flung operations is provided by the oil giant, Exxon. Exxon has a controller, a vice-president who has responsibility for monitoring compliance with all types of corporate rules—from environmental protection to accounting rules. Each region (for instance, Esso Europe) has a regional controller, and each subsidiary within the region has a controller. In addition to reporting directly to the chief executive of the subsidiary, the local controller has an important dotted-line reporting relationship through the regional controller up to the controller's office in New York. Even though the local organization is paying for its controller and the local auditing staff, the corporate controller ultimately determines the size of the local controller's work force. Auditors are therefore not tied to the purse strings of those whom they are auditing.

The controller is given responsibility for operational as well as financial auditing. Audits serve the dual purpose of improving operational efficiency and detecting deviations from proper bookkeeping procedures. Control activities, such as inventory, which were formerly independent of the auditing function, are now integrated into a total system of audit and control. Audits incorporate an assessment of whether standard operating procedures adequate to ensure compliance with company policies are in place, and whether these procedures are being consistently followed. An audit of a manufacturing facility includes, for example, an assessment of whether corporate industrial safety policies are being followed. Because of the range of skills that such operational audits demand, interdisciplinary teams that include engineers as well as financial auditors are used. The internal auditing function involves more than 400 people worldwide.

Responsibility for the accounting integrity side of the audit rests with the general auditor, who reports administratively to the vice-president and controller. However, the general auditor can bypass the controller and report directly to the audit committee of the board, which is composed entirely of outside directors.

Like U.S. Steel, Exxon therefore has centralized monitoring of compliance, albeit covering a more all-embracing range of areas of compliance under one controller function. Even though Exxon has much more centralized rule making than U.S. Steel, with detailed manuals of standard operating procedures being issued by the controller in New York, there is provision for local units to engage in principled dissent from the manuals. For example, deviations from corporate accounting principles are allowed, but must be approved "by the appropriate Regional Controller and Regional General Auditor in writing, and will be recorded in a central registry in the regional office, and at the affiliates' offices" (Exxon Corporation, 1973).

The controller function aims to create an organization full of "antennas." It was set up in response to top management's shock when it was discovered that bribery was happening on a massive scale in its Italian subsidiary during the 1970s. But like U.S. Steel, and like all companies with outstanding compliance systems, control is a line—not a staff—responsibility. The job of the controller's staff is to monitor and ring alarm bells to top management when corporate policies are not being enforced by line management. In the words of the controller: "Audit is not the control. Audit is the monitor of the control."

An underlying principle of the Exxon system is that no one is to have unaccountable power. Consider the question, "Who audits the auditors?" This problem is dealt with by peer review. The headquarters auditing group might audit the Asian Regional Auditing Group and the European Regional Group might audit the headquarters auditing group. Auditors are auditing other auditors all over the world.

In addition to formal audits, all subsidiaries have a kind of self-audit in the form of a triennial "business practice review." In this review, managers, after having refreshed their memories on the objectives of corporate ethics policies, assess all their current practices—bookkeeping, bidding, making gifts to customers, expense accounts, the lot—to root out any areas that leave open the possibility of abuse. It is a kind of corporate "cultural revolution," an attempt to keep alive among the masses the fervor to be watchful against unethical practices. Business practice reviews were introduced in 1976 in part as a way of dealing with Exxon's morale problems from the Italian bribery disclosures. Exxon management wanted to make their employees believe in the honesty and integrity of the company. The business practice reviews achieved that goal. By involving middle and junior managers in the campaign to eliminate unethical practices, Exxon convinced its own people that it was serious about its new ethics policy. Some company units found that the reviews were so effective and so good for morale that they involved lower-level employees, such as salespeople, in the process. The controller had never really intended that the reviews widely involve these lower levels; but he was happy enough with the result. Quite apart from the other favorable effects, he felt that the reviews had helped managers in the field to understand the reasons for many of the requirements imposed on them, and therefore made the task of the auditors easier. The reviews must also help keep the controller's staff on its toes to ensure that a problem that should have been identified does not surface in a business practice review.

IBM

To ensure compliance with its corporate policies—indeed, in all areas of business—IBM relies heavily on its so-called contention system. The contention system sets up a friendly adversariness between staff and line. If the general counsel of a subsidiary makes an objection to the subsidiary chief over a marketing practice perceived as contravening company policy, and if that objection is overruled, this must be reported to division counsel. If the latter agrees with the local counsel, the objection is taken up with the division chief executive to whom the local chief answers. Should the division chief executive support the local chief whereas the division counsel supports the local counsel, the contention will move up to a higher level of the organization. Ultimately, it might be decided in a discussion between the chairman and the general counsel, in which the chairman will have the final say. Such a formalized contention system between the line and staff reporting relationships increases the probability that problems will be flushed out into the open.

At the outset, we said that the contention system was friendly. Organizations cannot afford to undermine cooperation by fostering a war of all against all, so certain informal codes of fair play are followed. When a staff person feels compelled to blow the whistle on a line manager up through the staff channels, good form is to warn the line manager before the event. This gives the line manager two possible "outs." Recognizing that the staff person means business, the line manager can back down. Or, the line can itself report the problem up through staff channels. The latter protects the line manager from any accusation that he or she was trying to cover up problems from staff scrutiny.

IBM has a control function run by the internal audit group that monitors compliance with both financial and nonfinancial policies in a way similar to the Exxon controller. As in Exxon, their role is to assist the control of top management over the total management system. A total of 260 internal auditors check compliance with all corporate policies within each subunit on approximately a three-year cycle.

IBM executives, like those at Exxon, argue that the costs of the control function are paid for by the savings it generates in rooting out inefficiency or catching employees who are ripping off the company. A pleasant irony of self-regulation is that programs to detect corporate crime also uncover crimes against the corporation by employees (Fisse and Braithwaite, 1983: 180). Overly costly controls are reduced or eliminated by challenging employees to identify controls that have proven cost-ineffective. The control function also pays its way through being vital to the corporation's system for monitoring performance. IBM is a corporation based on action plans, and individuals and subunits are evaluated according to comparisons between actual results and those that are projected in the action plan. An important efficiency rationale for the control function is, therefore, that it ensures that the performance indicated in the books (be it production, profits, or industrial accidents) reflects the reality. If you manage by commitment, control over the measurement of performance is essential. By ensuring that everyone's performance is measured by the same yardsticks, the control function minimizes the loss of motivation that comes from feeling that others are exceeding their targets because they are using different counting rules.

Important among the action plans are those that result from the discovery of deficiencies in audits. A determinate period for the implementation of measures to rectify the deficiency will be set, and at the end of the period there will be an audit of compliance with the remedial requirements. The IBM management system is based on the notion that "we don't want surprises." Each year the local controller sends up an "early warning system report" to the divisional controller and so on up to the corporate controller. The early warning report is to indentify any business control problem that may be emerging. It is a way of dealing with the problem of the executive who says, "I would have reported it up, but first I wanted to be sure that something was wrong." Any problem that suddenly emerges in full-blown form will attract a reprimand of "How come I wasn't seeing that in the early warning report?"

We asked representatives from the environmental, health, and safety management areas what they thought of the job that auditors did in ensuring compliance with environmental, health, and safety policies. The responses were guardedly critical. Executives from specialist areas see the internal audits as broad brush and, at three-year intervals, too infrequent for their specialized compliance purposes. Internal audits tend to ignore detail, which is vital to assessing environmental, health, and safety compliance (such as checking the calibration of equipment) and lack a sophisticated understanding of what constitutes reasonable levels of exposure to dangerous substances. Generalist auditors, in spite of any scientific training they might have, are seen as lacking the specialized training and experience to pick the real problems (which might have nothing to do with observance of the rules) that could cause an environmental or safety crisis.

On the other hand, there are important advantages in having nonfinancial compliance audits conducted together with financial audits. The whole point of the control function is to alert top management to control deficiencies. In contrast, normal environmental and health and safety management systems are not designed as vertical reporting systems right up to the top management suites. They are partly horizontal, partly vertical mixes of dotted- and solid-line reporting and/or advisory relationships that have built into them various possibilities for communication blockages capable of preventing "bad news" from getting up the organization. Hence, it would be undesirable to limit the controller's role or the role of the internal audit group to reporting up only financial violations unearthed in audits. Interdisciplinary auditors are capable of picking up many, if not most, gross deviations from prudent environmental, health, and safety standards. To the extent that auditors do expose such deviations to the purview of top management, middle managers with the power to prevent the deviations will get busy doing so.

It may be that corporations can get the best of both worlds with a dual system that combines (1) the total performance assessment of an interdisciplinary control function with its stronger guarantees that the bad news will reach the top, and (2) the more frequent and intensive specialized compliance audits by relevant technical experts with their stronger guarantees that the real problems will be identified. Further, when the former audit the latter there is a synergy unattainable under any other compliance structure. The specialists ensure that the real problems are identified and the control function ensures that these problems are communicated to top management and rectified to the satisfaction of top management. Both IBM and Exxon have such a dual system. The control function has by no means completely replaced environmental, occupational health and safety, and other specialist staff.

COMMUNICATION OF COMPLIANCE PROBLEMS

It has already been suggested that a fundamental requirement of effective internal compliance systems is that there be provision to ensure that bad news gets to the top of the corporation. There are two reasons for this. First, when top management gets to know about a crime that achieves certain subunit goals, but that is not in the overall interests of the corporation, top management will stop the crime. Second, when top management is forced to know about activities that it would rather not know about, it will often be forced to "cover its ass" by putting a stop to it. Gross (1978: 203) has explained how criminogenic organizations frequently build in assurances that the taint of knowledge does not touch those at the top:

> A job of the lawyers is often to prevent such information from reaching the top officers so as to protect them from the taint of knowledge should the company later end up in court. One of the reasons former President Nixon got into such trouble was that those near him did not feel such solicitude but, from self-protective motives presumably, made sure he did know every detail of the illegal activities that were going on.

There are many reasons bad news does not get to the top. Stone (1975: 190) points out that it would be no surprise if environmental problems were not dealt with by the board of a major public utility company that proudly told him it had hired an environmental engineer: The touted environmentalist reported to the vice-president for public relations! More frequently, the problem is that people lower down have an interest in keeping the lid on their failures. Consider how a cover-up of bad news about the safety and efficacy of a pharmaceutical product can occur.

At first, perhaps, the laboratory scientists believe that their failure can be turned into success. Time is lost. Further investigation reveals that their miscalculation was even more extensive than they had imagined. The hierarchy will not be pleased. More time is wasted drafting memoranda communicating that there is a prob-

lem, but in a gentle fashion so that the shock to middle management is not too severe. Middle managers who had waxed eloquent
to their supervisors about the great breakthrough are reluctant to
accept the sugar-coated bad news. They tell the scientists to "really
check" their gloomy predictions. Once that is done, they must
attempt to design corrective strategies. Perhaps the problem can be
covered by modifying the contraindications or the dosage level?
Further delay. If the bad news must go up, it should be accompanied by optimistic action alternatives.

Finally persuaded that the situation is irretrievable, middle managers send up some of the adverse findings. But they want to dip
their toes in the water on this. Accordingly, they first send up some
unfavorable results that the middle managers earlier predicted could
materialize and then gradually reveal more bad news for which
they are not so well covered. If the shock waves are too big, too
sudden, they'll just have to go back and have another try at patching
things up. The result is that busy top management get a fragmented
picture that they never find time to put together. This picture plays
down the problem and overstates the corrective measures being
taken below. Consequently, they have little reason but to continue
extolling the virtues of the product. Otherwise, the board might pull
the plug on their financial backing, and the sales force might lose
the faith in the product that is imperative for commercial success.

In addition, there is the more conspiratorial type of communication blockage orchestrated from above. Here, more senior managers
intentionally rupture line reporting actively to prevent low-level
employees from passing up their concern over illegalities. The
classic illustration was the heavy electrical equipment price-fixing
conspiracy of the late 1950s:

> Even when subordinates had sought to protest orders they
> considered questionable, they found themselves checked by
> the linear structure of authority, which effectively denied them
> any means by which to appeal. For example, one almost Kaf-
> kaesque ploy utilized to prevent an appeal by a subordinate
> was to have a person substantially above the level of his imme-
> diate superior ask him to engage in the questionable practice.
> The immediate superior would then be told not to supervise
> the activities of the subordinate in the given area. Thus, both
> the subordinate and the supervisor would be left in the dark
> regarding the level of authority from which the order had
> come, to whom an appeal might lie, and whether they would

violate company policy by even discussing the matter between themselves. By in effect removing the subject employee from his normal organizational terrain, this stratagem effectively structured an information blockage into the corporate communication system. Interestingly, there are striking similarities between such an organizational pattern and the manner in which control over corporate slush funds (in the 1970s foreign bribery scandals) deliberately was given to low-level employees, whose activities then were carefully exempted from the supervision of their immediate superiors [Coffee, 1977: 1133].

The solution to this problem is a free route to the top. The lowly disillusioned scientist who can see that people could be dying while middle managers equivocate about what sort of memo will go up should be able to bypass line management and send the information to an ombudsman, answerable only to the board or chief executive, whose job it is to receive bad news. General Electric, Dow Chemical, and American Airlines now all have such short-circuiting mechanisms to allow employees anonymously to get their message about a middle-management coverup to the top.

The ombudsman solution is simply a specific example of the general proposition that if there are two lines to the top, adverse information will get up much more quickly than if there is only one. For example, if an independent compliance group answering to a senior vice-president periodically audits a laboratory, scientists in the laboratory have another channel up the organization through the audit group. Naturally, the middle managers responsible for the laboratory would prefer that they, rather than the compliance group, give senior management the bad news. The control function at Exxon and IBM is in part a systematic approach to sniffing out bad news and reporting it to top management. But there are also ways of creating de facto alternative channels up the organization. Exxon has a requirement that employees who spot activities that cause them to suspect illegality must report these suspicions to the Law Department. In most companies, a financial auditor who noticed in the course of his or her work a memo suggesting an antitrust offense would ignore such evidence because it is not his or her responsibility and because of the reasonable presumption that he or she is not expected to be an expert in antitrust law. Exxon internal auditors, however, would be in hot water if they did not report their grounds for suspicion to the Law Department.

Once a violation is reported, there is an obligation on the part of the recipient of the report to send back a determination as to whether a violation has occurred, and if it has, what remedial or disciplinary action is to be taken. Thus, the junior auditor who reports an offense and hears nothing back about it knows that the report has been blocked somewhere. He or she must then report the unresolved allegation direct to the audit committee of the board in New York. At the time of the field work, this free channel to the top has never been used by a junior auditor. However, the fact that it exists, and that everybody is reminded annually that it does, makes it less likely that it will have to be used. The most effective control system is one incorporating such strong situational incentives to compliance that it never has to be used.

Of course, many communication problems are more mundane than the failure of top management to become aware of the slush funds that were being used to pay bribes at Exxon. A worker notices chemicals dripping from a pipe outside the plant and does not think or bother to report it to someone with responsibility for environmental matters. A design engineer notices a claim in an advertisement for a technical capacity of a company product that he or she knows it does not have, yet does not report this to the advertising department. Getting the bad news to the right desk is not always easy in large organizations. But any organization can do at least three things:

(1) Make sure that routine formal reporting relationships are designed well enough and appropriately enough for the unique environment of the company, to ensure that most recurrent problems of noncompliance are reported to those with the power to correct them.
(2) Make sure there is a free route to the top, bypassing line reporting relationships, to reduce the likely success of conspiratorial blocking of bad news.
(3) Create a corporate culture with a climate of concern for compliance problems that are not an employee's own responsibility, an organization "full of antennae." There are formal ways of fostering communication of problems that fall outside routine reporting relationships, from the Japanese ringi (Clark, 1979) to the free-floating matrix management of many high-tech American companies (Kanter, 1983). But the fundamental solution is not formal—it lies in the corporate culture. Corporations must strive for a culture of compliance, a commitment to being alert, to noticing and

reporting how others, as well as oneself, can solve compliance problems.

TRAINING AND SUPERVISION FOR COMPLIANCE

It is not enough for top management to know when noncompliance is occurring and then to tell those with clearly defined responsibility for the problem to bring the company into compliance. Often the problems are complex and formal and systematic training is needed to ensure that all employees know *how* to comply in their area of responsibility, and supervision is needed to ensure that the lessons of the training have been learned.

Thus, all legal and marketing personnel require training in antitrust law and related corporate policies. Industrial relations staff need training in labor relations law. All production people need occupational health and safety training. The mistake that many noncompliant companies make is in communicating the relevant knowledge to middle management and then glibly assuming that they will pass it down.

The five coal mine safety leaders were all characterized by extraordinary measures to ensure that first-line supervisors were training and supervising their workers. At U.S. Steel, for example, department heads are responsible for developing training plans ensuring that foremen provide all workers with training in a set of safe job procedures that are written by the foreman for the job of each employee in his or her care. Each foreman must make at least one individual contact each week with each employee under her or his supervision to consolidate this training. With inexperienced workers, these contacts are usually "tell-show" checks whereby the worker is asked to explain what should and should not be done and why the approved procedure is the safest one. Foremen are required to make at least two planned safety observations of each employee each month. The safety observations are planned so that they cover systematically all job operations for which the employee has received instruction. In addition to the safety observations, which are planned and scheduled at the beginning of each week, foremen are expected to perform additional "impromptu observations" following chance recognition of unsafe practices. Whenever a foreman observes an unsafe condition or work method, whether in a planned or impromptu safety observation, he or she must correct it immediately and report the occurrence to higher management or a "supervisor's safety report." The foreman can tell whether a worker who deviates from a procedure or rule has been trained in it by looking at the employee's record. For all employees a record is maintained by their foreman, noting their safety history—basic training, safety contacts, planned safety observations, unsafe acts, violations, discipline, and injuries. When workers move from foreman to foreman, their records move with them, so a new foreman can discover at a glance what safety training a worker lacks for a new job.

In short, effectively self-regulating companies do not tell middle managers how to comply and assume they will tell the troops; they have training policies and programs to guarantee that training is happening and working down to the lowest reaches of the organization. They audit compliance with compliance training programs as assiduously as they audit compliance itself.

WATCHING PRESSURES FOR NONCOMPLIANCE

Having covered the five basic principles for creating an effectively self-regulating company, consideration might be given to another even more basic principle. This is that companies must be concerned not to put employees under so much pressure to achieve the economic goals of the organization that they cut corners with the law. The role of excessive performance pressures on middle managers in creating corporate crime has been frequently pointed to by the literature (Clinard, 1983; Cressey and Moore, 1980: 48). *Corporate Crime in the Pharmaceutical Industry* illustrated the problem thus:

Take the situation of Riker, a pharmaceutical subsidary of the 3M corporation. In order to foster innovation, 3M imposes on Riker a goal that each year 25 percent of gross sales should be of products introduced in the last five years. Now if Riker's research division were to have a long dry spell through no fault of its own, but because all of its compounds had turned out to have toxic effects, the organization would be under pressure to churn something out to meet the goal imposed by headquarters. Riker would not have to yield to this pressure. It could presumably go to 3M and explain the reasons for its run of bad luck. The fact that such goal requirements do put research directors under pressure was well illustrated by one American executive who explained that research directors often forestall criticism of long dry spells by spreading out discoveries—scheduling the programme so that something new is always on the horizon.

Sometimes the goal performance criterion which creates pressure for fraud/bias is not for the production of a certain number of winners but simply for completing a predetermined number of evaluations in a given year. One medical director told me that one of his staff had run 10 trials which showed a drug to be clear on a certain test, then fabricated data on the remaining 90 trials to show the same result. The fraud had been perpetrated by a scientist who was falling behind in his workload and who had an obligation to complete a certain number of evaluations for the year [Braithwaite, 1984: 94].

One might say that this is an inevitable problem for any company that is serious about setting performance goals for its people. But there are differences in the degrees of seriousness of the problem. At one extreme are companies that calculatedly set goals for their managers that they know can only be achieved by breaking the law. Thus, the pharmaceutical chief executive may tell her regional medical director to do whatever he has to do to get a product approved for marketing in a Latin American country, when she knows this will mean paying a bribe. Likewise, the coal mining executive may tell his mine manager to cut costs when he knows this will mean cutting corners on safety.

The mentality of "Do what you have to do but don't tell me how you do it" is widespread in business. Eliminating it is easy for executives who are prepared to set targets that are achievable in a responsible way. It is a question of top management attitudes. IBM is one example of a company that we found to have the approach we have in mind to target setting. IBM representatives do have a sales quota to meet. There is what is called a "100 Percent Club" of representatives who have achieved 100 percent or more of their quota. A majority of representatives make the 100 Percent Club, so the quotas are achievable by ethical sales practices. IBM in fact has a policy of ensuring that targets are attainable by legal means. Accordingly, quotas are adjusted downward when times are bad.

As Clinard (1983: 91-102, 140-44) found, unreasonable pressure on middle managers comes from the top, and most top managers have a fairly clear idea of how hard they can squeeze without creating a criminogenic organization. In the words of C. F. Luce, Chairman of Consolidated Edison: "The top manager has a duty not to push so hard that middle managers are pushed to unethical compromises" (Clinard, 1983: 142).

This "duty," however, takes us back to the fundamental problem of self-regulation. Companies have got to want to make themselves comply with the law sufficiently strongly to let this override other corporate goals. This sixth "principle" therefore really reduces to companies being motivated to be effectively self-regulating. As we said earlier, we believe companies can be so motivated both from their internal deliberations as moral agents and, more important, from external pressures calculated to make effective self-regulation an attractive policy. The design of these external pressures is the topic for another publication.

FROM CORPORATE TO TRADE ASSOCIATION SELF-REGULATION

Most of the discussion in this chapter has been about self-regulation by individual corporations rather than by associations of corporations. We believe that the same general principles of effectiveness are applicable to self-regulation at both levels, and for the same reasons. That is, effective self-regulation programs run by trade associations will

(1) give a lot of informal clout and backing from top management of member companies to compliance personnel employed by the trade association;
(2) ensure that managers in member companies who will be responsible for ensuring action on noncompliance detected by the association are identified in advance;
(3) monitor compliance performance carefully and let companies know when it is not up to standard;
(4) have effective communication of compliance problems to those capable of acting on them (for example, having mechanisms for ensuring that communication blockages within the trade association to protect favored member companies do not occur); and
(5) emphasize training and supervision for compliance.

Skepticism has often been voiced about the efficacy of self-regulation through trade associations. This is partly because of instances where such self-regulation has patently failed (see, for instance, Blakeney and Barnes, 1984), and partly because of the antitrust law implications of cooperative self-policing within an industry (Baum, 1961; Page, 1980; Zwicker, 1984). But assuming that trade associations could be spurred into running stauncher programs of self-regulation, and putting aside problems of antitrust violation, does self-regulation by trade associations have the same potential for compliance as that apparent in the context of self-regulation by particular corporations? Several critical differences suggest a negative answer.

One difference is that self-regulation by a trade association presupposes a transcorporate system of compliance rather than a system geared to the operations of one company. To the extent that compliance depends on an approach that is universalistic throughout a given industry rather than particularistic in relation to each member of an industry, it is likely to be less effective. In terms of command structure, access to information, and personnel loyalty, trade associations necessarily lack the capacity that each corporate member of an association has to police its own organization. Trade associations are outsiders attempting to pull the levers of intracorporate controls.

A second major difference lies in the difficulty trade associations have in mounting credible sanctions. At the level of informal sanctions, trade associations tend to lack the authority or influence that is found in many companies. We surmise that use of formal sanctions against noncompliant employees is not a necessary characteristic of effectively self-regulating companies because informal social control inside well-run companies can be so effective. In this sense, companies are like families; we do not expect the effectiveness of socialization in families to be necessarily related to how frequently children are smacked. However, nothing could be less like a family than an industry association. They are commonly uneasy alliances of companies that are trying to do each other in. It would be expecting a lot for informal social control to work in such a setting. There is no credible basis for shaming or for executives to turn away from disapproved conduct in the hope that this will earn "brownie points" for some future reward such as promotion. Thus, trade association self-regulation is likely to be only a faint symbolic activity unless breaches are punished by means of formal sanctions.

Trade associations can and sometimes do resort to formal sanctions—termination of membership, curtailment of membership benefits for a period, fines, press releases directing adverse publicity at the behavior of the offending company, or requests for regulatory action by the relevant government authority. However, it is notorious that even where formal sanctions are available they are rarely used (Blakeney and Barnes, 1984). The benefits offered by membership of a trade association tend to be less tangible or rewarding than the benefits offered by employment in a company, and hence a trade association lacks the control over vital contingencies necessary to impose formal sanctions with teeth. Here it is instructive to contrast the position of corporate trade associations with that of professional associations, some of which are empowered to discipline their members with the highly potent sanction of disqualification from practice.

To sum up, self-regulation by industry associations is devoid of any solid foundation for either informal or formal social control, and lacks the potential that self-regulation has at the level of the single company.

CONCLUSION

Our empirical research of the past eight years suggests to us that there are organizational characteristics distinguishing companies that are effectively self-regulating from those that are not. Equally, our data question some conventional wisdom—such as that relatively large compliance staffs are necessary for effective self-regulation.

Second, we have argued that there are grounds for pessimism that the most compliance-conscious trade associations can ever deliver the self-regulation of which the most compliance-conscious individual companies are capable. It follows that there is more mileage for regulators in strategies to elicit intracorporate private policing than trade association policing.

Such strategies exist. Direct regulatory enforcement—by prosecution, license suspension, adverse publicity, or other means—is one outstandingly important way of putting pressure on companies to self-regulate. Indeed, given what we have said about the greater resources, expertise, and capacity to get to the truth available from corporate compared to government compliance efforts, government regulatory strategies should be evaluated less in terms of their direct deterrent effect on deviant managers and more in terms of how successfully they trigger corporate controls to bring deviant managers to heel.

Regulatory agencies do not have to sit back and hope that their direct enforcement efforts will trigger self-regulatory enforcement. They can actively negotiate social contracts with individual companies. In the absence of convincing evidence that certain of the self-regulatory guarantees discussed in this chapter are in place, companies can be told that they will be targeted for more interventionist direct enforcement. Alternatively, self-regulatory practices proven to be effective by the most vigilant companies, in some circumstances might appropriately be made mandatory for all companies.

In short, understanding what makes self-regulation tick is not a field of interest only to optimists who see appeals to corporate social responsibility as the best route to ethical corporate conduct.

REFERENCES

BAUM, D. J. (1961) "Self regulation and antitrust: supression of deceptive advertising by the publishing media." *Syracuse Law Review* 12: 289-304.

BLAKENEY, M. and S. BARNES (1984) "Advertising deregulation: public health or private profit," in R. Tomasic (ed.) *Business Regulation in Australia*. Sydney: CCH.

BOULTON, D. B. (1978) *The Grease Machine: The Inside Story of Lockheed's Dollar Diplomacy.* New York: Harper & Row.

BRAITHWAITE, J. (1982) "Challenging just deserts: punishing white-collar criminals." *Journal of Criminal Law and Criminology* 73: 723-763.

———(1984) *Corporate Crime in the Pharmaceutical Industry.* London: Routledge & Kegan Paul.

———(1985) *To Punish or Persuade: Enforcement of Coal Mine Safety.* Albany: State University of New York Press.

———and B. FISSE (1985) "Varieties of responsibility and organizational crime." *Law and Policy,* 7: 315-343.

CLARK, J. (1979) *The Japanese Company.* New Haven, CT: Yale University Press.

CLINARD, M. (1983) *Corporate Ethics and Crime: The Role of Middle Management.* Beverly Hills, CA: Sage.

———and P. YEAGER (1980) *Corporate Crime.* New York: Free Press.

COFFEE, J. C., Jr. (1977) "Beyond the shut-eyed sentry: toward a theoretical view of corporate misconduct and an effective legal response." *Virginia Law Review* 63: 1099-1278.

CRANSTON, R. (1984) *Consumers and the Law.* London: Weidenfeld and Nicholson.

CRESSEY, D. and C. A. MOORE (1980) *Corporation Codes of Ethical Conduct.* New York: Peat Marwick and Mitchell Foundation.

Exxon Corporation (1973) *Policy Statement, Financial Controls—Internal Auditing.* New York: Author.

FISSE, B. and J. BRAITHWAITE (1983) *The Impact of Publicity on Corporate Offenders*. Albany: State University of New York Press.

GEIS, G. (1973) "Victimization patterns in white-collar crime," in I. Drapkin and E. Viano (eds.) *Victimology: A New Focus, vol. 1*. Lexington, MA: Lexington Books.

———(1982) *On White-Collar Crime*. Lexington, MA: Lexington Books.

GRABOSKY, P. N. (1984) "Corporate crime in Australia: an agenda for research." *Australian and New Zealand Journal of Criminology* 17: 95-107.

GROSS, E. (1978) "Organizations as criminal actors," in P. R. Wilson and J. Braithwaite (eds.) *Two Faces of Deviance: Crimes of the Powerless and Powerful*. Brisbane, Australia: University of Queensland Press.

KANTER, R. M. (1983) *The Change Masters: Corporate Entrepreneurs at Work*. London: Unwin Paperbacks.

KATZ, R. N. [ed.] (1976) "Industry self-regulation: a viable alternative to government regulation," in R. Katz, (ed.) *Protecting Consumer Interests*, Cambridge, MA: Ballinger.

PAGE, A. C. (1980) "Self regulation and codes of practice." *Journal of Business Law* 24-31.

REIMAN, J. H. (1979) *The Rich Get Richer and the Poor Get Prison*. New York: John Wiley.

REISMAN, W. M. (1979) *Folded Lies: Bribery, Crusades and Reforms*. New York: Free Press.

Securities and Exchange Commission (1969) *35th Annual Report*. Washington, DC: Author.

SHEARING, C. D. and P. C. STENNING (1981) "Modern private security: its growth and its implications," in M. Tonry and N. Morris (eds.) *Crime and Justice: An Annual Review*. Chicago: University of Chicago Press.

STONE, C. (1975) *Where the Law Ends: The Social Control of Corporate Behavior*. New York: Harper & Row.

———(1985) "Corporate regulation: the place of social responsibility," in B. Fisse and P. French (eds.) *Corrigible Corporations and Unruly Law*. San Antonio, TX: Trinity University Press.

WICKMAN, P. and T. BAILEY (1982) *White-Collar and Economic Crime*. Lexington, MA: Lexington Books.

ZWICKER, D. (1984) "Trade associations in Germany and the U.S.A.—antitrust restrictions on the ability of trade associations to regulate themselves." *Antitrust Bulletin* 29: 775-831.

Chapter 10

THE WIDENING WEBS OF SURVEILLANCE:
Private Police
Unraveling Deceptive Claims

NANCY REICHMAN

Private policing is expanding rapidly. As early as 1970 the number of private police was roughly equivalent to the number of public police (Shearing and Stenning, 1983). With retrenchment in the public sector and expansion in the private, private police are now believed to outnumber public police by approximately two to one (Cunningham and Taylor, 1983). Even these numbers may greatly underestimate the extent of private policing. Surveillance of private places and transactions is being conducted by actors who traditionally have not been counted as among the rank and file of private police. Insurance adjusters who monitor insurance claims, corporate risk managers, and "loss consultants" often are not included in estimates of private police strength.

The growth in private policing has been linked to socioeconomic changes demanding more extensive, intensive, categorical, and preventively oriented social control (Foucault, 1977; Spitzer and Scull, 1977; Donzelot, 1979; Spitzer, 1979; Shearing and Stenning, 1981, 1982, 1983; Mathieson, 1983; Bottoms, 1983, as well as others). The extension of corporate involvement into all facets of economic life has led to greater private interest in social regulation (Spitzer and Scull, 1977; 25). The development of "mass private property," shopping centers, high-rise buildings, manufacturing complexes, and the like has increased the amount of public life that occurs in privately owned places, and consequently is subject to

AUTHOR'S NOTE: This research was funded in part by the National Institute of Justice, grant 81-IJ-CX-0044.

private control (Shearing and Stenning, 1983). Similarly, the "administrative revolutions" of capitalist development (for example, techniques of social engineering and information management) have changed the problem and practice of social control. Exclusionary regulation has been abandoned in favor of more inclusionary, penetrating, and private forms (Spitzer, 1982). The focus of social control has shifted from the management of individuals to planned manipulation of whole groups and categories (Mathieson, 1983).

Changes in the nature of transactions have argued for greater penetration and intensity in policing activities as well. In contemporary society the growth in bureaucracies has meant a significant increase in the proportion of transactions occurring within organizational contexts (Coleman, 1982). Property transactions take place against bureaucratic "backgrounds," away from public scrutiny and control. New, more penetrating techniques and agents are required to surface violations deeply embedded in organizational process or "lost" within complex organizational structures (Vaughan, 1984).

Policing needs also have changed as increased specialization and reliance on fiduciaries have diffused responsibility for specific acts (Shapiro, 1985). "Symbolic commodities" such as insurance policies, pensions, stock options, patents, and royalties (Shapiro, 1984) are not easily monitored through face-to-face interaction. Events must be evaluated retroactively as when insurance agents investigate claims for loss of income due to injuries suffered some time prior to claim filing.[1] Retroactive reviews of transactions involving symbolic commodities often require third-party, documentary accounts (Rule et al., 1983) which are subject to falsification, fabrication, and other forms of data manipulation (Shapiro, 1984; Vaughan, 1984; Reichman, 1983; and Bowyer, 1982). And, because transactions and data about them often are spread over time and across institutional space, regulators can no longer afford to be tied to a single form of surveillance and control.

The demands for more extensive and intensive surveillance are being met with a variety of new surveillance techniques. Electronic beepers, video scanners, computer matches, light-amplifying devices, parabolic microphones, breathalyzers, brain-wave scanners, voice stress analyzers, and toxic drug screens have profoundly changed the nature of surveillance (Marx, 1985). By transforming the meaningless (for instance, sound waves) into the meaningful (a conversation), by joining what was heretofore unjoinable (matching heretofore disparate data), and by making what was hidden (body chemicals) apparent, these new surveillance techniques have increased the intensity and scope of what can be watched and what can be revealed. (For a discussion of some of these techniques see Rule et al., 1983; Marx and Reichman, 1984; Marx, 1984.) Social control has become "front loaded" as data are collected and analyzed on all individuals, not just those one has reason to suspect.

New configurations of surveillance agents also have appeared. We are beginning to witness the blending of private and public authorities and the creation of new public-private enterprises. (See Marx, this volume.) Specialized security personnel, such as computer security experts, have emerged to patrol and protect new forms of property (see also Shearing and Stenning, 1983.) At the same time, surveillance has been added to the routine activities of many organizational actors. Insurance adjusters, bank tellers, welfare workers, as well as others have added surveillance to the list of their official duties. Finally, existing private police authorities have expanded the range of their operations to include new types of investigation. There appears to be a ready market for the private police entrepreneur.

The topography of current private police practice reflects an interesting dialectic between the trend toward increased specialization in social control functions and attempts to integrate social control into other forms of social interaction. One consequence of these concurrent trends is likely to be a widening and deepening of the social control net (Cohen, 1979).[2]

Until recently, however, little research has focused on the dynamic configuration of private policing authorities. Scholarly interest in the comparison of state and private police has drawn our attention away from examining differences among and links between private forms. The following discussion represents one effort to fill in the gaps.

This chapter explores the organizational dispersion of private policing by examining the interlocking webs of surveillance woven around insurance transactions.[3] Rather than taking a broad view of private policing trends, I focus on the set of actors and the range of private interests involved in the investigation of one type of violation—specifically, fraudulent auto theft insurance claims. Although standing alone each private agent has relatively little power, this configuration of surveillance combined represents a potentially formidable mechanism of private regulation. Included in this discussion are non-state actors involved in the investigation of fraudulent auto thefts. Because of the focus of this volume, state actors (that is, traditional law enforcement personnel and agents of state-run fraud bureaus) who may be called in for assistance are excluded. (For a discussion of the latter, see Reichman, 1983.)

DECEPTIVE INSURANCE CLAIMING: THE CASE OF AUTO THEFT FRAUD

The insurance mechanism is a means for sharing and thus reducing individual uncertainty. A group of individuals subject to the same peril (such as auto theft) contributes to a shared "risk pool," most often organized and administered by a private insurance company. In return for their monetary contributions to the risk pool policyholders receive the promise of indemnification (compensation sufficient to restore them to their previous financial status) should they suffer a loss. The insurance contract formally establishes the insurance relationship.

Trust is essential to insurance success. Those paying premiums trust that by purchasing insurance their assets are protected. Companies assuming risk trust that the risks they assume are objective ones[4] and that policyholders have been truthful in their representations before and after losses occur. All too often, this trust can be misplaced.

Insurance industry officials estimate that nationwide from 10% to 20% of auto theft claims are being filed for thefts that never occur (Aetna Life and Casualty, 1980). Insurance policyholders fabricate loss circumstances and reports to make it appear that their cars have been stolen when, in fact, they have been ditched into lakes, intentionally crushed, burned, or sold. The "victims" call the police, report the "theft," and file theft claims complete with details about where and when the vehicles were last seen.

Whatever their specific motive, fraud offenders typically operate under the assumption that the potential insurance settlement will be more valuable than the property itself. This may be because the car has become defective and the cost of repair and replacement is greater than the owner is willing to pay. Or it may simply be that the car has become obsolete. As long as the insurance settlement matches or exceeds the car's market value, "selling the car to the insurance company"—that is, receiving compensation for a theft that never occurred—is a profitable exchange.

Exposure to fraudulent auto theft claims became a source of insurance industry concern in the late 1970s. The problem was threefold. First, although precise data were not available, industry personnel believed that the amount of fraudulent activity was increasing significantly over that occurring only a decade ago (*New York Times,* July 6, 1982). Second, rate relief was no longer adequately covering greater loss exposures. Third, because auto theft frauds involve a high percentage of unrecovered vehicles, companies could no longer use traditional methods for recovering claim costs. Technically, when an insurance company pays an auto theft claim it purchases the title of the vehicle from the owner. If the car is later recovered, the company can sell it and use that money to reduce its overall claim liability.[5] But, when auto theft fraud is involved, there are no cars to sell.

Faced with increased company costs many of the larger insurance companies intensified their efforts at controlling auto theft fraud. They did so by adding surveillance to the existing responsibilities of insurance actors, by creating new specialized personnel to review claims, by engaging private investigators, and by supporting industry-wide efforts to reduce fraud opportunities.

THE EXPANDING SURVEILLANCE WEB

The insurance industry's perspective on policing fraudulent auto theft differs from that of public authorities.[6] In contrast to conventional law enforcement who watch in order to apprehend suspects, the object of surveillance in the insurance context is to minimize insurance losses—to lower insurance settlements or reduce opportunities to engage in fraudulent behavior.[7] The strategies available for loss control include: (1) mitigating fraud effects by agreeing to pay less than the amount claimed; (2) denying the claim; (3) invoking criminal sanctions and hopefully deterring would-be offenders; and (4) more effective tracking of vehicle ownership and insurance company liabilities.

To carry out these objectives a multiagent, loosely coupled enforcement network was established. The network represents a variety of surveillance forms including ad hoc surveillance embedded into existing insurance practices; purposeful and focused surveillance conducted by specialized units; generalized surveillance conducted by entrepreneurs; and automated surveillance conducted by industrywide regulators. Some of the dimensions or ways that these private forms of surveillance can be compared are: (1) objective or interest; (2) derivation of cases; (3) patterns of intelligence;

(4) level of intensity; (5) level of extensity; (6) measure of performance; (7) degree of specialization; and (8) degree of integration. After a brief description of each form of surveillance, the chapter concludes with a discussion of how the combination of these differences (that is, interlocking webs of surveillance) provides a wide-ranging system of surveillance.

Ad Hoc Surveillance Embedded Into Other Organizational Activities

One piece of the fraud-control program focused on integrating surveillance into the existing routines of insurance adjusters. Adjusters or claims service representatives are responsible for reviewing *all* theft claims submitted to insurance companies. Their job is to clarify the parties' obligations under the insurance contract and to arrive at an appropriate amount of compensation. In the course of their review they consider the vehicle's condition at the time of loss, identify individuals with insurable interests,[8] and compare loss events (where, when, and how losses occurred) with the documentation of loss submitted by claimants. Because many auto insurance company claimants are also clients, claim evaluation is often tempered by the need to protect positive images of client service (Webb et. al., 1981). Good service (prompt, fair, and acceptable loss adjustments) is important for attracting new insurance business and retaining old (Pfeffer, 1974).

Establishing the cause of loss and extent of damages are central to determining the extent of a company's obligation to pay a claim. Consequently, much of the adjusters' attention is focused here. Claims personnel interview claimants, obtain official records of loss events, and contact witnesses in their effort to document loss details and the extent of damage sustained.

Because many thefts leave no evidence to inspect, this type of claim poses special problems for insurance adjusters. Because the cars are legitimately missing, adjusters are forced to rely on the truthfulness of after-the-fact accounts of property characteristics and loss details. Complex information requirements, heavy workloads, goal conflicts, ambiguous rules, and information overload often prevent them from verifying and confirming all the data they do receive. (For a discussion of these constraints see Reichman, 1983.)

Recognizing these constraints and yet faced with increasing exposure to fraudulent auto theft claims, industry officials developed a series of profiles to enhance fraud recognition by adjusters. These profiles are actually a set of "red flags" that outline factors associated with several fraud scenarios. One interesting consequence of the profiling system is that claimants are asked at the outset to supply adjusters with information that previously would have been asked only if the claims required further investigation. In addition, certain types of auto theft claims, such as cars recovered totally burned, are immediately suspect. (For a more in-depth analysis of these profiles see Reichman, 1983.)

Adjusters use the profiles to analyze and screen data they receive as part of the normal adjustment process. Cases that match the profiles are flagged for further investigation. Because of the constraints already outlined, they rarely conduct these investigations themselves. Instead, these claims are passed on to more specialized fraud investigators for more intensive review.

Purposeful Surveillance by Specialized Units

Many of the larger insurance companies responded to the "fraud problem" by creating units specializing in fraud detection and investigation.[9] Special Investigative Units (SIUs) were established first in Massachusetts, noted for its high auto theft rate and unique regulatory structure, [10] but quickly spread to other states. The units were designed to expand the scope of claim review beyond the details of the claimed loss. Rather than simply attending to the amount the company was obligated to pay (the adjuster's function), SIU investigations were designed to focus on the legitimacy of the claim itself, specifically on the claimant's motive for filing the claim. This required inquiries of significantly larger scope and intensity than could be managed by an adjuster. Included in SIU review is information related to the car's history (prior owners, maintenance, and past damage) as well as information on the claimant's activities and lifestyle.[11]

Cases are referred to the Special Investigative Unit from field or desk adjusters on the basis of similarity to fraud profiles. The decision to investigate any one case referred depends on the depth and documentation of the adjusters' initial suspicions as well as workload pressures of the investigators. Investigators usually conduct 8-10 investigations per month.

The investigations are purposeful—that is, directed to insurance outcomes related to claim payments. [12] Investigators begin by gathering all the relevant documents: the claim; police report; vehicle title; and then interviewing the claimant. Interviews are conducted in the claimants' homes. Investigators use these opportunities to "eyeball" the claimants, that is, to assess whether the claims make sense given the individuals' living circumstances. Are they likely to own the type of car they claim was stolen? They continue researching the claimant by running a credit check, verifying employment, examining previous claims filed, and contacting local police.

To establish the vehicle's condition at the time of the alleged "theft," investigators then construct a history of the car. They obtain a list of previous owners, and documents of the most recent servicing of the car. If the car has not been recovered, information on who serviced the car and when it was last serviced is obtained from the claimant and verified through interviews. If the car is recovered, this information can be obtained from service stickers inserted on the inside of the driver's door. Investigators verify the last inspection, find witnesses who can verify the car's condition at the time of loss; and contact anyone who has a lien on the car. They also will contact the agent who wrote the insurance policy, if one did so, to determine whether the agent ever inspected the car before the policy was written.

The Special Investigative Units are evaluated in terms of the net dollar savings that their actions bring to the company. Savings are calculated by tabulating the claim dollars that would have been paid if not for the actions of the SIUs. [13] Companies calculate savings by totaling the figures for claims that were denied outright plus dollar differences between claims submitted and actual claims paid. Thus, if after SIU investigation a claim was reduced from $100 to $50, the company would cite a $50 savings. Commercial Union, one of the SIU leaders, noted that the first nine months of their two-person operation racked up almost a quarter of million dollars in such savings (*Beacon* August/September, 1978: 3) Perhaps a larger and unmeasured effect of SIU activities is deterrence. [14] Investigators interviewed believe that nonprofessionals are "scared off" by the Special Investigative Unit whereas professionals take their business to companies that do not have them. [15]

In attempting to increase company savings SIU investigators expand the web of surveillance beyond details of the specific insurance transaction (the auto theft claim). Starting from the theft itself, the investigation reaches outward to include extra-insurance details that might shed light on the method and motive of fraud. Investigators often conclude their investigation with a different, more credible, version of the car's disappearance developed during their investigation.[16]

In addition to increasing the scope of investigations, Special Investigative Units have forged new links between surveillance agents (see also Ghezzi, 1983.) SIU investigators working in a particular city meet regularly to discuss their cases. The informal network has streamlined the cross-company inquiry system so that information useful to a particular fraud investigation can be exchanged in a timely fashion. Legislation providing insurance companies with immunity from civil prosecution when they exchange information in the course of an auto theft investigation has facilitated the growth of SIU networks and cooperation with public police.

Generalized Surveillance by Surveillance Entrepreneurs[17]

When information needs extend beyond what company employees can do for themselves, either because no qualified investigators are on staff or because of the type and amount of information required, "consultants" might be brought in. This is more likely to occur when an insurance fraud involves a substantial dollar loss (multiple claims) or has a high probability of ending up in court. Deceptive claims may become civil court cases if the company refuses to pay the claim and the claimant sues for recovery. Most frauds can be criminally prosecuted under a variety of theft and fraud statutes.

In contrast to SIU investigators who investigate for a specific purpose (establishing their company's liability), private investigators investigate to produce information that someone else (an insurance company) will use.[18] They are information brokers. It is the profitable sale of the information they generate, not insurance company savings, that drives their operation.

Without a client, someone who is willing to "foot the bill," the agency will not continue its investigation, no matter what stage the investigation is in when the funding stops. Consequently, the nature of the investigation is determined by how much money the client is willing to spend on the investigation, an amount often negotiated before any investigatory action is taken.[19]

A team approach to investigatory activity reinforces the agency's interest in gathering information for its own sake. A single case is divided into tasks that are assigned to the staff. Investigators are responsible only for their piece of the puzzle. Sometimes an investigator's "pieces" add up to the entire case; most often, they do not. In the spirit of information brokering, investigators appear ready to follow any lead that might arise, particularly when it means increased revenue for the firm. The case files are full of odd pieces of information jotted down by investigators "just in case" that information should prove useful on that or any other future case.

Many of the activities they engage in were similar to those of the insurance company investigator. They research public and private documents and interview individuals who can shed light on the claimants or on the circumstances surrounding the loss. But, in their search for information private investigators penetrate far more deeply into the backgrounds of their subjects than do insurance company investigators or adjusters. They are not tempered by any client relationships with the subjects of their investigation. They routinely have access to more sophisticated tools of surveillance (such as parabolic microphones and infrared cameras) than do insurance company employees. They are more likely to observe their subjects for extended periods of time, to go undercover to infiltrate suspected fraudulent organizations, and to look for past associations that would link apparently unrelated actors.

Because they sell their information and their time, investigators are careful to document their activities. They always take notes, even during interviews that are recorded. Documents are photocopied while information obtained from them is taken down in note form. Field notes are organized into memos detailing an investigator's activities. Despite this extensive recording of their activities agency investigators are often unaware of the final dispositions of their cases. For them, when the report is sent to the client, the case is closed.[20]

Private investigators produce an intensity in investigation not found in the Special Investigative Units. This intensity can be associated, in part, with the "gumshoe" role. Agents played their parts well. Yet another source for their greater intensity can be found in the reward structures of each. SIU investigators are rewarded for reducing claim costs with little regard for how that is accomplished. Private investigators are rewarded for drawing the best (most complete) picture of their surveillance subject. A private investigator's performance is measured in terms of how much information can be obtained, not in how it is ultimately used. Private investigators will continue to dig and dig as long as someone agrees to foot the bill.

Automated Surveillance by Industrywide Regulators

Established in 1912 the National Auto Theft Bureau (NATB) assists insurance and law enforcement communities in the recovery and identification of stolen vehicles and prevention of future auto thefts. A nationwide organization supported by nearly 500 insurance companies, NATB acts as a clearinghouse for auto theft information. NATB agents also are authorized to represent the insurance industry in signing criminal complaints. They help initiate criminal prosecution in cases where heretofore it was "not practical" for individual insurance companies to do so.

Maintaining the North American Theft Information System (NATIS) is the keystone of NATB's activity. Many states have adopted legislation requiring law enforcement officials and/or insurance personnel to submit auto theft reports to the NATB. The index contains pertinent information on thefts of passenger vehicles, trucks, trailers, boats, and construction vehicles. Data collected include identifying numbers, insurance information, and loss details. An on-line computer system, which by the end of 1979 held 1.5 million records, provides immediate access to NATB information by vehicle identification number (VIN) or NATB record number. They also have access to manufacturers' production records on microfiche. These records are the first chapter of the vehicle's biography and can be used to verify VINs at the time of manufacture, to provide information about where the vehicle was shipped after leaving the assembly plant, to trace vehicles and/or to verify a claimant's statement about where and when the vehicle was purchased. NATB is the exclusive recipient of the "confidential" Vehicle Identification Number (VIN) used to identify vehicles when their outward appearances have been altered substantially. All of this information is available to law enforcement officials investigating vehicle thefts and to insurance companies who are attempting to verify claims (also see NATB Annual Report, 1979).

In the late 1970s, NATB added its most important weapon in the fight against insurance fraud, a computerized index of salvage information. This index contains records of all vehicles reported stolen and all vehicles reported "totaled" and sold as salvage. (According to insurance definitions a car is totaled when the cost of repair exceeds the "book value" of the car.) These records are used to detect "paper car" schemes. Fraud offenders who employ this scheme purchase certificates of title for salvaged vehicles, use the titles to insure nonexistent vehicles; and then report the nonexistent vehicles stolen. Because the cars never existed, they cannot be recovered.

When a new auto theft report is entered into the NATB system, a routine search is conducted of the existing data base to determine whether the Vehicle Identification Number of the car now reported stolen had been previously entered as a total loss. A match suggests that the new claim involves a paper car.

As the official record keepers for an entire industry and an entire class of events, NATB agents have a unique surveillance perspective. Centralized data bases increase the organizational memory of the industry as a whole, and, by doing so, increase the potential to recognize patterns of fraud. Unlike SIU or private investigators they can view a great number of fraudulent transactions all at the same time while remaining divorced from particular persons or events. They offer a type of "direct checking" (Rule et. al., 1983) by which organizations are able to obtain information about individuals directly from other organizations. With computerization, information they obtain can be "freeze dried"[21] for analysis and used at a much later date and in ways unrelated to its initial collection. (For a more complete discussion of the impact of computerization on surfacing rule violations, see Reichman and Marx, 1985.)

In contrast to the increased intensity that private investigators provide, the NATB offers more extensive and categorical surveillance. The data collection strategies of the NATB widen and in many ways deepen the surveillance net. Electronic data links break down many of the structural barriers that prevented information sharing and exposure. More important, data are now collected and retained on all auto related transactions, not just those that insurance companies have reason to suspect.

A COMBINATION OF DIFFERENCES

The set of actors that can be engaged to review suspicious claims demonstrates on a small scale the breadth of surveillance that can be activated to review even a single type of economic transaction.

Organizational differences between adjusters, SIU investigators, private investigators, and NATB agents create different surveillance opportunities for these different actors. It is the combination of differences along the dimensions cited earlier that widens the web of private surveillance.[22]

Few actors have the capacity to see it all. There is no necessary panoptic vision here. Each type of surveillance agent has its own perspective, a slightly different angle on a similar problem. Taken together, these varied agents weave a blanket of surveillance with the potential to cover a significant number of fraudulent transactions.

Differences in the goals or objectives of surveillance produce investigations of qualitatively different scope and depth. Compare the activities of agents of insurance companies to agents of the NATB. SIU investigators are employed directly by insurance companies. Their incentives to look for fraud are associated with the job pressures and rewards that emerge directly from their specific insurance organizations. They investigate in an effort to reduce their companies' liability to pay specific claims. NATB agents, supported by a consortium of insurance companies, serve more general interests. Rather than relating their activities to specific insurance outcomes, they are rewarded organizationally for their ability to help "suppress" opportunities for thefts and false claiming and for facilitating the prosecution of fraud offenders generally. Thus, at the same time that SIU investigators are engaging in activities to control the actions of specific insurance claimants, NATB agents are attempting to restructure the claiming environment.

As Shapiro (1984) found when investigating the detection strategies available to Securities and Exchange Commission (SEC) investigators, structural location of a detection strategy or agent has a significant influence on what can be revealed. Claims personnel, for example, rarely extend their surveillance beyond the details of a specific theft claim. NATB agents, located at the periphery, can oversee the movement of cars and documents about them nationwide. Private investigators who are not tied to particular authorities are the most fluid in surveillance perspective. They are able to move in and about the social fabric. Moreover, because they are less visible than other agent types, they are less likely to be monitored by third parties other than their direct clients. Fewer restrictions on their activities often permits greater penetration into the inner sanctums of fraudulent activities.

Surveillance on the periphery (such as the SEC's market surveillance or NATB's salvage index) is likely to uncover offenses larger in scope than surveillance conducted more toward the center of fraudulent activity. Increasing the potential to catch larger frauds is not without cost in investigatory precision, however. The information uncovered at the center tends to be more accurate and of greater depth than that revealed from further afield.

Different types of lenses used by surveillance agents also are likely to produce qualitatively different types of cases as well. Because of the kinds of documents they use and their reliance on computerized data, NATB agents, for example, are best at discovering standardized or typical patterns of violation that can be specified well in advance. (For discussions of the implications of standardized discovery see Marx and Reichman, 1984, and Reichman and Marx, 1985.) Similarly, because cases referred to Special Investigative Units by insurance adjusters are sent to them because they match a predetermined profile of violation, SIU investigators tend to be locked into particular case types. Private investigators who are not bound to particular organizational locales or routines are more likely to unravel more idiosyncratic or atypical frauds.

The different surveillance agents have access to different types of sanctions as well. Agents who are employed directly by insurance companies—adjusters and special investigators—work with the authority of capital and have access to the legal, economic, and social power that such authority implies. As recognized elsewhere (Shearing and Stenning, 1983), the economic sanctions available to private police are often more varied and discretionary than the physical sanctions available to those who police with the state's authority. In the insurance context sanctions include the denial of insurance compensation and restriction of future access to insurance services. Because auto theft insurance is mandatory for those who purchase automobiles on credit, these sanctions can be very severe indeed.

But private authorities are not restricted to imposing economic sanctions. Again, here is where we see the strength of deploying a combination of policing agents, rather than a single one. Organizations like the NATB were established, in part, to bridge the gap between private and public sanctioning authority. Although NATB agents have no direct sanctioning authority themselves, because of the services they perform for public authorities, they provide the insurance industry with access to more physically coercive state sanctions. Thus, by utilizing a web of surveillance private authorities can extend the range of sanctioning options available to them.

CONCLUSION

Because of the implicit state-private comparison, many studies of private police have tended to view them as all of a kind. To the extent that they have been explored, differences tend to focus only on the range of investigatory services a private policing authority might provide. This chapter offers an alternate view.

The complexity of economic life and the fluidity of transactions demands a more intensive and extensive system of surveillance than can be managed by a single type of surveillance agent. As the theatre of policing becomes ever more the theatre of everyday life, social control becomes enmeshed into the routines of organizations with different sets of goals and objectives. "Tiny theatres" of private control supplement the more centralized state apparatus. Because they are linked with other forms of social interaction and appear more limited in individual scope, these private forms of policing often seem less threatening, less intrusive, and less important than state forms.

The apparent insignificance of individual private efforts, at least as measured against more coercive and centralized state power, should not blind us to their potential strengths. Standing alone, some of the private policing authorities as described are more powerful than others. Combined they become even more powerful. Interlocking private webs of surveillance increases the number and kinds of transactions that can be watched, as well as the sanctions that can be employed. This raises an important new question for social control. We should not only ask how powerful do we want specific social control agents to become. We also need to ask what are the links—technical, organizational, economic, and political—that might join agents with quite different surveillance objectives and perspectives. Similarly, what new possibilities of neutralization might emerge given the dispersal of social control?

NOTES

1. Compare these investigations to those in which regulators conduct on-site inspections or to the routine patrol of city streets or shopping malls for evidence of infractions.

2. As Marx (1985) correctly suggests recent rock-and-roll songs reinforce the dispersion of social control thesis. Consider, for example, the song by Rockwell: "I always feel like somebody's watching me. Can't get no privacy."

3. Because the surveillance of false auto theft insurance claims is not organizationally bound, data for this chapter were derived from a number of different

sources. A total of 62 interviews were conducted with insurance claims managers and fraud investigators. In order to interview representatives from companies that had significant experience with fraud, yet varied in terms of size and clientele, a sample of companies writing auto insurance in one eastern state was derived. The sample included the top 5 companies with respect to 1979 market share for particular property-casualty lines in each of three company categories outlined by A.M. Best, the major reporting agency for the industry. From that list interviews were secured with a number of representatives from 23 different companies. Interviews were conducted with at least one staff member in the eight special investigative units operating in one major metropolitan area. Among other questions respondents were asked to describe normal claims procedures, typical fraud cases encountered, and control strategies. Two special investigators permitted me to observe their daily routine. Observations were limited to a few days in each case. An additional 12 interviews were conducted with law enforcement personnel and with representatives from industrywide organizations providing fraud detection and control services to insurance companies. Finally, I spent 30 days observing the routines of one small private investigative agency. Interviews were conducted with the agency director before and after my visit. The purpose of my visit was to review extensive case files of fraud investigations. During that time informal interviews were conducted with all agency personnel. Unless otherwise noted, all observations are drawn from my interviews and observations.

4. The theoretical basis for insurance, neoclassical models of utility and welfare, assumes the independence of events as well as equality among individuals making choices.

5. Historically, as many as 75% of stolen cars were eventually recovered. Since a car's parts are sometimes worth more than the whole, close to the total amount paid to the claimant can be recovered through such sales.

6. Many states have criminal statutes prohibiting the filing of false auto theft claims. Auto theft fraud can be prosecuted under a number of general theft and fraud statutes as well.

7. These objectives are consistent with those outlined by Shearing and Stenning (1983) as those that apply generally to private policing.

8. Insurable interest is defined as a relation between an individual and the risk insured such that in the event that the contingency occurs, the individual would suffer financial and economic harm. Banks holding property mortgages have insurable interests in their property.

9. Private fraud squads have begun to crop up in other insurance areas as well. Fraud units are being established among medical insurance companies "not just to weed out suspicious claims but to build criminal cases against doctors, and other health care providers and sometimes even subscribers whom they suspect are cheating" (Mills, 1985: 29).

10. For a discussion of why the Massachusetts regulatory structure was a significant factor in the development of the SIU, see Ghezzi (1983).

11. Special investigative units varied in size from one investigator to four or five. In the larger units a supervisor was responsible for case assignments and review. SIU staffs bring to the units a varied array of backgrounds and prior experiences. Some units are staffed by former claims representatives who have proved to be solid investigators. The larger units often include a combination of former claims personnel and former law enforcement agents. The ideal situation seems

to be a combination of claims personnel and property appraisers who bring insurance experience to the unit and former law enforcement officials who bring investigatory training and law enforcement contacts to insurance investigations. Individuals are not recruited directly into the special investigative units unless they are recruited from the ranks of former police officers. Insurance personnel who enter the units do so only after a significant period of employment as insurance adjusters (no less that five or more years).

12. One of three actions will result: (1) If SIU investigation reveals no fraud on the part of the claimant, the claim will be paid. (2) If in the course of their review, SIU personnel discover that certain parts of the claim are, indeed, fraudulent, those pieces may be disallowed in the settlement. (3) If SIU staff find evidence of fraud sufficient enough to stand the test of a civil challenge by the claimant, the entire claim may be denied. In some rare cases (less than 5% of all cases) criminal prosecution is pursued. These cases usually involve fraud rings defrauding several insurers who band together and present their case to the authorities. By joining together, no one company is stigmatized as either a fraud victim or as aggressively pursuing claimants.

13. The problems with this type of measurement are twofold. First, it is not clear that these savings would not have occurred without SIU intervention. Second, with respect to claims denied, it is not clear that the companies would have paid the total claim. In fact, normal adjustment might have reduced the claim by 50%. If so, the savings attributed to the SIU would be far less than claimed. Finally, we do not know whether the claim denials will be upheld in civil court, and, if not, if the companies will ultimately pay more than the original claim. At the time of my research many of cases had not been tried and thus their ultimate dispositions are not known.

14. This position is consistent with white-collar crime literature, which suggests that deterrence is likely to be greater for those who commit white-collar or economic crimes than for conventional street criminals (see Braithwaite and Geis, 1982, and Gibbons, 1983, on "mundane" crimes).

15. It would be interesting to see whether control agents similarly "shop around" for the easiest people to catch.

16. It is difficult to determine how successful they are here. Most units report their success only in dollars saved, not number of claims.

17. This discussion of private investigators is drawn from an in-depth study of one private investigative firm involved in a variety of insurance cases including arson, auto theft, property theft, and art theft. Although many of the cases I researched involved arson, not auto theft, the steps of investigation tend to be similar across all case types. Moreover, this case study provides insights into the private investigator's interests in insurance fraud investigation.

18. Private investigators who conduct insurance fraud investigations are organized in many different ways ranging from lone operators to complex organizations where fraud investigation is one of many different functions performed by organization members. Interviews with a number of private investigators suggest that firms differ according to size, personnel (background, training, competence), and style. Although clearly important, further research is needed before any informed analysis of comparative types of private investigators can be drawn.

19. Some investigations are stopped far short of their stated goals. One company, for example, financed only a partial investigation when they simply wanted to enhance their bargaining position with the claimant. Of course, this could also

mean that some investigations are drawn out to fill out the negotiated amount. No systematic pattern in company decisions to follow through on investigations was readily apparent. Although claim size was clearly a factor, other factors—principally the ongoing relationship between investigators and clients—seems to play an important role as well.

20. Why wouldn't investigators try to learn about the ultimate disposition of their cases? Perhaps because they saw no benefit to doing so. They were paid. It is not clear that they would have any incentive to spend time finding out what happened with their investigations.

21. See, for example, Godwin and Humphreys (1982).

22. The web of surveillance may have the "absorbency" that Brodeur (1983) associates with "high policing."

REFERENCES

Aetna Life and Casualty (1980) Public Policy Issues Inventory. Hartford, CT: Author.

BOWYER, J. (1982) Cheating: Deception in War and Magic, Games and Sports, Sex and Religion, Business and Con Games, Politics and Espionage, Art and Science. New York: St. Martin's Press.

BOTTOMS, A. (1983) "Neglected features of contemporary penal systems," pp. 166-202 in D. Garland and P. Young (eds.) The Power to Punish. Atlantic Highlands, NJ: Humanities Press.

BRAITHWAITE, J. and G. GEIS (1982) "On theory and action for corporate crime control." Crime and Delinquency. 28: 292-315.

BRODEUR, J.-P. (1983) "High policing and low policing: remarks about the policing of political activities." Social Problems 30, 5: 507-520.

———(1984) "Policing: beyond 1984." Canadian Journal of Sociology 9, 2: 195-207.

COLEMAN, J. (1982) The Assymetric Society. New York: Basic Books.

CUNNINGHAM, W. C. and T. H. TAYLOR (1983) "Ten years of growth in law enforcement and the private security relationships." Police Chief 50, 6: 28-40.

DONZELOT, J. (1979) "The poverty of political culture." Ideology and Consciousness 5: 73-87.

FOUCAULT, M. (1977) Discipline and Punish: The Birth of the Prison. New York: Pantheon.

GIBBONS, D. C. (1983) "Mundane crime." Crime and Delinquency 29: 213-227.

GHEZZI, S. G. (1983) "A private network of social control: insurance investigation units." Social Problems 30, 5: 521-531.

GODWIN, G. and L. HUMPHREYS (1982) "Freeze dried stigma: cybernetics and social control." Humanity and Society (November): 391-408.

MARX, G. T. (1984) "I'll be watching you: the new surveillance." Dissent (Winter): 26-34.

———(1985)"The iron fist in the velvet glove: totalitarian potentials within democratic structures." Revised version of paper presented at the annual meeting of the American Sociological Association, San Antonio, TX, August 1984.

———and N. REICHMAN (1984) "Routinizing the discovery of secrets: computers as informants." American Behavioral Scientist 27, 4: 423-452.

MATHIESON, T. (1983) "The future of control systems—the case of Norway,"
pp. 130-1454 in D. Garland and P. Young (eds.) The Power to Punish. Atlantic Highlands, NJ: Humanities Press.
MILLS, D. (1985) "Insurers use police tactics to snare doctors who file false
claims." Wall Street Journal (April 26): 29.
PFEFFER, I. (1974) Perspectives On Insurance. Englewood Cliffs, NJ: Prentice-
Hall.
REICHMAN, N. (1983) "Ferreting out fraud: the manufacture and control of
fraudulent insurance claims." Doctoral dissertation, Massachusetts Institute
of Technology.
———(1984) "Screening, sorting, classifying and excluding: social control in
the welfare state." Presented at the Annual Meeting of the American Society
of Criminology, Cincinnati, Ohio.
———and G. T. MARX (1985) "Generating organizational disputes: the impact
of computerization." Presented at the Annual Meeting of the Law and Society
Association, San Diego.
RULE, J., D. McADAM, L. STERNS, and D. UGLOW (1983) "Documentary
identification and mass surveillance in the United States." Social Problems.
31: 222-000.
SHAPIRO, S. (1984) Wayward Capitalists. New Haven, CT: Yale University
Press.
———(1985) "The social control of trust." Unpublished manuscript, New York
University.
SHEARING, C. D. and P. C. STENNING (1981) "Private security: it's growth
and implications," pp. 193-245 in M. Tonry and N. Morris (eds.) Crime and
Justice—An Annual Review of Research, vol. 3. Chicago: University of Chicago Press.
———(1982) "Snowflakes or good pinches? Private security's contribution to
modern policing," pp. 96-105 in R. Donelan (ed.) The Maintenance of Order
in Society. Ottawa: Canadian Police College.
———(1983) "Private security: implications for social control." Social Problems 30, 5: 493-506.
SPITZER, S. (1979) "The rationalization of crime control in capitalist society."
Contemporary Crisis 3: 187-206.
———(1982) "The dialectics of formal and informal control," in Richard Abel
(ed.) The Politics of Informal Justice, vol. 1. New York: Academic Press.
———and A. SCULL (1977) "Privatization and capitalist development: the case
of the private police." Social Problems 25, 1: 18-29.
VAUGHAN, D. (1984) Controlling Unlawful Organizational Behavior. Chicago:
University of Chicago Press.
WEBB, B. (1981) Insurance Company Operations, vol. 2 Malvern, PA: American Institute for Property and Liability Underwriters.

Chapter 11

PROSECUTORIAL AND ADMINISTRATIVE STRATEGIES TO CONTROL OF BUSINESS CRIME: PRIVATE AND PUBLIC ROLES

MICHAEL CLARKE

In this chapter I shall maintain that there are two fundamental strategies for the control of business crime, criminal prosecution and administrative action. I shall also argue that not only are there grounds for preferring the administrative to the prosecutorial strategy, but that that there is a variety of both pragmatic and more deeply rooted reasons why it is increasingly being used now and the pro-secutorial strategy abandoned. This is by no means to say, how-ever, that this trend is without difficulties, either of principle or in social practice. I will consider, by way of examples of the prob-lems of achieving control, recent developments in three industries: cargo shipping, pharmaceuticals, and the Britsh financial sector of the City of London. Before doing so, however, I will attempt to clarify some of the issues of principle that are involved as these frequently become confused in the heat of political responses to real situations.

Perhaps the easiest way to begin is by a brief characterization of the two strategies. The prosecutorial involves the determination of responsibility and guilt and envisages the imposition of sanctions. Rooted as it is in the courtroom trial, it is highly individualistic in its assignation of responsibility. Because of these features it is hedged with the constraints of due process to protect the accused from innuendo, unsubstantiated allegation, frame-ups, prejudice, scapegoating, and so on. The implicit objective of prosecution may

AUTHOR'S NOTE: I am indebted to Clifford Shearing for his comments on an earlier version of this chapter.

be said to be the legitimation of the imposition of sanctions that are held to be just punishment for offences, and may deter repetition. In most of these respects prosecution contrasts with administrative control, the implicit objective of which is not sanction but prevention of recurrence. The concern of administrative action is with the achievement and maintenance of standards, and attention is directed therefore not so much at individual offenders as at the category (or in this case industry) to be regulated. The objective is to identify the main risks of dangerous or antisocial conduct and to take action to minimize actual offensive behavior by publicizing standards, requiring proof of competence and good character from practitioners, requiring disclosure of accounts and other records, inspections of business activities, and the like, the exact pattern depending on the hazards posed by the industry in question. Administrative control is obviously lacking in due process, but this need not become an issue at the stage of truly preventive work because the agency involved should always be able to tell practitioners how they may meet its standards.

The problem with both the prosecutorial and the administrative mode is the offender. The prosecution process tends to be ineffective in cases where offenses are committed in a business environment for a variety of reasons. The prosecutor will find it hard to obtain adequate early access to the records of the business, and these may be, or may be deliberately made, deficient. Even when there is clear evidence in the records and through outside witnesses of an offense, it is often hard to assign responsibility. True, there are simple cases such as employee theft, but there are also far more complicated cases, such as when poor accounting is to be held reckless or negligent or, indeed, false; at what point the company's assets are being distributed as dividends; and who was responsible for a contaminated batch of product. The orientation of the administrative strategy is, of course, to get procedures and structures established that clarify these problems, but the fact remains that where these are not established, or not followed, it may make much more sense to say that the guilt lies with the inadequate organization of the business than with an arbitrary individual. Indeed, the administrative solution to this dilemma is to go further down the road of laying down good practice. Administrative and regulatory agencies are increasingly empowered not only to appraise applications to enter an industry but to establish, in consultation with the industry, codes of good practice and minimum standards, with disclosure and inspection provisions that are mandatory. Where these are found wanting activities may be suspended by the regulatory agency. The business is thus left to put its own house in order, without on the one hand there being an implication that the failing in question was culpable negligence, sharp practice, or sheer bad luck, nor, on the other hand, that the business has any right to claim due process.

It is due process that is the bugbear of the administrative strategy. The logic of the latter is prevention, and the administative agency is hence at its weakest when prevention fails and offenses are committed. This weakness becomes compounded in cases where publicity about the offenses makes it evident that the motives of the identifiable principals involved were certainly nefarious if not clearly criminal. The public and political call for individual sanctions via prosecutions then becomes embarrassing. Yet the attempt to assign individual responsibility is not only fraught with difficulty for the reasons already identified, but the whole business of individual accusation and sanction is liable to alienate the industry as a whole and involve wider demands for due process in all the operations of the administrative agency, or indeed the withdrawal of all such agencies and the establishment of "a clear framework of law" within which the industry can operate.

This only points to the necessary dependence of administrative agencies upon the industries they regulate, and to the evident irrelevance of law to much of their operation. Much of what takes place in modern industries is too complex, technical, and esoteric to be effectively enshrined in law, and in any case organizations and their techniques change too rapidly. It is precisely for these reasons that administrative regulation becomes essential, and for these reasons too that cooperation between the administrative agency and the industry is essential so that the standards that are established are relevant and realizable. Yet this very relationship creates a continuing dilemma: If the regulatory agency is too close to the industry, its independence and effectiveness in setting and enforcing standards is weakened. If it is too distant, the cooperation of the industry is threatened, and demands for due process begin to be made that, if successful, emasculate the regulatory agency. An inherent problem with the administrative strategy is whether control of it is to rest with the industry or with the state. The interests of the public are thus frequently seen to be in conflict with those of the industry.

It is at this point that it is worth commenting on the relative roles of public and private agencies in the control of business crime and on the curious features of the literature on private policing.[1] The latter seems to have concentrated not only on one type of private policing that most closely parallels conventional state-provided public policing, but also to have implied a stark contrast between wholly private and wholly public police. The concern of the differentiated and often uniformed contract and in-house security officers that are the focus of the majority of the literature on private policing is the maintenance of security on behalf of private businesses and other self-contained entities (hospitals, universities, and so on) against the depredations of employees and the public. The work of these officers is then contrasted with that of the public police officer, the most marked aspect of this being that private security is oriented to prevention, and that investigation with a view to prosecution is limited and usually handed over to the public police. Partly in consequence, private security involves low levels of skills, training, status, and pay. Although the stereotypical mirror-image notion of private policing is at times recognized as too limited—for example, in that responsibility for in-house security is recognized to be at times diffused quite widely as part of (especially managerial) employees' roles—in practice it ignores, first, that there is a continuum between state and private policing occupied by the regulatory and self-regulatory agencies, and, second, that offenses against the public interest as well as those against the private interest of the business enterprise have to be policed, and that here again there is a continuum rather than a sharp contrast between public and private interests. Thus, there are cases where unsafe products or services are marketed contrary to the public interest, in contrast to employee theft of employer's property against a private interest; there are also cases of unsafe manufacturing processes hazardous to employees; predatory practices by businesspersons upon other businesspersons within and outside their industry; frauds against clients and investors, some of them also businesses, and some of them guilty of negligence and sharp practice in their own involvement in them. The issue of what private policing is, is thus much wider and more complex than is in practice allowed by the literature. This too will be a theme in the examination of the industry cases that follow this introduction.

To summarize the position I have argued so far, the administrative strategy is increasingly recognized as more effective than the prosecutorial in the control of business crimes because of the difficulty, and at times the irrelevance, of determining individual guilt and appropriate sanctions in most cases. It presents two continuing problems, however. It is a preventive strategy that is at a loss when offenses nonetheless occur. Further, there is always a dilemma over the extent of its cooperation with the industry that is highlighted when offenses occur and are publicized. Due process features as the joker in this situation. It can be successfully exploited to escape conviction by offenders, and be demanded by the industry when it is felt that it is being oppressively treated by the administrative agency. Yet such is the entrenchment of due process in the political mores of the Western world that it is hard to refuse to respond to a realistically based call for it.

The industry cases that will be discussed are presented in order of the complexity with which they raise the issues discussed. In the case of cargo shipping it is shown that, in the absence of realistic possibilities for prosecutorial remedy against fraud, much has been achieved by limited administrative means. The new international regime established has not yet reached the stage of strength and control at which the other issues that have been discussed become involved. In the second industry, pharmaceuticals, these issues have arisen and been the subject of bitter contest until the establishment relatively recently of an effective regulatory regime in the United States. This outcome has involved a shift in the balance of power to the state in the shape of the Food and Drug Administration, which has taken place because of public pressure in the wake of scandals involving unsafe pharmaceutical products. There are thus special reasons for this apparent victory for effective administrative regulation. Matters are much less clear in the final and most complex industry case, the city of London, where the political attractiveness of the prosecutorial strategy is still evident and where dilemmas as to the best balance of power between the industry and the state and the new regulatory agencies, and problems of due process, abound unresolved. This review of the way in which the issues have emerged in quite varied ways in different industries leads to a final section that discusses in the light of them the dilemmas and prospects of due process and the effectiveness of the administrative control of business crime, and the wider issue of their part in the demise of the rule of law in the modern industrialized capitalist democracy.

INTERNATIONAL MARITIME FRAUD

A good example of the effectiveness of relatively simple administrative measures is provided by the development of the International

Maritime Bureau, which is documented by Ellen and Campbell (1981). As they put it,

> In latter years there has been a marked escalation of fraud in the maritime field, and in 1979 there were an average of three frauds a month reported, each of which represented a loss of approximately US $1,000,000. Taking into account the fact that the greater number of charter party and documentary frauds are never aired in public, the 1979 figures may only represent the tip of the iceberg.

> In those cases which were reported it was found that (a) the majority of the vessels involved were over 15 years of age; and (b) that the majority of the vessels were on single voyage charter.

> An analysis of 93 cases reported up to November 1979 showed the following involvement of vessels by flags: Greece, 46; Panama, 24; Cyprus, 16; Spain, 2; Liberia, India, Singapore, South Korea and Sharjah 1 each [Ellen and Campbell, 1981: 2].

All these figures are affected by the large proportion of the world's shipping tonnage with Greek and Panamian registration, and by the absence of references to major shipping nations such as the United States and Japan among them; also the well-known status of the countries of registration as flags of convenience in the cases analyzed is significant. Another study (Ellen and Campbell, 1981: 62) analyzing 52 cases of nondelivery or misdelivery of cargo identified flags of convenience, single-ship ownership, ships over 15 years old, and of 5,000 to 10,000 tons as significant factors. Ellen and Campbell continue their analysis:

> In earlier days, the frauds were centred around Nigeria and the Arab countries of the Middle East. In these areas ports were in the developmental stage and a rapid increase in imports caused ships to be delayed for weeks and even months whilst waiting for a discharge of cargo.

> In some instances shipowners and charterers found themselves unable to wait because of economic and operational pressures and landed their cargo elsewhere. It did not take long for some to realise that this expedient, born of necessity, could be turned to their own criminal advantage and they could sell the cargo. This they did, making use of those countries where the law on this type of activity was either defective or non-existent. As countries became aware of the problem, and tightened

their laws, the action shifted to other areas, notably the Lebanon [Ellen and Campbell, 1981: 2].

One might suppose that this combination of circumstances would be such as to defeat any attempts at control: flags of convenience allowing vessels in almost any condition to remain registered, Third World countries with inadequate legal provisions and poor policing and administration, wide proliferation of ship ownership throughout the world, and a steady increase in world trade in cargo shipping. The rapid rise of "rust-bucket" scuttling frauds, of illegal cargo deviation and sale, and of documentary frauds in the 1970s and 1980s seemed to provide ample evidence of this. There was and is no international maritime police legally capable and adequately funded and staffed to investigate and prosecute such offenses, only a series of rudimentary international cooperative bodies and international maritime legal conventions. Frauds involving parties outside national jurisdictions tend to be regarded as impossible to process in many countries, and where the victim is outside national jurisdiction the case may fall very low in order of priority for action by limited skilled manpower. Even if resolute investigation does ensue in particular cases, jurisdictional problems are formidable. Cooperation from police and other investigative agencies in different countries may not be forthcoming, access to vital documents may be blocked, offenses not recognized in the same way, and extradition may be difficult or impossible. Ellen and Campbell (1981: 79-80) cite one extreme case of this kind of legal difficulty, in which information on a fraud suspected by the Fijian police to have been committed by a company based in Fiji was passed on the Hong Kong police for investigation in respect of the company's operations in Hong Kong. This was done, but the company successfully applied for a court ruling to ban the passing of the information uncovered in Hong Kong back to Fiji: Due process was successfully exploited to evade prosecution. The case is all the more remarkable given the commonwealth status of the two countries and the similarity of their legal and investigative traditions. A further indication of the limitation on the effectiveness of legal measures against maritime fraud is provided by the most celebrated recent case, that of the *Salem,* in which 193,000 tons of crude oil was illegally diverted to South Africa, and the ship, a large modern tanker, was then scuttled off the coast of West Africa in 1979-1980. This caused widespread reaction, with the South African government being eventually forced to admit receiving the oil and the insurers taking a lively interest in the claim for loss both of the hull and the cargo. Although the crew were interviewed and an inquiry held in Liberia, they were subsequently released following a change of government, and it was British police inquiries in South Africa that revealed the sanctions-breaking diversion of oil. The eventual trials of some of the principals did not begin in Greece and the United States until 1984 and 1985, and even then others said to have even larger interests in the affair were alleged to have escaped (Ellen and Campbell, 1981: 56-60).

In the case of maritime fraud, then, control clearly cannot be achieved by the enforcement of criminal law. As Ellen and Campbell point out, the situation in the 1970s and early 1980s was the outcome of the collapse of the British, and to a lesser extent the American, merchant fleets, which had imposed strict regulations on vessels registered under their flags during the days of their hegemony over world maritime trade, running back into the nineteenth century. With the diffusion of control through the world of shipping registration and the lack of preparedness and capacity in many countries for it, flags of convenience were only the final straw. Ellen and Campbell are able to show, however, that remedial action was possible, even with relatively limited means and that as a result many of the worst areas of fraud have since been cut back.

One example of effective short-term action was the initiation of enquiries in 1979 by the Far East Regional Investigation Team (FERIT), under the auspices of the Salvage Association, into extensive losses by piracy, scuttling, and other frauds in the South China Sea. Cooperation with local police, particularly in Hong Kong and Singapore, was good, and in four months extensive documentary evidence of fraud was gathered, resulting in a reduction of frauds in the region as the main criminals and their methods were identified and increased vigilance aroused. More widely and permanently, the increased interest of the Commonwealth Office in promoting international cooperation to control maritime and other frauds, and particularly the establishment of the International Maritime Bureau, has been significant and effective. The IMB was sponsored by the International Chamber of Commerce and established in London in the early 1980s as a focal point and clearing house for information on maritime fraud. It offers a number of services: advice to members on how to improve the skills of their staff in controlling maritime fraud, general information through publications to keep members abreast of latest developments, advice to members as to whether potential trading partners have been involved in fraudulent or suspect activity in the past, authentication of documents for banks and others, advice to others who suspect they have been defrauded, searches for vessels thought to have been illegally diverted from their declared destination, and in-depth surveys into particular losses. In sum, the objective of the IMB is to facilitate the reestablishment of an adequate system of control of international shipping now that there is genuinely a worldwide system. Ellen and Campbell are able to cite cases in which advice of the sort available from the IMB has been effective in preventing fraud, and it is evident that the worst abuses are now coming under control, even though the problem of maritime fraud in general is very far from adequate management and will require much more extensive international cooperation on such difficult matters as extradition, territorial jurisdiction, international conventions, and flags of convenience before it can be achieved.

The case of international maritime fraud amply illustrates the ambiguity of the categories of public and private policing and of any categorization of the interests protected by such policing as either those of the industry (private) or public. Although the industry has been the principal sufferer from the depredations of recent years, clients whose goods have been shipped and lost have also suffered widely. Although the individuals involved in trying to establish control of maritime fraud have been sponsored in the first instance by the industry, they could not have achieved what they have, and they certainly will not achieve a satisfactory regime in the future, without the formal and informal cooperation of governments, involving the exchange and training of specialist police manpower—public and private interpenetrate. Thus far the dilemmas of the administrative strategy have not emerged with respect to international maritime fraud because the system is not fully developed enough to coerce the recognition and at least nominal compliance of all shippers. One can foresee considerable resistance, for example, by governments and shipping companies at present making the most profitable use of flags of convenience, if international conventions to outlaw their abuse look imminent.

FRAUD IN THE PHARMACEUTICAL INDUSTRY

The case of pharmaceuticals provides a marked contrast. In this case, particularly, such are the hazards of unsafe products that strong public interest predominates and powerful state agencies have been created to enforce compliance by extensive adminstrative powers. The years when the industry could attempt to rely on self-regulation were brought to an end by tragedies such as that of thalidomide, and private interest and private policing, and even cries for due process, have been ridden over roughshod. It is in the sphere of pricing and profits that the industry has retained a substantial measure of control and this, coupled with the lucrative patenting process, is the reason it has been able to live so successfully with a strict state-imposed safety regime.

Readers have ready access to Braithwaite's extensive and recently published investigation into corporate crime in the pharmaceutical industry, and I shall not attempt to duplicate it here (Braithwaite, 1984). The industry is dominated by multinationals, and Braithwaite interviewed senior members of management in Britain, Australia, and the United States concentrating on the latter. Although by no means the only concern of the book (see Clarke, 1984), a theme running through it and the topic of a long concluding chapter is the problem of controlling offenses, particularly those involving product safety as regards reliable manufacturing processes, claims for product effectiveness made on the basis of research, and employee safety. Braithwaite is in no doubt of two things in this connection: that administrative sanctions can be effective where legal ones are not, and that the current regime administered by the U.S. Food and Drug Administration (FDA) is capable of securing compliance where the earlier system was not. These conclusions he sums up in the phrase "clout is what counts." This involves a recognition of the power of the corporations to resist and evade control, power that was freely exercised as recently as the 1960s. To quote one researcher of that period cited by Braithwaite (1984: 376), "You can stand and piss in the batch and turn around and shake the FDA inspector's hand. He's going to tell you that's not right, but when you go to court they won't find you guilty. . . . They haven't been able to make this law stick." Braithwaite argues that the effectiveness of FDA control today derives not from refinements of law and legal procedure, which are still susceptible to delay and diversion by the army of well-funded corporation lawyers, but from the deliberate use of the FDA's discretionary powers. The law is weak, not only in being slow and cumbersome and tying up great amounts of the regulatory agency's resources, but also in that even when convictions are obtained they are in a sense anomalous and certainly ineffective. It is exceedingly hard for the regulatory agency to be sure that it is pinning blame on the person in a corporation responsible for a particular misdeed: Should it be those operationally involved, their direct supervisor, or a senior manager responsible for the maintenance of standards in that division? The issue is the more obscure when the corporation, as usually happens, is itself prosecuted. The corporation is legally a person distinct from its owners and managers, but clearly cannot act except through them. What Braithwaite shows is that fines imposed on corporations are absurdly small in relation to profits and turnover, and that personnel are very rarely more than fined. The hazards of individual sanctions are well recognized in corporatons and the necessity is recognized of having someone who will bear responsibility in prosecutions to the extent that Baithwaite talked to management in one corporation with a designated "vice-president responsible for going to jail." From the point of view of the weakness of the sanctions actually imposed by the law on conviction, of the difficulties of obtaining a conviction for offences, and of the absurdities of criminal proceedings against corporations as entities, the law is an inappropriate and ineffective weapon.

Administrative sanctions, by contrast, can be highly effective because they hit at the core of the corporation: at its right to manufacture and distribute, at its public reputation, and at its profits. The FDA can use its powers to inspect premises at any time to coerce compliance.

> Some companies complained of situations where they had resisted an FDA request to comply with a particular regulation and had consequently been deluged with weekly FDA inspections for a time after. "It wasn't worth it. We won the battle but lost the war. Every plant in this country has violations that can be dug up if the inspector looks hard enough. If they are after you, they can make it very difficult" [Braithwaite, 1984: 377].

Inspections are, of course, a less drastic measure than closing a plant down for safety reasons, a measure that would also attract adverse publicity. Publicity has been used against corporations making exaggerated claims for products, with the FDA forcing them to take out advertisements in professional journals admitting their excesses on pain of having their product licenses suspended.

Braithwaite points out that the bargaining power of the FDA is great because of its wide responsibilities within the industry. "They approve new drugs, withdraw old ones, force product recalls, control good manufacturing practices, good labour practices, advertising, and often prices" (Braithwaite, 1984: 377). Further, he maintains that both parties prefer negotiation to litigation as it permits maximum effectiveness with minimum disruption. At the very end of his book, he expresses concern at the situation he is describing, in which huge corporations responsible for most of the drugs dispensed to the population are negotiating with powerful state agencies about the actual standards that will prevail in the industry. His concern is sharpened because of his conviction that such administrative controls are essential, and, indeed, he goes on to argue for an umbrella Department of Business Regulation to include the FDA, Occupational Safety and Health Administration, the Environmental Protection Agency and others so as to facilitate interagency communication and effectiveness, eliminate the chances of agencies becoming the creature of the industries they supervise, and to ensure that they have adequate muscle to enforce the regulations. Yet, as he points out, this will give enormous discretionary powers to the state and would more or less abandon legal constraints. He is aware of the need for such powers to be tempered by checks upon their use but does not give any detailed indication of the way in which these might work. He offers a general political remedy:

> The best guarantees against the abuse of administrative discretion are provided by diligent investigative journalists, active oversight committees of elected representatives, vocal consumer and trades union movements, aggressive industry associations which are willing to use the political process to defend their members against such abuses, freedom of information statutes with teeth, free access of the scientific community to the raw data on which regulations are based, and a requirement that regulatory agencies publicly justify their decisions and publicly hear appeals against them [Braithwaite, 1984: 380].

Of these the last is probably the most politically feasible and most effective. The concatenation of remedies as a whole, if politically feasible and operational, would, of course, probably be effective, but it really amounts to no more than saying that the only security against the overweening powers of state agencies is an organized and vigilant population willing to direct considerable energy to keeping these agencies in line. Democracies may at times be active and vigilant, but rarely remain on red alert for extended periods; entrenched bureaucratic power fattens and spreads with time and practices its arts daily.

I do not dissent from Braithwaite's conclusion that administrative rather than legal control of the pharmaceutical industry is the only effective method and is hence essential. Braithwaite does not, however, give sufficient recognition to the unique characteristics of the industry he is investigating in regard to the legitimation of the mode of control he proposes. The reason that it is essential to have effective control of the pharmaceutical industry is not, as he tends to argue, that it is large, powerful, and dominated by multinational corporations. These characteristics are not distinctive of pharmaceuticals, whose uniqueness lies in their involvement with the health of nations of individuals who consume its products. Although the industry has successfully promoted itself beyond the bounds of rational appraisal of its real contribution in this respect,[2] there seems little doubt that the pharmaceutical industry, as suppliers of drugs to hospitals and doctors who are directly responsible for maintaining the life and health that the citizens of industrialized nations have come to expect, is in a position of emotional, symbolic, and political leverage. The means to health are obscure to the population: the magic bullets. This means that a condition of the security of the industry that has so successfully persuaded them that health management should be through pharmaceuticals is that the public must retain confidence in them. It is that confidence that the regulatory agencies can threaten to shatter by the two cries, "ineffective" and "unsafe." They are credible cries in the ears of the public because of disasters such as thalidomide (Sjostrom and Nillson, 1972), amphetamines (Grinspoon and Hedblom, 1975), and the industry is now in an increasingly vulnerable position because of rising public doubts about a wide variety of drugs—the minor tranquillizers (Melville, 1984), for example, and indeed about drug-based routes to health in general. What this legitimates is public acceptance of very stringent control administered with a good deal of administrative discretion in the regulation of the industry. As in so many cases in the past, tough government standards of enforcement enhance public confidence and hence secure the market for the products.[3] In this case, it is arguably state guarantees of minimum standards of effectiveness and safety following well-publicized disasters that have restrained much wider public abreaction against consuming pharmaceuticals at all. Given this, the fact that the industry is dominated by big, bad corporations who are so powerful they need big, tough, unfettered state agencies to control them, and that corporations are not people and so people are not really hurt by sanctions against corporations (a half truth), is merely an additional factor making for the acceptability of administrative control.

The point here is that the uniquely direct concern of the pharmaceutical industry with health, and the fact of its domination by multinationals, may legitimate administrative rather than legal control on the grounds of expediency and effectiveness. However, this has few implications for its unfettered implementation elsewhere, even in the corporate sector. The implications of state regulation were argued in quite the opposite direction 20 years ago by Charles Reich. Reich (1964) documented at some length what he termed state largesse, which included state powers to grant, withhold, and revoke passports, citizenship for immigrants, pensions, and licenses to trade in restricted industries, as for example taxi drivers, broadcasters, or airlines. Although deregulation and the reduction of state regulation in some of these areas has recently taken place, the role of the state as regulator and licensor is still very extensive. Reich's point was that the state had in practice, as he was able to show by repeated examples, very great discretion in distributing its largesse, which in most cases powerfully affected the well-being and livelihood of the citizens involved. Why should there be no constraint upon the state, asked Reich, when the loss of a license to trade or practice, the loss of welfare, or of citizenship benefits, could be catastrophic for the citizen? His recommendation was the creation of a "new property" whereby the rights of the citizen would be legally protected where state largesse is concerned, so that the state's powers of discretion were made subject to a court hearing in all cases, in just the same way as they are if the state seeks to expropriate other property. The issue that Reich raises is thus precisely that which Braithwaite minimizes, namely the legitimacy of administrative controls. In brief, he raises the bogey of the big, bad state where Braithwaite raises that of the big, bad corporation and industry. He does not doubt that the state can be effective in its controls, though he does, by implication, raise questions as to the overall efficiency and economic desirability of discretionary state power, which may well deter the best candidates from entering a field if they believe that they will never be able to be secure from state oppression in any success they achieve.

REFORM OF FINANCIAL INSTITUTIONS
IN THE CITY OF LONDON

These are the kinds of questions that have been raised in the course of current reforms of the institutions of the City of London, in banking, insurance, financial services, and the Stock Exchange.[4] Pressure for substantial reforms has been brought about by a persistent series of scandals at the expense of clients and investors, which existing regulatory machinery in various sectors proved unable to control effectively, and by pressure of international competition, with rapid developments in trading aided by the transformation of telecommunications and information processing. These pressures have been recognized by the British government, which has insisted on reform, and promoted several important measures to this end in Parliament.

There are two points in particular toward which attention has been directed in order to secure effective control of abuses in the City. The first of these is the self-regulatory agencies by which various institutions and sections of the City govern themselves. Traditionally these have been select, private, patrician clubs acting informally and discreetly to put pressure on members suspected of overstepping the limits of propriety. In recent years, the capacity of such organizations for effective control came to be doubted, in part because of the rapidly increasing size and numbers participating in the various markets and the gradual breakdown of pervasive upper-class management of them; in part because of the increasing evidence that some of the more outrageous offenders were very much part of the establishment and yet showed little inclination to bow to its gentlemanly pressures; and in part because of a rising distaste for the social exclusiveness, and indeed cartel-like restrictive practices of the City—a distaste shared by a government committed to promoting the participation of a large section of the population in the central institutions of capitalism, and hence disposed to a dismantling of social barriers to access. In place of the traditional informal, closed, and exclusive clublike self-regulatory agencies, a series of much more public, formal, and bureaucratic agencies are being established, substantially manned by members of the relevant financial institutions, but with state-nominated members also, and formal constitutions with an emphasis upon compliance tests, inspections, and disclosure, as well as formal disciplinary machinery and with oversight by state agencies. What were formerly viewed as private matters of self-regulation are increasingly seen as issues involving the public interest, and in consequence state involvement in their regulation is seen as necessary.

Despite the much greater involvement of the state and its readiness to go further if the new regime proves ineffective in stemming abuses, the reforms have been greeted with skepticism in some quarters. "I suspect that one or two convictions (for fraud) coupled with stiff sentences would do more for investor protection than any number of state backed self-regulatory codes of conduct" (Raw, 1982), remarked one financial journalist with a strong record in investigating such abuses. It was a view echoed by the Council for the Securities Industry, an umbrella body representing practitioners, in its response to a government commissioned report on investor protection.

> Unquestionably the greatest weakness of the present scheme of regulation lies in what is a government responsibility, but one that goes wider than the Department of Trade [the main Ministry concerned], the failure to deal effectively with commercial and financial frauds. Anyone who commits an elaborate fraud knows that he probably will not be prosecuted, and that if he is prosecuted it will take years to formulate charges and he will probably escape the main charges. There is little point in improving the finer points of conduct if gross fraud goes unpunished [cited in Robinson, 1983].

Such views reflect well-known difficulties in securing convictions for major commercial frauds in Britain. One recent case lasted three months and cost half a million pounds, only for the trial to collapse, and this is by no means an isolated example. The practice of the Director of Public Prosecutions, whose sanction is necessary in fraud trials, came under increasing criticism. Decisions on cases where clear evidence had been amassed by the proceedings of self-regulatory agencies were delayed for reports by leading counsel, with time lags becoming so long that prosecutions became impossible because of the staleness of the evidence and difficulties in obtaining witnesses because of death, retirement, infirmity, and removal abroad. Although delay was justly criticized, the DPP's caution is understandable, given the costs, the court time, and the uncertainty of gaining convictions.

In an attempt to remedy some of these deficiencies, the government took two cautious steps. The first was the establishment on a formal basis in 1985 of the Fraud Investigation Group to coordinate the work on fraud by the police fraud squads, the Department of Trade, whose inspectorate investigate suspect companies, and the DPP's office, with a view to avoiding duplication of work and expediting decision making in prosecutions. It is too early to say how effective this will be. The second is the Committee of Inquiry under Lord Justice Roskill into the improvement of legal procedure in the prosecution of fraud. At the time of this writing, the committee has yet to report, but from its initiation in 1984 it was public knowledge that it was considering recommending the abolition of jury trial in at least some fraud cases on the grounds that juries, or at any rate those drawn randomly from the population, were incapable of following the complexities of fraud cases. The weight of evidence given to the committee seems, however, to be against such a drastic break with British legal tradition. A number of other areas for the improvement of procedure have been suggested that might go some way to making fraud trials shorter and more to the point, such as ensuring a full pretrial review of the outline of the case between the trial judge and leading counsel for both parties, and perhaps involving disclosure of both prosecution and defense positions to eliminate needless waste of court time during the trial in lines of argument that prove in the event to be uncontested. In addition, the relaxation of some of the rules might allow more effective use of modern techniques of graphic presentation in court to improve the intelligibility of the case for all concerned.

In cases involving frauds in the financial sector, then, as in the case of offences involving the pharmaceutical industry and maritime fraud, one major difficulty is investigation of the offense and the coordination of the hard-won evidence, often of several different agencies, to mount a prosecution against the right target. In all three cases, also, trials are likely to be complex and lengthy, both because of the complexity of the technical issues involved and because of the capacity of the defendants to mobilize high-powered legal defense teams that will delay and divert as well as fight the case tooth and nail in court. The law, too, is not of the greatest assistance in allowing relevant charges to be credibly brought in the case of financial fraud. As one legal commentator has remarked of British law,

In some cases where there is a specific serious offence which fits the circumstances, as in those involving fraudulent and misleading prospectuses and similar frauds, there will be a reasonable chance of success. But there are no such serious specific offences in respect of many other forms of City frauds, notably those which involve the improper abstraction of funds from the company or the manipulation of a market. In such cases the prosecution is faced with a choice between attempting to establish less appropriate "real" crimes or falling back on less serious preventive or regulatory offences. If defendants are charged with "real" crimes like theft or obtaining by deception there may be considerable difficulty in persuading a jury that what has been done matches the plain man's conception of such offences. If less precise charges of conspiracy to defraud or deceive are laid the defense will be able to take full advantage of the current legal distaste for vague general charges [Hadden, 1983: 506].

The state of British criminal law on fraud and related offences no doubt leaves something to be desired and the effectiveness of prosecution could probably be improved, but Hadden concludes his analysis as follows: "Traditional criminal prosecution is not an appropriate mechanism for the day to day regulation of companies and the securities market. It is unlikely to be cost effective as a means of securing compliance with all but the simplest requirements of the law" (Hadden, 1983: 509). For petty regulatory offenses Hadden recommends automatic but limited penalties for noncompliance, like parking tickets. For more important offenses,

> Much of the preventive role of the criminal law may also be carried out more effectively by administrative than by legal procedures. There is a choice, in this context, between governmental and self-regulatory systems. In either case, the objective should be to achieve as much as possible through licensing and prior vetting rather than by prosecution and punishment after the event [Hadden, 1983: 510].

Hadden's conclusion in respect of the City of London, then, is much the same as Braithwaite's in respect of the pharmaceutical industry: Legal proceedings are an instrument of doubtful effectiveness. In the case of the financial sector, perhaps even more than pharmaceuticals, the law's difficulty is further compounded by the speed at which changes in practice take place, as financial institutions and the products and services they develop alter. Practitioners are adept at identifying new ways to make a good profit that involve ever changing relationships with clients. The relevant bodies for the supervision of this are the sectoral self-regulatory agencies and the state supervisory bodies whose duty it is to keep abreast of the latest developments and to lay down clearly what is good practice and what is unacceptable practice. The danger—and here we come back to the issues discussed at the beginning of this section on the City of London—is that the regulatory agencies, both professional and state, are unwilling or unable to give clear leadership and take firm action in cases of breaches of the rules and impose sanctions that exclude serious offenders from participation in the markets they have abused, either temporarily or permanently, and deter others. Reforms in the City have been largely directed to this end of ensuring that regulatory bodies are effective, and there is some evidence, especially in the severe penalties imposed by the new sanctions machinery of Lloyd's insurance market, that this is happening.

One wonders, however, whether the issue of the management of regulation by the relevant practitioners is not something of a red herring. When self-regulatory agencies are genuinely autonomous they are suspected of featherbedding and not being tough enough. Hence the skepticism of commentators at the beginning of this section. In consequence, they are leaned upon by the state to reform themselves, become more public and formal, and accept state representatives and oversight. They produce stricter codes and start slapping members down more vigorously. But in this case are they really more than the cat's paw of the state, doing its dirty work for it? To judge from the reaction of City institutions, this is not the case, because they have fought hard and long to retain at least the semblance of continued self-regulatory powers, and presumably believe that even if they have been usurped by the state, having their own representatives well established in the machinery enables them to ensure that it functions reasonably fairly with respect to their members. The fundamental point at issue may be put more bluntly. If you want control of malpractice in a complex, intractable, and rapidly evolving sector of the economy you are not likely to get it by making laws—so much has been the initial point of the work reviewed in this chapter. You are likely to get it by funding and staffing regulatory agencies adequately and by granting them substantial investigative and sanctioning powers. Much of the same could be, and frequently is, said of the police, but at least the police, for all that they may violate many aspects of due process and civil rights in attacking a crime wave with public support, have at the end of the day to submit to criminal trial.[5] True, they have their ways of bullying, tricking, and bargaining for the outcome they want, which work fairly effectively for the largely impoverished, undereducated, and politically impotent defendants they process, but the implication of transfer of sole responsibility to the state or state-backed administrative machinery is the abdication of any formal concern with due process and the rule of law (see Skolnick, 1966, for a classic study of police methods). It may be that such a move will be sanctioned as expedient, as Braithwaite seems to be saying with respect to the FDA's hegemony over the pharmaceutical industry, but the point is that given the similar weakness of the law in other sectors of the economy and the need for effective control, can purely administrative means in principle be approved, and, if so, what happens to due process and the rule of law?

The British government, faced with this dilemma over the reform of the City of London, and determined to have malpractices stopped, but in need of an answer to City practitioners complaining of potentially oppressive arbitrary and authoritarian state agencies that would have an adverse effect in the longer term in blunting the drive and entrepreneurial ingenuity of financial sector business, thought it had the answer in self-regulation. Introducing its White Paper on Reform of Investor Protection, it claimed that "there is a wide measure of support for a regulatory system which can most simply be described as self-regulation within a statutory framework" (Her Majesty's Stationery Office, 1985). In support of this strategy the government argued that

> it offers the best possibility of combining adequate investor protection with a competitive and innovative market. Regulation is more likely to be effective if there is significant practitioner involvement in devising the rules and in encouraging observance of high standards of conduct. A private body is able to make and enforce rules and have a greater flexibility in its operations than a body unable to change its rules other than by Parliamentary legislation. Practioners are best equipped to spot breaches of the rules, and to take swift and effective enforcement action. A private sector body would be established and brought to a high degree of readiness by the time the legislation received Royal Assent: the legislation and the practical preparation can go forward together rather than consecutively. Day-to-day regulatory action is distanced from the government [Her Majesty's Stationery Office, 1985].

There seems to be something in it for everyone, but the issue of concern in this chapter, of what happens to due process and the rule of law, is fudged: The objective is to keep everyone happy, the government because it distances itself from responsibility, the investor because he or she gets effective control, the practitioner because he or she retains some control over enforcement. So the circle is squared, but, of course, more apparently than really. The only guarantee of effective enforcement is that the government will insist on it. To the extent that it demands tougher rules and acts to ensure this, the practitioner loses control. Conversely, to the extent that practitioners gain independence, there is a danger explicitly recognized in the White Paper that self-regulatory agencies will "degenerate into cosy clubs or cartels."

Now, it is arguable whether this is more appropriately called fudge or compromise, but this really misses the point about the necessity for administrative rather than legal control and the roots of the apparently relentlessly advancing necessity for a shift away from reliance upon the law. After all, administrative control was not always there—the state had neither the powers nor the economic resources to impose it in Western industrialized societies until, arguably, at least the end of World War I.

ADMINISTRATIVE CONTROL
AND THE RULE OF LAW

To pose this question properly we have to go back to Reich and ask a question that he did not when discussing state largesse: namely, why did the state get so big and powerful? Did it do so by sleight of hand behind the backs of the electorate, as it were, or with electoral consent? There seems no doubt that whether one is talking about Britain and other European countries where powerful socialist parties lent their ideological support to the extension of the state, or the United States where no such parties have ever been powerful, the answer is the latter. Whether linked to socialist rhetoric or not, the importance of welfare provision in a mature capitalist economy is undeniable as the basis of sustaining the legitimacy of the capitalist regime, by controlling poverty and offering a limited security to the population in respect of health, education, housing, and income. Provision for these welfare goods has been one major basis for the extension of the state's power, and the withholding or withdrawing of them in individual cases was one ground of Reich's complaint against the arbitrary power of the state. Despite current talk, and a good deal less practice, about rolling back the frontiers of the state, the basic provisions of the welfare state still command very substantial popular political support, and energy is more effectively directed at improving delivery, quality, and value for money.

The other major source of increased state influence has been consumerism, that is, the demand for minimum standards of quality and safety in consumer goods and services. The enormous powers of the FDA are but the most extreme example of this, and the consumer movement continues to flourish and achieve wider and wider victories in imposing controls on industries hitherto unregulated. Take, for example, financial services, where a good part of the British government's impetus to secure effective regulation derived from its desire to secure much wider participation by the population in financial institutions. It could not be achieved if the public was justifiably suspicious that the industry was run by a closed group of upper-class wealthy operators, some of whom were not above exploiting investors, and who were protected from serious sanction when doing so by their collegues. It is not without importance in this connection that the Thatcher government, whose hostility to state and quasi-state agencies was great enough to result in at least one major purge of them in the interests of cost and of freeing citizens from the state, should have continued to lend its substantial support to the Office of Fair Trading (OFT), whose remit is at once to ensure that free and open competition prevails in all sectors (including finance) and also to ensure that products and services are of a minimum quality agreed between the OFT and the industry, and that adequate means of redress are open to the aggrieved consumer. All the licensing and state supervision of quality that Reich complains of are the outcome of such consumerism, and where welfarism seems to have expanded at least as far as it will go and to be foundering on problems of cost, consumerism continues to flourish, led and proseletyzed as it is by the biggest consumers in the population, the middle class.

The point of this digression is that if state power has grown, and if its administrative discretion through a host of agencies now makes a mockery of the rule of law in many areas, this is not to be redeemed by any easy means, certainly not by removing the state's powers and scope to any great extent, as they have grown largely with the popular will. To complete the account of the reasons for the expansion of the state one must add that it has also, even under free market-orientated governments, come to have a very substantial role in managing the economy; indeed, it is this issue that normally

forms the center of election campaigns and government strategies in the industrialized capitalist democracies. Economic management, in turn, has been made the more necessary by the ever
greater concentration of industries into monopolies and oligopo-
lies, whose propensity to the less desirable habits of cartels must
be checked, and who in recent years have frequently needed state
financial aid as well as the support of the state as a major purchaser
of products, salesman for them abroad, and manipulator of tariffs
in their favor.

The convenient label for these developments is *corporatism*. I
do not wish to enter here upon the now extensive debate as to the
precise meaning and implications of corporatism,[6] but only to use
it as a means of recognizing the substance of major changes in the
representation of interests. The points I have made earlier about
welfarism, consumerism, and economic management are aspects
of corporatism, one practical implication of which has been the
enormously expanded administrative responsibilities of the state
through myriad agencies, on the one hand, and, on the other, the
pattern of representation of interests from interest and pressure
groups that are recognized in and through these agencies. Indeed, I
would maintain that so wide, diverse, and complex has the state's
remit become, that it is only by encouraging representation in and
through interest and pressure groups that it can obtain a constant
supply of reliable information, formulate sensible policies and
avoid inefficiencies, frustration, and constant sporadic outbursts of
protest, which can be politically very damaging. An inspection of
any directory of pressure groups will reveal how many have been
established since the 1950s in response to the increasing size of the
state and the need to make collective representations to its agencies
in order to have an impact upon policy.

I am by no means alone in arguing that the enormous rise in the
size and powers of the state has important implications for the rule
of law (see, for example, Unger, 1976). It would require considerably more space than I have here to substantiate by subsidiary contention that this growth in state administration has led to a growth in
interest and pressure groups that is as important to the stability and
effectiveness of the state as it is important as a source of resources
and policy developments to them. The point I wish to address in
these concluding paragraphs is the practical implications of these
developments for the rule of law—not, that is, for the rule of law
as a vague ideology, but for what it has in the past secured for the

citizen or the corporation as a guarantee against the abuse of state power.

The answer to this may, I think, be summed up in the word "certainty." Legal regulation has ensured that what is and is not permitted is publicly laid down in a tolerably clear formula, and that the state's powers of intervention are limited to clear breaches of the rules. Now, as we have seen, there are good indications that legal regulation does not work for many business offenses, and it has been superseded by state or state-supervised administration. The point of the foregoing argument about the growth of the power of the state and the development of corporatism was to give some context to this shift in the system of control. The main argument in its favor appears to be the practical necessity for it. Does this mean that the certainty provided by the rule of law must be abandoned?

I believe it does not, provided certain prejudices about the nature of rule of law are rejected. The principal of these is that law implies some single system of centralized judicial authority: a central legislature and a centralized hierarchical court system. Corporatism is essentially sectoral in its operation. This does not mean that there is no central authority, but it is intrinsic to corporatist relations that negotiations as to practice and policy within the sector are agreed among the local parties represented. As we have seen, one of the reasons for this is the rapid rate of change in different sectors of the economy and the technical complexity of some of the issues dealt with. The merit of the element of devolution inherent in corporatism is that it allows for discussion and agreement of these issues in detail and with rapid alteration, if need be, at the periphery. The disadvantage is that, in the words of the British White Paper on Investor Protection, such arrangements can turn into cosy clubs or cartels; that is, exclude the interests of those not represented, including those of the wider society.

There is, however, no reason why regulatory agencies operating in various sectors should not successfully aspire to build due process and certainty into their proceedings. Braithwaite's point that proceedings and agreements should be public is also pertinent here. It should be possible to devise publicly agreed to procedures for processing changes in regulations and providing for appeal to outside bodies in the event of sustained disagreements. It is also possible to provide that no sanctions be imposed unless regulations are breached—no retrospective regulation or arbitrary sanctions. Equally, the bodies to be regulated must allow inspection and comply with adequate disclosure requirements.

It is easy to claim that this is no more than the "legalization" of administrative control, which will strangle its effectiveness the closer it approaches the legal form. To that it can be replied, first, that the degree of legal formalization may vary from sector to sector and over time, and second, that one may point to the very similar developments in the quasi-legal system of tribunals in Britain, which have their counterparts in other societies, concerned with the adjudication of claims on, for example, land tenure, pensions, and welfare payments. These vary widely in the degree of their formality and their articulation with the central court system, but they all recognize the merits of establishing a clear body of regulation, providing clear and reasoned decisions on cases, allowing representation, and other elements of due process and certainty. Whether full certainty is seen as a merit, as against the importance of dealing with each case on its merits, varies from one kind of tribunal to another (see Adler and Bradley, 1975).

We come back finally to Braithwaite's point about the need for a vigilant population to require effective administration. The same argument can be mounted against the rule of law. Due process and civil liberties may be guaranteed by statute and constitution, but be of no practical benefit to the poor, ignorant, and isolated defendant, who is subject to the organized might and experience of the police and the desire of courts to process cases as rapidly as possible. Corporatist arrangements may have their formal disadvantages in leading to fragmented administration and jurisdiction, inadequate codification and unclear procedure, not to say a good deal of fudging and muddle, but they do offer the likelihood of a more balanced political representation of the interested parties than do much of the everyday proceedings of the criminal law. To that extent, I believe one should cease regretting the demise of the rule of law with respect, at any rate, to business offenses and set about trying to ensure that the system of administrative controls that replaces it—as it seems virtually certain that it will—is both effective in controlling abuses and fair to those it regulates, and incorporates as much as possible of the practically beneficial of the features of certainty.

NOTES

1. The work of Shearing and Stenning (1981, 1983) provides a percipient review and assessment of the main lines of research on private policing. The work of South and Scraton (1984) similarly reviews developments in the field, but with

more emphasis upon politico-historical analysis of the reasons for them. (See also South, 1983, 1984.)

2. There is now a quite substantial literature arguing this point. A radical version was propounded some time ago by Illich (1976). One of the more recent, well-documented, and presented examples is Melville and Johnson (1982).

3. Compare the development of federal regulation of the U.S. meat packing industry in the early part of the twentieth century, when after initial resistance major companies came to realize that government inspection constituted a guarantee of quality that was invaluable in their export trade in beating off Argentine competition, whose government was in no position to offer a guarantee of similar international standing. See Chambliss (1974), which makes use of Kolko (1963).

4. They are reviewed more extensively in Clarke (1986).

5. There are many examples of this now documented. A classic one is Balbus (1973).

6. It is impossible to provide a fully representative bibliography here. I have found the following useful, not only in themselves but for the sources they cite: Schmitter and Lehmbruch (1979); Lehmbruch and Schmitter (1982); Cawson (1982); Harrison (1984); and Offe (1984).

REFERENCES

ADLER, M. and A. W. BRADLEY (1975) *Justice, Discretion and Poverty.* London: Professional Books.

BALBUS, I. (1973) *The Dialectics of Legal Repression.* New York: Russell Sage Foundation.

BRAITHWAITE, J. (1984) *Corporate Crime in the Pharmaceutical Industry.* London: Routledge & Kegan Paul.

CAWSON, A. (1982) *Corporatism and Welfare.* London: Heinemann.

CHAMBLISS, W. J. (1974) "The state, the law and the definition of behaviour as criminal or delinquent," in B. Glaser (ed.) *Handbook of Criminology.* Indianapolis, IN: Bobbs Merrill.

CLARKE, J. M. (1984) "Review: corporate crime in the pharmaceutical industry," by J. Braithwaite. *Journal of Law and Society, 11* (2): 271-275.

———(1986) *Regulating the City.* Milton Keynes, England: Open University Press.

ELLEN, E. and D. CAMPBELL (1981) *International Maritime Fraud.* London: Sweet and Maxwell.

GRINSPOON, L. and P. HEDBLOM (1975) *The Speed Culture.* Cambridge, MA: Harvard University Press.

HADDEN, T. (1983) "Fraud in the City: the role of the criminal law." *Criminal Law Review.*

HARRISON, M. C. [ed.] (1984) *Corporatism and the Welfare State.* London: Gower Press.

ILLICH, I. (1976) *Limits to Medicine.* Toronto: McLelland and Stuart.

KOLKO, G. (1963) *The Triumph of Conservatism.* Glencoe, IL: Free Press.

LEHMBRUCH, G. and P. C. SCHMITTER [Eds.] (1982) *Patterns of Corporatist Policy Making.* Beverly Hills, CA: Sage.

MELVILLE, A. and C. JOHNSON (1982) *Cured to Death.* London: Secker and Warburg.

MELVILLE, J. (1984) *The Tranquiliser Trap*. London: Fontana.

OFFE, C. (1984) *Contradictions of the Welfare State*. London: Hutchinson.

RAW, C. (1982) "City cops out of policing plan," *Sunday Times*, June 20.

REICH, C. A. (1964) "The new property." *Yale Law Journal* pp. 733-787.

ROBINSON, P. (1983) "Time to tighten up policing of the fraud law," *Times*, November 10.

SCHMITTER, P. C. and G. LEHMBRUCH [eds.] (1979) *Trends Towards Corporatist Intermediation*. Beverly Hills, CA: Sage.

SHEARING, C. D. and P. C. STENNING (1981) "Modern private security: its growth and implications," in M. Tonry and N. Norris (eds.) *Crime and Justice: An Annual Review of Research*. Chicago: University of Chicago Press.

———(1983) "Private security: implications for social control." *Social Problems* 30: 493-506.

SJOSTROM, H. and R. NILLSON (1972) *Thalidomide and the Power of the Drug Companies*. London: Hammondsworth.

SKOLNICK, J. (1966) *Justice Without Trial*. New York: John Wiley.

SOUTH, N. (1983) "The corruption of commercial justice: the case of the private security sector," in M. J. Clarke (ed.) *Corruption: Causes, Consequences and Control*. New York: St. Martin's.

———(1984) "Private security: the divisions of policing labour and the commercial compromise of the state," in S. Spitzer and A. Scull (eds.) *Research in Law, Deviance and Social Control*, vol. 6. Greenwich, CT: JAI Press.

——— and P. SCRATON (1984) "The ideological construction of the hidden economy: private justice and work-related crime." *Contemporary Crises* no. 1.

UNGER, R. M. (1976) *Law in Modern Society*. Glencoe, IL: Free Press.

United Kingdom Government White Paper (1985) *Financial Services for the U.K.: A New Framework for Investor Protection*, Cmnd. 4320. London: Her Majesty's Stationery Office.

Chapter 12

IRONIES OF COMPLIANCE

PETER K. MANNING

In liberal democracies, the state attempts to control various markets through shaping the political economy of those markets. It can do so by a variety of methods, strategies, and tactics. There appears to be some relationship between the ways in which government attempts to control organizational life and the activities that are the named target of such attempts at control. Explanations for these apparent correlations vary, however. Most attempts to explain them have been broad views of the nature of the regulatory process, and have characterized or typified this process in some fashion. In general, these typifications are directed to speculations about the impact of the regulatory process, rather than explanations of why it works as it does, or accounts of successful regulation (Bardach and Kagan, 1982; Wilson, 1982).

If one sees the political or normative constraints in regulation as being broad, then the range of possible means of attaining a given end are also quite wide. Explanations for a present pattern of regulation, whether it focuses on failures or limits, assume that forms of regulation produce a given sort of content, and that the choice of form is related in an invariant fashion to the nature of the activities regulated. Such explanations therefore confuse indices of the activities regulated with indices of the activities of the regulatory body, and vice versa. By stating a description of the current practice, they may have confused description of a state of affairs with a normative or political question that concerns the choice and form of regulation and related practices. The point of this chapter is to emphasize the need to examine carefully the broader context within which

AUTHOR'S NOTE: I am grateful to Patrick Healy for his very valuable comments on a previous draft and for sharpening the focus of my argument.

governments act, rather than to assume a priori how they ought to act. By seeing that activities are themselves subject to *definition*—including a definition of both relevant activities and the nature of the problems to be regulated—and *regulation,* descriptive and normative questions can be disentangled.

Conventional explanations for regulatory form and failure need to be examined prior to addressing the analytic questions. Primary among these theories of regulatory "failure" is Bernstein's "capture theory," which asserts a degree of collusion between the regulated and the regulatee as a result of shared experiences in the marketplace, shared ideologies, and circulation of members between the industry and the government bodies designated as controllers (Bernstein, 1955). Lowi (1970), on the other hand, finds this pattern to be unexceptional, viewing it merely as a reflection of the inability of the liberal state to regulate. Rather, in the nature of the political and legal organization there is a structured acceptance of economic activities coupled with symbolic efforts to regulate. The potential tension between the economy and the state is replaced by the appearance of control. Similar arguments, by Gusfield (1966, 1981), Edelman (1964, 1971) and Manning (1977, 1980), advance a slightly more radical interpretation of government, seeing it as severely limited with regard to control, regardless of intent, resources, structure, and organization. Governmental regulation, therefore, is a dramaturgical performance, displaying a concern for and marking the interests of the whole in action (see also Lasswell, 1960). These three broad views are *interpretative* rather than functional.

There are two important *functional* views concerning the relationship between regulation and the regulated. These are the Marxist view, that the state acts in the interests of both the state and of the capitalist classes or segments (see Offshe, 1985), and information-based explanations that on the basis of the structure of information juxtapose the regulatory system and aims of the state (for example, see Reiss, 1983; Reiss and Biderman, 1980). Reiss (1983: 94-95), for example, provides a very concise summary of the conditions under which a system that seeks compliance rather than punishment is found:

> Compliance law enforcement systems have occurred under a variety of historical conditions. Two sets of conditions seem conducive to compliance law enforcement. When the goal of law enforcement is to prevent the consequences of violations either because they are too costly for the society to bear or

because the conditions of uniformity must be assured to continue activities, compliance law systems usually exist. It also opts when the processes of detecting violations and sanctioning violations are so complex and protracted or so costly that they are regarded as inadequate remedies for continuing harm.

Such overall characterizations of regulation are drawn at a very high levels of abstraction, and use the typification of the sanctioning system and the legal resources available as *indices* of the nature of the activities of the regulatory bodies. Often, the "data" used are drawn from court cases, official government records, and congressional hearings. What is unrevealed in these data and even in sensitive ethnographic depictions of processes of social regulation is the political and economic context within which types of regulatory systems emerge, and how this political context constrains enforcement. Although there is an implicit theory of motivation and choice in the Marxist view of regulation in Western societies, it does not provide an explanation for the choice of a particular form of regulation. Rather, it asserts that whatever the choice is, it serves the interests of the state. Marxists and neo-Marxists do provide an important insight absent in other explanations for regulatory form—they are sensitive to the issue of *choice* and its relationship to the market pattern, the political system, and historic conditions (see Carson, 1970). Functional and information-based explanations for extant systems are therefore valuable tools, for they explicate the conditions under which such sanctioning systems operate.

The thesis of this chapter, which draws on an ongoing study of the British Nuclear Installations Inspectorate,[1] is that systems of regulation can be seen as the result not only of historic and economic market conditions, but also of governmental choice. Choices to develop a system of control (whether sanctioning- or compliance-oriented), a sanctioning *strategy* (how and when to apply whatever *sanctions* are thought to be appropriate to achieve a given end), and *tactics* (the implementation of the strategy) are political. Furthermore, within the process of enforcement the points of decisions within a field of values outlined by the government make some outcomes rather than others more likely.

The argument here thus accepts the symbolic or dramaturgical aspects of regulation, but explores the conditions under which they are chosen to symbolize the interests of the whole that the government seeks to mobilize. In addition, the very nature, meaning, type, and availability of information is predetermined by the system of regulation that is put in place (Manning, forthcoming a). This chapter critically examines both functional and information-based models of regulation.

On the basis of a historical analysis it is argued that a compliance sanctioning system was chosen and has been repeatedly affirmed in the face of periodic criticisms and crises in nuclear safety since 1956. The centrality of the industry to national defense, its governmental monopoly status, and the complexity of its technology are unique. As a result, it is a governmental function rather than an industry subject to surveillance, evaluation, and sanctioning. A more exact statement of this argument is that it is virtually impossible to describe the NII without recognizing that government participation is so direct and persuasive that it might easily be mistaken for just another aspect of direct governmental action (Healy, 1985). Compliance is therefore fraught with irony and nuance, a kind of dancing in the shadow of the law.

MODES OF RULE ENFORCEMENT

It is claimed that there is a discernible relationship between the organization of social life and the modes of policing it that have evolved in Anglo-American societies (Reiss, 1983). Reiss has made perhaps the most parsimonious connection between compliance law enforcement systems and what he terms "historical conditions." In his description, two broad means are available for enforcing rules. The sanctions, rewards, or punishments available to force or encourage rule obeisance can be used as a basis for creating general types of rule-enforcement systems. These typifications of very complex processes select a few key points or dimensions around which they differ—questions of the moral intent of the enforcement, the state of affairs sought, the kinds of activities to be controlled, the nature of the adjudication and resolution of disputes arising, and the kind of discretion produced. In some ways, these types of systems cross-cut forms of law (such as civil, criminal, and administrative), types of penalties (fines, custodial sentences, restitution), and given institutions and agencies. Many agencies may be involved in both systems of rule enforcement in spite of their apparent focus on one. For example, the police are often engaged in compliance-focused rule enforcement, and civil agencies may invoke criminal sanctions (Bittner, 1972; Ericson, 1982). Furthermore, the two systems are not mutually exclusive in that they both may be used in a given event or sequentially over time, and this is indeed another form of political choice often left to the regulatory body. As Hawkins has observed, in some sense these systems transcend conventional classifications of types of law (Hawkins, 1984: 7ff).

In a *sanctioning system,* punishment for breaking a rule is sought for an evil or breach thought to require strict evidential proof, judicial processing, and binary outcomes (guilty or not guilty). There is usually a victim and an event of brief and marked duration in which harm is claimed to have been done. Prosecution is frequent, with a concern for the effective use of resources. The employed standards are legal rules and social conventions, and enforcement is seen as appropriately neutral and objective. Discretion is accepted if nevertheless criticized and subject to frequent public outcry. Consistent with this, and with judicial procedures to establish guilt and innocence, are appeal procedures available in both the relevant civil or criminal law. In some sense, such sanctioning systems and the associated strategies or styles of sanctioning, penal or adversarial, aim to establish guilt with respect to identified past events. The actions of the agents represent a stipulative moral consensus and shared sense of justice. The connection is made between the state, morality, and the law, as much as these simultaneously may be seen as standing in some state of dynamic tension (Manning, 1977; Douglas, 1971).

In a *compliance system,* on the other hand, conformity with a condition or state specified in rules is sought with the aim of preventing harm. Inspection or surveillance may be used to assure compliance, prevent occurrences, or minimize damage, and graduated outcomes, rarely based on court decisions, are sought. Appeal is unusual and it may not be available, or available only in special tribunals, review boards, or by administrative (internal) review. It may in fact be statutorily prohibited. The notion of an individual victim is not clearly relevant, because the ongoing nature of the process surveyed and the continuous nature of the potential harm are accepted. Its actual extent and appearance are to be determined by routine examination. Prosecution is seldom invoked. Because the primary aim of activity is to maintain the current state of affairs, to reinforce the status quo in a sense, prosecution is a secondary option when the primary and preferred means have failed. Indeed, it may be avoided with the purpose of ensuring continuous cooperation in monitoring the consequences of the routinely acceptable harm involved. The government may have determined that the costs of prosecution or detection are too great, or that the aim is continuous reduction in risk or establishing acceptable risk ("safety"), inasmuch as the process regulated is essential to economic well-being (see Lowrance, 1976; Fischoff et al., 1981). A concern may be expressed for efficiency or best use of resources available rather than effectiveness or a sought-for measurable impact, regardless of cost. Standards are likely thus to be administrative guidelines or guidance notes, with agencies "filling in" in the principles of procedure.[2] Enforcement tends to take the form of interpersonal bargaining within the context of a license, a consent, or permit, and often takes place in morally uncertain territory in which values, technology, and business practice intersect (Hawkins, 1984; Carson, 1970; Bardach and Kagan, 1982). A considerable element of "personalization" and particularization of enforcement eventually occurs, raising questions of social and natural justice as well as horizontal and vertical equity in treatment. Appeals—and, indeed, any formal action that might require appeal—are rare; conciliatory styles of enforcement are adopted with an aim to maintaining the market or product, reaching a future state, or securing a level of conformity consistent with mutual aims.

Compliance systems resemble private systems of justice or even self-help (Black, 1982) insofar as different moral contexts and standards are accepted as a basis for negotiation. Law hovers, its power in abeyance, somehow legitimating the process and acting as a source of potential sanction. The state stands even further removed, metaphorically at least, for its aims and concerns are not with the breach, but with achieving reasonably practicable outcomes and future compliance. To further emphasize, as government established the nature of the preferred status quo and the conditions under which it acts, the actions available once this fails are predetermined to be few and to be reluctantly adopted, because they represent evidence of a contravention of a contract with itself. In this sense, regulatory bodies such as the NII are governmental bodies directing action toward other governmental bodies.

THE POLITICAL NATURE OF
REGULATORY STRUCTURES

There is a large literature on the development of organizations with legal powers, and on the passage of laws and acts that establish organizations with new legal powers (Selznick, 1966; Messinger, 1960; Gusfield, 1962; Pressman and Wildavsky, 1973; Becker, 1963; Carson, 1970; Dickson, 1968). Organizations can emerge from moral crusades that attempt to criminalize acts (such as sexual practices, use of drugs, pollution of the air, water, or earth), or increase civil penalties of various kinds for constriction of trade, and broadly all matters of social and economic regulation (Becker, 1963). The pattern of moral crusades and moral entrepreneurial activity by which groups attempt to mark their social, political, and legal interests (whether they be rights to property, security, personal lifestyle or other entitlements) with the law, is also the subject of a large literature. In addition, there is published research on the emergence of new government bureaus or governmental expansionism (compare Becker, 1963, with Dickson, 1968).

Although the aims, political ideologies, and leadership patterns of these sources of emergent organizations vary, they act to produce additional legitimated structures of rules with general applicability. The existence of rules produces, necessarily, rules about their application, about changing them, or changing the practices that are affirmed by the policy. Variations in codification, and in the sorts of controls on those who exercise choices about the existence of such rules, and rules about those rules, are also thus created. Rules are enforced or not enforced within a hierarchy both of other rules and of authority to apply or interpret them. As has been discussed elsewhere (Manning, forthcoming b), rules do not provide a necessary and sufficient definition of organization, but they are a central feature of it.

In an important sense, the growth of a regulatory structure and the growth of a given industry must be mutually determinate (see, for example, Carson, 1982: chap. 5). Perhaps the most important distinctions are to be made between industries that emerged within an ongoing structure of regulation into which they were fitted (as were the new technologies of Silicon Valley and the postwar electronic industry, for example), industries that grew prior to and with the regulatory structure (as with heavy industry in Britain, especially mines and factories) and those industries that were deemed so dangerous at the time of their emergence that they were regulated from the beginning with specially created rules, organizations, and laws (as was the case with the nuclear power industry and biotechnology). In nuclear power generation some hazards were anticipated in advance. Others were identified in crisis periods (see Patterson, 1983; Bertell, 1985). This feature is not inconsistent with the connection of the industry with the national interest and defense, as well as the importance of the nature of the *perceived risk,* or images of danger associated with the industry (Carson, 1982: chap. 3; Perrow, 1984).

The history of Britain's involvement with atomic energy and the generation of electricity by nuclear reactor has been described by Gowing (1974). In 1946, the United States passed the McMahon Act, which forbade the transmission of atomic data to other countries. As a result, the British were practically excluded from information necessary to participate in a joint project, and began their own project in 1947. Gowing (1964, 1974) and others (Valentine, 1985; Patterson, 1983, 1984; Williams, 1980; Pocock, 1977) have indicated that initial efforts were directed primarily to military requirements for atomic bombs. According to Williams (1980), the first formal program in Britain for producing civil nuclear power was begun in February 1955.

The interplay of economics, international competition for reactor designs, and safety considerations resulted in a series of protracted and frequently reversed decisions by the British (Gowing, 1974, 1978; Williams, 1980). Throughout the period from 1953 to 1978, conflicts developed between the commercial interests involved in building the reactors, the central government, the civil service, and environmental groups. As well, there was continuing conflict between the three groups responsible for developing the nuclear industry, the United Kingdom Atomic Energy Authority (UKAEA), the Central Electricity Generating Board (CEGB), and the consortia who were to design and construct the planned reactors (Williams, 1980: 27). Paralleling these events were military developments of experimental reactors. Perhaps the most important development in the nuclear power field in Britain in 20 years has been the Sizewell Inquiry, which was called to assess the safety, economic feasibility, environmental consequences, and waste management associated with the proposal of the CEGB to build a new reactor.

Against this brief overview of the origins and development of the nuclear power industry in Britain can be set the primary aim of the government with regard to nuclear power in postwar Britain. This was to establish a plutonium-generating capacity; that domestic power could be produced by harnessing the heat emitted by the reaction in the thermal piles was merely a positive externality[3] associated with plutonium production and national defense. Whether this view of the process is emphasized or whether, conversely, plutonium is viewed as a positive externality associated with domestic power production, both are characterized as public or collective goods. This feature of electric power in general, and of nuclear reactor-generated power in particular, serves to explain some anomalous features of the industry with respect to costs, pricing, and safety assessment, as well as some of the political constraints in evidence.

The national political constraints noted in the discussion of origins of the nuclear power industry in Britain were embedded in a series of external constraints, such as the economic market structure of the nation, the governmental and party system, the political forces of opposition and support, and international economic factors such as changing rates of inflation, fuel costs, and interest rates. The British situation, like that of other nations producing electrical power by nuclear reactors (see Campbell, 1984; Sweet, 1983; Camillieri, 1984), has a specific politicoeconomic character. Political interpretations within the industry itself also shape the development of nuclear power and its regulation. Choosing one locally available natural resource over another, a locally available fuel over an internationally available one, or to subsidize one form of fuel or another at some level creates variations within the national strategy. Centralizing decision making shapes strategies as well. Sweet (1983: 26) notes:

> Where the state is exercising monopoly power as seller and buyer, this means that the influence of the market is diminished and indeed the industry can be cushioned against pressures, both political and economic, that might otherwise force changes unwelcome to itself. The difference in institutional structures of the US and the Federal Republic of Germany where the private sectors are predominant and the UK and France where the state is predominant are basic for understanding the effective moratorium on nuclear power in the former and the relative immunity from both market forces and public opposition in the latter.

Economic factors, such as the costs of replacing old generators and building new ones, are even more elusive in Britain than they are in the United States. Because of the substantial economic risks and costs, and government interest involved, governments in centralized nations have taken primary decision-making roles in shaping the industry. These strategies are based upon the special sort of collective good that nuclear energy is said to represent.

Arguments around the notion of a collective good have been developed in detail elsewhere (Manning, forthcoming) and will be briefly summarized here. The accepted definition of collective goods derives from Samuelson (1954: 387) who identified two kinds of goods: private consumption goods, which can be individually parceled out in distinguishable units or amounts and which can be attached to particular persons exclusively, and collective goods, "which all enjoy in common, in the sense that each individual's consumption of a good leads to no subtraction from any other individual's consumption of such a good." The benefit of a collective good is simultaneously derived by each and every individual and by the collectivity. The state, or any organized group, produces collective goods such that if any person in the group consumes those goods, they cannot be readily withheld from the others in that group (Olson, 1970: 14). The state dispenses collective goods in aggregate, not individual terms. Both benefits (such as enhanced air quality in the absence of coal smoke and jobs produced) and costs (such as the risk of actual accidents, waste disposal, pollution, and health dangers associated with exposure to radiation) are "externalities" associated with production of the collective good. Because of the special nature of nuclear power, these costs and benefits are quite difficult to identify and measure. Consumers, strictly speaking, cannot judge the quality of the collective good generally distributed. One cannot exercise a choice among producers and products, nor can one "exit" (Hirschman, 1970). Given the nature of the consumer's relationship to the production of nuclear power—that is, consumption—the quite disparate nature of the other costs and risks may be obscured (see Lowrance, 1976).

It could be argued that nuclear regulation is directed to reducing negative externalities associated with a "semi-collective good" (Thomas, personal communication, January 1984) and is not in this sense directly comparable with other collective goods, such as education, defense, and sewage and rubbish disposal. It is not something that all enjoy in common—there are clear inequities in terms of who benefits and who pays. It could, ironically, be a public good with respect to costs to society while not so with respect to benefits.

The political nature of nuclear reactor-generated power further defines several features of this collective good. Massive governmental subsidies for the development of nuclear power were supplied to the industry, as were subsidies for rates of electricity, thus obscuring the actual costs to the consumer and to the society. In addition, the government has taken responsibility for waste disposal, radioactivity standards, transport controls, and fuel reprocessing. Each government since the war has had the stated aim of encouraging production and stimulating demand. The government implements and enforces the rules establishing and shaping the industry, and confirms the rules governing the safety and operation of reactors producing electrical power and plutonium. Safety is a political matter (Lowrance, 1976: chap. 3) and a value concept.

In presenting a case analysis of the NII, it will be argued that political choice more than environmental or social structural determinism operates with respect to the nature of the regulatory pattern developed for the nuclear industry in Britain. The pattern of nuclear industry regulation in Britain, in other words, is a result of government decisions about the organization of the industry. Regulation is by no means of a compliance system.

A BRIEF DESCRIPTION OF THE
NUCLEAR INSTALLATIONS INSPECTORATE

The Inspectorate was established in April 1960 following the introduction of the Nuclear Installations (Licensing and Insurance) Act 1959. As is often the case, the NII came into being partly as a result of a crisis and public response—in this case, a fire at the Windscale Fuel Reprocessing plant in 1957 in which, at one point, 11 tonnes of uranium were ablaze, spewing radioactivity into the atmosphere around the plant (see Patterson, 1983; Fleck Hearings, 1957). It was shifted from the Ministry of Energy to the Health and Safety Executive, under the Minister of Employment, in a consolidation of health and safety inspectorial functions in 1975.

The resistance of the industry to regulation has been rather modest. All the relevant parties are (part of) the state. The industries involved are nationalized producers of essential services tightly linked to national defense. Governmental policy, on the whole, has been to pursue nuclear energy in various degrees of enthusiasm since about 1945 (see Gowing, 1964, 1974; Williams, 1980; Patterson, 1983). At key points in the debate concerning nuclear power, groups have opposed the building of further plants (in 1964, 1965, and 1979, and at the Sizewell hearings of 1983 through 1985), and have raised the issues of safety in fuel reprocessing and environmental pollution (Fleck, 1957; Flowers, 1976; see also Black, 1984, on the incidence of cancer in and around Windscale). Opposition has arisen from environmental groups, local community groups, and some governmental groups such as the Greater London Council (see Barker, 1984).

The NII is an inspectorate of some 100 people located in five branches with responsibility for policy, current reactors, reactors in progress, fuel reprocessing, and future reactors. Each branch other than the policy branch contains specialist assessors as well as inspectors, but the line is not sharply drawn, because all inspectors are specialists, and assessors may do site inspections. Inspections are made at the discretion of the Inspectorate. Its work is activated in large part by requests made by the licensees. There are three nationalized licensees, the Central Electricity Generating Board (CEGB), the South of Scotland Electricity Generating Board (SSEGB), and British Nuclear Fuels (BNFL). There is a strict liability provision as regards accidents, although this is confined by the 1965 Act. No legal or quasi-legal review of decisions can be taken on decisions to revoke consent or license, or impose fines. There are some standards, such as those relating to dosage of radioactivity to workers and others, but on the whole, the model is one of negotiation, bargaining, and setting of the practical implications of some rather general statements.

The rules used by the NII are of three types: rules associated with radioactivity applied within and around the plant, some of which are international standards (Her Majesty's Stationery Office: 1); rules concerning the design, operation, commissioning, and decommissioning of the reactor; and rules concerning the safety of the plant and employees (such as those dealing with the storage of hazardous wastes and fire regulations). These arise in the first instance from international bodies and the National Radiation Protection Board, from the industry itself (the operating and plant specification rules), and from the Health and Safety at Work Act and its related guidance notes. The standards are absolute, but the rules surrounding functions and safety are mediated by the general notion that what should be done is within reasonably practicable means. This gives individual inspectors great flexibility in interpreting various levels and kinds of rules governing reactor safety and operations.

The *strategy of enforcement* is reactive.[4] The NII responds to requests, anticipated modifications, license applications, and inquiries from the three licensees. Theoretically the inspectors spend about one-quarter of their time on site. The Inspectorate sees itself as an objective judge of the adequacy of a "safety case" put to it by the industry. Although it is possible to prosecute under civil and/or criminal law for dereliction on the part of the industry, the NII has not practiced this, preferring to act informally and non-legally to induce compliance and set mutually agreeable lines of authority, modes of correction, and plant modification. Because all the costs of inspection and clerical work associated with the licensing and inspection activities of the Inspectorate are billed to the industry, the NII recovers about 60% of its costs.

IRONIES OF COMPLIANCE IN THE NUCLEAR SAFETY FIELD

The apparent aims of regulation in the nuclear field are to maintain the market in electrical power, maintain the production of plutonium (not a publicly stated goal), and encourage the regulated industry to accept their general duty to do what is "reasonably practicable." What is regulated produces valued public goods, well-being, and income. From the perspective of the industry, regulation in its various forms is seen as an additional cost added to production. The form of control, licensing, is generally used in a monopoly market or nationalized industry in order to ensure a lowest level of performance as an entry criterion, or to grant an exception to a given standard, such as pollution by effluents. The consumer is assumed to be ignorant or information-free, or unable in any case to judge the quality of the goods and services produced.

As noted previously, these features are consistent with a compliance model of enforcement. In spite of the centrality of compliance as the defining characteristic of the enforcement pattern in nuclear regulation, the concept itself is often obscured. Compliance can be seen as a *process* including a number of states in flux, subject to assessment and bargaining. This is a common administrative notion for assessing industries in normal operation. Compliance can also refer to the *degree of fit* between what the law requires and what is actually the case at any given time or inspection. Compliance, in some sense a value judgment concerning what the law requires, is always to some degree absent, and variations around the principles are accepted. In the case of nuclear safety, principles of safety assessment are coupled with standards for radiation exposure that guide administrative behavior.

Compliance can also be conceived as a binary relationship, an isomorphism between organizational practices and standards held by an agency or in the written law. A reactor, for example, is either complying (and, therefore, licensed) or not with requirements. This definition is atemporal, and collapses the range of systems that are covered in a given license, such as management, safety systems, reactor maintenance schedule, and workers' exposure to radioactivity.

In an important sense, compliance is a function of the capacity of the inspecting agency to penetrate private domains, to monitor the regulation organization's functions, and to obtain information on operations. This requires data-analytic capacity, data storage and retrieval systems, and the development of generalizable categories of error, causation and crime. Training in the use of techniques and technologies must be provided. Thus, compliance depends upon the social organization of information gathering as well as a degree of cooperation between the regulated industry, and between the industry and the Inspectorate.

Public opinion trends that might guide the relationship between the industry and the Inspectorate are suffused with ambivalence. There is no consensus about the degree of risk involved in nuclear power, about the likelihood of accident and its consequences, and the routine costs and exposure levels associated with power generation (Perrow, 1984). As a result, the meaning of a given violation, what should be done as a result, and whether it represents harm or potential harm are problematic. To whom the harm evolves and what the precise tariff, if any, ought to be if a dereliction comes to light are unclear. Public opinion polls show divisions among the public and a tendency to trust the experts (Henderson, 1985; Eiser et al., 1985). Experts disagree (Mazur, 1981; Nelkin, 1971). Interviews suggest that the Inspectorate does not view as its primary concern responding to public opinion. Nor do they consult public opinion data, which might indicate general trends in fear of nuclear accidents or radiation. Unlike the police who may rely on fear of crime data, victim surveys, or the crime rate to monitor performance, the Inspectorate views public conceptions of risk or safety as of little use.

In an important sense, whether compliance obtains in the nuclear industry is an administrative decision (Hawkins, 1984: 23ff; Becker, 1963). The rules and standards developed are set by the government, in this case the Inspectorate, for its own operation. This distinguishes regulation of nuclear safety from other forms of regulation involving sanctioning and penal strategies. It also differentiates the British from the American model (see note 2).

Conceptually, compliance is best seen as an administrative construction defined by technique and activities developed within the Inspectorate, and as having a tacit relationship to moral and political notions of *safety*. In general operation, compliance is indicated by licensing patterns, not by the assessment of safety, or by risk analysis. The NII does not assume that nuclear power generation is problematic, or indeed that reactors are inherently unsafe. The central belief is that the industry is a responsible body that produces an essentially valuable product by a proven and safe technology. These beliefs anticipate and guide the process of negotiating a license. The aim of the licensing process is to produce electricity safely. That is a given from the outset, and not to be determined in the course of investigation, inspection, audit, or negotiation.

The Health and Safety at Work Act (1973) places duties on a licensee and operators for general and nuclear safety. These are to be achieved by "reasonably practicable" means that are to take into account the economic well-being of the industry, the current state of the plant, and what is practical. A corollary of this, when combined with the licensing procedure, is *variation* in safety requirements. Reactors were built at different times, with different designs, by several construction consortia. There have been no requirements to "back fit" reactors to current safety standards, nor to alter licenses to a uniform length and set of conditions. The Inspectorate develops through case-by-case decisions a body of precedents, loosely held as analogously relevant, which are serially unique, and are geared to avoidance of complaint, the maintenance of authority, and the feasibility of the requirements (Reiss, 1985). To some degree, the state of play between the industry, the management of a given site, and the Inspectorate, and moral conceptions of the reactor are important in shaping the negotiating frame. Some reactors, and some management, are said to be more cooperative than others; management at some sites are more willing to negotiate, to share information and problems, and to be more forthcoming in the event of requests by the Inspectorate for information.

Nuclear safety is assessed in many ways, both in advance and after the reactor is constructed. These include risk analysis, the reasonably practicable means test, inspection and monitoring, and techniques of assessing the safety of the reactor itself, such as the use of high-frequency sound and X-ray tests for leaks, simulations of releases, and testing procedures for the reactor's pressure, temperature, and performance (see O'Riordan et al. 1985).

As previously noted, the Inspectorate responds to requests made by the licensees. It relies on the industry for information, test results, and research data on reactor performance.

This occurs in at least four important ways. First, the industry develops the rules and plans that govern its operation at the plant level. Modification of administrative rules or plants are negotiated with plant, regional, or central officials. Second, when the industry has decided to build a reactor, within the confines of government policy the perceived task of the NII is to determine the *relative safety* of the proposed reactor, given the current state of the art. Third, determinations of safety through risk analysis and levels of risk may be used. They are almost entirely notional. Nuclear safety concerns events that have not occurred, or are so rare that they are statistically highly unlikely. Simulations are based upon *assumptions* about the nature of the site, the prevailing winds, the level of the release, the number of persons to be affected, and the sort of reactor in question. This simulation is not based on actual events or "real data," but is a hypothetical treatment of artificial data (see Short, 1984). The limits of risk analysis are well reviewed elsewhere (Perrow, 1984; Short, 1984; Manning, forthcoming). Fourth, the nature of the events to which the NII should direct attention is variable.[5] Each reactor station is required to keep a book in which incidents are to be recorded, but there are no written or formal criteria for inclusion. Matters reported to the Energy Secretary are those the NII and the licensees deem relevant for ministerial attention. This loose system was introduced in 1979, when public revelations about an accident at a reactor embarrassed the Energy Minister, who had not been informed (Patterson, 1983: 161). There is a patterned ambiguity in the sorts of incidents that should be reported and how they are reported and to whom. Even if compliance with all required safety cases is attained and confirmed by administrative decision (that is, nonaction or intervention in the operation), an accident or release may still occur. An accident rate will vary around a statistical mean, regardless of changes in plant safety practices. Furthermore, the relationship between compliance and the inspection function is hopelessly confounded by the fact that compliance is defined by inspectors. Compliance and its consequences are rather subtle and indistinct.

The risks associated with nuclear power generation are debated by many and governments have taken the view that questions of safety—the valuation of risks to which people are exposed—are to be assessed by government through and by its own agents. Thus, although in many respects modern life is less subject to many risks experienced in the past, especially those of infectious diseases, it is dramatically subject to the risks associated with high technology. Licensing and compliance systems of enforcement act in tentative areas of innovation as well as in those industries thought to be central to national defense and well-being (Wildavsky and Douglas, 1983).

THE FUNCTIONALIST MODEL OF NUCLEAR SAFETY REGULATION

Reiss has argued a functionalist position that implies, among other things, that there are determinate features of regulatory systems that reflect a clear and precise or "best-guess" approach to the control of harm or, conversely, the likelihood of safety for the public. He argues that compliance systems are found when the costs of violations are too great for society to bear and/or where detection and sanctioning offenders is too difficult or expensive. This further implies that there is a degree of unity in the motivation and aims of the statutory agencies involved in regulation, and that the regulatory body is charged with and produces the conditions of compliance.

Each of these features is a political issue that has a symbolic meaning in the sense that the state and the law act in ways that signal the values, meanings, and intention of the state toward various social groups. These groups in turn invest in the actions of the state symbolic meanings conditioned by their own social position (Gusfield, 1981). It may be that rather than arising as a result of social conditions that can be easily verified, compliance systems are instead a residual category of regulation in which questions of general or natural justice, consensually based punishments, and notions of harm are not clear. Costs of violations are indeterminate and not sought or calculated in any precise fashion, rather than clearly defined and identified as too great to be borne.

In the case of the NII, as has been suggested, regulative activities are not violation-focused, and perhaps could not be. In fact, the concept of violation is not used by the Inspectorate or by the electricity generating boards. Breaking rules is not relevant in this regulatory context. Rather, the question is how to determine the reasonable level practicable for modifications that are seen as improving the safety of the operation. The costs to society cannot and could not be calculated, and thus must be symbolic or potential in character. It is not *known* costs, harm, or rule-breaking violations that lead to the development of compliance systems. It is instead that the matters to be regulated are representative of moral and political concerns that cannot be determined, or are such a potential source of dissent and conflict that precise regulation would dramatically reveal the interests of the powerful and the state.

It is in the interests of the state to avoid intervention in Anglo-American societies when the level of harm is unknown, and/or to maintain a degree of public ignorance. It is not the presence of *knowledge* that leads to the emergence of compliance systems of regulation rather than deterrent ones, but the absence of knowledge combined with a willingness to pursue the level, kinds, distribution, and consequences of harm issuing directly or indirectly from a form of production.

The aims of the regulators need not be speculated about, nor any typology of motivations of either regulators or regulated created. Nor is there a good reason to assume that the aims of an agency or Inspectorate could be typified in any meaningful way. In other words, the appeal to motives and to intentions, and the link between these and societal goals or aims is false and misleading (Winch, 1958). The specific point here is that motives vary within the Inspectorate according to function and level. At the top, the interest is in procedure, in the appearance of objectivity and professionalism, whereas within the middle management of the Inspectorate far more concern is given to the control of subordinates and the flow of paper connected with the regulatory process (such as the licensing of a reactor). At the lower level, the inspectors and the assessors direct far more concern to the moral credibility and trustworthiness of the management of a plant, with a willingness to accede to requests, suggestions, hints, jokes, and other nuances of persuasion. Conversely, offenses against the "face" of the inspector, against his or her dignity and respectability, and an unwillingness to bargain or to provide information when asked, will be of concern. In all of this, the question of "safety" plays an often indirect role. It is quite clear from a number of studies that abstract questions of justice, enforcement, policy, and even law become subsumed under the general, moral, and practical perspectives of the enforcers (see Skolnick, 1966; Westley, 1970; Manning, 1977; Lipsky, 1977; Hawkins, 1984). Any typification of "intent" is misleading and, strictly speaking, ad hoc. In addition, it is difficult to establish the aim of the state, or the goal of the regulatory body.

All regulation is in some sense *symbolic;* this appears incontrovertible. The question is to determine what aspects of regulation achieve an instrumental impact, and can be shown to have such an impact, and what aspects serve to dramatize and define social values, to set apart certain social relationships for evaluation and control, and to reassure society of the merits of regulation. It has been argued elsewhere that crime control is a symbolic matter (Manning, 1977, 1980), but this does not omit the consequences of crime in terms of loss of property and lives, and human misery. Figures demonstrate rates of crime, degrees of personal loss, and the failure of police to clear crime. The costs to society of the criminal justice system can be estimated, but they cannot establish finally what this loss *means* to various groups in the society, nor to the police mandate. In other words, police actions and crime statistics conflate two meanings and communicate both—the instrumental (the indicators of the existence of crime) and the symbolic (the indicators of the moral status of the society and its control agents).

The relative degree to which nuclear safety can be measured evaluated, and assessed varies; whether one calls this uncertainty in the environment, lack of consensus about the aims of the organization, or "market failure," it remains variable. Nuclear safety is uncertain in several ways. Long-term data about the safety of reactors are unavailable because experience with the technology is brief; reactors have been operative for only 30 years. Operating data on reactors are gathered by the management of the reactors, and sent only in summary form to the NII. "Safety" itself is defined in at least four different ways, using risk analysis, principles of exposure to radiation, and up-to-date safety case following start-up and maintenance, and merely the possession of a license.

Finally, as has been noted previously, the nature of the danger associated with the production of the electrical power by means of nuclear reactors is of a special kind: invisible, chronic, life threatening, and potentially massive in character. It is furthermore a collective and nonvoluntary risk that would be experienced by all should exposure to radiation occur due to an accident. The fear or dread cannot be reduced by the facts of exposure nor by presentation of rates of cancer. The dread has a foreboding and generalized level that resonates with basic fears of termination of social, personal, psychic, and generational continuity (Lifton, 1969).

Technological change constantly modifies standards and practices. In the case of nuclear technology questions still remain as to safety and exposure, and the consequences of accidents. Governments in the past have concealed the results of tests, nuclear accidents, exposure to radioactive waste, and current risks associated with work in reactors (see Hilgartner et al., 1983). This is partly because the question of risk and exposure is still under debate and partly because of the national interest in producing material for weapons. The nuclear industry represents a new form of power production, and new forms of social and political organization were developed as a result. Government aims to reduce electrical costs, to enhance national defense, and to strengthen the electricity industry interact with perceived public interests. These values are in conflict and in flux, and the modes of regulation appropriate to such activities are therefore likely to be noncriminal in nature.

CONCLUSION

Social processes embed governmental regulation of economic life. Regulatory practices are perhaps more dramatic when institutional patterning is shown to determine rule enforcement in the most sacred domains of collective life—those involving the quality of water, air, and the environment.

Regulatory efforts in Britain with respect to the control of the risks and safety of electricity generation by nuclear power are in part a product of government interests in maintaining the health of the industry and in part a product of organizational exigencies surrounding the licensing process. The NII employs bargaining and negotiating to protect the safety of the plant and nearby community and to implement the required standards of radiation protection. It utilizes rules arising from joint consultation and negotiation, with the exception of radiation standards, and does not focus on "violations" or complaints as a basis for justifying its existence or establishing its neutrality. It is presumed to act as an objective judge of the technical adequacy of the reactor and the power station. It has very high discretion at all levels, and engages in problem solving and bargaining in the shadow of the law, rarely having other than consultative arrangements with solicitors [lawyers]. It has adapted to uncertainty in the safety domain by focusing on the technical aspects of reactor safety. With regard to the broader political and economic questions, it adopts the view that its role is to implement government energy policies, judging only their safety correlates and responding to the licensing applications of the industry. The use of the reasonably practicable means approach permits the introduction of economic considerations in a semiformal and commonsense manner.

Because the Inspectorate focuses its attention upon the licensing process—assuming that reactors are essentially safe—its approach to the task is on a case-by-case basis, permitting variations by reactor design and construction, contemporary standards of safety, and economic constraints. This means that the traditional concerns of regulation, discretion, and horizontal and vertical equity disappear. No single moral standard determines the viccissitudes of the licensing process. An absolute conception of moral order and of safety are rejected.

Because in a sense the government is acting as a private actor within a legal framework when it licenses a nationalized industry to produce a public good, it is in fact establishing the conditions under which it expects its agencies to operate. It establishes the contractual conditions for its own operation by means of what Healy (1985) terms *bilateral voluntarism*. Such agreements of government might be considered regulation, but as contractually legitimated modes of private operation. If the latter is so, it is a form of self-policing analogous to that found in private security companies, industries, insurance companies, and stock markets.

NOTES

1. This study is funded by a grant from the Health and Safety Executive to the Centre for Socio-Legal Studies, Wolfson College, Oxford, and provides support for four years from April 1983 to April 1987. The research incorporates economic, legal, historical, sociological, and social-psychological perspectives and data, and includes, at various levels of time obligation, some 8-10 persons. Details are found in Center for Socio-Legal Studies (1982). My work includes a joint project with Keith Hawkins on decision making generally, as well as the study of the NII. To date, the work consists of fieldwork in three of the branches of the Inspectorate including meetings, site visits, and correspondence, interviews with some 21 staff from the chief inspector to inspector, and field notes. It also includes analysis of official documents, transcripts of the Sizewell Inquiry (1983-

1985), histories of the origins and development of nuclear power in Britain, France, and the United States, and newspaper clippings from 1982 to present on nuclear energy in Britain and related problems such as waste disposal, the economics of electrical energy, pollution, and international developments in nuclear power.

2. Although the aims of regulation may be similar in the United Kingdom and in America, the approach differs insofar as Congress in the United States attempts to write very specific standards and rules governing the administration and implementation of a law, whereas these same functions are delegated to Ministers in the United Kingdom. A number of important differences in approach and in enforcement practices in the two countries are suggested in the works of Vogel (1983), which is explicitly comparative, and Hawkins (1984), which details one British agency's practices (see also Reiss, 1985; and Abel, 1985, on comparative practice).

3. A positive externality is defined as a benefit that results from a production process other than that defined as the primary product, good, or service. A negative externality is a cost derived analytically in the same fashion. As these are value judgements based on definitions of the primary product and the externalities associated with it, as well as hypothecated preferences, they are somewhat controversial even in economics.

4. This is misleading insofar as these are communications or transactions precipitated by a license request. It could be argued that once a request is made, the NII actively seeks confirmation of the desired state of affairs.

5. The NCR, as Ford (1982) points out, does not analyze these incidents; it simply stores them.

REFERENCES

ABEL, R. (1985) "Risk as an arena of struggle." University of Michigan Law Review 83, 4: 772-812.

BARKER, T. (1984) "Inquiries in Britain." Presented to the Law Faculty, University of Oxford, November.

BARDACH, S. and R. KAGAN (1982) Going by the Book. Philadelphia: Temple University Press.

BECKER, H. S. (1963) Outsiders. New York: Free Press.

BERNSTEIN, M. (1955) Regulating Business by Independent Commission. Princeton: Princeton University Press.

BERTELL, M. (1985) No Immediate Danger. London: Women's Press.

BITTNER, E. (1972) The Role of the Police in Modern Society. Washington, DC: Government Printing Office.

BLACK, D. (1983) "Self-help." American Sociological Review 48.

———(1984) Investigation of the Possible Increased Incidence of Cancer in West Cumbria. London: Her Majesty's Stationery Office.

CAMILLIERI, J. (1984) The State and Nuclear Power. Brighton, England: Wheatsheaf Books.

CAMPBELL, J. (1984) "Can we plan? The political economy of commercial nuclear energy policy in the United States." Doctoral dissertation, Department of Sociology, University of Wisconsin, Madison.

CARSON, W. G. (1970) "White collar crime and the enforcement of factory legislation." British Journal of Criminology 10: 192-206.
———(1982) The Other Cost of Britain's Oil. Oxford: Martin Robinson.
Center for Socio-Legal Studies (1982) An Agenda for Socio-Legal Research Into the Regulation of Health and Safety at Work. Wolfson College, Oxford, England.
DICKSON, D. (1968) "Bureaucracy and morality: an organisational perspective on a moral crusade." Social Problems 16: 143-1XX.
DOUGLAS, J. D. (1971) American Social Order (Chap. 2). New York: Free Press.
EDELMAN, M. (1964) Symbolic Uses of Politics. Urbana: University of Illinois Press.
———(1971) Political Language. Chicago: Markham.
EISER, R., R. SPEARS, and J. van der PLIGT (1985) "Community attitudes to proposals for new nuclear power stations." Presented to the meeting of the Institute of British Geographers, Leeds.
ERICSON, R. V. (1981) Making Crime. Toronto: Butterworths.
———(1982) Reproducing Order. Toronto: University of Toronto Press.
FLECK, R. (1957) Report on Windscale Accident. Comnd. paper 338, December. London: Her Majesty's Stationery Office.
FLOWERS, B. (1976) Report of Royal Commission on Environmental Pollution. London: Her Majesty's Stationery Office.
FISCHOFF, B. et al. (1981) Acceptable Risk. Cambridge, England: Cambridge University Press.
FORD, D. (1982) Three Mile Island. New York: Viking.
GOWING, M. (1964) Britain and Atomic Energy, 1939-45. London: Macmillan.
———(1974) Independence and Deterrence. London: Macmillan.
GUSFIELD, J. (1963) Symbolic Crusade: Status Politics and the American Temperance Movement. Urbana: University of Illinois Press.
———(1981) The Culture of Public Problems. Chicago: University of Chicago Press.
HAWKINS, K. (1984) Environment and Enforcement. Oxford: Clarendon Press.
HEALY, P. (1985) Notes for a Descriptive Model of Compliance and the Forms of Governmental Action. Wolfson College, Oxford.
HENDERSON, J., J. BROWN, and J. SPENCER (1985) "Psychological impacts of the siting of nuclear facilities: some paradoxes and coping strategies." Presented to Methods and Experiences in Impact Assessment Conference, Utrecht, Holland, July.
Her Majesty's Stationery Office (1982) The Work of a HM Nuclear Installations Inspectorate. London: Author.
HILGARTNER, S., R. BELL and R. O'CONNOR (1983) Nukespeak: Nuclear language, Visions and Mindset. New York: Penguin.
HIRSCHMAN, A. (1970) Exit, Voice or Loyalty. Princeton: Princeton University Press.
LASSWELL, H. (1960) Psychopathology and Politics. New York: Viking.
LIFTON, R. J. (1969) Death in Life. New York: Vintage.
LIPSKY, M. (1977) Street Level Bureaucracy. New York: Russell Sage.
LOWI, T. (1970) The End of Liberalism. New York: W.W. Norton.
LOWRENCE, W. W. (1976) Of Acceptable Risk. Los Altos, CA: Kaufmann.

MANNING, P. K. (1977) Police Work. Cambridge, MA: MIT Press.
———(1980) Narcs' Game. Cambridge, MA: MIT Press.
———(forthcoming a) Secularised Dread: The Regulation of Nuclear Safety.
———(forthcoming b) "The Limits of Knowledge," in K. Hawkins and J. Thomas (eds.). Regulation and Policy.
MAZUR, A. (1981) The Dynamics of Technical Controversy. Washington, DC: Communications Press.
NELKIN, D. (1971) Nuclear Power and Its Critics. Ithaca, NY: Cornell University Press.
OFFSHE, C. (1985) Disorganised Capitalism. Oxford, England: Basil Blackwell.
OLSON, M. (1970) The Logic of Collective Action. New York: Schoken.
O'RIORDAN, T., R. KEMP, and M. PURDUE (1985) "How the Sizewell B inquiry is grappling with the concept of acceptable risk." Journal of Experimental Psychology 5: 69-85.
PATTERSON, W. (1983) Nuclear Power. Harmondsworth, England: Penguin.
———(1984) The Plutonium Business. London: Paladin.
PERROW, C. (1984) Normal Accidents. New York: Basic Books.
PRESSMAN, J., and A. WILDAVSKY (1973) Implementation. Berkeley: University of California Press.
POCOCK, R. F. (1977) Nuclear Power: Its Development in the United Kingdom. London: Allen & Unwin.
REISS, A. J., Jr. (1983) "The policing of organizational life," pp. 78-97 in M. Punch (ed.) Control of Organizational Life. Cambridge, MA: MIT Press.
———(1985) "Compliance without coercion." University of Michigan Law Review 83, 4: 813-819.
———and A. BIDERMAN (1980) Data Sources in White-Collar Law-Breaking. Washington, DC: Government Printing Office.
SAMUELSON, P. (1954) "The pure theory of public expenditure." Review of Economics and Statistics 36: 387-390.
SELZNICK, P. (1966) TVA and the Grass Roots. New York: Harper Torchbooks.
SHORT, J. (1984) "The social transformation of risk analysis." American Sociological Review 49: 711-725.
SKOLNICK, J. (1966) Justice Without Trial. New York: John Wiley.
SWEET, C. (1983) The Price of Nuclear Power. London: Heinemann.
VALENTINE, J. (1985) Atomic Crossroads. London: Merlin.
VELJANOVSKI, C. (1982) The New Law-and-Economics. ESRC. Centre for Socio-Legal Research, Oxford.
VOGEL, D. (1983) "A comparison of environmental regulation in Great Britain and the United States." Public Interest (Summer):
WEICK, K. (1979) The Social Psychology of Organizing. Reading, MA: Addison-Wesley.
WESTLEY, W. (1970) Violence and the Police. Cambridge, MA: MIT Press.
WILDAVSKY, A. and M. DOUGLAS (1983) Risk and Culture. Berkeley: University of California Press.
WILLIAMS, R. (1980) The Nuclear Power Decisions. London: Croom Helm.
WILSON, J. Q. [ed.] (1982) The Politics of Regulation. New York: Basic Books.
WINCH, P. (1958) The Idea of a Social Science. London: Routledge & Kegan Paul.

Chapter 13

SAY "CHEESE!":
The Disney Order That Is
Not So Mickey Mouse

CLIFFORD D. SHEARING
PHILIP C. STENNING

One of the most distinctive features of that quintessentially American playground known as Disney World is the way it seeks to combine a sense of comfortable—even nostalgic—familiarity with an air of innovative technological advance. Mingled with the fantasies of one's childhood are the dreams of a better future. Next to the Magic Kingdom is the Epcot Center. As well as providing for a great escape, Disney World claims also to be a design for better living. And what impresses most about this place is that it seems to run like clockwork.

Yet the Disney order is no accidental by-product. Rather, it is a designed-in feature that provides—to the eye that is looking for it, but not to the casual visitor—an exemplar of modern private corporate policing. Along with the rest of the scenery of which it forms a discreet part, it too is recognizable as a design for the future.

In these last few pages of the book, we invite you to come with us on a guided tour of this modern police facility in which discipline and control are, like many of the characters one sees about, in costume.

The fun begins . . .

AUTHOR'S NOTE: This chapter is largely extracted from "From the Panopticon to Disney World: The Development of Discipline," pp. 335-349 in A. Doob and E. Greenspan (eds.) *Perspectives in Criminal Law: Essays in Honour of John Ll. J. Edwards* (Aurora: Canada Law Book, 1984). We would like to thank the Canada Law Book company for granting permission to reprint part of this essay here.

the moment the visitor enters Disney World. As one arrives by car one is greeted by a series of smiling young people who, with the aid of clearly visible road markings, direct one to one's parking spot, remind one to lock one's car and to remember its location and then direct one to await the rubber-wheeled train that will convey visitors away from the parking lot. At the boarding location one is directed to stand safely behind guard rails and to board the train in an orderly fashion. While climbing on board one is reminded to remember the name of the parking area and the row number in which one is parked (for instance, "Donald Duck, 1"). Once on the train one is encouraged to protect oneself from injury by keeping one's body within the bounds of the carriage and to do the same for children in one's care. Before disembarking one is told how to get from the train back to the monorail platform and where to wait for the train to the parking lot on one's return. At each transition from one stage of one's journey to the next one is wished a happy day and a "good time" at Disney World (this begins as one drives in and is directed by road signs to tune one's car radio to the Disney radio network).

As one moves towards the monorail platform the directions one has just received are reinforced by physical barriers (that make it difficult to take a wrong turn), pavement markings, signs and more cheerful Disney employees who, like their counterparts in other locations, convey the message that Disney World is a "fun place" designed for one's comfort and pleasure. On approaching the monorail platform one is met by enthusiastic attendants who quickly and efficiently organize the mass of people moving onto it into corrals designed to accommodate enough people to fill one compartment on the monorail. In assigning people to these corrals the attendants ensure that groups visiting Disney World together remain together. Access to the edge of the platform is prevented by a gate which is opened once the monorail has arrived and disembarked the arriving passengers on the other side of the platform. If there is a delay of more than a minute or two in waiting for the next monorail one is kept informed of the reason for the delay and the progress the expected train is making towards the station.

Once aboard and the automatic doors of the monorail have closed, one is welcomed aboard, told to remain seated and "for one's own safety" to stay away from open windows. The monorail takes a circuitous route to one of the two Disney locations (the Epcot Center or the Magic Kingdom) during which time a friendly disembodied voice introduces one briefly to the pleasures of the world one is about to enter and the methods of transport available between its various locations. As the monorail slows towards its destination one is told how to disembark once the automatic doors open and how to move from the station to the entrance gates, and reminded to take one's possessions with one and to take care of oneself, and children in one's care, on disembarking. Once again these instructions are reinforced, in a variety of ways, as one moves towards the gates.

It will be apparent from the above that Disney Productions is able to handle large crowds of visitors in a most orderly fashion. Potential trouble is anticipated and prevented. Opportunities for disorder are minimized by constant instruction, by physical barriers which severely limit the choice of action available and by the surveillance of omnipresent employees who detect and rectify the slightest deviation.

The vehicles that carry people between locations are an important component of the system of physical barriers. Throughout Disney World vehicles are used as barriers. This is particularly apparent in the Epcot Center, the newest Disney facility, where many exhibits are accessible only via special vehicles which automatically secure one once they begin moving.

Control strategies are embedded in both environmental features and structural relations. In both cases control structures and activities have other functions which are highlighted so that the control function is overshadowed. Nonetheless, control is pervasive. For example, virtually every pool, fountain, and flower garden serves both as an aesthetic object and to direct visitors away from, or towards, particular locations. Similarly, every Disney Productions employee, while visibly and primarily engaged in other functions, is also engaged in the maintenance of order. This integration of functions is real and not simply an appearance: beauty *is* created, safety *is* protected, employees *are* helpful. The effect is, however, to embed the control function into the "woodwork" where its presence is unnoticed but its effects are ever present.

A critical consequence of this process of embedding control in other structures is that control becomes consensual. It is effected with the willing co-operation of those being controlled so that the controlled become, as Foucault has observed, the source of their own control. Thus, for example, the batching that keeps families together provides for family unity while at the same time ensuring that parents will be available to control their children. By seeking a definition of order within Disney World that can convincingly be presented as being in the interest of visitors, order maintenance is established as a voluntary activity which allows coercion to be reduced to a minimum. Thus, adult visitors willingly submit to a variety of devices that increase the flow of consumers through Disney World, such as being corralled on the monorail platform, so as to ensure the safety of their children. Furthermore, while doing so they gratefully acknowledge the concern Disney Productions has for their family, thereby legitimating its authority, not only in the particular situation in question, but in others as well. Thus, while profit ultimately underlies the order Disney Productions seeks to maintain, it is pursued in conjunction with other objectives that will encourage the willing compliance of visitors in maintaining Disney profits. This approach to profit making, which seeks a coincidence of corporate and individual interests (employee and consumer alike), extends beyond the control function and reflects a business philosophy to be applied to all corporate operations (Peters and Waterman, 1982)

The coercive edge of Disney's control system is seldom far from the surface, however, and becomes visible the moment the Disney-visitor consensus breaks down, that is, when a visitor attempts to exercise a choice that is incompatible with the Disney order. It is apparent in the physical barriers that forcefully prevent certain activities as well as in the action of employees who detect breaches of order. This can be illustrated by an incident that occurred during a visit to Disney World by Shearing and his daughter, during the course of which she developed a blister on her heel. To avoid further irritation she removed her shoes and proceeded to walk barefooted. They had not progressed ten yards before they were approached by a very personable security guard dressed as a Bahamian police officer, with white pith helmet and white gloves that perfectly suited the theme of the area they were moving through (so that he, at first, appeared more like a scenic prop than a security person), who informed them that walking barefoot was, "for the safety of visitors", not permitted. When informed that, given the blister, the safety of this visitor was likely to be better secured by remaining barefooted, at least on the walkways, they were informed that their safety and how best to protect it was a matter for Disney Productions to determine while they were on Disney property and that unless they complied he would be compelled to escort them out of Disney World. Shearing's daughter, on learning that failure to comply with the security guard's instruction would deprive her of the pleasures of Disney World, quickly decided that she would prefer to further injure her heel and remain on Disney property. As this example illustrates, the source of Disney Productions' power rests both in the physical coercion it can bring to bear and in its capacity to induce co-operation by depriving visitors of a resource that they value.

The effectiveness of the power that control of a "fun place" has is vividly illustrated by the incredible queues of visitors who patiently wait, sometimes for hours, for admission to exhibits. These queues not only call into question the common knowledge that queueing is a quintessentially English pastime (if Disney World is any indication Americans are at least as good, if not better, at it), but provide evidence of the considerable inconvenience that people can be persuaded to tolerate so long as they believe that their best interests require it. While the source of this perception is the image of Disney World that the visitor brings to it, it is, interestingly, reinforced through the queueing process itself. In many exhibits queues are structured so that one is brought close to the entrance at several points, thus periodically giving one a glimpse of the fun to come while at the same time encouraging one that the wait will soon be over.

Visitor participation in the production of order within Disney World goes beyond the more obvious control examples we have noted so far. An important aspect of the order Disney Productions attempts to maintain is a particular image of Disney World and the American industrialists who sponsor its exhibits (General Electric, Kodak, Kraft Foods, etc.). Considerable care is taken to ensure that every feature of Disney World reflects a positive view of the American Way, especially its use of, and reliance on, technology. Visitors are, for example, exposed to an almost constant stream of directions by employees, robots in human form and disembodied recorded voices (the use of recorded messages and robots permits precise control over the content and tone of the directions given) that convey the desired message. Disney World acts as a giant magnet attracting millions of Americans and visitors from other lands who pay to learn of the wonders of American capitalism.

Visitors are encouraged to participate in the production of the Disney image while they are in Disney World and to take it home with them so that they can reproduce it for their families and friends. One way this is done is through the "Picture Spots", marked with signposts, to be found throughout Disney World, that provide direction with respect to the images to capture on film (with cameras that one can borrow free of charge) for the slide shows and photo albums to be prepared "back home". Each spot provides views which exclude anything unsightly (such as garbage containers) so as to ensure that the visual images visitors take away of Disney World will properly capture Disney's order. A related technique is the Disney characters who wander through the complex to provide "photo opportunities" for young children. These characters apparently never talk to visitors, and the reason for this is presumably so that their media-based images will not be spoiled.

As we have hinted throughout this discussion, training is a pervasive feature of the control system of Disney Productions. It is not, however, the redemptive soul-training of the carceral project but an ever-present flow of directions for, and definitions of, order directed at every visitor. Unlike carceral training, these messages do not require detailed knowledge of the individual. They are, on the contrary, for anyone and everyone. Messages are, nonetheless, often conveyed to single individuals or small groups of friends and relatives. For example, in some of the newer exhibits, the vehicles that take one through swivel and turn so that one's gaze can be precisely directed. Similarly, each seat is fitted with individual sets of speakers that talk directly to one, thus permitting a seductive sense of intimacy while simultaneously imparting a uniform message.

In summary, within Disney World control is embedded, preventative, subtle, co-operative and apparently non-coercive and consensual. It focuses on categories, requires no knowledge of the individual and employs pervasive surveillance. Thus, although disciplinary, it is distinctively non-carceral. Its order is instrumental and determined by the interests of Disney Productions rather than moral and absolute. As anyone who has visited Disney World knows, it is extraordinarily effective.

While this new instrumental discipline is rapidly becoming a dominant force in social control . . . it is as different from the Orwellian totalitarian nightmare as it is from the carceral regime. Surveillance is pervasive but it is the antithesis of the blatant control of the Orwellian State: its source is not government and its vehicle is not Big Brother. The order of instrumental discipline is not the unitary order of a central State but diffuse and separate orders defined by private authorities responsible for the feudal-like domains of Disney World, condominium estates, commercial complexes and the like. Within contemporary discipline, control is as fine-grained as Orwell imagined but its features are very different. . . . It is thus, paradoxically, not to Orwell's socialist-inspired Utopia that we must look for a picture of contemporary control but to the capitalist-inspired disciplinary model conceived of by Huxley who, in his *Brave New World,* painted a picture of consensually based control that bears a striking resemblance to the disciplinary control of Disney World and other corporate control systems. Within Huxley's imaginary world people are seduced into conformity by the pleasures offered by the drug "soma" rather than coerced into compliance by threat of Big Brother, just as people are today seduced to conform by the pleasures of consuming the goods that corporate power has to offer.

The contrasts between morally based justice and instrumental control, carceral punishment and corporate control, the Panopticon and Disney World and Orwell's and Huxley's visions is succinctly captured by the novelist Beryl Bainbridge's observations about a recent journey she made retracing J. B. Priestley's celebrated trip around Britain. She notes how during his travels in 1933 the centre of the cities and towns he visited were defined by either a church or a centre of government (depicting the coalition between Church and State in the production of order that characterizes morally based regimes).

During her more recent trip one of the changes that struck her most forcibly was the transformation that had taken place in the centre of cities and towns. These were now identified not by churches or town halls, but by shopping centres; often vaulted glass-roofed structures that she found reminiscent of the cathedrals they had replaced both in their awe-inspiring architecture and in the hush that she found they sometimes created. What was worshipped in these contemporary cathedrals, she noted, was not an absolute moral order but something much more mundane: people were "worshipping shopping" and through it, we would add, the private authorities, the order and the corporate power their worship makes possible.

REFERENCES

BAINBRIDGE, B. (1984) Television interview with Robert Fulford on *"Realities"* Global Television, Toronto, October.

FOUCAULT, M. (1977) *Discipline and Punish: The Birth of the Prison.* New York: Vintage.

PETERS, T. J. and R. H. WATERMAN, Jr. (1982) *In Search of Excellence: Lessons from America's Best-run Companies.* New York: Warner.

PRIESTLEY, J. B. (1934) *English Journey: Being a Rambling but Truthful Account of What One Man Saw and Heard and Felt and Thought During a Journey Through England the Autumn of the Year 1933.* London: Heinemann & Gollancz.

ABOUT THE AUTHORS

JOHN BRAITHWAITE is Senior Research Fellow in the Department of Sociology, Research School of Social Sciences, Australian National University, Canberra. Formerly a research criminologist at the Australian Institute of Criminology, from 1982 to 1984 he was director of the Australian Federation of Consumer Organizations. Braithwaite is the author of a number of books in the fields of sociology and criminology, including *Inequality, Crime, and Public Policy, Corporate Crime in the Pharmaceutical Industry,* and *To Punish or Persuade.*

MICHAEL CLARKE was educated at the Universities of East Anglia, Manchester and Durham, England, and has been a lecturer in Sociology at the University of Birmingham since 1971. He is the author of a number of books and articles, including *Fallen Idols: Elites and the Search for the Acceptable Face of Capitalism* (1981), *Corruption: Causes, Consequences and Control* (1983), and *Regulating the City: Competition, Scandal and Reform* (1986).

BRENT FISSE is Professor of Law at the University of Sydney, Australia. A Bicentennial Fellow in Criminal Law and Administration at the University of Pennsylvania Law School in 1968-1969, he has held several university posts in the United States, including that of Mitchell Visiting Distinguished Professor at Trinity University, Texas. His publications include *The Impact of Publicity on Corporate Offenders* (with John Braithwaite), *Corrigible Corporations and Unruly Law* (edited with Peter French), and "Reconstructing corporate criminal law: deterrence, retribution, fault, and sanctions," in the *Southern California Law Review.*

STUART HENRY is Assistant Professor in the Department of Sociology and Criminal Justice at Old Dominion University. He received his Ph.D. in 1976 from the University of Kent at Canterbury, England, for a study of amateur trading in stolen goods, which was published as *The Hidden Economy,* (1978). He worked on a study of self-help and mutual aid support networks at the University of London's Addiction Research Unit and coauthored *Self-help and Health* (1977). More recently during research and teaching appointments at Middlesex and Trent Polytechnics his study of informal processes has turned to a detailed look at non-state justice systems in capitalist society which resulted in the edited collection *Informal Institutions* (1981) and his most recent book *Private Justice* (1983).

PETER K. MANNING specializes in phenomenological analyses of complex social systems within subfields of criminology and medical sociology. He has taught or held positions at the University of Missouri, Michigan State, State University of New York, Albany, MIT, The Centre for Socio-legal Studies, Wolfson College, Oxford, and Balliol College, Oxford. Dr. Manning has published a number of books, articles, and chapters, including *Police Work* (1977) and *Narc's Game* (1980) and is the author of the forthcoming *Signifying Calls*. For the past two years he has been studying the regulation of nuclear power production in Britain and is preparing a book. He is also writing (with Keith Hawkins) *Legal Decision-Making*. He is currently Professor of Sociology, Psychiatry, and Criminal Justice at Michigan State University.

GARY T. MARX is Professor of Sociology at Massachusetts Institute of Technology. He is the author of *Protest and Prejudice* and *A Necessary Evil: The Paradoxes and Problems of Undercover Police Work in America*. He is currently engaged in research on the sociology of surveillance.

NANCY REICHMAN is Assistant Professor of Sociology at the University of Denver. Her current research involves the use of new technologies for social control and the regulation of financial markets.

ALBERT J. REISS, Jr. is William Graham Sumner Professor of Sociology and Lecturer in Law at Yale University. He is the author of *The Police and the Public* and is a frequent contributor of writings on crime and law enforcement.

SUSAN P. SHAPIRO is currently a Fellow at the Gannett Center for Media Studies at Columbia University, where she is investigating the problem of credibility and the social control of the mass media. She will be joining the Department of Sociology at Northwestern University and the American Bar Foundation. Her research interests also include stock fraud and securities regulation, the social control of white-collar crime, and the sociology of trust. She is the author of *Wayward Capitalists: Target of the Securities and Exchange Commission*.

CLIFFORD D. SHEARING, of the Centre of Criminology, University of Toronto has published primarily on policing and sociological theory. He is currently doing a study of self-regulation within a North American Stock Exchange, with Philip Stenning.

PHILIP C. STENNING, of the Centre of Criminology, University of Toronto, has published primarily on policing, prosecutions, firearms control, and criminal law topics. He is currently doing a study of self-regulation within a North American Stock Exchange, with Clifford Shearing.

NIGEL SOUTH is Research Associate in the Centre for Ciminology, Middlesex Polytechnic and Research Sociologist, Institute for the Study of Drug Dependence, London. He has taught in London and New York and previously written on aspects of private justice, the informal economies, cultural studies, and drug-related problems and services. He is the author of the forthcoming study, *Private Security*, and coauthor of *Helping Drug Users* (1985) and *Message in a Bottle* (1983).

AUSTIN T. TURK is Professor of Sociology at the University of Toronto and immediate past president of the American Society of Criminology. He has written extensively on the linkage between legal power and social conflict, and is currently at work on studies at sociolegal development and a book on critical criminology. His most recent major publication is *Political Criminality: The Defiance and Defense of Authority* (Sage, 1982).

ROBERT P. WEISS is Associate Professor of Sociology at the State University of New York at Plattsburgh. In addition to private policing, his research interests include community crime prevention, private prisons, and the historical development of penal sanction. He has published articles in *The Historical Journal, The Insurgent Sociologist*, and *Crime and Social Justice*. He is also interested in correctional education, and, since 1976, he has taught courses in criminology to prisoners in four state systems.

W. GORDON WEST is Associate Professor of Sociology in Education at the Ontario Institute for Studies in Education, and Centre of Criminology, University of Toronto. He has previously studied juvenile delinquency, youth culture, juvenile courts, and diversion, with a special interest in critical ethnographic and participatory research methods in relation to recent European theories of the state. Dr. West has published *Children's Rights: Educational and Legal Issues* (1978) and *Young Offenders and the State: A Canadian Perspective on Delinquency* (1984), as well as numerous articles in journals and books. He has visited Nicaragua four times and spent his sabbatical there in 1985 as a researcher at La Corte Suprema; he is presently a member of the Nicaraguan team of the Comparative Social Control project of the Grupo Critica de Criminologia.

NOTES